JOB READY
JAVA®

JOB READY JAVA®

HAYTHEM BALTI
CO-AUTHORED BY ALAN GALLOWAY

WILEY

ISBN: 978-1-119-77564-5
ISBN: 978-1-119-77656-7 (ebk)
ISBN: 978-1-119-77565-2 (ebk)

Manufactured in the United States of America

For general information on our other products and services please contact our Customer Care Department within the United States at (877) 762-2974, outside the United States at (317) 572-3993 or fax (317) 572-4002.

Wiley publishes in a variety of print and electronic formats and by print-on-demand. Some material included with standard print versions of this book may not be included in e-books or in print-on-demand. If this book refers to media such as a CD or DVD that is not included in the version you purchased, you may download this material at booksupport.wiley.com. For more information about Wiley products, visit www.wiley.com.

Library of Congress Control Number: 2020951893

SKY10024858_021021

About the Authors

Haythem Balti is the director of curriculum at Wiley's Software Guild and mthree. Haythem has created courses used by thousands of Software Guild and mthree students for Java, Python, Go, and other development and data science skills. Prior to Wiley, he was a data scientist with Humana and a software architect with White Clay. Haythem earned his PhD in computer engineering and computer science from the University of Louisville.

Alan Galloway is the director of instruction at Wiley's Software Guild and mthree. Alan supervises a team of instructors who deliver large-scale training programs in various technology areas. Prior to Wiley, Alan worked as a professional software developer, information technology specialist, and design engineer for more than 19 years. His experience spans multiple industries including applications such as hardware service request management, health spending account management, release coordination, and automated deployments. He has managed teams on the development of web applications, written middleware utilities, and worked on batch processing applications.

About the Technical Writer

Bradley Jones is the owner of Lots of Software, LLC. He has programmed in a variety of languages such as C, C++, C#, JavaScript, and Java) as well as tools such as Unity. He has written code for platforms that include the Internet, Windows, mobile devices, and even mainframes. He's even built virtual reality apps for fun. In addition to programming, he has authored books on C, C++, C#, Windows, the Web, and many more technical topics and a few nontechnical topics. Bradley has been recognized in the industry as a community influencer as well as a Microsoft MVP, a CODiE Judge, an international technology speaker, a bestselling technical author, and more.

About the Technical Editors

Kim Weiss is a veteran course developer, specializing in Computer Science courses since 2002. She was an assistant professor in Computer Science for over ten years before deciding to focus exclusively on course design. She has worked with multiple universities as well as corporate training settings to develop interactive instructional content appropriate for the target learners and course goals.

Janeice DelVecchio has been a professional Software Developer for 10 years, and has had a lifelong love of programming and computers. She has served as technical editor on several other titles, including the Java 11 OCP Certification books. Editing is a fun task for her because she likes finding and fixing defects of all types.

For her day job, she works in the financial industry using a very broad range of skills with technologies including cloud computing, process automation, advanced unit testing and devops. She also volunteers at CodeRanch.com where she runs the Java class known as the Cattle Drive.

She is an expert with the Java programming language. If you ask her which language is the best, she will tell you that languages are tools and to pick the one that fits your use case. The first language she learned was BASIC, and one day she hopes to learn gaming development.

In her spare time, she enjoys cooking, solving puzzles, playing video games, and raising chickens. She loves eating sushi, drinking craft beer, and petting dogs — her guilty pleasure is 80's pop music. She lives in Litchfield County, Connecticut.

Acknowledgments

Although Alan and Haythem are the main authors of this book, this book would not have been possible without the hard work of the content development and instruction teams at the Software Guild and mthree.

Specifically, this book will not be possible without the expertise and countless reviews and improvements by the following contributors:

Paul Menefee

Calvin Moser

David Hunnicutt

Sean Palm

Ronnie Jones

Kyle Rudy

David Smelser

Amir Gill

Irina Cudo

Randall Clapper

Ishwar Joshi

Phil Williams

Quinten Lambert

Randy Hash

Pat Toner

Austyn Hill

Contents

PART IV: Intermediate Java   531

Lesson 28: Exploring the Service Layer   532

Lesson 29: Pulling It All Together: Coding the Class Roster Service Layer   538

Introduction

Programming computers can be a fun and exciting career. Before you begin your journey as a programmer, you need to decide which programming language to learn. You may wonder which one makes you the most marketable. There are many viable answers to this question, but Java is a flexible and widely used language.

There are many reasons that Java makes a great choice. As a general-purpose language, Java can be used to build applications that run on a variety of platforms ranging from desktop computers to mobile devices. Java applications can also be created to run on the Web as well as on other architecture. Regardless of the platform, you can use the same Java syntax on whichever Java-supported platform you choose. You'll learn that syntax in this book.

Java is widely used across the globe. In the rankings of programming languages, Java is often at or near the top. For example, on the Tiobe index, which ranks interest in programming languages, Java is generally in the top one or two spots and has not been lower than third since 2001.

> **NOTE** You can find the Tiobe index for Java at `www.tiobe.com/tiobe-index`.

There are many open positions waiting for candidates who know Java programming. At the time of this writing, more than 38,000 Java jobs were listed on `Monster.com`.

Job Ready Java provides you with the foundation you need to be ready to take on some of the Java jobs that are out there. This book is quite different from other Java books. This book is based on a professional Java course. Additionally, the structure of the book presents not only the Java information you need to know to program Java for a job but also the features that help you to be better prepared to apply what you've learned.

A Java Course within a Book

This book contains a full-fledged Java course: the Software Guild's Java Bootcamp: Object Oriented Programming course. Many people have paid thousands of dollars to take the Software Guild's course.

The Software Guild is recognized as one of the best bootcamps and a leading authority on coding education. They have helped future developers to gain the wide range of understanding they need. The focus is not on teaching you lessons in a purely academic fashion, but rather to help you go further.

Features to Make You Job Ready

Job Ready Java provides a number of features that not only teach you Java, but also help you apply it. If you read through this book, enter the listings, and try the code, then you'll get an experience like many other books. If you also take a hands-on approach to doing the exercises, you'll be better able to take what you learned to the next level.

Most importantly, this course goes beyond what many books provide by including lessons that help you pull together everything you are learning in a way that is more like what you would need to do within a job. This includes building a more comprehensive example than what you get in the standard short listings provided in most books. If you work through the "Pulling It All Together" sections and lessons, then you will be better prepared for many of those Java jobs that are available.

WHAT DOES THIS BOOK COVER?

As mentioned, this book is a complete Java course. The course is broken into several parts each containing a number of lessons. By working through the lessons in this course, you will learn Java programming as well as prepare yourself for a job in Java programming.

Part I: Getting Set Up   The first part of the book focuses on getting you set up to use Java. This will include help for installing Java and setting up the tools you'll need to work through this book. You'll also be shown how to enter, compile, and run Java programs using the Java IDE.

Part II: Basics of Object Oriented Programming   In Part 2, you will learn the basic constructs needed to use the Java programming language. This will include the syntax, how to control program flow, how to organize your code using methods, and how to organize your data using arrays. Because it is easy to make a mistake, you will also learn about identifying and fixing issues in your code.

Part III: Fundamentals of Classes and Objects   The third part takes you deep into object-oriented programming. You'll take the syntax you learned in Part 2 and begin to build classes, interfaces, and more.

Part IV: Intermediate Java   In Part 4, you'll go beyond the basics of Java and object-oriented programming to delve into aspects such as the service layer, doing unit testing, and working with code that is stateful and stateless. You'll also learn useful information on working with big numbers, dates, and times.

Part V: Advanced Java   In Part 5, you'll learn about resources to help make your coding more robust such as using the Spring Framework and Maven.

Part VI: Appendices   You will also find appendices that provide a coding checklist as well as a list of concepts to study to show that you know Java should you consider interviewing for a Java job. There is also a checklist for taking an agile approach to building CRUD applications, which is a topic you'll learn about within this course.

READER SUPPORT FOR THIS BOOK

There are several ways to get the help you need for this book.

Companion Download Files

As you work through the examples in this book, you should type in all the code manually. This will help you learn and better understand what the code does.

However, in two of the lessons, download files are referenced. You can download the Lessons 27 and 36 files from www.wiley.com/go/jobreadyjava under the "Downloads" links there.

How to Contact the Publisher

If you believe you've found a mistake in this book, please bring it to our attention. At John Wiley & Sons, we understand how important it is to provide our customers with accurate content, but even with our best efforts an error may occur.

To submit your possible errata, please email it to our Customer Service Team at wileysupport@wiley.com with the subject line "Possible Book Errata Submission."

PART I

Getting Set Up

Lesson 1
Installing Java

Welcome to the world of learning Java. In this first lesson, we will set up everything needed to write Java programs. We will then write our first program together called "Hello, World!"

It is important to know that, by itself, Java code doesn't do anything. It is just text. To make it useful, we need to install the Java Development Kit (JDK). The JDK contains the compiler and other tools needed to create executable Java programs. After the JDK is installed, we will check the configuration by creating, compiling, and running the obligatory "Hello, World!" program.

LEARNING OBJECTIVES

By the end of this lesson, you will be able to:

- Differentiate between the JDK and Java custom runtimes
- Compare OpenJDK to Oracle JDK
- Install a JDK and verify the installation
- Trace the steps to create a "Hello, World!" program using a text editor
- Define syntax as it relates to development
- Explain the pieces of the compiler
- Trace the development of a program through the various parts of compilation and execution of a program

THE JAVA UNIVERSE

Before we get into downloading and installing the Java tools and writing our first program, let's first take a look at the bigger picture: the Java universe, if you will. A little history will help to make sense of where Java is today.

The development of the Java language was led by James Gosling at Sun Microsystems. The initial development started in the early 1990s, and the language was originally called Oak. The first official release of Java was in 1996. Now, in Internet time, 1996 seems like, I don't know, a million years ago. And it seems that Java has this reputation for being an old and creaky language because there are all these newer and cooler languages out there—you know, like Ruby and Python and JavaScript.

But wait—the first version of Ruby was also released in 1995 and the first version of Python was started in 1989, so they aren't really newer languages. JavaScript was called LiveScript when it came on to the scene in 1995. Maybe Java isn't an old language after all.

Java was originally a closed source project, meaning that developers had to purchase a license to use it, and the code that runs Java was accessible only to Sun Microsystems developers. In 2006, however, Sun decided to make the project open source under a newly defined General Public License (GPL). In short, Sun decided to let any developer use Java to write software programs for any purpose at no cost. In addition, the GPL allows developers to access the code that runs Java to tweak it for their own purposes.

In 2010, Oracle bought Sun Microsystems and took over stewardship of Java. Oracle continues to maintain, distribute, and support Java and its related tools, including the JDK and the JVM.

The Java Development Kit

The Java Development Kit is a software package that contains tools that allow developers, like you, to write new Java programs. These tools include things like the Java compiler, which converts the code you write into bytecode that the Java Virtual Machine can read, as well as the JVM itself and tools that allow you to package your creations to distribute to other users.

> **NOTE** We will be downloading and installing the JDK later in this lesson.

There are two basic versions of the JDK, both maintained and distributed by Oracle: OpenJDK and Oracle JDK. OpenJDK is the open source *reference implementation* of the JDK. This means that it is the standard from which all other JDK implementations are derived. OpenJDK is released under the GPL v2 license and is completely open to the community. It contains the core code that makes Java work.

The Oracle JDK is based on OpenJDK, but it is a commercial implementation released under the Oracle Binary Code License Agreement.

The two versions have nearly identical code, but the Oracle JDK has a few more classes (some closed source) and some additional bug fixes. Businesses generally use the Oracle JDK because it tends to be a bit more stable; however, most Oracle JDK versions are distributed under a relatively restricted license. You can download the software for free, but you are only allowed to use the free version for personal, noncommercial projects. The free Oracle JDK license excludes the ability to create software that you want to sell or distribute for others to use. Many businesses choose to pay for commercial-use licenses because Oracle Java JDK includes support features not included in the open source versions.

We include instructions in the following sections to install OpenJDK for use in this course. You are welcome to use Oracle JDK instead, if you prefer. We use the open source OpenJDK here because it is completely free for any purpose you want to use it for, including creating and selling your own software packages. While Oracle does allow developers to use its Java JDK at no cost for personal projects, the free license does not allow commercial use. Many businesses choose to purchase licenses for Oracle's Java JDK to take advantage of the additional support that Oracle provides with the commercial version. However, because the JDK is very much behind the scenes when developing software using Java, you are not likely to notice much difference between the two.

The Java Virtual Machine

One of the problems with writing software today is that we normally want our programs to be compatible with as many different types of computers as possible. What good is a killer app if it will run on only one brand of smartphone? What about a custom enterprise application that will run only on a Windows machine, even though many employees may use Apple computers? This is where Java has an advantage over other coding languages.

The Java Virtual Machine (JVM) is a software layer between the Java code and the machine running the software. A virtual machine (VM) is essentially a piece of software that acts like a computer, and it performs many of the same input/process/output operations that a physical computer does.

Essentially, the JVM (which is included in the JDK) acts as a translator between the compiled Java code and the machine's bytecode. This means that our program will run on any computer that the JVM recognizes, so we can write one app that will work on many different devices, rather than writing multiple versions of the same app for different platforms. The result is that we can write once and run anywhere, a process Sun Microsystems named WORA to promote the use of Java.

The Java Runtime Environment

As a Java developer, you may also hear about the Java Runtime Environment (JRE). Through Java version 8, anyone who wanted to run a Java application on their computer had to first install a compatible JRE, which included the JVM required to run compiled software but did not include the tools used to develop software.

Starting with Java 9, however, the JDK includes a packaging process that creates an executable package that does not require a separate JRE on the end user's computer. This streamlines the distribution process a bit, making it even easier to write once and run anywhere when we use Java.

Java 8 is still widely used in many enterprises, however, so it's not impossible that you will run across the need to have a JRE installed to run software written in Java.

INSTALLING OpenJDK

You will need to install the JDK for this book because it has the tools needed to develop Java applications. As mentioned, the JDK also contains the Java runtime, which is the component that allows us to run the Java programs that we (and others) write. You might have a Java runtime already installed on your system because Java is widely used to write software.

> **NOTE** When we install the JDK, it will simply replace any existing JDK.

For this course, we will use OpenJDK, which you can also use for any project in the future. The following instruction sets can be used to check your current installed version of a JDK and to install OpenJDK if you do not already have it. The following sections cover

- Installing on Microsoft Windows
- Installing on macOS

We recommend installing the most recent long-term support (LTS) version of OpenJDK, which was version 11 at the time of this writing. While you will see newer versions (such as 14), you should choose an LTS version because it will be more stable than newer versions that are still in development. Each version is based on a previous version, however, so you don't want to choose a version that comes before 11—there may be newer features we use in this course that are not available in older versions.

Additionally, while we provide added guidance here for installing a JDK on Microsoft Windows and macOS, you can also install it on other operating systems including various versions of Linux and AIX. The installation would be similar to what is shown here, including starting at the same website.

> **NOTE** At the end of the day, the JDK is being used to compile and run our Java programs.

Installing OpenJDK on Microsoft Windows

The following instructions walk you through checking for an existing copy of the JDK on Microsoft Windows 10. You'll then install and verify an installation of OpenJDK. If you are using macOS, skip ahead to the next section.

Checking for an Existing JDK on Windows

Start by checking to see whether you already have a JDK installed. This can be done by opening a command prompt window and using the command line.

You can open a command prompt window by clicking the *Start* menu, searching for *cmd*, and selecting *Command Prompt* in the search results. Figure 1.1 shows how to use the Windows Search box to find the command prompt window.

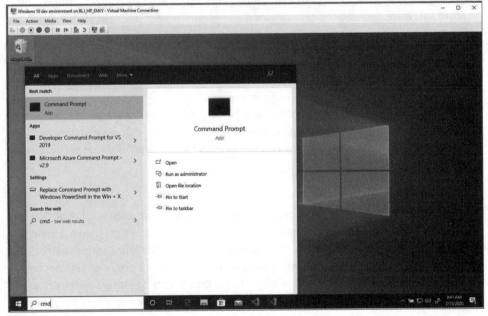

Figure 1.1 Running the command prompt window

In the command prompt window, key the following command as shown in Figure 1.2:

```
java -version
```

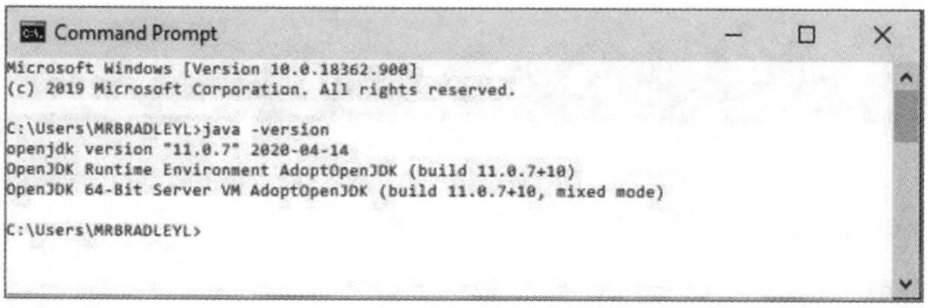

Figure 1.2 Checking the version in the Command Prompt

Windows will display the current version of Java installed on your computer. In this screenshot, the results are as follows:

```
openjdk version "11.0.7" 2020-04-14
OpenJDK Runtime Environment AdoptOpenJDK (build 11.0.7+10)
OpenJDK 64-Bit Server VM AdoptOpenJDK (build 11.0.7+10, mixed mode)
```

If your results are similar to those displayed in Figure 1.2 and you see *openjdk* with a version number that starts with 11, you already have the correct version of OpenJDK on your computer, and you can skip to "Creating Your Java First Program."

In the rare case that Java is not installed, you might see a message such as this:

```
'java' is not recognized as an internal or external command,
operable program or batch file.
```

If you get this message, simply continue to the next section for installing OpenJDK.

Installing OpenJDK

If you don't have the latest version—or any version—then you'll need to install the OpenJDK. Use your browser to navigate to AdoptOpenJDK.net, as shown in Figure 1.3.

Verify that the page has identified your computer platform (e.g., Windows, macOS, or Linux) correctly and select OpenJDK 11 with the Hotspot JVM. Click the *Latest release* button and save the file to a known location on your computer.

> **NOTE** The screenshots here use release 11.0.7+10.2. It's fine if you have a slightly different version, as long as the first number is 11.

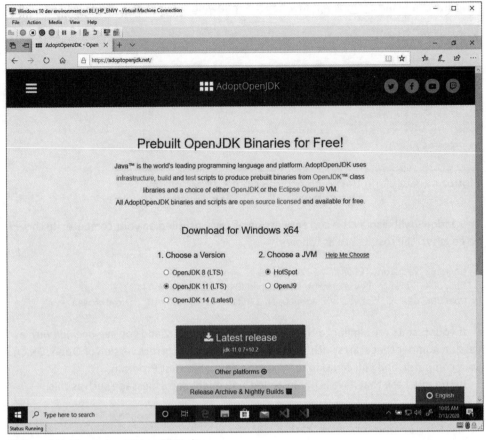

Figure 1.3 The AdoptOpenJDK site

Open or run the saved file. If prompted as shown in Figure 1.4, confirm that you want to launch the installer.

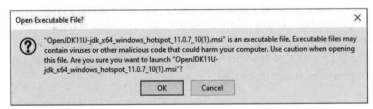

Figure 1.4 Prompt for running the launcher

The installer will launch the setup wizard to install the AdoptOpenJDK JDK, as shown in Figure 1.5.

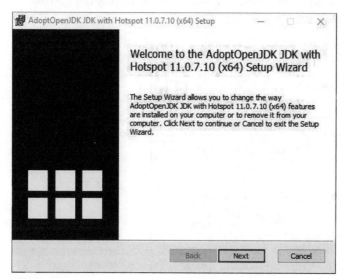

Figure 1.5 The AdoptOpenJDK setup wizard

You should verify that it will install JDK 11 and click *Next*. This will show the end-user license agreement, as shown in Figure 1.6.

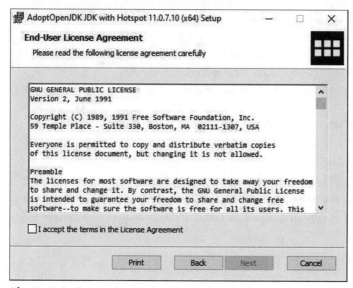

Figure 1.6 The end-user license agreement

The license on AdoptOpenJDK is a GNU General Public License, which means that it is open source, and anyone can use it in any way, as long as credit is given to the original developers. Accept the license agreement and click *Next*. This will display the Custom Setup settings, as shown in Figure 1.7.

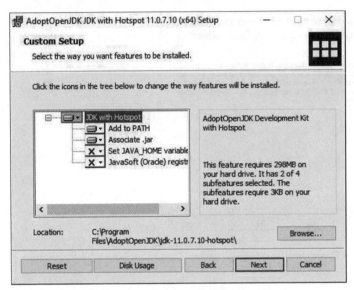

Figure 1.7 The Custom Setup settings

Accept the default settings in the Custom Setup window. You should note the location where the JDK will be installed in this window. You will need it later.

Click *Next* to be taken to a window similar to Figure 1.8.

Click *Install* to begin the actual installation of the JDK. Windows will ask if you want to allow the app to make changes to your account (Figure 1.9). Click *Yes*.

The installation will start and run automatically (Figure 1.10). The installation will take several minutes to complete.

You will see a confirmation window when the installation is complete (Figure 1.11).

Verifying the Installation

Verify that you have Java 11 installed on your computer. Follow the same steps you did earlier to see what version you had installed. Open a command-line window by clicking the *Start* menu, searching for *cmd*, and selecting *Command Prompt* in the search results. This was shown in Figure 1.1.

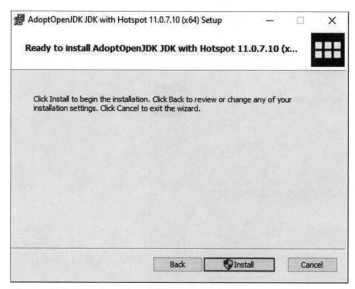

Figure 1.8 Ready to install

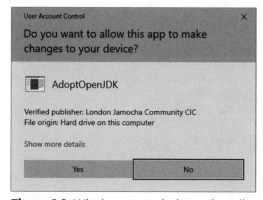

Figure 1.9 Windows permission to install

As shown in Figure 1.2, type the following command into the command prompt window:

```
java -version
```

Windows will confirm that Java is installed by returning the version number. We show this again in Figure 1.12. You should now see a version that starts with 11 as the first number in the version number. We are now ready start working with the Java and the JDK.

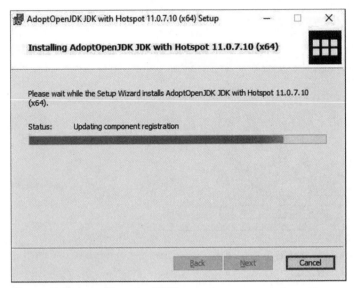

Figure 1.10 Installing the JDK

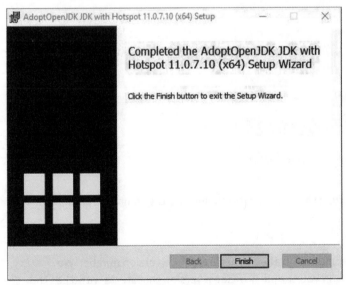

Figure 1.11 Installation completed message

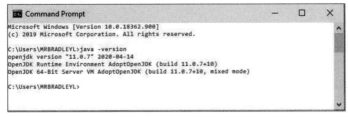

Figure 1.12 Verifying the JDK was installed

> **NOTE** If you do not see OpenJDK 11 as the Java version and you didn't get any error messages, then try to reinstall the JDK.

Installing OpenJDK on macOS

The following instructions walk you through checking for an existing copy of the JDK on macOS. You'll then install and verify an installation of OpenJDK. If you are using Windows, skip ahead to the next section to see how to use the JDK with a Java program.

Checking for an Existing JDK on macOS

Check the version of Java installed on your computer by opening Terminal (using Spotlight Search, Siri, or Launch Pad) and entering the following command:

```
java -version
```

As you can see in Figure 1.13, the results are as follows:

```
openjdk version "11.0.3" 2019-04-16
OpenJDK Runtime Environment AdoptOpenJDK (build 11.0.3+7)
OpenJDK 64-Bit Server VM AdoptOpenJDK (build 11.0.3+7, mixed mode)
```

If you see openjdk version 11 in the results, you do not need to install Java. You can skip to the next section to create your first program in Java.

Installing OpenJDK

Use your browser to navigate to AdoptOpenJDK.net. You should see a page similar to what is presented in Figure 1.14.

Verify that AdoptOpenJDK recognizes your operating system as macOS x64. Select OpenJDK 11 on the left and Hotspot on the right and then click *Latest release*. In Figure 1.14, the file is jdk-11.0.3+7, but you may see a slightly different version number. As long as the first number is 11, it's fine.

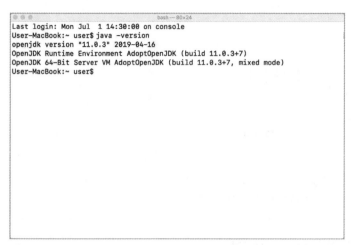

```
                                     bash — 80×24
Last login: Mon Jul  1 14:30:00 on console
User-MacBook:~ user$ java -version
openjdk version "11.0.3" 2019-04-16
OpenJDK Runtime Environment AdoptOpenJDK (build 11.0.3+7)
OpenJDK 64-Bit Server VM AdoptOpenJDK (build 11.0.3+7, mixed mode)
User-MacBook:~ user$
```

Figure 1.13 Checking the version number

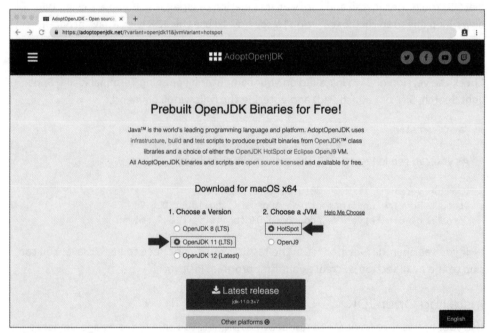

Figure 1.14 The AdoptOpenJDK website

Your browser will download the file. Open the saved file after the download is complete to start the Installer. This should display a dialog similar to Figure 1.15.

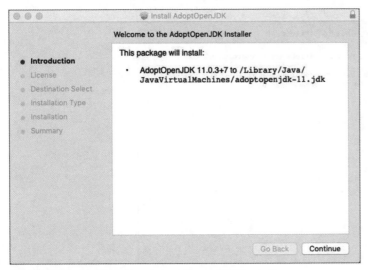

Figure 1.15 Starting the AdoptOpenJDK install

Click *Continue* to start the installer. When prompted, you must accept the license agreement, as shown in Figure 1.16.

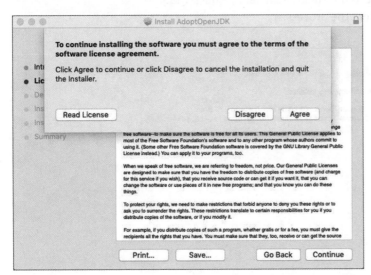

Figure 1.16 Accepting the licensing

Click *Agree* and then click *Continue*. You'll be taken to the dialog shown in Figure 1.17 that shows that, by default, the files will be installed on the computer's main disk.

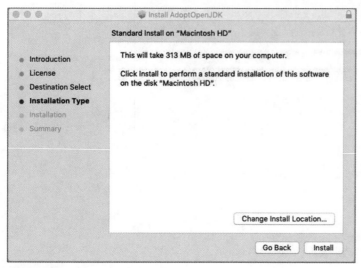

Figure 1.17 Location for the install

You can change the location if you want, but most users should use the default setting. Click *Install* to continue. This will start the installation. When the installation is completed, you will see a confirmation similar to Figure 1.18.

Click *Close* to complete the process.

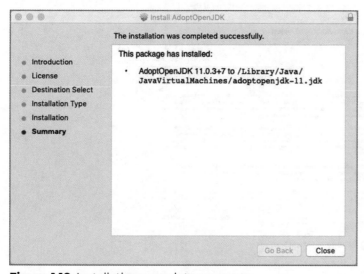

Figure 1.18 Installation complete message

Verifying the Installation

Confirm the version of Java installed on your computer by opening Terminal (using Spotlight Search or Launch Pad) as you did before and entering the following command:

```
java -version
```

You should see results similar to what are shown in Figure 1.19. The results are as follows:

```
openjdk version "11.0.3 " 2019-04-16
OpenJDK Runtime Environment AdoptOpenJDK (build 11.0.3+7)
OpenJDK 64-Bit Server VM AdoptOpenJDK (build 11.0.3+7, mixed mode)
```

```
                              bash — 80×24
Last login: Mon Jul  1 14:30:00 on console
User-MacBook:~ user$ java -version
openjdk version "11.0.3" 2019-04-16
OpenJDK Runtime Environment AdoptOpenJDK (build 11.0.3+7)
OpenJDK 64-Bit Server VM AdoptOpenJDK (build 11.0.3+7, mixed mode)
User-MacBook:~ user$
```

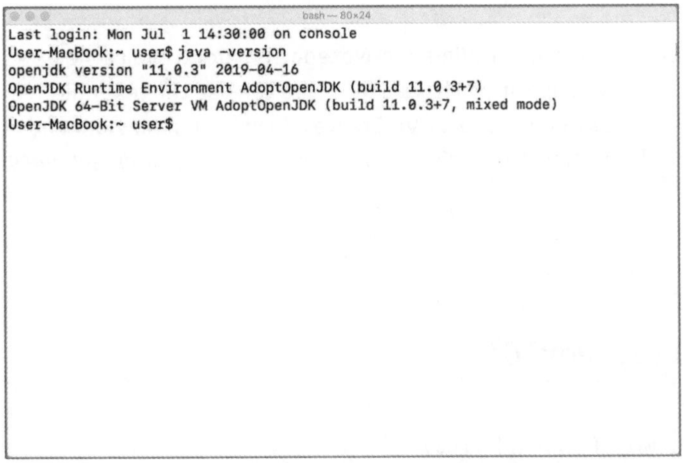

Figure 1.19 Verifying that the installation was successful

If you see openjdk version 11 in the results, you are ready to go to the next step.

> **NOTE** If you do not see OpenJDK 11 as the Java version, try reinstalling the AdoptOpenJDK.

CREATING YOUR FIRST JAVA PROGRAM

Now that we have a JDK installed, we are ready to create our first Java program. We will use a text editor for this process and then walk through how your computer runs a program written in Java. You're not going to understand all of the words in the syntax here, which is fine. What we want to do at this point in time is get you writing your first program and running it!

Writing the Program

When learning a new language, it is customary that your first program simply print out "Hello, World!" to the screen. We'll do this following these steps:

1. Open a text editor.
2. Type in the Java code.
3. Save the file as Hello.java.
4. Compile the code with the Java compiler (*javac*).
5. Run the program.

Open a text editor on your computer. For Windows, Notepad is a good choice; however, you can use any text editor you like. If you have a Mac, you can use the text editor. On Linux, there are editors such as Gedit, nano, or Vi. Create a new file if necessary and then type the code presented in Listing 1.1. Don't worry about what any of it means; we'll get to that soon enough.

LISTING 1.1

Hello.java: "Hello, World!"

```
public class Hello {
    public static void main (String[] args) {
        System.out.println("Hello, World!");
    }
}
```

> **NOTE** Save the file as *Hello.java* your Documents library. Make sure that *.java* is the filename extension, rather than *.txt* or something else.

There are several things to notice about this file. First, you should note that the program creates something called a *public class* in the first line. A Java program is a *class*, which is a basic container for code in Java. This public class has the name Hello. It is important that when you enter this program into your editor and save it, you use this same name for the file. As such, you will need to save the program as Hello.java. If you are using a text editor in Windows, you'll want to make sure that .txt doesn't get added to the end of the name.

In addition to a Java program being a class, this class will also have a main method in it. A method is another container for Java code. A method must be placed inside a class. It is a named block of code that can be executed to accomplish some task. Here, it just prints "Hello, World!" You will learn more about classes and methods in future lessons.

The main method is a special method that is the entry (or starting) point for every Java program. The first line of the main method (public static void main (String[] args)) must be written exactly as in Listing 1.1, and it must be contained inside a class.

The curly braces, {}, denote the beginning and ending, respectively, of code blocks. You'll see that there are two sets of curly braces in our program. One is nested inside the other.

This leaves one more big line of code to mention:

```
System.out.println("Hello, World!");
```

This line is the magic code that sends things to the console. In this case, this code is going to write what is between the two quotes to the console. We'll learn much more about this later. For now, make sure you include the periods and the semicolon where they are shown in this line of code. You also need to make sure you capitalize the word System as shown. These small details are important for making sure the program works as expected.

Compiling and Running the Program

Now that you've written the Java program, you are ready to compile and run it.

To be able to run the program, we need to convert it into what is known as a *class file*. That class file contains what is known as bytecode. It is bytecode that the Java runtime environment, in particular the Java virtual machine, is able to interpret and run as our program. To do that, we can run the Java compiler.

To run the Java compiler, we type in javac. That's the name of the program. Javac is looking for one or more Java files to compile. In our case, we just want to pass in Hello.java. When we do this, the compiler will read Hello.java, and it will convert that into a class file called Hello.class.

Open your command-line interface and use the cd command to open the directory where you saved the Hello.java file. You saw how to open the command-line interface earlier to check the version of your JDK.

- In Windows, click *Start* and use *cmd* to open the command prompt.
  - Enter **cd Documents** and hit Enter.

- Enter **dir** at the prompt and verify that you see `Hello.java` in the results.

- In Mac (or Linux), open Terminal.

  - Enter **cd Documents** and hit Enter.

  - Enter **ls** at the prompt, hit Enter, and verify that you see `Hello.java` in the results.

We will now compile our program by running the following command on the command line:

`javac Hello.java`

When you run this command, it will compile your code and create a Java program that can be executed. If you entered everything correctly, you won't see any feedback. If you entered something wrong, then any errors will be displayed. If an error is displayed, review the code in Listing 1.1 and make sure what you typed into your editor is identical, including semicolons and periods.

After our program is compiled, we can run it. We need to tell Java what program to execute. We'll run the Java program by using the `java` command on the command line followed by the name of the class we are running, in this case, `Hello`.

`java Hello`

Note that we did not include any extension, but rather just use the name of the class we are running. When this command is executed, it will print "Hello, World!" to the screen, as shown in Figure 1.20.

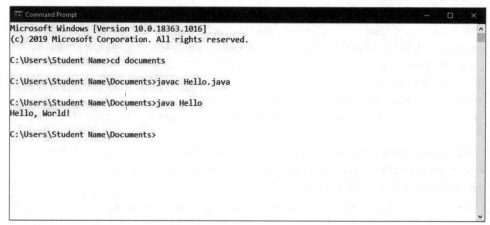

```
Microsoft Windows [Version 10.0.18363.1016]
(c) 2019 Microsoft Corporation. All rights reserved.

C:\Users\Student Name>cd documents

C:\Users\Student Name\Documents>javac Hello.java

C:\Users\Student Name\Documents>java Hello
Hello, World!

C:\Users\Student Name\Documents>
```

Figure 1.20 `Hello.java` output

> **NOTE** Technically, with the current version of Java, single class execution is supported. This means that if your program is a single class, then you don't have to compile your program before calling Java to run it. Generally, however, most of your programs in a corporate environment are going to have more than one class.

Dealing with Syntax Errors

Syntax is the sequence of characters that make up well-formed statements in a programming language. You can think of syntax like the spelling, punctuation, and grammar rules of the programming language. The compiler is good at detecting syntax errors and will tell you when you type something that is not syntactically correct.

If you make a mistake in your program by leaving off a punctuation mark, capitalizing something that shouldn't be capitalized, or forgetting a bracket, it can cause a syntax error. If you entered Listing 1.1 perfectly, then it would have compiled without any issues. If, however, you made a mistake, then you might have gotten feedback.

Remove the semicolon from the end of the following line in Listing 1.1:

```
System.out.println("Hello, World!")
```

If you compile the listing again, the following is the output you'll receive:

```
C:\Users\JavaStudent\java>javac Hello.java
Hello.java:3: error: ';' expected
        System.out.println("Hello, World!")
                                           ^
1 error
```

As you can see, the Java compiler is providing you with information on your syntax error. This will help you determine what needs to be fixed.

> **TIP** Sometimes a single mistake can cause multiple errors.

> **NOTE** All syntax errors will cause a compiler error. Not all compiler errors, however, are syntax errors.

USING THE COMPILER AND JAVA VIRTUAL MACHINE

The flow chart in Figure 1.21 represents the steps that happen behind the scenes when we compile and run our program.

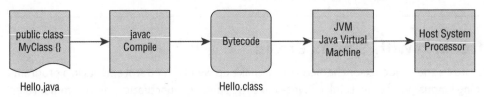

Figure 1.21 Behind the scenes while compiling and running

1. We created the Hello.java file using normal text and Java syntax. It includes a public class that defines what we want the computer to do when we run the program.

2. When we ran the command javac Hello.java in the second step, it invoked the Java compiler. The compiler converts the text that we typed in Hello.java into bytecode.

3. Bytecode is a set of instructions for the JVM. When we ran the command java Hello, we were running the bytecode version of the program that the JVM can read and interpret.

4. The JVM is basically a virtual computer that runs in a layer between the software and the operating system. Because all Java programs use the JVM to run, we can run the same program on any platform that supports Java, including Windows, macOS, and Linux.

5. The JVM interprets the bytecode from your program and converts it into machine code that can run on the processor of your machine.

SUMMARY

In this lesson, we went over what a JDK is and why we need one as Java developers. We compared Oracle JDK with OpenJDK and then installed OpenJDK for use in this book.

We then created, compiled, and ran our first Java program called `Hello.java`. We learned the following:

- Java programs consist of a class that contains a `main` method. The `main` method is the special starting point for every Java program.

- Curly braces, {}, mark the start and end of code blocks in Java.

- `System.out.println("Hello, World!");` is the magic code that sends text to the console to be displayed.

Finally, we learned about the Java Virtual Machine and the process that a Java file goes through from creation to execution.

While it is possible to write any Java program using a plaintext editor like we did in this lesson, larger programs are much more complicated than this one is and often include many individual files that must work together as a single project. In the next lesson, we'll install an integrated development environment (IDE), which includes tools that can identify syntax errors as we are coding before we say to compile the program, keep related files together in a single project, and compile the code when we want to test it.

Lesson 2

Installing a Development Environment: NetBeans

This lesson walks you through the process of installing NetBeans 12, which you can use for the remaining lessons in this book.

LEARNING OBJECTIVES

By the end of this lesson, you will be able to:
- Know the value of using an integrated development environment (IDE)
- Understand the core parts of an IDE
- Install NetBeans using the automated installer
- Install the NetBeans binaries
- Be able to start NetBeans

NOTE To install NetBeans, you must first have a Java Development Kit installed on your computer, which you did in the previous lesson. If you did not go through Lesson 1, you will need to complete those steps prior to continuing with this lesson.

GETTING STARTED

NetBeans is a Java IDE, which stands for *integrated development environment*. The IDE is where a developer does most of their work when developing software programs, and it includes tools that help identify errors in the code as well as an interface for complicated development projects.

In this course, we will use NetBeans 12. If you already have NetBeans 12 installed and you can open it without errors, then you can skip this lesson. If you have problems opening NetBeans 12, see the troubleshooting steps near the end of each set of instructions in the following sections, depending on your operating system.

UNDERSTANDING THE VALUE OF AN IDE

The IDE is the single most important tool in your developer toolbox. The IDE is where you will write and compile, debug, and run your Java programs. The better you know the ins and outs of your IDE, the better a developer you are likely to be.

The main purpose of the IDE is to give developers a single application to use for creating software. It is a one-stop shop for writing and editing source code. It also provides for compiling and building your programs and provides debugging. Most IDEs also have hooks into various source code control repositories, giving a truly comprehensive environment for developing software.

Let's take a look at the three biggest features of an IDE.

- The source code editor
- The build automation tools
- The debugger

Using the Source Code Editor

The source code editor, on its face, is a place to type in the characters that make up a program. But really, it's much, much more. Source code editors do a lot to help the developer. First, source code editors will automatically format and indent your source code. This is a great help when working in teams because the IDE can be configured with rules that format everyone's code to look the same, making it much easier to work on other people's code.

Second, most source code editors color code the source code that is entered. This is known as *syntax highlighting*. This is a huge help for developers because it identifies different parts of the source code. For example, the color coding makes it easy to spot language keywords or comments or strings. You will see this in the next lesson when we rewrite "Hello, World!" in the IDE.

Third, source editors can provide hints and autocompletion of code. Autocompletion features greatly improve developer productivity because they can help you type the command you are entering, help you determine parameters that are needed, and much more. Similarly, the editor can provide immediate feedback for syntax errors. The code editor will let you know if you've typed something that is invalid, similar to the automatic spell-check in Microsoft Word.

> **NOTE** If you have used Microsoft development tools such as Visual Studio, then you might have heard them call their autocomplete feature *IntelliSense*.

Using the Build Automation Tools

The second big feature we want to mention is the build automation tools. In the previous lesson, we wrote our first program using a text editor. To compile and run the program, we had to do everything by hand, which wasn't too bad because we had only one file in our program. But imagine having to manually run the compiler for a Java program with hundreds of files. That is not as easy as compiling one file.

This is where the build automation tools of the IDE come to the rescue. Most IDEs for doing Java development can build your Java program no matter how many files you have. They also can integrate with external build tools such as Maven and Gradle. You don't have to worry about the details right now; just know that NetBeans will build and run your project for you with the click of a button.

> **NOTE** We'll take advantage of this integration ability in this book. You will learn to use the Maven build system.

Using the Debugger

Finally, let's talk about the debugger. The debugger is worth its weight in gold but is often overlooked by the novice developer. A debugger allows you to stop the execution of your program, essentially freezing it in time, and to look at exactly what the program is doing at that moment.

Once you've had a look around, you can resume the execution of the program. This is an invaluable feature when you are trying to figure out why your code is not doing what you expected. You will learn how to use a debugger within this book.

> **NOTE** The IDE contains the tools of our craft. The better you learn how to use the tools and features of the IDE, the better a developer you'll become. Remember, a master of any craft is also a master of the tools of the craft.

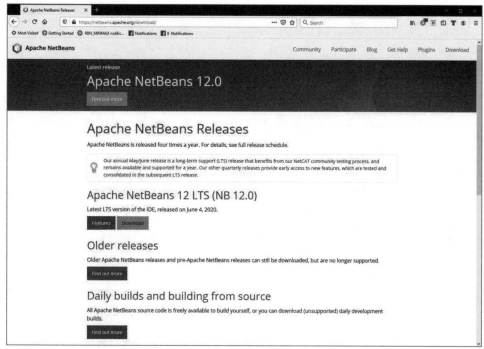

Figure 2.1 The Apache NetBeans download page

INSTALLING NETBEANS

Now that you've had a quick overview of what an IDE is and why it's important, it is time to get and install one on your computer. Before you can install a new IDE, you must first get a copy of it. You can download a copy of Apache NetBeans 12 from netbeans.apache .org/download/. If you go to this page, you should see something similar to Figure 2.1.

From this page, click the *Download* button to get to the page that lists the Apache NetBeans 12 download files, as shown in Figure 2.2.

The page shown in Figure 2.2 gives us a couple of options for installing Apache Net-Beans. Either we can download the binary files that are in a zip file or we can run an installer program. In this lesson, we'll run through both. We will start with the installer.

Using an Installer

On the web page, you can see a section labeled *Installers*. These are programs that you can run that will do the download and installation of NetBeans. As you can see in Figure 2.2, there were three installers available at the time this book was written.

Figure 2.2 Downloading Apache NetBeans 12.0

Choose the one that corresponds to your platform. Your options are for Windows on a 64-bit machine, Linux on a 64-bit machine, or macOS.

Clicking the option for Windows (`Apache-NetBeans-12.0-bin-windows-x64.exe`) takes you to a page like that shown in Figure 2.3. If you pick the Linux or macOS options, you will be taken to similar pages.

Click on the suggested link. This will start the process to open the installer file and install NetBeans on your machine. Simply follow the instructions. For Windows, you will be asked to open the executable file, as shown in Figure 2.4. If you are using a different operating system, you should see something similar but for your operating system.

At this point, what happens will be dependent upon your operating system. We show you what happens on Windows in the following steps. Jump to the next section if you are installing on macOS.

Installing on Windows

In the dialog that was shown when you clicked the link, click *Save File* to save the file. The file will download and save to your hard drive. Once it has downloaded, open it or click it to run the installer program. After approving the program to make changes on your system, the Apache NetBeans Installer will start, as shown in Figure 2.5.

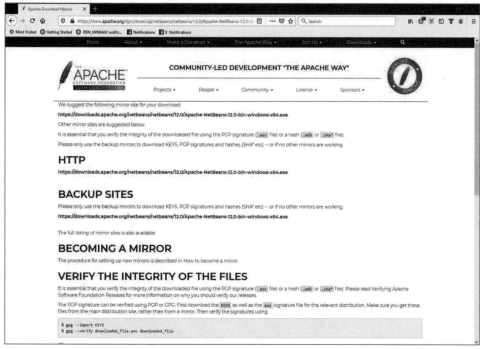

Figure 2.3 Installer for Windows

The program will configure the installer so that the program can be set up on your system. Once the installer has been configured, you will be able to click the Next button, as shown in Figure 2.6.

With the installer configured, click the *Next* button to continue. You will be shown a dialog similar to that in Figure 2.7.

With the installer configured, you are now ready to go. While you can click the *Customize* button on this page, we recommend you simply click *Next*. This will start the installer and take you to the licensing agreement shown in Figure 2.8.

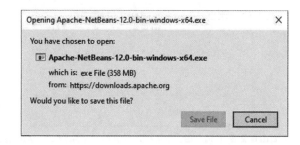

Figure 2.4 Prompt to open the installer file in Windows

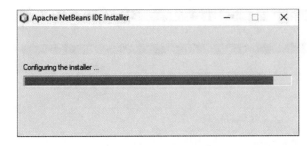

Figure 2.5 Running the Apache NetBeans Installer

In a nutshell, NetBeans is an open source program, distributed under the Apache License. The main points of the license agreement are the following:

- You can use as many copies of the software as you want, and you can distribute the software to others, as long as the distribution package includes the same licensing restrictions.

- You can modify the code and distribute your own version of the code, as long as your modified package includes the same licensing restrictions on the core code distributed by Apache Software Foundation.

- The software is distributed on an as-is basis.

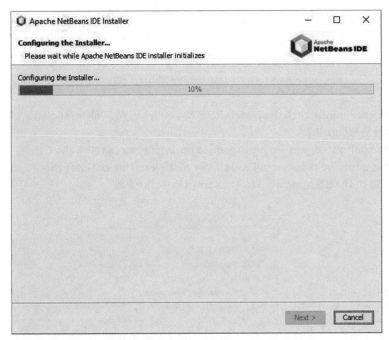

Figure 2.6 The installer configured and ready to go

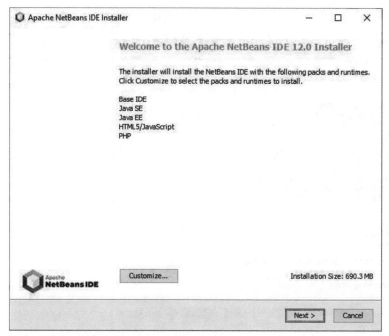

Figure 2.7 Welcome to the installer dialog

Review the terms and then check the box next to *I accept the terms in the license agreement* to be able to continue. Click *Next* to continue the installation process. The next step presented in Figure 2.9 determines where the program files will be installed on your computer.

This dialog asks you where you want to install the IDE and JDK. Unless you have a strong reason not to, you should use the default settings.

Note that this package will install both NetBeans and a compatible JDK. If you already have a JDK installed, this installation will replace it (if it is the same version) or install the JDK alongside any older JDKs you may already have on your computer.

Once you have set the locations, click *Next* to continue. This will take you to the summary page as shown in Figure 2.10, which is the last page before installation.

It is fine to leave the box checked that is next to *Check for updates*. If you are connected to the Internet during the installation process, NetBeans will look for any updated packages and install them at the same time as the other components of the program.

Click *Install* to begin the installation and to continue. The program will then display a dialog similar to Figure 2.11.

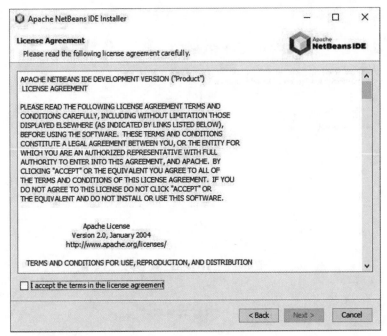

Figure 2.8 Apache NetBeans licensing agreement

The program will prepare to install the files. Once they're prepared, it will do the installation. The dialog shown in Figure 2.11 might change; however, it will inform you of what it is currently doing. Once the installation is complete, you will see a dialog similar to what is shown in Figure 2.12.

You can click the *Finish* button to close the window. At this point, Apache NetBeans should be installed on your system and be ready to use.

> **NOTE** The installation process is similar to the installation process you went through for installing the JDK in Lesson 1.

Installing on macOS

To install Apache NetBeans on your macOS, you should have the downloaded package on your system, as shown in Figure 2.13. The process for downloading the package was mentioned earlier in this lesson.

Double-click the package icon and allow the package to run, as shown in Figure 2.14. When you click *Continue*, the installation wizard will open, as shown in Figure 2.15.

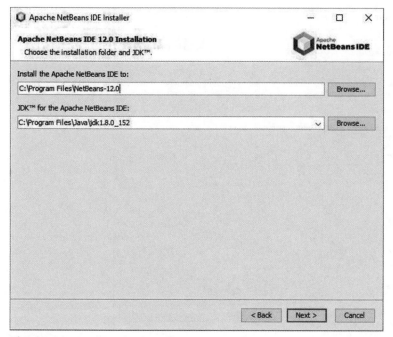

Figure 2.9 Setting the location

Click *Continue* to start the installation process. This will present the licensing agreement for using the software, as shown in Figure 2.16. You must agree to the license to continue with the installation.

In a nutshell, NetBeans is an open source program, distributed under the Apache License. The main points of the license are as follows:

- You can use as many copies of the software as you want, and you can distribute the software to others, as long as the distribution package includes the same licensing restrictions.

- You can modify the code and distribute your own version of the code, as long as your modified package includes the same licensing restrictions on the core code distributed by Apache Software Foundation.

- The software is distributed on an as-is basis.

NOTE You can find the Apache License at www.apache.org/licenses/.

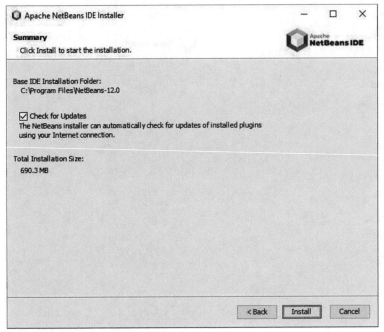

Figure 2.10 Confirming the settings

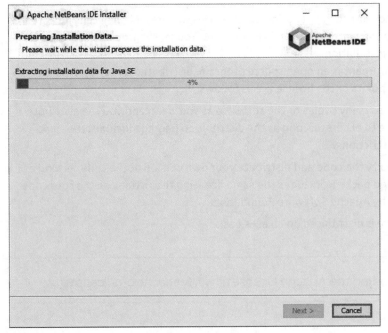

Figure 2.11 Installing the files

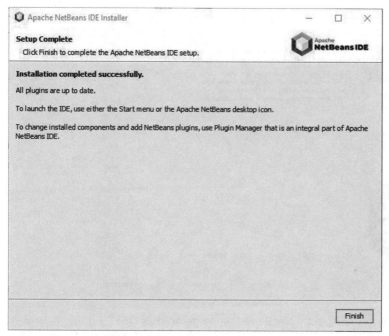

Figure 2.12 Installation complete!

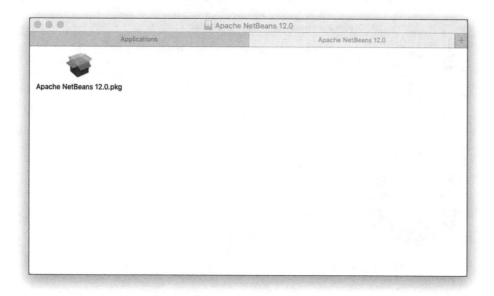

Figure 2.13 The installation package

Figure 2.14 Running the Apache NetBeans package on macOS

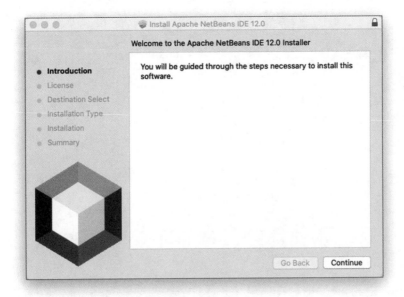

Figure 2.15 The installation wizard

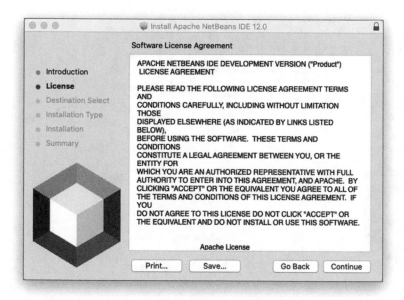

Figure 2.16 The licensing agreement

Review the terms and then click *Continue* and *Agree* to accept the terms in the license agreement.

The installer will present default installation settings, as shown in Figure 2.17. There is no need to change these settings unless you have a specific, unusual need.

Click *Install* to begin the installation. The wizard will proceed to install the program on your system, as shown in Figure 2.18. If necessary, enter your password to continue and then wait for the installation to complete.

You will see a confirmation window similar to that in Figure 2.19 when the installation is complete.

At this point, you have successfully installed NetBeans and may close this window.

Installing Binaries

An alternative way to install the IDE is to download the files and install them manually. This information is presented in case you want more control of how the installation is done. If you used the installer as shown earlier, then feel free to skip this section and jump right to "Running NetBeans."

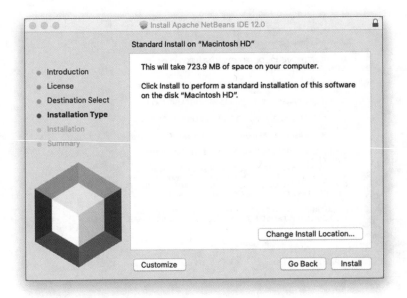

Figure 2.17 Installation settings for macOS

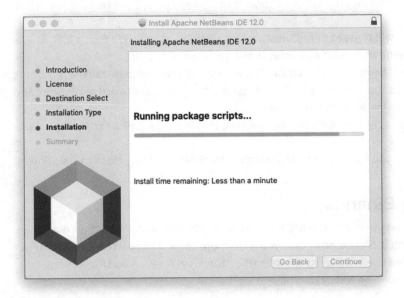

Figure 2.18 Installing the files

Figure 2.19 Installation complete message

The binary process is only shown for Windows; however, installing for other platforms is similar. To install the binaries on Windows, start by clicking the link next to *Binaries* in the list of options you saw in Figure 2.2 earlier. A new page similar to Figure 2.20 will open to confirm the download link.

> **NOTE** The filenames might be slightly different. The current version when this book was written was 12.0. If updates were made, then the version number might differ slightly.

It is fine to accept the suggested link that appears at the top of the page. Clicking that link will download a file named `incubating-netbeans-12.0-bin.zip`. Save the zip file to a known location.

The suggested site may be different from the one shown in the screenshot, based on your location and current traffic to the servers.

After saving the file to your computer, the process will be slightly different depending on whether you are installing on Windows or macOS/Linux. We'll focus on Windows here.

Figure 2.20 Download links for NetBeans binaries

Installing Binaries on Windows

After saving the file to your system, find the `.zip` file on your computer and unzip it. You can do this using the Windows extract tool.

1. Right-click the saved file.

2. Click *Extract All*.

3. Use the Extract dialog box to unzip file to a known location (e.g., Documents or Desktop).

After extracting the files, navigate to the selected location in the previous step. In the example in Figure 2.21, the folder was extracted to the Documents folder, in a subfolder named netbeans.

Open the netbeans folder. As shown in Figure 2.22, this folder contains the files required to run NetBeans, and you should not delete anything in this folder.

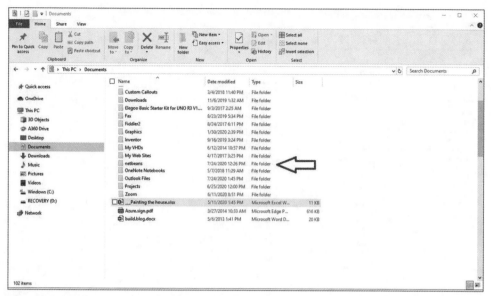

Figure 2.21 The extracted NetBeans files

To start NetBeans, open the `bin` subfolder and double-click the appropriate executable file for your computer. Most Windows users should use `netbeans64.exe`, but if you do not have a 64-bit system or if you have problems running that version, you can choose `netbeans.exe` instead.

The first time you run NetBeans, Windows is likely to display a message saying it does not recognize the application. If so, walk through the prompts to run the program anyway. You might need to click a "more info" link to get the option to click a *Run anyway* button.

If NetBeans opens correctly, you are ready to get started with the programs in the rest of this book. If you have problems, see the next section about adding the JDK.

NOTE The file with no extension is for macOS and will not open on Windows. Use it if you are using macOS.

TIP You can add a shortcut to the executable file to your Start menu or taskbar by right-clicking the file and selecting *Pin to Start* or *Pin to Taskbar* in the context menu.

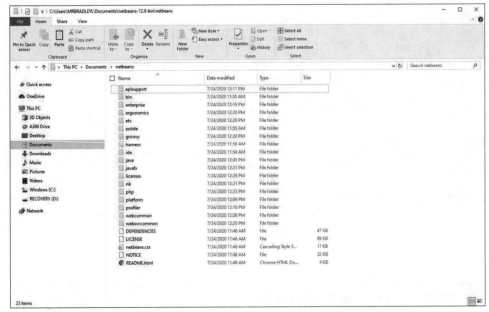

Figure 2.22 The netbeans folder

Adding the JDK

You may receive an error message that NetBeans cannot find Java the first time you open NetBeans. If so, follow these steps to resolve the problem:

1. In the root NetBeans folder, open the etc subfolder and then open the file named netbeans.conf using any text editor (such as Notepad or Notepad++).

2. Locate the line containing netbeans_jdkhome.

3. If this line is commented out (with # at the beginning of the line), remove the # to enable the setting.

4. Set its value to include the path to your JDK, so the line looks something like netbeans_jdkhome="C:\Program Files\AdoptOpenJDK\jdk-11.0.3.7-hotspot".

   a. If you just installed AdoptOpenJDK, use the path provided in that wizard.

   b. If OpenJDK 11 was already installed, locate the Java folder for your system (normally in C:\Program Files\) and use the path to the JDK file in that folder.

   c. The version number may be slightly different. As long as it starts with 11, it is the correct version.

   d. Save the changes to netbeans.conf and close the file.

   e. Launch NetBeans again.

Figure 2.23 The Net-
Beans splash screen

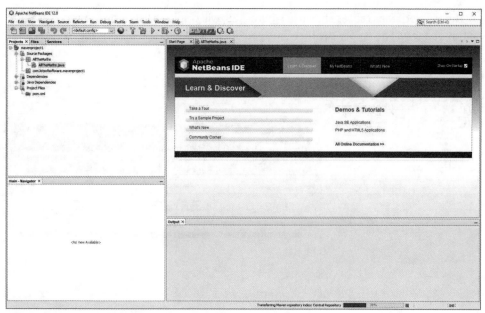

Figure 2.24 The NetBeans start page

RUNNING NETBEANS

The previous sections for Windows and macOS indicated how to open NetBeans to have it run. This was accomplished by running the appropriate NetBeans file as was indicated.

When NetBeans opens, you will first see a splash screen similar to Figure 2.23 that shows it is loading.

After the program is completely loaded, you will see the start page similar to Figure 2.24 that includes links for learning how to use NetBeans. If you don't see this, then click the *Learn & Discover* tab.

> **NOTE** The first time you run NetBeans, you might be prompted with a dialog asking you to help improve the NetBeans IDE. You can read the text and determine whether you would like to provide usage statistics.

The My NetBeans tab, as shown in Figure 2.25, will display a list of previous projects, but this page will be empty the first time you open NetBeans and before you have created any projects.

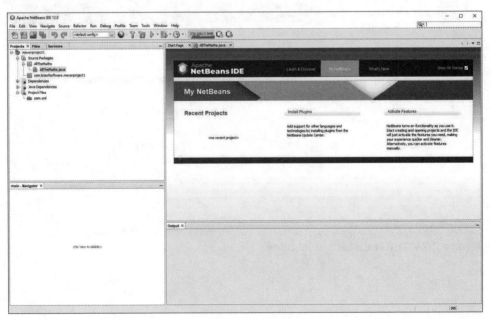

Figure 2.25 The My NetBeans tab in the IDE

SUMMARY

At this point, you have both OpenJDK 11 and NetBeans 12 installed on your computer and ready to use. With the IDE and JDK installed, you are ready to jump in and see the features we discussed early in this lesson. That is exactly what we will do in the next lesson!

Using an Integrated Development Environment

In this lesson, we will use an IDE to create a "Hello, World!" program and look at the tools that an IDE provides to developers.

LEARNING OBJECTIVES

By the end of this lesson, you will be able to:
- Start a new project using NetBeans
- Create a "Hello, World!" program using NetBeans
- Use IDE features to compile your program
- Explore how to start debugging a program

NOTE For this and the remaining lessons, you will need both OpenJDK and NetBeans 12 installed and working on your computer.

USING AN IDE

If you don't already have NetBeans open, open it now and explore it a little bit. As you saw in the previous lesson, when you first open NetBeans, it will normally open to a start page, which includes links to common tasks that are organized by tab. The Learn & Discover tab includes links to resources to help you learn how to use NetBeans and develop software programs using Java. The My NetBeans tab (as shown in Figure 3.1) includes links and shortcuts to recent projects that you have worked on in NetBeans, as well as links to plug-ins and other features available through NetBeans. The What's New tab includes links to news articles and blog posts about NetBeans development.

While the information on these tabs is useful, they don't really represent what Net-Beans can do for you as a developer.

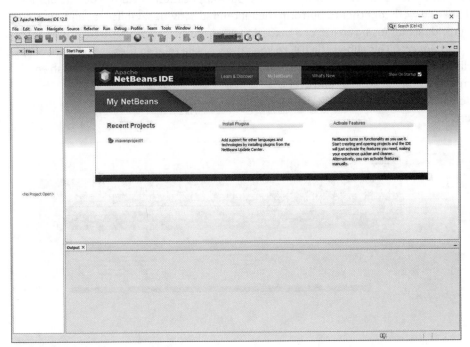

Figure 3.1 The My NetBeans tab

NOTE If you just installed NetBeans, then your projects list is empty because you haven't created anything yet, but that will change as you work through this course.

When we create a program in Java, we have to work through several steps before we can actually run the program. These steps are as follows:

1. Create a new NetBeans project.

2. Type in the Java code and save it using NetBeans.

3. Compile the code in NetBeans.

4. Run the program.

We will go through these steps now. We will also look at how we can use NetBeans to help us find problems in our code and add the new program to our GitHub repository.

Creating a New Project

Let's create a new project. Many (if not most) Java applications include a bundle of files that need to work together to perform their intended activities. While we can simply create individual files (using an IDE or a text editor), we normally use an IDE to group these files into *projects*. This allows the IDE to keep track of the related files as you work on an application, as well as to include all the required parts when you decide to publish and distribute the application to end users.

To create a new project, click the *File* menu and then click *New Project*, as shown in Figure 3.2.

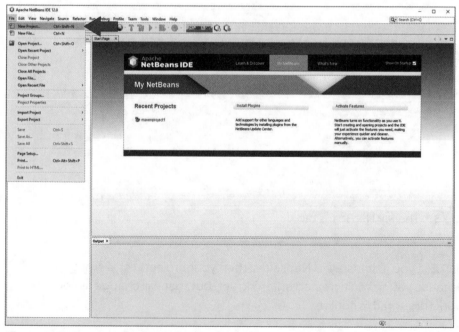

Figure 3.2 Creating a new project

Alternatively, you can simply click the *New Project* button (not New File) in the toolbar as shown in Figure 3.3, or you can use the shortcut Shift+Ctrl+N.

Figure 3.3 Clicking the New Project icon

When you create a new project, NetBeans asks you to start by choosing the type of program you want to create from the dialog, similar to what is shown in Figure 3.4.

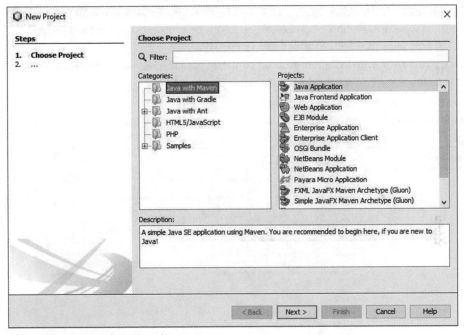

Figure 3.4 Choosing a project type

Maven is a widely used build management system for Java projects. Although Net-Beans has its own internal build management system, many teams use Maven (or something similar) so that their projects can be built without NetBeans. There are often many people on a software development team (quality control, systems administrators, build managers, etc.), and they have different automated processes (such as continuous integration servers) that need to build and deploy a Java project but don't need NetBeans because they aren't going to change the Java code itself. External build systems like Maven make it easy for everyone on the team to get their jobs done without dictating the use of a particular IDE. In this case, we will select *Java with Maven* in the Categories pane and *Java Application* in the Projects pane and then click *Next*.

INSTALLING MAVEN The first time you create a project with Maven, you may be prompted to download and activate content for that project. If you are, click *Download and Activate* to continue and walk through the steps to install the plug-in for those features. You should choose to include any libraries (such as mbjavac Library) and click *Next* to continue the installation process. You will also need to accept any licensing agreements to complete the installations. You might also need to give permission to install plug-ins. If you are using Windows, you should include the JavaFX Implementation for Windows. Once you've walked through the wizard, the installer will confirm when installation is complete. You might be prompted by the New Project Wizard to activate a new feature after it has been installed.

Once you have Maven installed, you can continue with the New Java Application dialog in the New Project Wizard, which is shown in Figure 3.5.

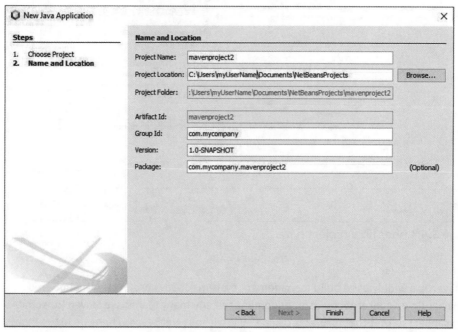

Figure 3.5 The New Java Application dialog in the New Project Wizard

Enter the following information in the dialog box:

Project Name:	HelloWorld
Project Location:	Browse to the folder where you'd like to save your project and select it. The default folder the first time you run NetBeans will be something like `C:\Users\MyUserName\Documents\NetBeansProjects`. You can use the default location if you are unsure.
Group Id:	We'll replace `mycompany` with `tsg`, but you should include your initials or a short username to identify yourself as the developer.
Version:	Leave the default `1.0-SNAPSHOT`, which indicates this is an initial version of the program that we don't plan to ship anywhere.

Let's look at a couple of these options in a little more detail.

The Group Id value essentially identifies who owns and maintains the code, similar to how a domain name works in a web address. We use `com.tsg` in our examples, because `tsg` is being used as an identifier for the Software Guild. NetBeans will automatically use whatever you choose here as the Group Id value for the next project you create, so it's a good idea to use something that identifies you as the developer of the program. A username or initials is appropriate to this end.

The Version value describes the current version of the program, and snapshots are Maven's take on versions. When you create a new program, Maven assumes you want to use SNAPSHOT 1.0. If you use version control software, such as Git or Subversion, Maven will automatically retrieve version numbers from that software and include them in its own documentation for the program.

There are a couple of items we did not include in the previous list. The Artifact Id value should default to the project name, and Package should default to the Group Id combined with the Artifact Id. It's fine to use these default values. Once you've made your changes, the dialog should look similar to Figure 3.6.

With the information updated, click *Finish*, and NetBeans will create an empty project, as shown in Figure 3.7.

Before going on, take a look at the different parts of the window.

The menu bar and the toolbar at the top of the window provide easy access to commonly used tools. Most common tasks (such as creating new projects or compiling and running programs) can be performed using either the appropriate menu option or a tool in the toolbar, and it's worth opening every menu and pointing to every tool to identify where these commands are.

In the left pane, you will find the Projects and Navigator panes, as well as tabs for Files and Services provided through NetBeans. We will use the Projects pane heavily in this book because it displays all the different files required by the current project, organized in directories based on the role that each of those files plays. The Navigator pane

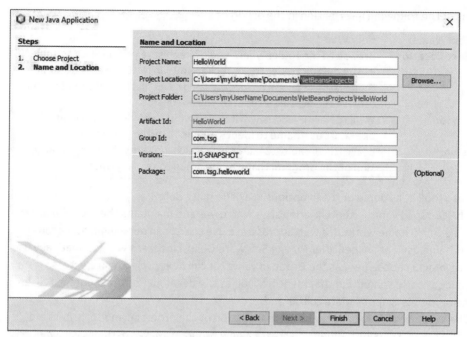

Figure 3.6 The completed Java Application dialog

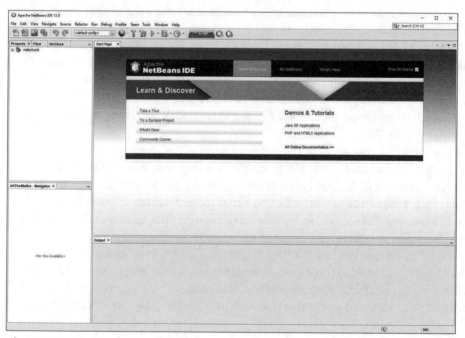

Figure 3.7 A new empty project

will be more useful in the more complicated programs we will create later in the book, because it displays the classes and other objects that have been defined in the code.

The larger pane on the right will display the code window, which we will look at in more detail when we start to code. You can also close the Start Page tab before continuing. You close the tab by clicking the x next to the tab title.

Coding the "Hello, World!" Program

A project is an organizational tool that developers use to keep related files together while we create applications. However, unlike most editors you have probably used in the past, a new project doesn't automatically create a new file for our code. This means we need to create the Java file for our "Hello, World!" program.

Click the + next to *HelloWorld* in the Projects pane. This will expand that directory to display subdirectories created for our Maven project, as shown in Figure 3.8.

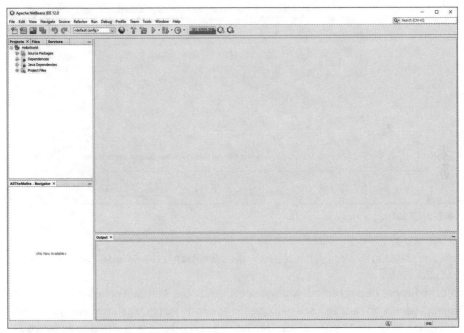

Figure 3.8 Expanding the HelloWorld in the Projects pane

We will look at how each of these subdirectories works in a project as we go further into the book. For now, we will use only the Source Packages subdirectory, which typically holds all the Java code files.

You can create a new Java file in one of two ways:

- Click the *Source Packages* icon in the *Projects* pane, click the *New File* button (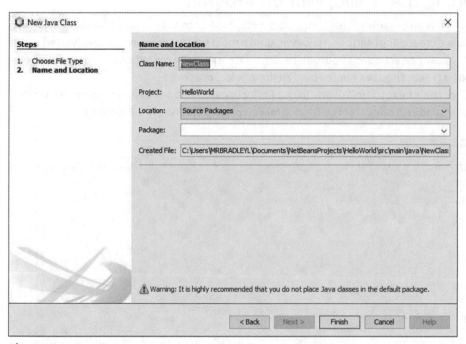) on the toolbar, and select *Java Class* in the *File Types* list in the *New File* dialog box.

- Right-click the *Source Packages* icon, point to *New*, and select *Java Class*.

This will open the New Java Class dialog, as shown in Figure 3.9.

Figure 3.9 Creating a new Java class

Name the class `Hello`. Verify that the new file's location is the Source Packages directory and click *Finish*.

After the file has been created, you will see it inside the Source Packages directory in the Projects pane, and the file itself will open in the code editor, as shown in Figure 3.10.

By selecting to create the new class, NetBeans has created the starting code for you, as shown in Listing 3.1.

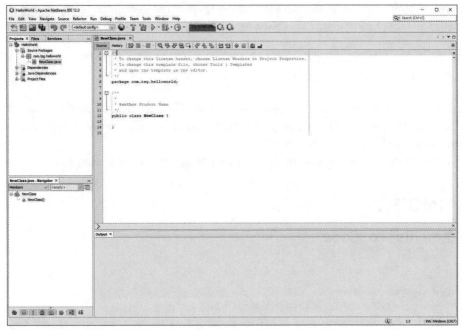

Figure 3.10 The new class file in the code editor

LISTING 3.1

The Default Code for the Hello Class

```
/*
 * To change this license header, choose License Headers in Project
Properties.
 * To change this template file, choose Tools | Templates
 * and open the template in the editor.
 */

/**
 *
 * @author Student Name
 */
public class Hello {

}
```

> **NOTE** Your default code might have a different value after @author. If so, that is okay! You are going to change this.

It is worth looking closer at this default code. As part of the default code, NetBeans includes comment placeholders (lines between /* and */) as well as the following code:

```
public class Hello {

}
```

It used the class name `Hello` because we named the file `Hello.java`. Using the same name for both the file and the class helps the IDE better identify classes that might be added to separate files within the project.

Now update the entire contents of the file by entering the code in Listing 3.2.

LISTING 3.2

The New Hello Code

```
/**
 *
 * @author Your Name
 */
package com.tsg.helloworld; // Use YOUR Group Id value here instead of com.tsg

public class Hello {
    public static void main(String[] args) {
        System.out.println("Hello, World!");
    }
}
```

Let's look at the changes:

- We removed the comments about licensing.
  - Per the instructions there, you can use the NetBeans Template tool to define the default text of new classes, if you want.
- We left the comment with the author information, a common practice to identify the author of a program.
  - While the sample here says *Student Name*, NetBeans likely added your Windows or macOS username here instead. If not, enter your name instead.
  - You can also include comments for @date or @purpose to provide even more details about the project.
- We identified the package that this class belongs to.
  - In this example, we used com.tsg as the Group Id, but you should have used your initials or other personal identifier instead. Change this line as needed for your program.

- The comment starting with // is optional, and you can leave it out of your code.
- We use class Hello to correspond to the name of the file we are using.
- public static void main tells Java where the program itself starts.
- System.out.println tells Java to print out the text inside the parentheses to the standard output, in this case the console.

> **NOTE** We will go over what this code is doing again in the next lesson, so don't be too concerned if you don't fully understand it now.

> **TIP** If you look at Figure 3.9, you will see that there is an option for entering the package. You could have used this drop-down to select existing package names, which would have automatically added the package line into your code. If your package doesn't exist, you can enter it.

Compiling the Code in NetBeans

Now that we have entered the code into the editor, we need to compile our program. Remember that our computer cannot read Java code directly, so we use a compiler to convert our text into language that the operating system can use.

In NetBeans, we compile a program by clicking the *Build* button—a button that looks like a hammer with a blue handle in the main toolbar, as shown in Figure 3.11.

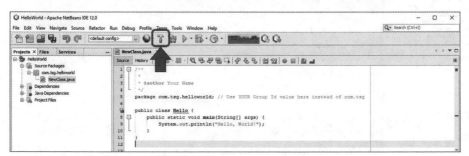

Figure 3.11 The Build button

Alternatively, you can also find the Build option in the Run menu, or simply tap the F11 key to build the current program.

After you click the Build button, the Output pane will open under the code editor, showing the status of the build, as shown in Figure 3.12.

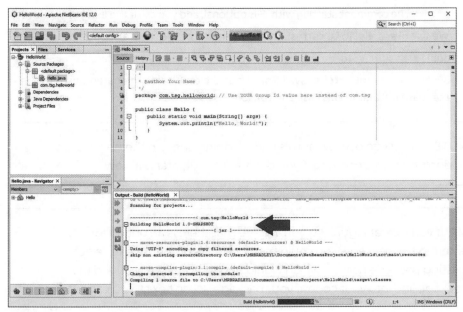

Figure 3.12 Building the Hello program

If the program compiled correctly, you will see a BUILD SUCCESS message in the output pane, as shown in Figure 3.13, along with other details about the build.

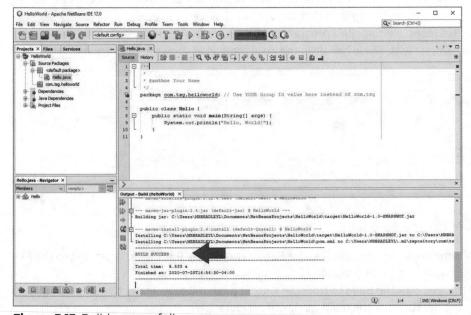

Figure 3.13 Build successful!

If you received an error message when you compiled the program, read the message carefully—it will likely tell you where the error is if not exactly what error it found. Correct the problem and use the Build button to compile the program again.

Running the Program

Now that our program is compiled, we can run it. Click the *Run Project* button (the green arrow icon) in the toolbar, as shown in Figure 3.14, or tap F6 to run the program.

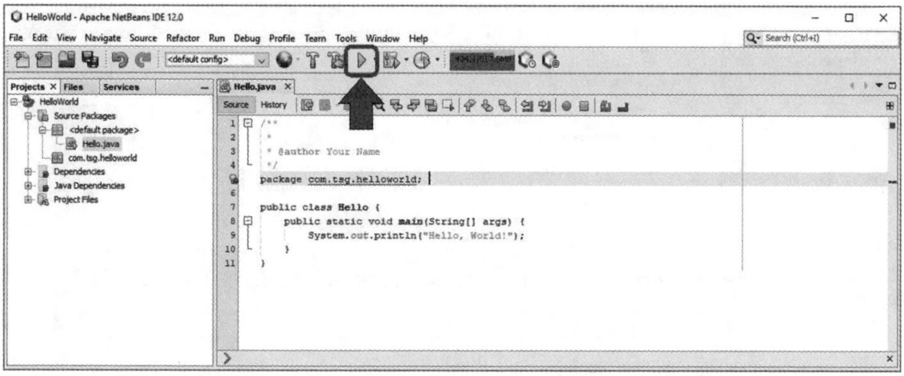

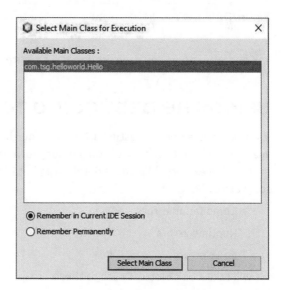

Figure 3.14 The Run Project button

You will be prompted to select a main class for execution, as shown in Figure 3.15.

Figure 3.15 Selecting the class to execute

We have to tell NetBeans and Maven which of our classes contains the main method that we want to run. This is an easy choice for this program since we have only one class: Hello. Click *Remember Permanently* and then click *Select Main Class*.

NetBeans will now run your program, and the text Hello, World! should appear in the output pane, as shown in Figure 3.16.

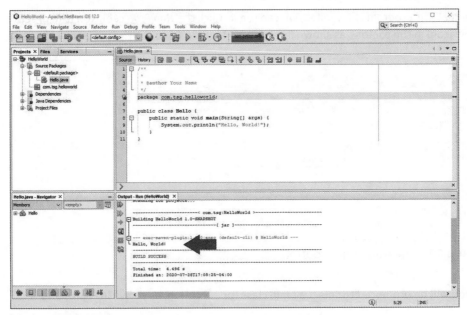

Figure 3.16 The program output

Congratulations! You have used an IDE to write, compile, and run your Java program!

USING THE DEBUGGING TOOLS

If you were able to enter Listing 3.2 without making any mistakes, then congratulations again on a job well done! Errors do happen, however. We will look at errors (more formally called *exceptions*) in more detail later, but in general, three types of errors occur in software code.

- Compilation errors
- Runtime errors
- Logic errors

We will take a quick look at each of these.

Compilation and Syntax Errors

Syntax errors—which include missing or misplaced characters—are the most common type of error, and they can prevent a program from compiling. A huge advantage of an IDE over a text or code editor is that the IDE can help us identify syntax errors before we even compile the code. When you compile code that includes syntax errors, they become compilation errors, and even one syntax error can prevent the code from compiling.

Chances are good that you typed at least one character wrong when you entered the code earlier, or maybe you left out a bracket or a semicolon. In either case, you should have seen red squiggle marks under the text where the error occurred, as well as a red dot next to the line number. In Figure 3.17, we can see that the word *String* is misspelled as *Sring*.

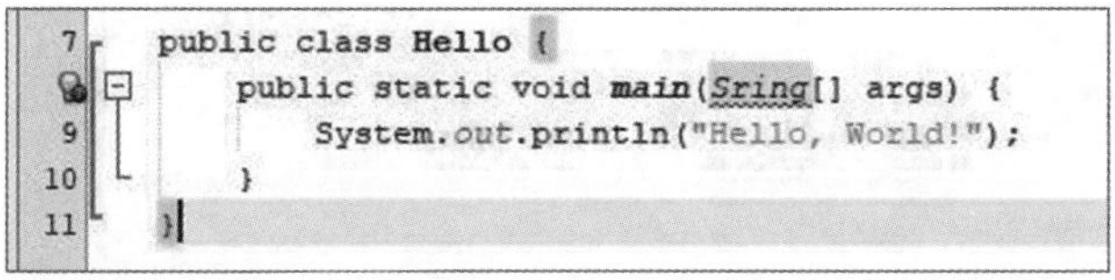

```
 7    public class Hello {
 8        public static void main(Sring[] args) {
 9            System.out.println("Hello, World!");
10        }
11    }
```

Figure 3.17 A syntax error

If you didn't actually enter the code into the editor but simply read it in this book, go back and do it. While it may seem time-consuming to type code while you are learning, you will learn to use the code better and faster if you actually take the time to type it and play with it.

NetBeans is programmed to recognize common compilation and syntax errors and point them out as you enter code. Paying attention to those signals can save you a lot of time in the long run. However, if you do miss them and try to compile anyway, NetBeans will help you identify the error output.

Go back to your program and delete a character, like the *t* in *String*. Because we have already compiled the program (at least once), we can simply rebuild the program instead of recompiling from scratch, by clicking the *Clean and Rebuild* button () next to the Build button (or simply press Shift+F11). The output this time should include a compilation error, as shown in Figure 3.18.

> **NOTE** The Build button completely recompiles all code in the program. The Clean and Rebuild button identifies code that has changed since the last build and recompiles only the classes that contain the changed code, which is more efficient in larger programs.

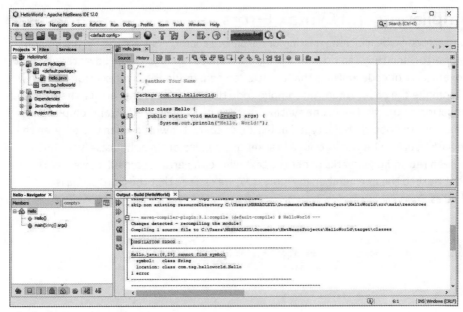

Figure 3.18 A compilation error

Looking at Figure 3.18, you can see that the error message in this example reads as follows:

```
COMPILATION ERROR :
com/tsg/helloworld/Hello.java:[8,29] cannot find symbol
  symbol:    class Sring
  location: class com.tsg.helloworld.Hello
1 error
```

The message includes details about what file the error is in (Hello.java), what line number the error is on (8), and the fact that it cannot find (or recognize) *Sring*.

Fix the error and click *Clean and Rebuild* to recompile the code and verify that the error was corrected.

> **NOTE** One of the values of using an IDE like Maven is that it will do some work in the background while you are creating your program. This work includes compiling and checking your code to find some possible compilation and syntax errors while you are entering your code. When you entered *String* wrong in the previous listing, you might have noticed that the IDE drew a red squiggly line under the word identifying that something was not right.

Runtime and Logic Errors

Exceptions and logic errors are harder to debug. Exceptions are errors that prevent the code from running after it has been compiled, and they include things like dividing a number by 0, which is mathematically impossible.

Logic errors are related to how we define the values that go into the code and that produce unexpected output, even when there are no syntax errors and the code runs without errors. For example, you may write a program designed to multiply 5 and 6 but get the result of 35 instead of 30.

Debuggers and Debugging

IDEs like NetBeans give us a debugging tool that uses *breakpoints* to help us find runtime and logic errors, by allowing us to see the values or output of specific lines of code as the code runs, rather than having to wait until the entire program runs.

It is hard to see how breakpoints work with only one line of executable code, so let's add a second print line. Listing 3.3 provides an update to our `Hello` class.

LISTING 3.3

A Hello Class with Another Line of Code

```
/**
 *
 * @author Your Name
 */
package com.tsg.helloworld;

public class Hello {
    public static void main(String[] args) {
        System.out.println("Hello, World!");
        System.out.println("My name is Harry!");
    }
}
```

If you rebuild and run the program again, you should see both lines print in the output window, as shown in Figure 3.19.

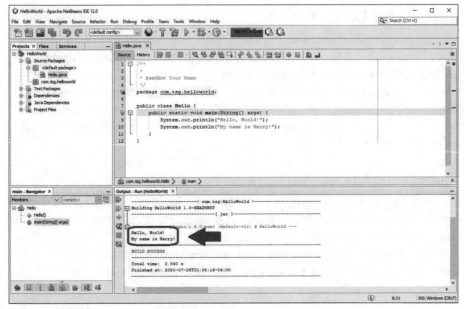

Figure 3.19 Output from the new `Hello` class

Adding a Breakpoint

We will add a breakpoint to the new line of code and then see how the debugger tool uses the breakpoint. We do this in several ways.

Right-click the line number next to the second print command, point to *Breakpoint*, and select *Toggle Line Breakpoint*, as shown in Figure 3.20. In this example, the line number is 10, but your line number may be different.

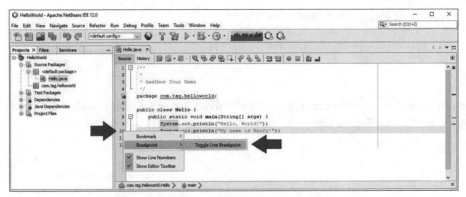

Figure 3.20 Right-clicking to set a breakpoint

A red square will appear on the line number, and the line itself will be highlighted in red to indicate that the breakpoint has been set on that line, as shown in Figure 3.21.

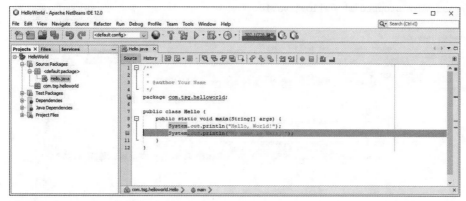

Figure 3.21 A breakpoint has been set.

NOTE You can also set a breakpoint by clicking the line of code where you want to set the breakpoint. Then select *Toggle Line Breakpoint* from the *Debug* menu in the IDE. You can also highlight the line where you want to set the breakpoint and then select Ctrl+F8.

After setting the breakpoint, click the *Debug Project* button (🔳), which is next to the Run button or use Ctrl+F5 to run the program in Debugger Mode, as shown in Figure 3.22.

NOTE If you see both lines of output, you probably hit the Run button instead of the Debug Project button.

NOTE The first time you run the debugger, you might be asked again to select the main class. Do this just as you did before when running the program.

As you can see in Figure 3.22, the Debugger pane will open under the code window with Variables, Breakpoints, and Output tabs, and the Debugger panel will open to indicate that the program is running and the debugger stopped at the breakpoint on line 10. You should see output similar to the following:

```
User program running
LineBreakpoint Hello.java : 10 successfully submitted.
Breakpoint hit at line 10 in class com.tsg.helloworld.Hello by thread main.
Thread main stopped at Hello.java:10.
```

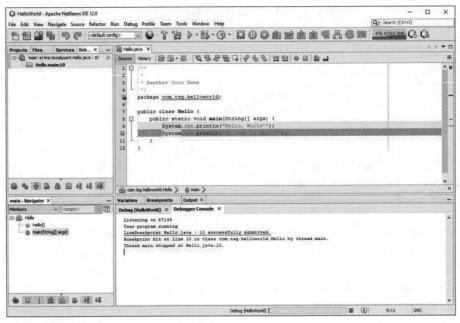

Figure 3.22 Running to a breakpoint

Click the tab that reads *Debug (HelloWorld)* to see the last output value, as shown in Figure 3.23.

As you can see in the Debug tab shown in Figure 3.23, the following information is displayed:

```
-------------------------------------------------------------------------
Building HelloWorld 1.0-SNAPSHOT
-------------------------------------------------------------------------

--- exec-maven-plugin:1.5.0:exec (default-cli) @ HelloWorld ---
Hello, World!
```

This tells us that the program stopped executing after outputting the phrase `Hello, World!`.

Hit the F5 key to tell the debugger to continue. The program should finish running and display the second line of text in the Debug output pane.

```
--- exec-maven-plugin:1.5.0:exec (default-cli) @ HelloWorld ---
Hello, World!
My name is Harry!
---------------------------------------------------------------------
BUILD SUCCESS
```

You can remove the breakpoint the same way you added it: right-click the square, point to *Breakpoint*, and click *Toggle Line Breakpoint*.

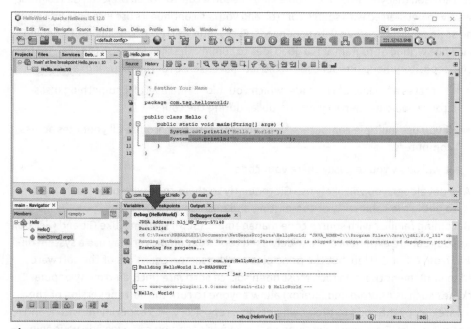

Figure 3.23 The Debug tab

NOTE In Lesson 11, "Debugging your Applications," we will go into greater detail on debugging.

UNDERSTANDING SOURCE CONTROL

Source control is an integral part of the software development process. The proper use of source control can be the difference between having a copy of files when they appear to be lost and really losing the files. Hard drive failures, files being accidentally over-written, and other catastrophes are hard to avoid; they just happen sometimes.

Source control management systems are designed to keep history and revision information about the files and projects stored within a repository, which is an online storage space usually maintained through a source control manager like GitHub or Bitbucket. By storing this information, we have a complete history of everything that happened to the projects within the repository. In the event of a catastrophe, we can recover a previously saved version. Also, by saving our changes, we can easily share work with other developers and collaborate on projects regardless of location.

It is advised that you always use some kind of source control for all projects. Git is a great, easy way to get started with source control, and you can continue its use into enterprise and large-scale projects. It grows with your needs. Every time you reach a meaningful stopping point while writing a program, it is a good idea to commit the files and push the changes to a GitHub repository. Keeping your code in GitHub makes sense for the following reasons:

- It creates a backup of the code, which you might find useful if something disastrous should happen to your computer during the course.

- If you use multiple computers, you can use Git to synchronize all your files across computers.

- It will allow you to easily share your code.

As a developer, you will likely use Git regularly to share code with other team members, so get in the habit early of committing and pushing code often.

Becoming familiar with source code management (SCM) systems (like Git and GitHub) gives you real-life experience in a widely used tool. Your employer may use a system different from Git or GitHub, but the principles are the same, regardless of the software used to implement them. In fact, most open source software (including many popular packages such as Android and Firefox) allow anyone to fork the current version of the software—copy the code to their own personal repository—to experiment with it and see how it works. Once you have some coding experience, you can even add your own features to an existing open source software package and submit them to the developer group of that package for review.

> **NOTE** You don't have to use Git or GitHub to use this book; however, when you start building applications for more than just learning the language, we highly recommend that you consider their use or the use of a similar version control product.

> **NOTE** You can find official documentation on getting started with Git at https://git-scm.com/book/en/v2/Getting-Started-Installing-Git.

SUMMARY

Congratulations! Here is what we covered in this lesson:

- We discussed and explored the main features of an IDE: code editor, debugger, and build automation.
- We created, compiled, ran, and debugged "Hello, World!" in NetBeans.
- We looked at the display of error messages and output in NetBeans.
- We looked at basic debugger operations in NetBeans.

With your tools set up, you are ready to go! In the next lesson, we will start digging into the Java programming language.

PART II

Basics of Object Oriented Programming

Lesson 4
Using Program Statements and Variables

Have you ever tried to learn another spoken language? Have you thought about what is involved in this process? Natural languages are composed of many things: language constructs (nouns, verbs, adjectives, etc.), word order, and tense, to name a few. These features are common to all natural languages, so to learn a new language, you must understand how these features work in that language.

Learning a programming language is similar—you must understand the language constructs and how to say something that makes sense in the language. When learning your first programming language, you have a couple of additional challenges. Not only do you have to learn the programming language, but you also have to learn the meta-language of programming. In other words, you must learn how to talk about programs and programming languages. You will also have to learn the language of the industry and how we talk about software, the process of software development, and computer technology in general. This is a lot to learn at once and can be quite difficult at first; however, it will get easier as you gain experience.

In this lesson, your journey begins with the smallest pieces of the Java language: programs, statements, and variables.

LEARNING OBJECTIVES

By the end of this lesson, you will be able to:

- Define the term *computer*
- Compare data and information
- Differentiate between program and programming
- Explain the importance of objects and specifications in creating programs
- Describe the difference between syntax and semantics
- Explain why the use of comments is so important in development
- Explain the purpose of an identifier
- Explain the difference between primitive data types and reference or developer-defined data types
- Identify literals in code
- Use variables in code
- Use expressions in code
- Know the Java operators and the order in which they are evaluated

APPROACH

We will take a bottom-up approach in this course. We will start with the smallest pieces of the language and build our vocabulary—at first, it will be a lot like "See Spot run," but we will quickly move on from there. As our vocabulary grows, we will look at more complicated statements and add larger and larger constructs.

Learning to write software is like learning how to write fiction or learning how to play an instrument. In fiction writing, you start with the basic vocabulary and build on it (after all, you cannot write the next great American novel if you only know six words). Then, you move on to more complicated sentences, paragraphs, chapters, and finally the novel itself. Similarly, when learning to play an instrument, you start with the individual notes, then scales, then more complicated rhythms, melodies, chords, and harmonies, and finally entire songs.

Learning to write software is a process: you must start at the beginning, build a strong foundation, and—most importantly—practice. A lot.

CONCEPTS

To begin, we will look at some concepts you will need to write good software: computers, data and information, programs and programming, models and metaphors, objects, specifications, and, finally, syntax and semantics. We must keep these concepts in mind because computer programs are not merely a sequence of characters on the screen, typed in the right order to magically make things happen. We write programs that instruct the computer to process data and to solve real problems.

Computers

So, what is a computer, anyway? Computers are seen and used every day, but what are they? One definition is as follows:

> An electronic device that processes data according to a set of instructions contained in a program.

This is a general definition that covers all the bases for our purposes. One thing to keep in mind is that it takes both the hardware (computer) and the software (program) to accomplish anything useful. Most people do not program computers—most people simply use them. You will be doing both as you go through this book.

Data vs. Information

Data and *information* are two words that are closely related and are often used interchangeably, but they have different meanings. Data is the raw material from which information is built. An example of data is a number like 120. You can recognize it as a number, but it does not have any meaning. Does it refer to your current speed? The temperature?

How much money you have in your pocket (in dollars or pennies)? Something else? Information is interpreted data, and it is the interpretation that gives it meaning. The computer processes data, but we give that data meaning and interpret the output as information.

Programs and Programming

What is a program? What is programming? A *program* is a set of instructions that, when run on a computer, solves a particular problem or performs a task. For example, maybe the program will add any two given numbers together and produce the sum. Programming is the act of writing those instructions for the computer to solve the problem. One thing to keep in mind is that the computer cannot and will not help you solve any problem; it simply does what you tell it to do.

> *You must be able to solve a problem on paper before you can tell the computer how to solve it!*

For the most part, programming is not about math—it is about solving problems, organization, and structure. It is what we do when we write these sets of instructions. This implies that you need to know what the problem is and know how to solve it before you can even begin to write a program. Knowing this is something that many beginning developers fail to understand.

Models and Metaphors

We use models and metaphors to help us program solutions to problems. If our programs are to solve real-world problems, they must distill the problem down to its essence, model the important pieces, and then calculate the result. One great example of a computer metaphor is the concept of a "desktop" on your computer. It is not really a desktop, but the metaphor is useful in helping us to organize files (folders and files are also metaphors) and icons that we use.

Objects

One of the most important metaphors that we use in Java is the object. This metaphor is not used in Java alone; it is used in all object-oriented languages. Objects represent things, and the world is full of things. Things have properties (weight, volume, color, etc.), and they have actions that they can perform (walk, turn left, fly, etc.). Objects model these properties and actions. We are not going to get into objects too deeply until Part 3, but keep the concept of objects in mind as we move through the lessons in this part.

Specifications

Specifications are important to the process of writing software. They tell us what problem we are to solve. Without a specification, there is no way of knowing what kind of program to write. Specifications do not have to be elaborate, but they do have to state the problem to be solved and any constraints around the problem.

Syntax vs. Semantics

One thing that can be frustrating to beginning programmers is how literal the compiler is. If you do not type in perfectly formed Java statements, the compiler will not understand what you mean. Beginning programmers spend a lot of time worrying about syntax—after all, if the compiler won't compile your code, you cannot run your program. You will learn proper Java syntax in this book (as discussed earlier, we'll build your vocabulary); however, the main emphasis of your learning will be on semantics: the meaning and purpose of the various language constructs and (most importantly) how and when to use them to solve problems.

LANGUAGE BUILDING BLOCKS

Now that we are familiar with some of the concepts involved in programming, we are ready to move on to the Java language itself. In the first two lessons of this unit, we wrote the simple "Hello, World!" program. We got familiar with the basics of a Java program, and now it is time to take a deeper look. We will start with some beginning vocabulary pieces and then look at the rules for how those pieces can be used. These pieces are all related, so we will cover all of them in this section.

Comments

Comments are used to document your code. Comments are important for us as developers, but not for the computer itself because the compiler and runtime will ignore these comments. Adding comments while developing and writing your code is an especially important habit to get into. These comments may be used by other developers who come along later to maintain or modify your code, but often these comments will be useful to you as well.

Comments are written clues that we leave for ourselves. What was I thinking when I did this, and why did I implement it the way I did? Comments can be extremely helpful if we come back to our code in two or three months. They are also helpful to our teammates who might have to review our code as well.

If you are new to programming, you should know that it is quite common to be asked to go back and enhance or fix code that you wrote perhaps six months or a year ago. It is likely that you would have worked on several projects since that original code was written, which makes it hard to remember why you did what you did. This is where code comments can save the day. One of my favorite quotes of software development is by Hal Abelson:

Programs must be written for people to read, and only incidentally for machines to execute.

Java supports three types of comments, which will each be covered in turn:

- Single-line (a trailing or end-of-line comment)
- Multiline (a traditional comment)
- Doc (or Document comment)

Single-Line Comments

Single-line comments begin with //. The compiler will ignore everything between the // and the end of the line. Single-line comments are handy if you just have to jot something down.

The following is an example of a line of Java code with a single-line comment at the end:

```
System.out.println("Hello, World!"); // print to console
```

Multiline Comments

Multiline comments begin with /*, can span multiple lines, and end with */. The compiler ignores everything between /* and */ inclusive. The following snippet of code has a multiline comment that begins on the first line and goes through the fifth line. This is then followed by three lines of Java code.

```
/*
    public static void main(String[] args)
    This is the entry point for the program.
    Prints "Hello, World!" to the console.
*/
public static void main(String[] args) {
    System.out.println("Hello, World!");
}
```

> **NOTE** Multiline comments are also known as *block comments*.

Doc Comments

Doc or document comments begin with /**, can span multiple lines, and end with */. The compiler ignores everything between /** and */ inclusive. Document comments may appear to be nearly identical to multiline or traditional comments, except that they differ in two ways. First, they have the extra asterisk at the beginning. Second, document comments are generally used in only specific locations in your code. Doc comments are used by the Javadoc utility to generate HTML documentation for your program. Because of this, doc comments can also be referred to as *Javadoc comments*. The following is an example of a simple document comment:

```
/**
    Documentation for a method
*/
```

Anytime we have that slash and two stars at the beginning, we know that it is a doc comment. Doc comments can document our classes and methods. Some of the Java tools you use that generate code are likely to add doc comments automatically for you when they generate code. For example, in the IntelliJ tool, if you put a slash followed by two asterisks and then hit Return, it automatically puts a doc comment block into the code.

Javadoc comments can also be used for each of the methods that you will create. They give you a chance to explain what the code is going to do as well as describe what it expects. This could include something like the entry point to the program as well as a description of any arguments that are used.

> **NOTE** Javadoc comments are good for classes and also good for methods; however, you don't generally put Javadoc comments on the main method because the main method is everywhere and is always the entry point into a Java program.

As you will be writing methods in the future, you might want to put doc comments on them. That way, people will understand how to use your methods or what you were thinking about when you created that method.

In a previous lesson you were introduced to a "Hello, World!" application, which you created using the NetBeans IDE. The IDE created some of the code, and then you added to it. Listing 4.1 presents part of the code presented in that lesson.

LISTING 4.1

"Hello, World!" Program

```
/*
 * To change this license header, choose License Headers in Project
 * Properties.
 * To change this template file, choose Tools | Templates
 * and open the template in the editor.
 */

/**
 *
 * @author Your Name
 */
public class Hello {
    public static void main(String[] args) {
        System.out.println("Hello, World!");
    }
}
```

In this listing, you can see two of the types of comments. In the first five lines of the listing, you can see a multiline comment. This starts with a slash followed by a single asterisk and ends with a single asterisk followed immediately by a slash in the fifth line. After this block comment, you see that the next code line starts with a forward slash followed by two asterisks. As you learned, this is the start of a doc comment. This doc comment continues for a couple more lines before ending with an asterisk followed immediately by a forward slash.

Using Comments

There are a couple things to note about comments. Even though your compiler will ignore them and even though comments will not really affect the way your program runs, you should be judicious about how you comment things. For instance, the single-line comment example in the previous example would not be a valuable comment. The comment says that the code prints to the console. That is what System.out.println does, so it really is not necessary to say that as a comment because it is redundant.

If, however, you have some kind of calculation you are doing such as a conversion of temperatures, then you could put a note in the comment to say that the formula converts from Fahrenheit to Celsius or from Celsius to Fahrenheit. If you have code that is kind of tricky, then you could put a comment to let other people know what is going on.

Be judicious, but make sure you include comments, because it does make it a lot easier for your teammates and a lot easier for yourself when you come back and look at your code. Of course, when maintaining your code, you should always remember to also maintain and update your comments.

> **TIP** A common use of comments is to temporarily disable lines of code during the development process. Commenting out code allows you to see what was there before you started experimenting with the code. To restore the code, you just remove the comment markers.

> **NOTE** You can read more about using comments in the online documentation at www.oracle.com/technetwork/java/codeconventions-141999.html.

Identifiers

An identifier is a sequence of characters used to name a variable, method, class, or package. You will learn about variables, methods, classes, and packages later. For now, you need to know that a Java identifier must follow these rules:

- It cannot span multiple lines.
- It must only contain numbers, letters, underscores (_), dashes (-), and dollar signs ($).
- It must start with a letter, underscore, dash, or dollar sign.
- It cannot contain any spaces.
- It cannot be an underscore on its own.

Java reserves the words shown in Table 4.1, which means you cannot use them as identifiers.

Table 4.1 Java Reserved Words (Keywords and Literals)

abstract	assert	boolean	break	byte
case	catch	char	class	const
continue	default	do	double	else
enum	extends	false	final	finally
float	for	goto	if	implements
import	instanceof	int	interface	long
native	new	null	package	private
protected	public	return	short	static
strictfp	super	switch	synchronized	this
throw	throws	transient	true	try
void	volatile	while	_	

Data Types

We have talked about data and information. You should already understand concepts such as numbers or text. But how do we tell the computer that we would like to do something with a number or keep track of a name? This can be done by telling the computer about the kind of data we want to deal with by using something called a type.

A *data type* describes the internal representation of a piece of data and the operations that can be applied to that data. A type has certain predefined characteristics. These characteristics include what kinds of things are valid and how big those things can be. You can think of types as defining the shape and size of the data that fits the definition.

For example, int is a data type in Java. Valid ints are whole numbers in the range from roughly negative two billion to positive two billion. The word *apple* is not an int. In fact, it is not even a number. And the number 12.45 is not an int either because it is not a whole number. While the number four billion is a whole number, it is too big to be an int. So, you can see that for something to fit the definition of a type, it has to meet all the criteria of the definition.

Java has two kinds of data types: *primitive* (which are part of the language definition) and *reference* (or developer-defined). We will cover primitive data types in this lesson.

NOTE It's also possible to create your own types. In fact, each class we write is actually a new type. For now, just concentrate on the concept of the type itself.

Table 4.2 presents the Java primitive data types. The table includes the type along with a description of what it can contain, the default value of the type, the amount of memory needed to store the data type (size), and then the range of values that can be placed into the type.

Table 4.2 Java Primitive Types

Type	Contains	Default	Size	Range
boolean	true or false	false	1 bit	NA
char	Unicode character	\u0000	16 bits	\u0000 to \uFFFF
byte	Signed integer	0	8 bits	-128 to 127
short	Signed integer	0	16 bits	-32768 to 32767
int	Signed integer	0	32 bits	-2147483648 to 2147483647

Type	Contains	Default	Size	Range
long	Signed integer	0	64 bits	-9223372036854775808 to 9223372036854775807
float	IEEE 754 floating point	0.0	32 bits	±1.4E-45 to ±3.4028235E+38
double	IEEE 754 floating point	0.0	64 bits	±4.9E-324 to ±1.7976931348623157E+308

It is worth noting that because computers are binary machines, they only understand whole numbers. As such, decimal numbers such as floats and doubles are really inherently imprecise. Floats and doubles should never be used for precise calculations for numbers such as currency.

Statically Typed Languages

A couple of terms that you will hear associated with types are statically typed and dynamically typed languages. Java is a statically typed language. This means we have to say the type of a piece of data before we use it. By doing this, we let the compiler know ahead of time the kind of data that is valid for particular purposes and at particular points in our program. In other words, all the types for all the data in our program are known at compile time.

Type Conversion

On occasion, you will need to convert one data type to another. In general, the compiler will automatically convert a narrower data type (i.e., one containing fewer bits) to a wider data type (i.e., one containing a larger number of bits) but will not do the reverse. In the reverse case, the developer is generally required to explicitly tell the compiler how to convert the data type with a cast operator, which will be covered later.

To illustrate this, imagine that you have a small carry-on piece of luggage for your trip. If you wanted to, you could easily fit the contents of the small carry-on into a larger suitcase. You wouldn't even have to think about it; everything would just fit. However, if you started with the large suitcase and wanted to switch to the smaller carry-on, you would have to make decisions as to what items (shirt? shorts? camera?) you would have to leave out. You would have to make some explicit decisions about what stays home and what goes with you.

> **NOTE** The ability of the compiler to check that all types are compatible is known as *type safety*, and it's one of the advantages of a statically typed language. The type safety feature saves you time and effort when coding because it will prevent you from doing things that are undefined or unexpected.

Literals

A *literal* is a sequence of characters that represents a data item in the source code. Java recognizes six data literals, listed here:

- **boolean**: The reserved words true and false are `boolean` literals.
- **char**: A `char` (character literal) is represented by a single character surrounded by single quotes ('B'), a Unicode escape sequence (u\000), or a regular escape sequence (\n).
- **Floating-point number**: Examples of floating-point literals are: 3.14, 2.56E+31, and 4.56D. The letter F or f can be used to specify a `float` data type; D or d is used to specify a `double` data type.
- **Whole number**: Integer literals can be written as decimal (104) or hexadecimal (0x19F). They are of the `int` data type unless followed by an uppercase or lower-case L, in which case they are of the `long` data type.
- **Null**: The reserved word `null` is a null literal. We will look at this in more detail in the next unit.
- **String**: This is a sequence of characters surrounded by double quotes. `"Hello, World!"` is a string literal.

Variables

Variables are used in combination with the Java type system that you saw earlier. A *variable* is a named piece of memory where you can stash the value of something. The reason that these spots in memory are called variables is because we can change the value of the data that we put in the spot in memory as our program runs.

To declare a variable, we simply type in the data type, for example, `int`, followed by the name that we want to give the variable, for example, `counter`. In short, you must declare your variable according to the following pattern:

```
data_type variable_name;
```

The following code snippet creates a variable on the third line that is called counter and is of the data type int. The code also creates a variable called isDone on the seventh line that is of the data type boolean.

```
public static void main(String[] args) {

        // declare an int called counter
        int counter;

        // declare a boolean called isDone
        boolean isDone;
    }
```

Once you have declared a variable, you can assign a value to it. The following code stores the value of 7 in the counter variable, and it stores the value of false in the isDone variable:

```
public static void main(String[] args) {

        // declare an int called counter
        int counter;
        // now assign the number 7 to counter
        counter = 7;

        // declare a boolean called isDone
        boolean isDone;
        // now assign false to isDone
        isDone = false;
    }
```

You can also declare a variable and assign a value at the same time, if you want:

```
public static void main(String[] args) {

        // declare an int called counter and assign the value 7
        int counter = 7;

        // declare a boolean called isDone and assign false
        boolean isDone = false;
    }
```

When assigning values to variables, you must be sure to assign the correct type. Failing to do so will result in a compilation error. For example, you cannot assign the number 34 to a variable that is of the type boolean.

The name of your variable should be descriptive of what you are going to use the variable for in your program. In our example, you would expect a variable called counter to, well, count something. Make sure your variable names are easy to read and clear on what they do. You might be tempted to just use c for the name of your counter, or ctr, but don't do it. Just name the variable what it is; for a counter, that would be the name counter.

Another important point to note when creating variables is the style of the variable name. In Java the convention is to use *camel case*, which means the variable name starts with lowercase but any new words are capitalized. In the previous examples, you can see that with isDone. If the variable name is one word, it is simply lowercased. It is important to note that this is not something enforced by the Java compiler, but it is the agreed-upon style that the vast majority of Java code written today will use.

Constants

On occasion, you will need to define constants, or "magic" numbers, in your code. *Constants* are similar to variables in that they are named pieces of data; however, once you set the value for a constant, it cannot be changed. For example, you may want to define a constant for pi or for min/max limits in a program.

The convention in Java is that the name of constants should be in all caps and should use underscores to separate words in the name. You should also declare constants using the final keyword as in the following examples:

```
final int MAX_AGE = 99;
final float PI = 3.14f;
```

It is good practice to use constants rather than literal values in your code. The use of constants makes your code more readable but also makes it more maintainable. Consider the case where the business rules change and MAXAGE goes from 99 to 109. If you are using a constant for MAXAGE, you only have to make this change in one place. If you are using literals, you will have to make the change everywhere you use the literal. What happens if you miss one?

Operators and Expressions

We now understand that Java requires types and that we can use variables to hold on to pieces of data for a particular type. We also understand how to declare variables and assign values to variables in our programs. But a big part of programming is figuring out how to actually get data into our variables and how to execute our programming logic.

For this we will need a new kind of statement called an *expression*. An expression is a statement that can be evaluated to produce a result. The actions that your program takes are expressed in statements. There are many types of statements in Java, and as we just mentioned, we have seen and used two of them: variable declaration statements and assignment statements. Now, we will look at another kind of statement, the expression.

Expression statements can calculate values, assign values, and compare values. An expression is a series of *operators* and *operands*. An operator is a symbol that represents an operation that returns a result. You should be familiar with basic operators and operands from everyday math. Operators are the symbols that do the work (such as +, -, *, /). The plus sign is an operator that we have used, and it returns a result that is a number.

An operand is a data element used by the operator. Using the plus sign, the operands would be the two things that we want to add. So, in this case, the result of the operator is a number. The process by which we get from 5 plus 10 to 15 is called *evaluation*. Figure 4.1 illustrates three expressions with operands and operators.

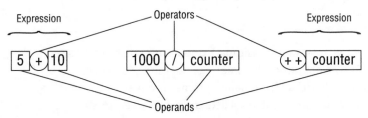

Figure 4.1 Operators and operands

One of the cool things about programming is that operands can come from anywhere. Operands can be literals, which means we directly type the values into the code. Operands can also be variables, and the value of that variable will be used in the evaluation. Finally, operands can be the result of method calls.

Three Flavors of Operators

Java as a language has a few more operators than grade-school math. It has 41, in fact. Operators come in three types: unary, binary, and ternary. The type depends on the number of operands that the operators requires.

Unary Operators

Unary operators require only one operand. (The negation operator is one example.) Unary operators can be either *prefix* (coming before the operand) or *postfix* (coming after the operand). Table 4.3 shows examples of unary operators.

Table 4.3 Unary Operators

Operator	Description
+	Unary plus operator (numbers are positive by default)
-	Unary minus operator
++	Increment operator
--	Decrement operator
!	Logical complement operator (inverts the value of a `boolean`)
~	Unary bitwise complement

> **NOTE** Note that while all the operators are being shown in this section of the book, some, such as the bitwise operators, might be unfamiliar to you. For now, just know that these operators exist. You will learn more about many of these throughout this book.

Binary Operators

Binary operators require two operands. (Basic math operations fall into this category.) Binary operators are *infix* (the operator is between the operands). Binary operators fall into several categories, including the assignment, arithmetic, equality/relational, conditional, and bitwise/bit shift operators. Table 4.4 lists the binary operators.

Table 4.4 Binary Operators

Operator	Description
Simple Assignment Operator	
=	Simple assignment operator
Arithmetic Operators	
+	Additive operator (also used for string concatenation)
-	Subtraction operator
*	Multiplication operator
/	Division operator
%	Remainder operator
Comparison Operators (Equality and Relational Operators)	
==	Equal to
!=	Not equal to
>	Greater than
>=	Greater than or equal to
<	Less than
<=	Less than or equal to
instanceof	Compares an object to a specified type

Operator	Description
Conditional Operators	
&&	Conditional-AND
||	Conditional-OR
Bitwise and Bit Shift Operators	
<<	Signed left shift
>>	Signed right shift
>>>	Unsigned right shift
&	Bitwise AND
^	Bitwise exclusive OR
|	Bitwise inclusive OR

As you can see, there are many categories of binary operators. The arithmetic operators work just like familiar math operators. The one that you might be less familiar with is the remainder (or modulus) operator, which returns the remainder of an operation. As such, if you did 7 % 2, the result would be 1 because the remainder after dividing is 1.

Another category of binary operators is the comparison operators. Comparison operators compare two values and producing a single value of true or false. Comparison operators are used in conditional statements, where the outcome of a program is dependent on the available input, rather than being predictable based on fixed values.

Conditional operators tend to be used with a comparison operator to allow for multiple tests to be done at once. In the case of &&, you are looking for both conditions to be true. In the case of ||, you are looking for one or the other of the two conditions to be true.

NOTE Bitwise operators are a more advanced topic.

Ternary Operators

Ternary operators require three operands. There is only one ternary operator in Java: the conditional operator, which is an infix operator:

?:   Ternary (shorthand operator for if–then–else statement)

You'll see the ternary operator in action when you learn about the if–then–else statement later in this book.

Operator Precedence

In addition to the different types and categories of operators, Java also has 14 different levels of operator precedence. *Precedence* is the order in which you evaluate expressions when they are grouped together.

For example, like in math, addition and subtraction are at the same level of precedence. As a result, if all you have are addition and subtraction operations, you can really do them in any order. In the following expression, you can choose to add the 3 to the 5 first, or you can subtract the 2 from the 5 first. In either case, the result will be 6.

$$3+5-2$$

When operators have the same precedence, they are typically evaluated from left to right. The exception to this is the assignment operator or the equal sign, and it is evaluated from right to left.

In your math classes, you might have learned the phrase "Please Excuse My Dear Aunt Sally" to represent the order of math operations: Parentheses, Exponents, Multiplication and Division, and Addition and Subtraction. Parentheses were always evaluated first, followed by exponents, then multiplication and division, and finally addition and subtraction.

NOTE You will find that as we explore expressions, many of the things you learned in math classes transfer over nicely to programming.

For the most part, as you use operators with their operands, you will find that the precedence in which they are evaluated is pretty logical. Java operates similarly to the precedence you learned in math classes with parentheses being evaluated first and so forth. Table 4.5 presents the levels of operator precedence in Java with the first level happening first, and the 14th happening last.

Table 4.4 Operator Precedence

	Operators	Precedence
1	Postfix	*expr++ expr--*
2	Unary	*++expr --expr +expr -expr* ~ !
3	Multiplicative	* / %
4	Additive	+ -
5	Shift	<< >> >>>
6	Relational	< > <= >= instanceof

7	Equality	== !=
8	Bitwise AND	&
9	Bitwise exclusive OR	^
10	Bitwise inclusive OR	|
11	Logical AND	&&
12	Logical OR	||
13	Ternary	? :
14	Assignment	= += -= *= /= %= &= ^= |= <<= >>= >>>=

> **NOTE** Because parentheses have the highest level of precedence, they can be used to dictate the order of precedence.

Pulling It All Together: Mathematical Expressions and Operators

We've covered a lot of material in this lesson on expressions, operators, operands, and more. Listing 4.2 is rather long, but it helps pull a lot of the information together for you to see it in action. Comments are used (since you learned about them in this lesson) to describe what the code is doing!

LISTING 4.2

Mathematical Expressions and Operators

```
/**
 * Program to show the use of expressions and operators
 * Comments provided throughout to explain what is happening!
 */
public static void main(String[] args) {
        // Declare variables to use in the examples
        int result;
        int operand1;
        int operand2;
        int operand3;

        //
        // Assignment
        //
        // Initialize result with the value of 0 by using the
        // assignment (=) operator. The assignment operator takes the
```

```
// value on the right and assigns it to the variable on the
// left
result = 0; // now result has the value of 0

// Initialize the operands
operand1 = 5;
operand2 = 7;

// Assignment works with variable values as well as literal
// values. We'll set operand3 to the same value as operand2
operand3 = operand2; // now both have the value 7

//
// Addition
//
// Addition is a binary infix operator.  It works with
// literals:
result = 42 + 53;  // result is now 95

// It also works with variables:
result = operand1 + operand2;  // result now equals 12

// It works with a combination of literals and variables:
result = 1 + operand1;  // result now equals 6

// You can chain addition operators together:
// result now equals 20
result = 1 + operand1 + operand2 + operand3;

// Finally, the += operator is used to add a value to a
// variable. result += operand1 is equivalent to
// result = result + operand1.
// NOTE: the initial value of result is used to calculate the
//       new value of result:
result = 2;  // set result to 2
result += 4;  // result is now equal to 6 (2 + 4)
result += operand1; // result is now equal to 11 (6 + 5)

//
// Subtraction
//
// Subtraction is a binary infix operator.  It works with
// literals:
result = 9 - 5;  // result is now 4
```

```
// It also works with variables:
result = operand1 - operand2;  // result now equals -2

// It works with a combination of literals and variables:
result = 15 - operand1;  // result now equals 10

// You can chain subtraction operators together:
// result now equals 0
result = 19 - operand1 - operand2 - operand3;

// Finally, the -= operator is used to add a value to a
// variable. result -= operand1 is equivalent to
// result = result - operand1.
// NOTE: the initial value of result is used to calculate the
//       new value of result:
result = 2;  // set result to 2
result -= 4;  // result is now equal to -2 (2 - 4)
result -= operand1; // result is now equal to -7 (-2 - 5)


//
// Multiplication
//
// Multiplication is a binary infix operator.  It works with
// literals:
result = 2 * 3;  // result is now 6

// It also works with variables:
result = operand1 * operand2;  // result now equals 35

// It works with a combination of literals and variables:
result = 2 * operand1;  // result now equals 10

// You can chain multiplication operators together:
// result now equals 490
result = 2 * operand1 * operand2 * operand3;

// Finally, the *= operator is used to add a value to a
// variable. result *= operand1 is equivalent to
// result = result * operand1.
// NOTE: the initial value of result is used to calculate the
//       new value of result:
result = 2;  // set result to 2
result *= 4;  // result is now equal to 8 (2 * 4)
result *= operand1; // result is now equal to 40 (8 * 5)
```

```
//
// Division and Modulus
//
// Division is a binary infix operator.  It works with
// literals:
result = 6 / 3;  // result is now 2

// It also works with variables:
result = operand1 / operand2;  // result now equals 0

// What?!?!?!?!  When dividing integers, integer division
// is used - we only get the whole number part of the
// quotient.  In this case, 7 goes into 5 0 times with a
// remainder of 5
// We use the modulus operator (%) to get the remainder:
result = operand1 % operand2;  // result now equals 5

// It works with a combination of literals and variables:
result = 20 / operand1;  // result now equals 4

// You can chain division operators together:
// result now equals 1
result = 245 / operand1 / operand2 / operand3;

//The /= operator is used to add a value to a
// variable. result /= operand1 is equivalent to
// result = result / operand1.
// NOTE: the initial value of result is used to calculate the
//       new value of result:
result = 40;  // set result to 40
result /= 4;  // result is now equal to 10 (40 / 4)
result /= operand1; // result is now equal to 2 (10 / 5)

//
// Postfix and Prefix operators
//
// Finally, you can use the postfix and prefix operators
// to add 1 to a variable. The postfix adds 1 after other
// things are done, the prefix operator adds 1 before.

operand1 = 10;        // set operand1 to 10
result = ++operand1;  // adds 1 to operand then sets result to 11

operand1 = 10;        // set operand1 back to 10
result = operand1++;  // sets result to 10, and then sets operand
                      // to 11
    }
```

SUMMARY

We covered a lot of information in this lesson. You learned about some concepts surrounding programs and programming, including information about computers, programs, programming, models, metaphors, and how data differs from information. You also were introduced to objects, specifications, syntax, and semantics.

You also jumped into the Java programming language. You learned about the basic building blocks of Java. You learned the different types of comments and how to identify and use them. You learned about identifiers, literals, and variables. You also learned about the various data types as well as the different categories of expressions. To tie some of this together, you learned about expressions including operators and operands. Not only did you learn a lot of core information about Java, you started the process of putting the pieces together to do something—a process you will build upon in the upcoming lessons.

EXERCISES

Now that you are digging into the Java programming language, it is time to introduce some coding exercises to help you practice what you are learning. You will find exercises at the end of many of the lessons in the rest of this book. These exercises are suggestions for things you can do to practice what you are learning. These are to do on your own, so most will not include answers.

The exercises for this lesson have you continue to use the IDE you installed previously. As you work through these exercises, remember the following:

- Java project names should not include spaces or other nonalphanumeric characters.

- Project names should be spelled using camel case, where the name starts lowercase but each next word in the name is capitalized.

- At this point, all projects should be Java Maven applications.

As you become more experienced with building projects in Java, you will use additional project types and files inside projects. For now, we are simply focusing on the basics. There are several exercises for you to apply what you learned in this lesson:

Exercise 1: ABeginning.java

Exercise 2: ProjectGutenberg.java

Exercise 3: CommentingCode.java

Exercise 4: AllTheMath.java

Exercise 5: BucketsOfFun.java

We will start with a couple of basic exercises to get used to creating text that will appear in the console window when we run an application.

Important!

Enter all the code for each exercise. As tempting as it is to copy and paste the code instead, you will learn more and understand the code better if you type every character yourself. Making mistakes is part of the process of learning to program. You will also learn how to take advantage of the shortcuts that your IDE offers.

Exercise 1: ABeginning.java

In this exercise, you will write text to the console. Using NetBeans in the same way you did in the previous lesson, create a new project, create a Java class file named ABeginning.java, and enter the code provided in Exercise Listing 4.1. The name of the file here is important, as Java code is written in files that end with .java.

EXERCISE LISTING 4.1

ABeginning.java

```java
package com.sg.foundations.basics.core;

public class ABeginning {

    public static void main(String[] args) {
        System.out.println("Hello World!");
        System.out.println("Hello from the Guild!");
        System.out.println("Typing code is easier than I thought ...");
        System.out.println("Typity Typity Type!");
        System.out.println("After I finish typing,");
        System.out.println("I'll compile my code.");
        System.out.println("And then when I run it,");
        System.out.println("The console will print out all my
brilliant words!");
        System.out.println("And it all starts with \'Hello World!\' ..");
    }
}
```

After you enter the code (and double-check it for errors), you can compile it by right-clicking your project file in NetBeans and selecting _Build. This takes all your Java code and turns it into bytecode. This is the code that will run on the JVM, and these particular compilations end with `.class`.

Next, you can do the even *more* exciting part, running your code! Right-click your file, and this time select *Run File*. If you have typed everything correctly, you should see output like the following:

```
Hello World!
Hello from the Guild!
Typing code is easier than I thought ...
Typity Typity Type!
After I finish typing,
I'll compile my code.
And then when I run it,
The console will print out all my brilliant words!
And it all starts with "Hello World!" ..
```

If your output does not match or if you see some red text in the output window, go back and double-check again: you have mistyped something, and you need to fix it! Remember, the computer *only* does what we tell it to do, so if there are errors, it is our fault!

Remember that NetBeans only looks at the code, not the text inside quotation marks that you want to appear in the console. Because the end users will see only the text output, you should also proofread that text for spelling errors.

Exercise 2: ProjectGutenberg.java

Like a modern Gutenberg, the `System.out.println()` method takes in information and prints it to the console terminal easily. We can print out whole books or even libraries this way. In this exercise, you again write text to the console.

> **NOTE** Random note: There are other printing methods too. `System.out` `.print()`, for example, takes in information does not also add a new line character. You can find more printing methods at docs.oracle.com/javase/tutorial/essential/io/formatting.html.

Complete the following steps:

1. Enter the code in Exercise Listing 4.2 into a Java class file named `Project-Gutenburg.java`.

2. Update the code as necessary so that it matches the expected output.

EXERCISE LISTING 4.2

ProjectGutenberg.java

```
package com.sg.foundations.basics.core;

public class ProjectGutenberg {
    public static void main(String[] args) {
        System.out.println("Did you know that in 1440 (or thereabouts),");
        System.out.println("Johannes Gutenberg invented the printing press?");
        System.out.println("He started out as a goldsmith!");
        System.out.println("His invention made it easy to print and");
        System.out.println("distribute books to anyone who wanted one.");
        System.out.println("We are like a modern Gutenberg,");
        System.out.println("printing vast amounts to the waiting console
with ease.");
    }
}
```

When you run this code, you should see the following:

```
Did you know that in 1440 (or thereabouts),
Johannes Gutenberg invented the printing press with moveable type?
He started out as a goldsmith!
His invention made it easy to print and
distribute books to anyone who wanted one.
We are like a modern Gutenberg,
printing whatever we want to the console with ease.
```

After you get the original code to produce the previous output, experiment using System.out.print instead of System.out.println. Change the code as necessary to make the output look like the following:

```
Did you know that in 1440 (or thereabouts), Johannes Gutenberg invented the
printing press?
He started out as a goldsmith!
His invention made it easy to print and distribute books to anyone who
wanted one.
We are like a modern Gutenberg, printing whatever we want to the console
with ease.
```

Exercise 3: CommentingCode.java

As you learned in this lesson, comments are used to add text to explain in plain speech what code is doing. Comments can also be useful as a way of reminding you why you used a specific version of the code, so you (or someone else on your team) know why you wrote the code a specific way later in the development process.

Let's experiment with some basic comment approaches. Create a new Java class file named CommentingCode.java using the code in Exercise Listing 4.3.

EXERCISE LISTING 4.3

CommentingCode.java

```
package com.sg.foundations.basics.core;

public class CommentingCode {

    public static void main(String[] args) {

        // Comments are written to explain code in an easily
        // understandable way
        // Basically for single lines
        // anything after // is considered a comment
        System.out.println("Normal code is compiled and runs ...");
        System.out.println("Comments however ... ");// do not execute!

        // Comments can be on their own line
        System.out.println("..."); // or they can share like this

        // However if you put the // BEFORE a line of code
        // System.out.println("Then it is considered a comment");
        // System.out.println("and it won't execute!");

        /*
            This is an example of a multi-line comment, which is useful if
            you want to comment out multiple lines of code quickly.
            Console.WriteLine("Java ignores everything inside the comment
markers.");
        */
    }
}
```

What appears in the console window when you run the program? Try moving or removing some of the comment markers to see what happens.

Exercise 4: AllTheMath.java

While it is pretty cool that we can make a computer display specific text, remember that computers can do so much more. One of the things they do really well is math. You just have to give a program the raw values, tell it what do to with those values, and then let it do the rest of the work for you.

As a refresher, here are some of the operators we use for math:

+	for adding (or concatenating!)
-	for subtracting
*	for multiplying
/	for dividing
%	for modulus (or remainders from dividing)

As you learned, these are binary operators, which means you can use only two values at a time with each of them. If you have a longer string (like 1 + 2 * 3), the computer will perform one operation at a time, using one pair of values, and then use the result of that operation as the second value in the remaining pair.

Another set of operators you saw in the lesson are comparison operators. Comparison operators are also binary, with the purpose of comparing two values and producing a single value of true or false.

==	equal to
!=	not equal to
>	than
<	less than
>=	greater than or equal to
<=	less than or equal to

If you entered the expression 4 > 2, you would get the result of true because 4 is greater than 2. If you entered the expression 4 > 4, you would get the result of false, because 4 is not greater than 4. Rather, they are equal. In a future lesson, you will learn that comparison operators are used in conditional statements, where the outcome of a program is dependent on the available input, rather than being predictable based on fixed values.

Let's see how to incorporate math statements into a Java program. Start by entering the code in Exercise Listing 4.4 (as is). Type this into a new class file named AllThe-Maths.java.

Build and run the code to make sure it works. If there are errors, fix the problems before going on. Once the code works correctly, change each of the "???" into the mathematical expression described in the comment for that operation, using the operators described earlier.

EXERCISE LISTING 4.4

AllTheMaths.java

```
package com.sg.foundations.basics.core;

public class AllTheMaths {
    public static void main(String[] args) {
        System.out.print("1 + 2 is: ");
        System.out.println(1 + 2);

        System.out.print("42001 modulus 5 is: ");
        System.out.println(42001 % 5);

        System.out.print("5565.0 divided by 22.0 is : ");
        System.out.println(5565.0 / 22.0);

        System.out.print("223 times 31 minus 42: ");
        System.out.println(223 * 31 - 42);

        System.out.print("Is 4 greater than -1? ");
        System.out.println(4 > -1);

        System.out.println("\n****** Now make the computer do some harder
math!");

        System.out.print("8043.52 minus 4.2 plus 23.0 divided by 56.0 times
-76.13 is: ");
        System.out.println("???");

        System.out.print("11111 modulus 3 minus 67 minus 1 plus 9 is: ");
        System.out.println("???");
```

```
        System.out.print("44 minus 22 minus 11 minus 66 minus 88 minus 76
minus 11 minus 33 is : ");
        System.out.println("???");

        System.out.print("22 times 3 minus 1 plus 4 times 6 minus -9 is : ");
        System.out.println("???");

        System.out.print("Is 67 greater than 4 * 5? ");
        System.out.println("???");

        System.out.print("Is 78 less than 4 * 5? ");
        System.out.print("???");
    }
}
```

> **NOTE** Update one chunk of code at a time, building and running the program after each update. That will help you identify errors earlier so you can learn from errors as you go, rather than having to fix lots of errors later.

Here is what the result should look like after making all the updates. Do your results match those shown here?

```
1 + 2 is: 3
42001 modulus 5 is: 1
5565.0 divided by 22.0 is : 252.954545454545
223 times 31 - 42: 6871
4 is greater than -1: true

****** Now make the computer do some harder math!
8043.52 minus 4.2 plus 23.0 divided by 56.0 times -76.13 is: 8008.05232142857
11111 modulus 3 minus 67 minus 1 plus 9 is: -57
44 minus 22 plus 11 minus 66 minus 88 plus 76 minus 11 minus 33 is : -89
22 times 3 minus 1 plus 4 times 6 minus -9 is : 98
67 is greater than 4 * 5: true
78 is less than 4 * 5: false
```

Exercise 5: BucketsOfFun.java

Did you know that you can declare tons of variables all on the same line? You can! Also, once you assign a value to a variable, you can use that variable to assign a value to another variable.

Let's try it out!

Enter the code from Exercise Listing 4.5 into a class called BucketsOfFun. Build and run the program to make sure it works. What operators are being used to show that the dog ate a bug? Why does the number of bugs not change when we change the number of butterflies? The answers to these questions are in the comments in the program.

EXERCISE LISTING 4.5

BucketsOfFun.java

```java
package com.sg.foundations.variables;

public class BucketsOfFun {

    public static void main(String[] args) {

        // Declare ALL THE THINGS
        // (Usually it's a good idea to declare them at the beginning of
        // the program)
        int butterflies, beetles, bugs;

        // Now give a couple of them some values
        butterflies = 5;
        beetles = 9;

        bugs = butterflies + beetles;
        System.out.println("There are only " + butterflies + " butterflies,");
        System.out.println("but there are " + bugs + " bugs in all.");

        System.out.println("Uh oh, my dog ate one.");
        butterflies--;
        System.out.println("Now there are only " + butterflies +
                                    " butterflies left.");
        System.out.println("But there are still " + bugs + " bugs left...");
        System.out.println("Wait a minute!");
        System.out.println("... maybe my computer can't do math, after all!");
    }
}
```

When you run this program, you should see the following output:

```
There are only 5 butterflies,
but there are 14 bugs in all.
Uh oh, my dog ate one.
```

```
Now there are only 4 butterflies left.
But still 6 bugs left, wait a minute!
Maybe my computer can't do math, after all!
```

> **TIP** The operators ++ and -- are unary operators, which means they take only one value (instead of two values, like a binary operator does). They are used to increment an existing value to the next higher or next lower value, as a shortcut for "+1" or "–1", respectively.

Lesson 5
Collecting and Parsing Input from the User

O ften, when we are dealing with input devices such as a keyboard or reading data from text files, the incoming data will be in string format. The string data often must be converted to other data types such as integers or decimals before we can use those values in our objects. The process of converting a string type to another type is commonly referred to as *parsing*.

In the first part of this course, we will be doing a lot of our work using the console window as the user interface, so we will use the console for now. Later, we can use the same techniques when we collect data from other sources, such as web forms or data sources.

LEARNING OBJECTIVES

By the end of this lesson, you will be able to:
- Use Scanner to collect input from a user
- Parse input into specific data types
- Use parsed data in a program

CONSOLE INPUT AND OUTPUT

In many programs, we need to be able to accept input from a user as well as define output that the user will see. We've already seen the output side of things: the "Hello, World!" application we started with is an example of this. Now we need to look at how we can get input from the user using the console.

> **TIP** We often use the abbreviation I/O to refer to "input/output" processes. In this lesson, we are using the console to accept input and create output, but I/O processes can also happen in other interfaces using similar options.

The ability to get input from the user allows us to write more interesting and useful programs. The programs we have seen so far do only one thing, and they'll always do only one thing unless we go in and actually change to source code. If we can get input from the user, we can write programs that adapt and react based on the data that the user gives us; this allows us to do much more than we could before.

We will use a combination of System.out.println and an object called Scanner to perform console input and output. To illustrate this, we will create a small program called Adder.

Adder Version 1

The first version of Adder shown in Listing 5.1 will just add two variables and print the results to the screen. The values of the variables are hard-coded, so this version is pretty boring.

LISTING 5.1

Adder.java: The Adder Program

```
class Adder {

public static void main(String[] args) {
```

```
    // declare sum and initialize it to 0
    int sum = 0;
    // declare and initialize our operands
    int operand1 = 3;
    int operand2 = 2;

    //assign the sum of operand1 and operand2 to sum
    sum = operand1 + operand2;

    // NOTE: In the output below, the plus (+) operator
    // is acting as the string concatenation operator
    // instead of the addition operator.  In Java, we use
    // the plus (+) operator to concatentate (or glue together)
    // string values.
    System.out.println("Sum is: " + sum);
  }
}
```

Enter this program into your Java IDE and then compile and run it. When you do so, you should see the following output in the console window:

```
Sum is: 5
```

Let's review this code to make sure you understand what is happening. This program starts like the other Java programs you've entered, with the creation of a public static void main routine followed by a string array called args. This routine contains the code that will be executed for the Adder program.

In this first version of the program, three variables are declared and initialized with assigned values. The first thing you are doing is declaring a variable called sum as an integer, so type int is being used. The sum variable is being initialized to 0 at the same time. After that, the two operands that will be used are declared and assigned values as well. You can see that these are called operand1 and operand2, and both are set to be of type int as well. At the same time these are declared, each is set to a value. In this case, operand1 is set equal to 3, and operand2 is set equal to 2.

At this point, you have declared three variables and initialized their values. Next you will want to assign the sum of operand1 and operand2 into the variable called sum. This is done by setting sum equal to operand1 plus operand2 using the addition operator you learned about in the previous lesson.

At this point in our program, sum is going to equal 5. So, the last thing to do is print that out to the screen using our friend system.out.printlin. You can see that system.out.printlin is being used to print a string ("Sum is: "). This string, however, is followed by a plus sign and the sum variable. In this case, the plus sign is not the addition operator, but rather is acting as the string concatenation operator. The result is that a string version of the value stored in sum will print, which is the number 5.

> **NOTE** When you deal with strings, the plus sign is what is known as the *string* concatenation operator.

Adder Version 2

The first Adder program showed output, but no input. Now we'll modify version 1 so that we ask the user for the value for operand1 and operand2. This is the technique we will use for all console applications going forward in this book.

Declaring and Initializing Our Variables

In the updated listing, we will create and initialize the same three variables; however, we'll set operand1 and operand2 to 0 as default values.

```
int sum = 0;
int operand1 = 0;
int operand2 = 0;
```

Setting Up a Scanner Object

To get the numbers (input) from the user, we'll need to set up a scanner object. A Scanner object is what allows you to read in information from the standard input, which is generally the console. A Scanner object is a nonprimitive data type. You are going to declare a scanner similar to how you declared an integer. You will say the data type followed by a variable name. In this case, instead of using int, you will use Scanner (with a capital *S*) as the type, and we'll call the new variable myScanner.

```
Scanner myScanner
```

Initializing a nonprimitive data type (in this case, your new scanner) is a little bit different from what you've seen before. Most of the time, nonprimitive data types get initialized by creating a new object. You'll learn more about objects and this initialization process in a later lesson. For now, just know that Scanner is an object. To instantiate an object, we have to use the new operator to create a new one, and we have to say that it is a new scanner that is being created:

```
Scanner myScanner = new Scanner();
```

Of course, you aren't done setting this up quite yet. The scanner needs to be pointed toward the thing that we want to read. In this case, it is System.in. At this point, our complete instantiation of our scanner now looks like this:

```
Scanner myScanner = new Scanner(System.in);
```

> **NOTE** When we want to display things, we print them. To do this, we print them to System.out. When we want to read things into our program from the console, we read them from System.in.

If you enter this line into your IDE, you are likely to notice some angry red squiggly lines under Scanner. The system doesn't really know what the scanner is because the scanner is in a different part of the Java source code. If you are using NetBeans, then if you hover your mouse over the word *Scanner*, you will see a message saying "cannot find symbol: class Scanner." To remedy this, we need to let our program know where the Scanner object can be found so that the Scanner code can be imported into our program. This is done with an import statement, as shown here:

```
import java.util.Scanner;
```

By adding this import statement to the top of our new listing, the Scanner object will be found, and the angry red squiggly lines will go away.

> **TIP** The IDE is your friend. If you are using NetBeans, you can right-click Scanner and select *Fix Imports* from the menu. This will automatically add the missing import for you. You can also press Ctrl+Shift+I, which will display a dialog asking if you want to add the Scanner import statement. Clicking *OK* will add it for you.

Understanding the Command Line

The import statement tells our class where to find the Scanner class and how to use it. With it added, we are ready to read values from the command line.

One of the things you must understand is that everything that comes in on the console command line is text, which is stored in strings. Because of this, two more variables are needed that can hold the strings that will be retrieved from the command line. We'll need one for each operand.

```
String stringOperand1 = "";
String stringOperand2 = "";
```

As you can see, two new variables are being declared with a data type of String. These are being initialized with a default value of "", which is an empty string.

With these two strings defined, we have a place to put the string representation of operand1 and operand2.

Getting the Values from the User

We are now ready to write the code to ask the user for the values. If we want the user to type something for our program to read, then we need to give them a message so they know what is expected. We have to let them know they need to type something in. We show this message just like we did with the "Hello, World!" program. The way we let the user know something or print something to the console is with System.out.println.

```
System.out.println("Please enter the first number to be added:");
```

With our message displaying to the user, we are ready to get the first number!

We are now ready to use the myScanner object we created to read in the first number and put it into stringoperand1.

```
stringOperand1 = myScanner.nextLine();
```

The scanner will read the next line the user types on the command line and assign that information to stringOperand1.

NOTE myScanner.nextLine() waits for the user to type something into the console and hit the Enter key. When the Enter key is pressed, nextLine() reads everything that the user typed on that line and assigns it to the variable on the left side of the = operator.

With the first number read, this same process of showing a message and reading a response can be done for the second operand value.

```
System.out.println("Please enter the second number to be added:");
stringOperand2 = myScanner.nextLine();
```

Going from Strings to Integers

With the values now gathered from the user, we need to add them together. But, they're in string format right now, which means they won't add together. As we saw earlier, using a plus sign with two strings concatenates rather than adds. We need to be able to convert stringOperand1 and stringOperand2 into the integers we set up (operand1 and operand2).

There is a handy method that allows us to convert strings into integers if we want. We can use the parseInt method within the Integer class to convert the string in stringOperand1 to a number to be stored in operand1 by doing the following:

```
operand1 = Integer.parseInt(stringOperand1);
```

We haven't talked much about methods in objects, so with this you're going to have to take what is happening in this line of code on faith. `Integer` is a class, and there's a method on it. There's a named bit of code that, if you hand it a string, will hand you back the integer representation of that string. If I hand in the string 10, it will return the `int` 10. In the previous line of code, we are passing in the string `stringOperand1`, and the integer being returned is being placed into `operand1`.

With the first operand converted, we'll do the same thing with `operand2`. So, `operand2` equals `Integer.parseInt` with the string value stored in `stringOperand2` being passed in.

```
operand2 = Integer.parseInt(stringOperand2);
```

WARNING Be careful here: if it can't convert the input to a number, it will throw an error (called an *exception*). We'll see how to handle these exceptions in a later lesson.

Adding the Numbers Together

At this point, you've gotten `operand1` and `operand2` as integers. You can then set the value of `sum` by just adding `operand1` and `operand2` together. You can then print `sum`.

You've now done everything to get two numbers from the user and print them. Listing 5.2 presents the completed listing.

LISTING 5.2

Adder2.java: The Adder Program with Input

```
import java.util.Scanner;

class Adder2 {

  public static void main(String[] args) {
    // declare the number variables and initialize to 0
    int sum = 0;
    int operand1 = 0;
    int operand2 = 0;

    // declare and initialize a Scanner object - the Scanner reads
    // input from the console
    Scanner myScanner = new Scanner(System.in);
```

```
// declare and initialize String (text) variables to hold the
// values that the user types in
String stringOperand1 = "";
String stringOperand2 = "";

// ask the user to input the first operand
System.out.println("Please enter the first number to be added:");

// now wait until the user types something in - put the value
// in stringOperand1
stringOperand1 = myScanner.nextLine();

// ask the user to input the second operand:
System.out.println("Please enter the second number to be added:");

// now wait until the user types something in - put the value
// in stringOperand2
stringOperand2 = myScanner.nextLine();

// in order to add the values input by the user we must
// convert the String values into int values.  We use the
// parseInt method for this:
operand1 = Integer.parseInt(stringOperand1);
operand2 = Integer.parseInt(stringOperand2);

// assign the sum of operand1 and operand2 to sum
sum = operand1 + operand2;

// print the sum to the console
System.out.println("Sum is: " + sum);
    }
}
```

What we have done here is add some interactivity within a program. Now when this program is running, nearly any two numbers can be added together, and we do not have to change the code! The following shows one example of output from this program:

```
Please enter the first number to be added:
35
Please enter the second number to be added:
53
Sum is: 88
```

> **NOTE** Scanner is a built-in Java class that helps us collect text input from the user in various ways. We'll use it frequently. See the official documentation at docs.oracle.com/en/java/javase/11/docs/api/java.base/java/util/Scanner.html for more on Scanner.

Using Loops to Gather User Input

One trick some programmers like to use is to create a loop when a user is required to enter some text. Loops will be explained in greater detail in Lesson 7, "Controlling Program Flow," so if you don't completely follow what is covered in the rest of this lesson, don't fret. It will make more sense after you complete Lesson 7.

In a nutshell, loops are used to create cycles in the code. This loop prompts for the data and then checks to see whether the entry is null or empty. If it is, it displays an error message and falls to the end of the code block, which returns to the top of the loop. If the value is not null or empty, the break keyword is used to end the loop. A generic sample of this style of code is shown here:

```java
while (true) {

    System.out.println("Enter some data: ");

    String input = myScanner.nextLine();

    if(input != null && !input.isEmpty()) {
        // User hits enter without any data. Display error message then back to
        // top of loop
        System.out.println("You did not enter anything!");
    } else {
        // User entered something, leave the loop
        break;
    }
}
```

Another way to check for user input is to use the while condition to check that the user has entered a value. This will also prompt the user to enter data until they enter something into the console.

```java
boolean isValid = false;
```

```
do {

    System.out.println("Enter some data: ");
    String input = myScanner.nextLine();

    if(input == null || input.isEmpty()) {
        System.out.println("You did not enter anything!")
    } else {
        isValid = true
    }

} while(!isValid)
```

PARSING DATA

Each primitive type, such as int, double, and boolean, has access to a method to parse strings (nonprimitive) types, such as LocalDate. In all these cases, the method takes a string value as input and then attempts to convert it to the proper type. If, for example, we wanted to read in an int from a string source like the console, the incoming data would be a String type, so we would use the Integer.parseInt() method to convert it to an integer, like so:

```
String input = myScanner.nextLine();
int number = Integer.parseInt(input);
```

One thing to note about the parseInt() method is that it will throw an exception at runtime if the inputted value cannot be converted. So, in the previous case, if the user typed in **banana**, the string could not be converted to an integer and the program would crash.

Because of this, Integer.parseInt() should be used only when we can fully trust the input. In other words, we must have a solid guarantee that the incoming data can be converted to the target type. One example of a trusted data source could be a text file generated by another machine, such as records from a database. Unlike a human user, a file generated by a computer should have a specific file format that we can test and be comfortable using without needing additional validation steps. In fact, if we have an agreed-upon format, we may want the program to throw an exception if bad data comes in.

For cases where we are dealing with human input or the potential for bad data is high, we'll have to handle a NumberFormatException. We should also double-check whenever we are converting any Strings to ints.

DEALING WITH BAD NUMBERS: NumberFormatException

If you check the documentation for `Integer.parseInt()` at docs.oracle.com/en/java/javase/11/docs/api/java.base/java/lang/Integer.html#parseInt(java.lang.String), you'll see `throws NumberFormatException`. We will go into more detail on exceptions later in the book but for now, what this means is that the `Integer.parseInt()` method is telling us that something is wrong, specifically, that the input cannot be converted to a number. Basically, if the input cannot be parsed into a number, this will happen instead of success.

To handle this problem, you'll have to surround your code with a try/catch block. Again, you'll learn more about these later, but let's look at an example of how it would work.

```
try {

    String input = myScanner.nextLine();
    int number = Integer.parseInt(input);

} catch(NumberFormatException ex) {
    // Think of this kind of like an 'else' block for now. This is the code
    // that will run
    // if the user doesn't enter a number.
    System.out.println("That was not a whole number!");
}
```

We can use this inside a loop similar to the loop we created for the required string example shown earlier. Instead of checking for any data at all, though, we will attempt to parse the data to determine validity.

```
boolean isValid = false;

do {
```

```
            try {
                System.out.println("Please enter a whole number: ");

                String input = myScanner.nextLine();
                int number = Integer.parseInt(input);
                isValid = true;

            } catch(NumberFormatException ex) {
                System.out.println("That was not a whole number!");
            }

        } while(!isValid)
```

This setup guarantees that when the loop exits, the variable output will contain a valid integer. If `Integer.parseInt()` fails, the program will print That is not a whole number, and the loop will execute again, prompting the user to enter a whole number.

As you can see with this and the required string sample shown earlier, this pattern can be used to force a user to input any sort of valid data. Simply adjust the `if` condition and prompts in the loop to suit your needs.

Say we wanted a value between 1 and 10. A few small modifications to our previous code will do the trick.

```
boolean isValid = false;

do {

    try {
        System.out.println("Please enter a whole number from 1 to 10: ");

        String input = myScanner.nextLine();
        int number = Integer.parseInt(input);

        if (number >= 1 && number <= 10) {
            isValid = true;
        }

    } catch(NumberFormatException ex) {
        System.out.println("That was not a whole number!");
    }

} while(!isValid)
```

SCANNER PROBLEMS

Before ending this lesson, it is worth talking a little more about what Scanner can do as well as some of the problems that can happen. As you learned earlier, we always read everything as a string, and then if we want to convert it, we convert it ourselves. This process might seem cumbersome, and it is. It's an extra step.

Scanner has the ability to read values other than strings directly into a variable. It could have been used to read our two integers directly into operand1 and operand2; however, it is worth taking a closer look to see some of the problems that we can get into with this. More specifically, it is worth exploring what can happen when you start going back and forth between reading in strings and numbers.

To illustrate this, we are going to write another program where we ask for a user's name, age, the number of computers they own, and hometown. We will ask in that order. Rather than jumping right to the program that does all of this, we'll start by first reading in the name and age. Listing 5.3 is the start of our program to do this, and it is based on what you saw earlier in Listing 5.2.

LISTING 5.3

MyScanner.java: Getting Just the Name and Age

```java
import java.util.Scanner;

class MyScanner {

  public static void main(String[] args) {
    // declare the number variables and initialize to 0
    String name = "";
    int age = 0;
    // int numComputers = 0;
    // String hometown = "";

    // declare and initialize a Scanner object - the Scanner reads
    // input from the console
    Scanner myScanner = new Scanner(System.in);

    // ask the user to input their name
    System.out.println("Please enter your name:");
```

```
    // now wait until the user types something in - put the value
    // in name
    name = myScanner.nextLine();

    // ask the user to input their age:
    System.out.println("Please enter your age:");
    // now wait until the user types their age
    age = myScanner.nextInt();

    // We will get the other values in the next listing!

    // print the information to the console
    System.out.println("Hi " + name + " your age is " + age );
  }
}
```

In reviewing the code in this new listing, you see that four variables are defined and initialized to hold our data. The third and fourth are actually not defined because they are commented out, since we are not using them yet.

You can see in the listing that the first variable is a string called name that will be used to hold the user's name. Then there is an int called age to hold the age for holding the user's age. The next two lines are commented out but will be used later. These are declarations of int numComputers for holding the number of computers and String hometown for holding the name of the user's hometown.

You can see that, instead of using the string variables and doing a parse as we did in Listing 5.2, this time we read directly into our variables. If you look at Listing 5.3, you'll see that we are using the scanner's nextLine to read a value from the console directly into the name variable. This is just as we did before. Of course, we are prompting the reader to enter a value before each call to myScanner.

You learned that nextLine sits and waits until the user hits Enter. When the user presses Enter, then the program knows to read the information that was typed into the console command line. In fact, a call to myScanner.nextLine actually reads the entire line *including* the return that the user typed in.

For reading the age, you can see in Listing 5.3 that we are using nextInt instead of nextLine. What you probably expect from nextInt is for it to sit and wait until the user enters an integer and presses Enter. You likely assume that when the user hits Enter, then we know that they are done. This is correct; however, there is one difference between nextInt and nextLine that is critically important. nextInt only reads the number that was entered, and it leaves the carriage return that the user entered. Additionally, if a value other than a number is entered, the program will throw an error.

If you run the program, you'll see that it is going to print the user's name and age that are entered. If you run it with the name Joe Smith with an age of 23, you should see output like the following:

```
Please enter your name:
Joe Smith
Please enter your age:
23
Hi Joe Smith your age is 23
```

What happens, however, if you mix things up a little bit? When it asks you to enter your name, what happens if you skip it? Run the program and simply hit Enter instead of entering a name. Go ahead and say an age as well. We entered 23. What happens? The program should still work, and you'll see output like the following:

```
Please enter your name:

Please enter your age:
23
Hi  your age is 23
```

What happens if you enter your name and choose to skip entering your age by simply pressing Enter? The program doesn't end but rather simply creates a new line and continues to wait.

```
Please enter your name:
Joe Smith
Please enter your age:
```

You are pressing Enter, but what is the program doing? Well, the program is trying to read the nextInt. The return is not an int, so it is ignored, and the program continues to wait for an integer. Unlike the name, you cannot skip entering the age. You will have to enter a value (such as 23). The nextInt method is not going to just wait for the carriage return of the return statement; it's going to wait literally for the next integer.

If the user doesn't enter an integer, the program is just going to stay there waiting. You can't just skip it. If we had read the age into a string like we read the operands in Listing 5.2 and then tried to convert it, that would have been fine. Then if you pressed Enter without a value, the program would have continued.

Let's look at another scenario. Listing 5.4 removes the comments from the declarations for numComputers and hometown. It also adds another nextInt to get the number of computers and a call to nextLine to get the hometown.

LISTING 5.4

MyScanner: Updated for All Four Values

```java
import java.util.Scanner;

class MyScanner {

  public static void main(String[] args) {
    // declare the number variables and initialize to 0
    String name = "";
    int age = 0;
    int numComputers = 0;
    String hometown = "";

    // declare and initialize a Scanner object - the Scanner reads
    // input from the console
    Scanner myScanner = new Scanner(System.in);

    // ask the user to input their name
    System.out.println("Please enter your name:");
    // now wait until the user types something in - put the value
    // in name
    name = myScanner.nextLine();

    // ask the user to input their age:
    System.out.println("Please enter your age: ");
    // now wait until the user types their age
    age = myScanner.nextInt();

    // ask the user to input their age:
    System.out.println("Please enter the number of computers: ");
    // now wait until the user types the number of computers
    numComputers = myScanner.nextInt();

    // ask the user to input their hometown:
    System.out.println("Please enter your hometown: ");
    // now wait until the user types their hometown
    hometown = myScanner.nextLine();

    // print the information to the console
    System.out.println("Hi " + name + " from " + hometown + ".");
    System.out.println("Your age is: " + age );
    System.out.println("Number of computers: " + numComputers );

  }
}
```

As you can see in this listing, we are now also asking for the number of computers. This is being done by saying `numComputers = myScanner.nextInt`. This is going to work pretty much the way you would expect in that the program will again wait for a number. Like what was seen before, the program is going to wait for a number because `nextInt` is being used. This number cannot be skipped either.

In addition to getting the number of computers, we are also going to ask the user for the hometown. In this case, we use `hometown = myScanner.nextLine` to get the string value for the hometown from the user.

Once we have the hometown, then we're good. At that point, we can print out the hometown along with the other information we have grabbed.

Go ahead and run the program. We should see output similar to the following:

```
Please enter your name:
Joe Smith
Please enter your age:
23
Please enter the number of computers:
5
Please enter your hometown:
Hi Joe Smith from .
Your age is: 23
Number of computers: 5
```

When we ran this, we entered Joe Smith for the name, 23 for the age, and 5 for the number of computers. But wait a minute, it just skipped my hometown! It didn't even give us a chance to enter anything!

Actually, you can see from the output that it did ask for the hometown, but it went by so fast that it wasn't seen. It didn't wait for an answer, and then it just jumped to the output and left the hometown blank.

Why is that? Well, remember the problem when we hit Enter when using `nextInt`? When I just hit Enter, the carriage return was ignored because `getInt` is looking for an `int`.

It's not looking for the Enter. And so, it's just going to wait until you type something in and it can read that next number. After reading that number, it doesn't consume any other characters or the carriage return statement that was also returned. So, once `getInt` has read the number of computers, which was 5 in our case earlier, then the carriage return is still sitting there waiting to be read.

With the number read, the program then comes to the prompt to enter your hometown. When we say `nextLine`, the carriage return is still waiting, so it looks like you just hit Enter and wanted to skip your hometown. The program can't tell the difference between you hitting the Enter key or the value of the Enter key already being there!

So, what can you do with this?

This issue is the reason why I say if you read everything in as a string, you read the entire line and you process it. You know what's going on and you convert it yourself. You have full control all the time, and it's always going to work.

You will learn later in this book how to take care of problems involving the user typing the wrong thing, such as the user typing characters when you want a number. For now, there is another way to resolve the problem with nextInt in Listing 5.4.

Because I know that I just read a number with nextInt, I know there's still a return waiting to be read. If we want to get rid of that return, why don't we just do myScanner.nextLine?

That would consume the carriage return, and we would be ready to go for the next value.

```
// ask the user to input their age:
System.out.println("Please enter the number of computers: ");
// now wait until the user types the number of computers
numComputers = myScanner.nextInt();

myScanner.nextLine();   //<-- added this line
```

Now when you run the program, the carriage return will be read and ignored, the prompt asking for hometown will be displayed, and you can enter a value such as Akron.

```
Please enter your name:
Joe Smith
Please enter your age:
23
Please enter the number of computers:
5
Please enter your hometown:
Akron
Hi Joe Smith from Akron.
Your age is: 23
Number of computers: 5
```

As you can see, adding the nextLine call resolved the issue. Adding the call is something you can do every time that you do a nextInt. Of course, this means you are now doing two steps: reading the number, then getting rid of the carriage return instead of doing the two steps of reading a string, and converting it.

> **NOTE** It's really up to you how you want to handle reading integers. Again, the best suggestion is to read everything as a string and convert it yourself. That way, you know things will work.

SUMMARY

Many of the modern framework tools we will reference in this book will parse incoming data automatically into the proper types. Regardless, it is important that you understand how to deal with string data manually in your code; oftentimes, smaller tasks such as batch jobs or small validation programs will not import those more powerful tools, and you will need to create your own validation methods. It is also common in interviews for code exercises to involve processing string data, which nearly always requires parsing of some kind.

As you work through the code examples and exercises, try to be mindful of opportunities to use patterns such as those shown in this lesson. In this lesson, you have had several code snippets, all very similar, that touch on the problem of "validating user input." While these snippets might not make complete sense now, they will become clearer as you work through this book. They are presented here because these snippets will form a foundation that can be adjusted and reused for nearly any user input validation case.

EXERCISES

The following are some additional coding exercises to help you practice what you are learning about the Java programming language. These are to do on your own, so most will not always include answers. Many of the exercises cover accepting user input via Scanner. There are several exercises for you to apply what you learned in this lesson:

Exercise 1: Quest for the User Input

Exercise 2: Don't Forget to Store It

Exercise 3: Passing the Turing Test

Exercise 4: Healthy Hearts

Exercise 5: Mini Mad Libs

Exercise 1: Quest for the User Input

Create a new program using the code in Exercise Listing 5.1. As you enter the code, decide what each line is supposed to do. Make sure that the program works before you go on to the next exercise.

> **NOTE** Remember when entering listings to create a filename with the same name as the class in your code. For this listing, the Java class file is named QuestForTheUserInput, so the filename would be QuestForTheUserInput.java.

EXERCISE LISTING 5.1

QuestForTheUserInput.java

```java
package com.sg.foundations.userinput;

import java.util.Scanner;

public class QuestForTheUserInput {

    public static void main(String[] args) {
        Scanner inputReader = new Scanner(System.in);

        String yourName;
        String yourQuest;
        double velocityOfSwallow;

        // We can use the Scanner's readLine to assign value to our strings
        // because its return type is string
        System.out.print("What is your name?? ");
        yourName = inputReader.nextLine();

        System.out.print("What is your quest?! ");
        yourQuest = inputReader.nextLine();

        // When we get to our double data type, we can use Scanner's
        // nextDouble method
        // or we can use the Double.parseDouble to convert the nextLine's String

        System.out.print("What is the airspeed velocity of an unladen
swallow?!?! ");
        velocityOfSwallow = Double.parseDouble(inputReader.nextLine());
        System.out.println();
        System.out.println("How do you know " + velocityOfSwallow +
                        " is correct, " + yourName + "?");
        System.out.println("You didn't even know if the swallow was African or
European!");
        System.out.println("Maybe skip answering things about birds and instead
go " + yourQuest + ".");
    }

}
```

When you run this program, you should see the following:

What is your name?? **Sir Lady FluffyBunnykins**
What is your quest?! **Smite Many Things**
What is the airspeed velocity of an unladen swallow?!?! **45**

How do you know 45.0 is correct, Sir Lady FluffyBunnykins?
You didn't even know if the swallow was African or European!
Maybe skip answering things about birds and instead go Smite Many Things.

Exercise 2: Don't Forget to Store It

Scanner takes care of collecting the input, but it's up to the programmer to put it somewhere. Right now, the following code will ask for (and accept) input, but it is a forgetful machine: once it's been taken, it's lost.

In this exercise, you'll create a new program with the code in Exercise Listing 5.2. Compile and run this program to make sure it works. Change the code so that the appropriate input is stored in the right variable. When you think you have that done, uncomment the last two lines in your main method to test it.

EXERCISE LISTING 5.2

DontForgetToStoreIt.java

```java
package com.sg.foundations.userinput;

import java.util.Scanner;

public class DontForgetToStoreIt {

    public static void main(String[] args) {

        int meaningOfLifeAndEverything = 42;
        double pi = 3.14159;
        String cheese, color;

        Scanner inputReader = new Scanner(System.in);
```

```
    System.out.println("Give me pi to at least 5 decimals: ");
    Double.parseDouble(inputReader.nextLine());

    // We've used Double.parseDouble but meaningOfLifeAndEverything is an INT
    // so we'll have to use Integer.parseInt

    System.out.println("What is the meaning of life, the universe and
everything? ");
    Integer.parseInt(inputReader.nextLine());

    System.out.println("What is your favorite kind of cheese? ");
    inputReader.nextLine();

    System.out.println("Do you like the color red or blue more? ");
    inputReader.nextLine();
//      System.out.println("Ooh, " + color + " " + cheese +"
//      " sounds delicious!");
//      System.out.println("The circumference of life is " +( 2 * pi *
//      meaningOfLifeAndEverything));
    }
}
```

Here's an example of what you should see. (This does not contain the last two lines of code that are commented out in the previous code, and your user input will be different.)

```
Give me pi to at least 5 decimals:
3.14159
What is the meaning of life, the universe, and everything?
42
What is your favorite kind of cheese?
brie
Do you like the color red or blue more?
blue
```

Exercise 3: Passing the Turing Test

The Turing test (named for Alan Turing, who first proposed it) is a test to see whether a computer can pass for a human in a conversation, a feat that typically means that the computer responds to human input appropriately.

This exercise is on your own. Create a new program that incorporates user input in a conversation, with the following steps:

1. Ask the user for their name.

2. Display that name and tell them yours (or your AI's name).

3. Ask them for their favorite color.

4. Display the color they enter in a conversational way.

5. Do the same thing with favorite food and number and then say goodbye.

6. Make sure you use the right variable with the right user input.

When you run this program, you should see something like the following:

```
Hello there!
What's your name? Zaphod

Hi, Zaphod!  I'm Alice.
What's your favorite color? Blue

Huh, Blue? Mine's Electric Lime.

I really like limes. They're my favorite fruit, too.
What's YOUR favorite fruit, Zaphod? Pawpaws

Really? Pawpaws? That's wild!
Speaking of favorites, what's your favorite number? 42

42 is a cool number. Mine's -7.
Did you know 42 * -7 is -294? That's a cool number too!

Well, thanks for talking to me, Zaphod!
```

Exercise 4: Healthy Hearts

Create a simple application to help your user monitor their health. You can call the class and filename HealthyHearts.java. The program should ask the user for their age, and then it uses this value to calculate and display the healthy heart rate range they should use for exercising.

- The maximum heart rate should be 220 minus their age.
- The target heart rate zone is 50%–85% of the maximum.

When the user runs the program, it should look something like the following:

```
What is your age? 50
Your maximum heart rate should be 170 beats per minute.
Your target HR Zone is 85 - 145 beats per minute.
```

Exercise 5: Mini Mad Libs

Write a program that lets you play Mad Libs. The program should ask the user for the following (unless you use a different Mad Lib):

- Noun
- Adjective
- Noun
- Number
- Adjective
- Plural noun
- Plural noun
- Plural noun
- Verb infinitive form
- Same verb but past participle

Then substitute all the entered words into the following passage (in order!):

‹1›: the ‹2› frontier. These are the voyages of the starship ‹3›. Its ‹4›-year mission: to explore strange ‹5› ‹6›, to seek out ‹5› ‹7› and ‹5› ‹8›, to boldly ‹9› where no one has ‹10› before.

The following is an example of what the user should see:

Let's play MAD LIBS!

I need a noun: **Chocolate**
Now an adjective: **spooky**
Another noun: **Dodo**
And a number: **10101**
Another adjective: **red**
A plural noun: **kittens**
Another one: **balls**
One more: **lettuce**
A verb (infinitive form): **sneeze**
Same verb (past participle): **sneezed**

*** NOW LETS GET MAD (libs) ***
Chocolate: the spooky frontier. These are the voyages of the starship Dodo. Its 10101-year mission: to explore strange red kittens, to seek out red balls and red lettuce, to boldly sneeze where no one has sneezed before.

Lesson 6
Pulling It All Together: Building a Useful Program

Now, let's pull everything we've learned together and build our first useful program. The purpose of the program is to calculate the total cost for home replacement windows. Here are the requirements:

PROGRAM OBJECTIVES

- Must prompt the user for the height of the window (in feet).
- Must prompt the user for the width of the window (in feet).
- Must calculate and display the area of the window.
- Must calculate and display the perimeter of the window.
- Based on the area and perimeter, it must calculate the total cost of the window.
  - The glass for the windows costs $3.50 per square foot.
  - The trim for the windows costs $2.25 per linear foot.

PLANNING THE PROGRAM

Before you boot up your IDE and start to write the code, you should always take time to plan any program you will write. This includes identifying any variables your program will need and how the variables are related to each other, as well as using pseudocode or a flowchart (or both) to identify the steps your program will need to complete.

> **NOTE** If you haven't worked with flowcharts before, don't fret! You'll learn more about creating a flowchart in Lesson 9, "Understanding Flowcharts and Algorithms."

Identifying the Variables

Looking through the requirements list, we will need the following variables:

- String variable for height (read from console)
- String variable for width (read from console)
- Float variable for height (converted from string; use float because we do not want to be limited to whole feet)
- Float variable for width (converted from string; use float because we do not want to be limited to whole feet)
- Float variable for area of window (calculated from height and width)
- Float variable for perimeter of window (calculated from height and width)
- Float variable for cost (calculated from area, perimeter, and costs)

Note that even though we want height and weight to be numbers (so we can use the input in calculations), we will accept them as strings through the console.

Planning the Steps

At this point, before we even start considering the code, take the time to plan the steps that the program will take. You might find it useful to write the pseudocode or sketch a flowchart to make sure you understand the steps the program will use.

Every developer tackles this stage in a slightly different way, so we won't tell you what it should look like. Instead, look over the steps we have already identified and plan them out in a way that makes sense to you and to other developers you may need to work with on this project.

As we go through the coding steps, take the time to map each line of code to your pseudocode and/or flowchart so that you can see how they work together. In future exercises, you will be expected to come up with the code on your own, and it is easier to write code if you understand the algorithms you need first.

CREATING THE CODE

Once the planning steps are done, we can start to code. Start a new program named *WindowMaster*.

Declaring the Variables

We'll start the coding by declaring the variables in the main method. We have already listed what we need, so we just need to code them at this point.

Declare the variables in the main method as shown in Listing 6.1.

LISTING 6.1

Declaring the Variables in the WindowMaster Program

```
public class WindowMaster {

  public static void main(String [] args) {
    // declare variables for height and width
    float height;
    float width;

    // declare String variables to hold the user's height and
    // width input
    String stringHeight;
    String stringWidth;

    // declare other variables
    float areaOfWindow;
    float cost;
    float perimeterOfWindow;
  }
}
```

There are a couple of things to note here. First, we do not have to declare the variables in the order we intend to use them in the program. You can declare them in any order. As such, it is best to organize your variables in a manner that is clear and makes sense.

Additionally, you'll see that we have used similar variable names for the height and width values, with the `string` prefix to distinguish console input that we need to convert. This not only makes it easy to know what the variables are being used to do, but also makes it easier to not mistakenly use the string variables for calculations.

Check that all the variables we identified earlier are represented in the code before going on.

> **NOTE** As with other coding exercises in this course, you should enter all the code shown in the listings rather than just reading it here in the lessons or copying and pasting it. Entering the code will help you understand the code better, as well as help you learn to use your IDE to help you resolve errors.

Getting Input

The next step is to accept user input for the height and width values. If you recall, we used a `Scanner` object to obtain values from the user. To be able to use `Scanner`, we needed to include the appropriate code by adding an `import` statement to our listing.

```
import java.util.Scanner;
```

You can see this `import` statement as well the new code for obtaining the input in Listing 6.2. The `import` statement is added to the top, and the remaining code is added to the bottom of the `main` method you had entered in Listing 6.1.

LISTING 6.2

Adding the Code for Getting Height and Width

```
import java.util.Scanner;

public class WindowMaster {

  public static void main(String [] args) {
    // declare variables for height and width
    float height;
    float width;
```

```
// declare String variables to hold the user's height and
// width input
String stringHeight;
String stringWidth;

// declare other variables
float areaOfWindow;
float cost;
float perimeterOfWindow;

// declare and initialize the Scanner
Scanner myScanner = new Scanner(System.in);

// get input from the user
System.out.println("Please enter window height:");
stringHeight = myScanner.nextLine();
System.out.println("Please enter window width:");
stringWidth = myScanner.nextLine();
    }
}
```

Remember from the earlier lessons that we have to use Scanner to accept user input in Java. We need to initialize the scanner and create a myScanner object for the input variables. Once we've done that, we use System.out.println() to display appropriate prompts to the user, with each prompt followed by a myScanner.nextLine(), which will wait for the user to enter a value and hit the Enter key.

As you should recall, the console input is a String type, so we use myScanner to store the inputs in the string variables we declared earlier. These are stringHeight and stringWidth.

Converting the Strings

With the information scanned from the user, the next step is to convert the strings to numbers, using parse:

```
// convert String values of height and width to float values
height = Float.parseFloat(stringHeight);
width = Float.parseFloat(stringWidth);
```

In a more robust program, we would add error handling to ensure that the input is valid. In this case, it will be our own fault if we don't enter appropriate values, so we'll skip that at this point. Just be aware that because this program does not have any validation, if you enter **Hello** (or anything else that isn't a number) for a height or width, the program will crash when it tries to parse.

We use `Float.parseFloat()` to convert the string input values to numbers that we can use in our calculations. You can see that the converted values are stored in their own variables, `height` and `width`.

> **NOTE** You will learn more about adding error handling in future lessons. This will include learning about the `try/catch` statements as well as using loops such as a `while` loop.

Calculating the Area and Perimeter

Next, we will need to add expressions to calculate the window area and trim to the code. We use the standard formula *height * width* to calculate the area of the window.

```
areaOfWindow = height * width;
```

The formula for the trim is twice the height plus twice the width. We could use a long formula like this:

```
perimeterOfWindow = height * 2 + width * 2
```

Or we could use a shorter version:

```
perimeterOfWindow = 2 * (height + width)
```

The longer version does not need parentheses because, as we learned in Lesson 3, "Using an Integrated Development Environment," about operator precedence, the program will do the multiplication operations first and then add the products. That said, we could write it as `(height * 2) + (width * 2)` if we wanted. The shorter version needs parentheses to force addition to precede multiplication.

The following is all the code we will add to our listing. We've used the shorter version here, but you can use the longer one if you want.

```
// calculate the area of the window
areaOfWindow = height * width;

// calculate the perimeter of the window
perimeterOfWindow = 2 * (height + width);
```

Calculating the Cost

We now need to calculate the cost of the window, adding together the glass (area * $3.50) and trim (perimeter * $2.25).

```
// calculate the total cost - use a hard-coded value
// for material cost
cost = ((3.50f * areaOfWindow) + (2.25f * perimeterOfWindow));
```

You'll note that we are using hard-coded values for the unit costs. This works here because we are just learning how all this works, but in a real program, you would want to use variables whose values can change as the prices change. Otherwise, a software developer would have to go in and recode the program every time the price goes up or the product goes on sale.

Note that we do not need the parentheses here. The multiplication will happen before the addition, even without the parentheses. However, including parentheses makes it much easier for human developers to read the formula.

Displaying the Results

Finally, we use System.out.println() to display the results to the user.

```
// display the results to the user
System.out.println("Window height = " + stringHeight);
System.out.println("Window width = " + stringWidth);
System.out.println("Window area = " + areaOfWindow);
System.out.println("Window perimeter = " + perimeterOfWindow);
System.out.println("Total Cost =  " + cost);
```

For the height and width, we chose to use the original string values input by the user, but we could have used the converted numbers instead. As you can see, we have provided output to show what was entered, what was calculated, and, most importantly, the total cost of our project.

With the variables set up, input obtained and parsed, calculations completed, and results displayed to the user, we've accomplished everything our program was tasked to do. Listing 6.3 presents the completed listing.

LISTING 6.3

The WindowMaster Listing

```java
import java.util.Scanner;

public class WindowMaster {

  public static void main(String [] args) {
    // declare variables for height and width
    float height;
    float width;

    // declare String variables to hold the user's height and
    // width input
    String stringHeight;
    String stringWidth;

    // declare other variables
    float areaOfWindow;
    float cost;
    float perimeterOfWindow;

    // declare and initialize the Scanner
    Scanner myScanner = new Scanner(System.in);

    // get input from the user
    System.out.println("Please enter window height:");
    stringHeight = myScanner.nextLine();
    System.out.println("Please enter window width:");
    stringWidth = myScanner.nextLine();

    // convert String values of height and width to float values
    height = Float.parseFloat(stringHeight);
    width = Float.parseFloat(stringWidth);

    // calculate the area of the window
    areaOfWindow = height * width;

    // calculate the perimeter of the window
    perimeterOfWindow = 2 * (height + width);
```

```
    // calculate the total cost - use a hard-coded value
    // for material cost
    cost = ((3.50f * areaOfWindow) + (2.25f * perimeterOfWindow));

    // display the results to the user
    System.out.println("Window height = " + stringHeight);
    System.out.println("Window width = " + stringWidth);
    System.out.println("Window area = " + areaOfWindow);
    System.out.println("Window perimeter = " + perimeterOfWindow);
    System.out.println("Total Cost =  " + cost);
  }
}
```

RUNNING THE PROGRAM

Compile and then run the program. When you run the program, you should see something like the following, using **10** and **15** as the input values:

```
Please enter window height:
10
Please enter window width:
15
Window height = 10
Window width = 15
Window area = 150
Window perimeter = 50
Total Cost = 637.5
```

If you get errors when compiling, remember what you learned in previous lessons. See what information the IDE is providing you, and make sure your code matches the code in the listing. A simple missing semicolon or extra space in the wrong place can cause your program to not compile.

SUMMARY

In this lesson, you reviewed what you have learned in the previous lessons. You took a problem, which was to calculate a cost, and then provided a programmatic solution to it. You saw the process of thinking through what needed to be done, and then you wrote the code for each section. By the end, you had pulled together everything you have learned up to this point into a full-fledged program.

> **NOTE** If you had trouble using your IDE or entering the code, now would be the time to go back and review the earlier lessons. Going forward, you will be digging deeper into the code.

EXERCISES

Run the program you created in this lesson to make sure it works as expected and then review what you have done. The following are suggested exercises to do on your own.

Exercise 1: Mapping Instructions to Code

Exercise 2: Adding Prompts for Costs

Exercise 3: Adding Multiple Windows

Exercise 4: Adding Validation

Exercise 1: Mapping Instructions to Code

Go back to the pseudocode or flowchart that you created before starting to code and map each instruction in the program with that plan.

- Does your initial plan include more steps than the program required?
- Did your initial plan skip any of the required steps?

Exercise 2: Adding Prompts for Costs

The program used hard-coded values of 3.50 and 2.25. Refactor the code to include the use of prompts and a Scanner to obtain these values for the cost of the window and trim from the user. Make sure that the updated code works and produces the expected results.

Exercise 3: Adding Multiple Windows

Refactor the code to prompt the user to enter the number of windows in addition to the height and width. Update the cost calculations to include the number of windows. Assume that all windows are the same size for this exercise.

Exercise 4: Adding Validation

Refactor the code to include a `try/catch` validation on the user input, using the pattern provided in the lesson on collecting console input.

> **TIP** When refactoring multiple parts of the code to do the same thing, it is often best to refactor *one* of the parts first to make sure it works as expected. Once you understand what the pattern is doing, it is easier to reuse it in other parts of the code.

Lesson 7
Controlling Program Flow

In this lesson, we are going to begin to look at how we can control the flow of a program. Specifically, we look at how we can make decisions and change the flow based on those decisions. To do that, you will be introduced to conditional statements and boolean expressions.

LEARNING OBJECTIVES

By the end of this lesson, you will be able to:
- Define boolean expressions
- Differentiate between conditional operators and relational operators
- Learn how to make decisions in your code to execute one code block instead of another
- Work with code that will branch to different code blocks depending on a value
- Explore conditional statements
- Discover a method for comparing strings

WHAT CAN OUR CODE DO?

So far, our programs have simply executed from beginning to end, one statement after another. We've added some code that allows us to get input from the user, but even with that, our code executes in a straight line—the same way every time. You would think there has to be more that can be done than this, and you'd be right. There is more but, surprisingly, not too much more. Here is what we can do in code:

- Execute statements one after another in a straight line
- Make decisions to execute one block of code instead of another based on some criteria
- Repeat a set of statements a certain number of times based on some criteria

That's it—there is no more. All programs are built from these building blocks. We've already covered creating code in straight lines. That's how all the prior programs in this book have flowed. In the rest of this lesson, you'll learn how to make decisions and change program flow based on the criteria. In the next lesson, you will learn the method for repeating a set of statements.

Conditional Execution

Conditional execution allows us to make decisions in our code. It allows us to choose one path over another.

DECISIONS AND BOOLEAN EXPRESSIONS

How do we make decisions that can change how our programs flow? What do the criteria for these decisions consist of? We make these decisions using an `if` statement.

NOTE There are additional ways you can make decisions that will change program flow; however, using `if` statements is the easiest and thus what we will focus on now.

---

if Statements

Often when you are writing programs, you want the program to do something only *if* something else is true. In Java, one way we control the flow of a program is using `if` statements along with a condition presented. This condition can be any valid boolean expression, which is simply any expression that evaluates to true or false.

When you write an `if` statement, you declare the condition you want the program to check inside parentheses, followed by the code you want it to execute if the condition is true. If the condition evaluates to being true, then the program will execute the block of code that is within the `if` statement's code block. If the condition evaluates to being false, then the program will skip the rest of the `if` statement completely.

The basic syntax looks like this:

```
if (condition) {
    // execute code if condition is true
}
```

The `condition` given to an `if` statement can use equity, relational, and conditional operators to create the boolean expression that determines whether a block of code should be executed. Because it is a boolean expression, it will always evaluate to either true or false. For example, the following is a simple snippet of code that checks to see whether a value stored in an age variable is greater than or equal to 18. If it is, then a message is displayed.

```
if (age >= 18) {
    System.out.println("You're old enough to vote!");
}
```

Table 7.1 presents the equality and relational operators. Relational operators operate, for the most part, on numerical operands and evaluate to true or false (boolean) values.

Table 7.1 Equality and Relational Operators

	Relational Operator	Meaning
Equal	operand1 == operand2	Evaluates to true if the two operands are equal, false otherwise
Not equal	operand1 != operand2	Evaluates to true if the two operands are not equal, false otherwise
Less than	operand1 < operand2	Evaluates to true if operand1 is less than operand2, false otherwise
Greater than	operand1 > operand2	Evaluates to true if operand1 is greater than operand2, false otherwise
Less than or equal	operand1 <= operand2	Evaluates to true if operand1 is less than or equal to operand2, false otherwise
Greater than or equal	operand1 >= operand2	Evaluates to true if operand1 is greater than or equal to operand2, false otherwise

Boolean Expressions

The condition inside the parentheses following the `if` command is a boolean expression. Boolean expressions are similar to mathematical expressions in that they are code statements that evaluate to data values. The main difference is that boolean expressions always evaluate to either true or false. Another big difference is that boolean expressions are formed using boolean and relational operators instead of mathematical operators.

Just like other Java statements, we can string together a series of `if` statements to control the output of a program. Java will evaluate each statement in turn: if the current statement is true, it will perform the action specified in the statement and move on to the next `if` statement. If the current statement is false, Java will skip it and evaluate the next `if` statement or instruction.

In Listing 7.1, we present a series of `if` statements. In the listing, we create a variable called day that has a number from 1 to 7. This number will correspond to a day of the week, with 1 being Monday and 7 being Sunday. The `if` statements are used to set the value of another variable, dayName, to the day of the week, which is then displayed.

LISTING 7.1

DayOfWeek.java Using an if Statement

```java
public class DayOfWeek {

    public static void main(String[] args) {

        int day = 4;
        String dayName = "";

        if (day == 1) {
            dayName = "Monday";
        }
        if (day == 2) {
            dayName = "Tuesday";
        }
        if (day == 3) {
            dayName = "Wednesday";
        }
        if (day == 4) {
            dayName = "Thursday";
```

```
        }
        if (day == 5) {
            dayName = "Friday";
        }
        if (day == 6) {
            dayName = "Saturday";
        }
        if (day == 7) {
            dayName = "Sunday";
        }

        System.out.println("The day is " + dayName);
    }
}
```

If we enter Listing 7.1 and run it, we will see the following output:

```
The day is Thursday
```

Thursday is printed because the value of day is 4. When the program executes, it checks to see whether day is equal to 1. When it is not, it jumps to the next command after the if statement, which in this case is another if statement that checks to see whether day is equal to 2, which it again is not. This continues until the day is equal to 4, at which point the code within that if statement is executed, assigning the variable dayName the value of Thursday. Once this is completed, the execution of the code continues to the next if statement, which checks to see whether day is equal to 5, which it again is not. Execution continues to check all the if statements before finally using println to display the day of the week.

> **NOTE** Change the value of day from 4 to a different number to see how it changes what is displayed.

if-else Statements

The code in Listing 7.1 might not seem to be the most optimal, and it is not. While a basic if statement can be useful, the problem is that each statement is evaluated independently of each other, meaning that any (or none or all) of the statements can produce an outcome, based on the input and conditions.

Sometimes, though, we want the program to perform one action if the condition statement is true and a completely different action if the conditional statement is false, without having to consider other conditions. This is where if–else is useful. With an if–else statement, we consider only one conditional statement and then direct to one of two possible outcomes. With the if–else statement (also known as the if–then–else statement), our program will execute a certain block of code if a certain condition is true and will execute a different block of code if the condition is false. It looks like this:

```
if (condition) {
    // execute code if condition is true
} else {
    // execute code if condition is false
}
```

For example, if a person is 18 or older, they can vote. If they are not, then they can't vote. With a single condition, we can evaluate to a true or false and act upon the result.

```
if (age >=18) {
    System.out.println("You're old enough to vote!");
} else {
    System.out.println("You'll have to wait to vote!");
}
```

Listing 7.2 puts an if–else statement to work. In this listing, we check to see if a number is positive or negative.

LISTING 7.2

PositiveNegative.java

```
import java.util.Scanner;

public class PositiveNegative {

    public static void main(String[] args) {

        int number = 0;
        String stringValue = "";

        Scanner inputReader = new Scanner(System.in);
        System.out.println("Enter a number: ");
        stringValue = inputReader.nextLine();
        number = Integer.parseInt(stringValue);

        if (number >= 0) {
            System.out.println("The number is positive");
```

```
            } else {
                System.out.println("The number is negative");
            }
        }
    }
```

Note that in Listing 7.2, we added code that should look familiar from Lesson 5, "Collecting and Parsing Input from the User," which asks the user to enter a number. We read the number in as a `String` and then convert it to an integer. If this code is confusing, go back and review Lesson 5.

Once we have the integer converted and stored in our number variable, we use an if-else statement to do our magic. If the number is greater than or equal to zero, then the if statement is true, and we print out a message saying the number is positive, as shown in the following output:

```
Enter a number:
5
The number is positive
```

If the number is not greater than or less than zero, then the code jumps to the else statement and prints a message saying the number is negative.

```
Enter a number:
-435
The number is negative
```

> **NOTE** If you enter a value into Listing 7.2 that is not a number, your program will give an error because we haven't included exception handling. This is something you will learn in a future lesson.

Chaining if-else Statements

If we want to consider multiple conditions, then if-else statements can be chained together in your code as shown here:

```
if (condition1) {
    // execute code if condition1 is true
} else if (condition2) {
    // execute code if condition2 is true
} else if (condition3) {
```

```
        // execute code if condition3 is true
    } else {
        // execute code if all conditions above were false
    }
```

This lets us check multiple conditions in our code to get to a single outcome. If we look back at Listing 7.1, you can see that once we find the day of the week, there is really no need to continue with checking more `if` statements. Listing 7.3 rewrites Listing 7.1 to use chained `if-else` statements. Once a true continue is found, execution drops out of the `if-else` chain.

LISTING 7.3

`DayOfWeek.java` Using an `if-else` Statement

```java
public class DayOfWeek {

    public static void main(String[] args) {

        int day = 4;
        String dayName = "";

        if (day == 1) {
            dayName = "Monday";
        } else if (day == 2) {
            dayName = "Tuesday";
        } else if (day == 3) {
            dayName = "Wednesday";
        } else if (day == 4) {
            dayName = "Thursday";
        } else if (day == 5) {
            dayName = "Friday";
        } else if (day == 6) {
            dayName = "Saturday";
        } else if (day == 7) {
            dayName = "Sunday";
        } else {
            dayName = "Oops!";
        }

        System.out.println("The day is " + dayName);
    }
)
```

When we run Listing 7.3, we get the same result as we did running Listing 7.1.

```
The day is Thursday
```

There are, however, two differences. The main difference is that once the program finds that day equals 4, it sets the value of dayName equal to Thursday and then jumps to the end of the entire if–else chain.

The second change was the addition of a final else statement at the end of the chain. If the day is not equal to any of the values checked in the chain of if statements, then when the last if check evaluates to false, its else statement will be executed. We can see this happen if we change the value of day to a number greater than 7 or less than 1 and run the program again. We see that the final else catches the mistake.

```
The day is Oops!
```

> **NOTE** It is important to mention that the evaluation of a chain of if and else statements is evaluated from top to bottom. If at any point a condition is true, then the code block will execute, and the rest of the conditions after it will be skipped. If it is possible for multiple conditions to be true, then only the topmost one will be executed since we call it first.

> **NOTE** You can learn more about the operators shown in this lesson on the Oracle site at docs.oracle.com/javase/tutorial/java/nutsandbolts/op2.html.

Evaluating Multiple Conditions

So far with our flow control, we have been using single-part conditionals. That is to say, we've been writing expressions that do a single comparison and evaluate to true or false. What happens if we want to check multiple conditions?

You have a couple of options. The first is to nest one if statement inside another.

```
if (condition) {
   if (condition) {
   }
}
```

While this works, there is another option: conditional expressions can be compounded using conditional-and (AND) or conditional-or (OR) operators.

Conditional-And and Conditional-Or Operators

With a conditional-and operator, both conditions must be true for the conditional expression as a whole to be true. For example, if there is precipitation AND the temperature is below freezing, it will snow. If one or both of those conditions is false, it will not snow.

With a conditional-or operator, the conditional expression is true if at least one of the conditions is true. If both are false, the conditional expression as a whole evaluates as false. For example, if it is raining OR snowing today (or even if it just cold enough to rain and snow at the same time), I will need an umbrella to stay dry if I go outside. The only case where I won't need an umbrella is if it is neither raining nor snowing.

Both conditional-and (represented as &&) and conditional-or (represented as ||) are logical operators and are used in the following manner:

```
if (conditionA && conditionB)  //an AND condition
{
    // code;
}

if (conditionA || conditionB)  //an OR condition
{
    // code;
}
```

To fully understand these, let's look at them in action. Listing 7.4 includes both the conditional-and and conditional-or operators.

LISTING 7.4

AboutYou.java: Using Conditional Operators

```
public class AboutYou {

    public static void main(String[] args) {
        int age = 19;
        boolean registered = true;
```

```
        // See if a person can vote!
        if( age >= 18 && registered == true){
            System.out.println("You can vote!");
        }

        // See if they are not allowed to vote!
        if(age < 18 || registered != true ){
            System.out.println("You not eligible to vote!");
        }
    }
}
```

In Listing 7.4, there is more than one condition within an if statement. The code is a bit redundant but works for showing how conditional-and and conditional-or work. In the first if statement, we are checking to see whether a person can vote. To vote, they must be 18 years of age or older *and* they must be registered. Each of these conditions is created using expressions with relational operators that evaluate to either true or false. It is either true or false that they are older than 18, and it is either true or false that they are registered to vote. If both resolve to true, then the && results in the entire if statement resolving to being true, and thus the message is displayed.

The second if statement is a bit redundant with the first but is good for illustrating the conditional-or statement. In this case, we are checking to see whether the age of the person is younger than 18, and we are also checking to see whether the person has not registered to vote. If either their age is younger than 18 or they are not registered (registered is not true), then they are not eligible to vote, so we display a message to let them know.

When you run this program, the output you see should look like the following:

```
You can vote!
```

If you change the value of age to something less than 18 and then compile and run the program again, you'll see a different result. Change the age to various values and change registered to false instead of true to see what differences it makes when you run the program.

> **NOTE** Operator precedence puts the conditional operators at a lower level than the relational operators. As such, the conditional operators will always be evaluated after the relational operations have occurred. If you want to make sure your code is clear, you can use parentheses to separate the expressions.

```
if( (age >= 18) && (registered == true)) {
    ...
```

> **NOTE** The conditional-and (&&) and conditional-or (||) are called *short-circuit operators* because they will only evaluate the second operand if they must. The & and | operators will always evaluate both operands.

Exclusive-Or

There is actually a third operator we can use as well, the exclusive-or (^). The exclusive-or (^) or XOR operator checks to see whether the operand on either side is true but also checks to make sure both are not true. Table 7.2 summarizes the three operators we've talked about that can be used for combining multiple conditions.

Table 7.2 Operators

Operator Type	Operator		Meaning
Conditional	&&	AND	Evaluates to true if both operand1 and operand2 are true, false otherwise
Conditional	||	OR	Evaluates to true if either operand1 or operand2 or both are true, false otherwise
Logical	^	Exclusive-Or (XOR)	Evaluates to true if either operand1 or operand2 but not both are true, false otherwise

Bitwise Operations

We covered the logical boolean operators in this lesson. The Java language also has bitwise boolean operators and bit shift operators. These are not commonly used, but Oracle has a brief intro at docs.oracle.com/javase/tutorial/java/nutsandbolts/op3.html.

When you use the operators from Table 7.2, your expression will be evaluated to a true or false result. Table 7.3 summarizes the results of using the three operators on two different operands.

Table 7.3 Operator Results

A	B	a && b	a || b	a ^ b
False	False	False	False	False
True	False	False	True	True
False	True	False	True	True
True	True	True	True	False

TERNARY OR CONDITIONAL OPERATOR

It is worth mentioning a special operator in Java, the ternary operator (?:), which is also called the *conditional operator*. This operator is the only operator that has three operands.

The ternary operator is used to provide a shortcut for an if-else statement. The difference between the ternary operator and a standard if statement is that the ternary operator assigns a value to a variable. The format of this operator is as follows:

```
result = (condition) ? true_result : false_result;
```

The operator will evaluate a condition, which is a standard boolean expression that will evaluate to a true or false answer. Depending on the result of the boolean expression, one of two answers will be assigned to the variable on the left. If the condition evaluates to true, then the first expression (true_result) after the question mark will be assigned to the variable (result). If the condition evaluates to false, then the second expression (false_result) that appears after the colon will be assigned to the variable. This operator is roughly equivalent to the following if-else statement:

```
if (condition) {
    result = true_result
} else {
    result = false_result;
}
```

It should be clear that the benefit of the ternary operator is to allow for a condition to be used to quickly place a value into a variable. Listing 7.5 gives a simple example of using a ternary operator.

LISTING 7.5

Using a Ternary Operator

```
public class VotingAge {

    public static void main(String[] args) {

        int age = 19;
        String result = "";
```

```
        result = (age >= 18) ? "You can register!" : "You are not old
enough to vote";
        System.out.println(result);
    }
}
```

When you run Listing 7.5, you should see the following:

```
You can register!
```

When the program runs, one of two strings is placed into the results variable, which is then printed. The result that is displayed is determined by the ternary operator. If the condition that checks to see whether age is greater than or equal to 18 evaluates to true, then the first message, You can register, is assigned to result. If the condition evaluates to false, then the second message is assigned.

SWITCH STATEMENT

In several of the listings, we used if statements to use a number to determine the day of the week. In looking at Listing 7.3, you might believe that there must be a better way to accomplish the same result without having so many if statements.

The switch statement is an alternative construct that allows for conditional execution. The switch statement checks a condition against any number of cases. If a case matches, then the code associated with that case is executed. The basic form is as follows:

```
switch (expression) {
    case constant:
        // execute code if expression == constant
        break;
    case constant2:
        //execute code if expression == constant2
        break;
    default:
        //execute code if no match found
        break;
}
```

The main body of a switch statement is called the switch block. The switch block is composed of one or more cases or default labels. The code associated with the default label is executed if none of the cases matches the expression.

A big difference between switch statements and if statements is that the conditions tested in an if statement must be boolean expressions, whereas the expressions evaluated in a switch statement can be byte, short, char, int, enumerated types (more on these later), strings, or the wrapper classes for byte, short char, and int (more on this later). The switch statement simply checks whether the evaluated expression matches any of the cases.

Another thing to notice about switch statements is the break statement. The break statement terminates the switch—in other words, after a break statement is executed, the program continues with the first statement after the switch block. The break statements are necessary because all statements after a matching case label are executed in order until either a break statement or the end of the switch block is encountered, regardless of the values of the subsequent case labels. This is known as *falling through*. The best way to see this in action is to look at some code. In Listing 7.6 we take advantage of this feature to improve the day of the week program.

LISTING 7.6

DayOfWeek Using a switch Statement

```java
public class DayOfWeek {

    public static void main(String[] args) {

        int day = 4;
        String dayName = "";

        switch (day) {
            case 1:
                dayName = "Monday";
                break;
            case 2:
                dayName = "Tuesday";
                break;
            case 3:
                dayName = "Wednesday";
                break;
            case 4:
                dayName = "Thursday";
                break;
            case 5:
                dayName = "Friday";
                break;
```

```
        case 6:
            dayName = "Saturday";
            break;
        case 7:
            dayName = "Sunday";
            break;
        default:
            dayName = "Invalid day";
    }

    System.out.println("The day is " + dayName);
    }
}
```

Running this listing gives the same result as Listing 7.3.

```
The day is Thursday
```

The switch statement is taking day as the expression it will evaluate. It will compare the value of day to each of the cases until it finds one that matches. Once it finds the match, it will execute the code within that case until it gets to either the end of the switch statement or a break command. If it reaches a break command, execution will jump to the end of the switch statement.

If the day does not match any of the cases, then program flow will go to the default case, labeled default. The code in the default section will then execute. The default block operates a lot like an else statement.

TIP It is a good practice to always include a default case even if you don't believe it will ever be used. It's a good safety check for your code.

Falling Through with a switch Statement

There are times when you want to run the same code for several values in a switch statement. In such situations, we can just stack up the case statements one after another.

For example, in Listing 7.7, we want to determine the type of day for a given number. In other words, we want to know whether it is a weekday or a weekend.

LISTING 7.7

Falling Through in a switch Statement

```
public class DayOfWeek {
```

```java
public static void main(String[] args) {

    int day = 4;
    String dayType = "";

    switch (day) {
        case 1:
        case 2:
        case 3:
        case 4:
        case 5:
            dayType = "Weekday";
            break;
        case 6:
        case 7:
            dayType = "Weekend";
            break;
        default:
            dayType = "Invalid Day";
    }

    System.out.println(dayType);
}
}
```

Looking at the code in Listing 7.7, you see that if the value for day is 1, 2, 3, 4, or 5, then dayType is Weekday. But, if the value of day is 6 or 7, the dayType value is Weekend. When you run the code, you should see that day 4 is a weekday:

Weekday

NOTE Switch logic can be achieved with if and else-if statements. Using it is really just a matter of preference. Some developers find it more readable, but others don't, so using it is really up to you. The key difference is that for a switch statement you need to have a list of acceptable values that are being compared to the same thing.

NOTE All switch expressions can be converted to if-else logic; however, not all if-else expressions can be converted to a switch.

COMPARING FOR EQUAL STRINGS

It is easy to do conditional statements with numbers, but comparing strings works a little differently. When comparing strings, we need to call an approach similar to calling the println() method to display information.

To compare strings, we call the equals() method. This is done by adding .equals() to the string we want to compare and including the string we want to compare to it in the parentheses. For example, we used a variable called dayName earlier to store the name of the day of a week. Using the .equals() method, we could check to see whether the dayName value was equal to Saturday by doing the following:

```
dayName.equals("Saturday")
```

If dayName is equal to the string between the parentheses, then this expression will evaluate to true. If they are not equal, the expression will evaluate to false. Listing 7.8 is an update of Listing 7.6.

LISTING 7.8

DayOfWeek Where We Look for a Weekend

```java
public class DayOfWeek {

    public static void main(String[] args) {

        int day = 4;
        String dayName = "";

        switch (day) {
            case 1:
                dayName = "Monday";
                break;
            case 2:
                dayName = "Tuesday";
                break;
            case 3:
                dayName = "Wednesday";
                break;
            case 4:
                dayName = "Thursday";
                break;
```

```
            case 5:
                dayName = "Friday";
                break;
            case 6:
                dayName = "Saturday";
                break;
            case 7:
                dayName = "Sunday";
                break;
            default:
                dayName = "Invalid day";
        }

        System.out.println("The day is " + dayName);

        if(dayName.equals("Saturday") || dayName.equals("Sunday")) {
            System.out.println("It is the weekend!");
        } else {
            System.out.println("It is a weekday.");
        }
    }
}
```

If we look near the end of Listing 7.8, we see that we have added an `if` statement that checks to see whether `dayName` is equal to Saturday or Sunday. We've done this using a conditional OR operator (||) as well. If the value is equal to one of these two days, then we know it is a weekend. When you run the listing, you will see the following output:

```
The day is Thursday
It is a weekday.
```

If you change the value of `day` to 7, then when you compile and run the listing, you see the following:

```
The day is Sunday
It is the weekend!
```

> **TIP** For more information on String's `equals()` method, check out the Java tutorial on comparing Strings at docs.oracle.com/javase/tutorial/java/data/comparestrings.html.

The `compareTo()` method is another method that can be used to check for equality of strings. Whereas the `equals()` method returns a boolean value (true or false) if the strings are equal, the compareTo() method returns an integer. It the strings are equal, it returns 0. If the string passed to compareTo() is greater than the original string, then a value greater than zero is returned. If the passed string is less than the original string, then a value less than zero is returned. Listing 7.9 is a super-simple listing that shows you the result of calling compareTo() a couple of times.

LISTING 7.9

Comparing Two Strings

```
public class CompareStrings {

    public static void main(String[] args) {

        String stringOne = "apples";
        String stringTwo = "bananas";
        String stringThree = "grapes";


        int result = 0;

        result = stringOne.compareTo(stringTwo);
        if (result == 0) {
           System.out.println( stringOne + " equals " + stringTwo);
        } else if (result < 0) {
            System.out.println( stringOne + " is less than (before) " +
stringTwo);
        } else {
            System.out.println( stringOne + " is greater than (after) " +
stringTwo);
        }

        result = stringThree.compareTo(stringTwo);
        if (result == 0) {
            System.out.println( stringThree + " equals " + stringTwo);
        } else if (result < 0){
            System.out.println( stringThree + " is less than (before) " +
stringTwo);
        } else {
            System.out.println( stringThree + " is greater than (after) " +
stringTwo);
        }
    }
}
```

> **NOTE** It is worth clarifying what one `String` being greater than or less than another `String` means. Strings are sorted based on their characters. In fact, numbers come first, then uppercase letters, then lowercase letters. This means that "a" is less than "b" and that 1 is less than "z". It also means that the String "Abc" would come before (is less than) "abc" and that the String "Zzz" would come before (be less than) the String "aaa" because the capital letter *Z* comes before the lowercase letter *a*.

When you run this listing, you should see the following output:

```
apples is less than (before) bananas
grapes is greater than (after) bananas
```

This listing creates three string variables and assigns value to them. It then uses comparisons to determine whether one string is equal to, less than, or greater than another. In this case, `apples` come before `bananas`, and `grapes` comes after `bananas`. You can change the strings to see how it impacts the results.

> **NOTE** You saw two different ways to determine whether `Strings` are equal. When writing programs, it is not uncommon to have multiple approaches that can solve the same problem.

SUMMARY

In this lesson, we looked at how we can control the flow of a program. Specifically, we looked at how we can make decisions and change the flow based on those decisions. In going through this lesson, you discovered many core elements of the Java programming language including:

- The `if-else` statement
- The `switch` statement
- The relational operators
- The conditional operators including the conditional AND (&&) and conditional OR (||)

You also learned a method for comparing strings, the `.equals()` method.

That's it for this lesson, but it isn't the end of controlling programming flow. In the next lesson, you will continue to dig into the Java language and learn commands for directing your program flow to repeat or loop.

EXERCISES

This section includes coding exercises to introduce flow control. Now that you are learning to control the flow of the program, you will be able to do a lot more. This lesson has more exercises than other lessons to help you make sure you understand what you learned in the lessons up to this point, plus to show you the variety of things you are now able to do with the Java statements you've learned.

Exercise 1: What Month Is It?

Exercise 2: Guess Me

Exercise 3: Birthstones

Exercise 4: Trivia Night

Exercise 5: Space Rustlers

Exercise 6: Picky Eater

Exercise 7: Field Day

Exercise 1: What Month Is It?

Create a class that uses `if-else` statements to convert a number from 1 to 12 to the correct month. You can use Listing 7.3 as a starting point.

Exercise 2: Guess Me

Let's play a game with the user. We choose a number, ask the user to guess the number, and produce a response based on how well their choice matches the number we started with. Create a new program called *GuessMe* that includes the following:

- Create a new class named `GuessMe`. (You'll want your file to be named `GuessMe.java`.)
- Write a program that that has an integer of your choice stored in a variable.
- The program asks the user to pick a number.
- Regardless of the choice, the program should print out what the user entered as part of the response.
- If their choice is equal to the number, print `Wow, nice guess! That was it!`
- If their choice is less than the number, print `Ha, nice try - too low! I chose #.`
- If their choice is greater than the number, print `Too bad, way too high. I chose #.`

You're on your own for the code. The following example shows a sample output, but you can change the wording if you want:

```
I've chosen a number. Betcha can't guess it!
Your guess: 11

11? Ha, nice try — too low! I chose 44.
```

Exercise 3: Birthstones

Now let's try a lookup application, where the user enters one value and the program returns a specific value from a list in relation to the input. In this case, we will ask the user for a month number and tell the user the corresponding month and birthstone. The following table shows a common list of birthstones that you can use for this program:

Month	Birthstone
January	Garnet
February	Amethyst
March	Aquamarine
April	Diamond
May	Emerald
June	Pearl
July	Ruby
August	Peridot
September	Sapphire
October	Opal
November	Topaz
December	Turquoise

Create a new file named BirthStones.java for this exercise. The program should perform the following steps:

- Ask the user for a number.
- Match that number against the month number.
- Print out the name of the month and its corresponding birthstone.
- If the user enters a value that doesn't correspond to a month number, display an appropriate error message.

The code and wording are completely up to you, as long as the program runs and meets the criteria listed earlier.

As an example, if the user entered a value of 12, the output might look like the following:

```
What month's birthstone do you want to know? 12
December's birthstone is Turquoise.
```

If the user entered -1 as the month, the output might look like the following:

```
What month's birthstone do you want to know? -1
I think you must be confused, -1 doesn't match a month.
```

> **NOTE** Try doing this with a chain of `if` statements and then convert your solution to a `switch` statement.

Exercise 4: Trivia Night

Now let's create a program that uses everything you've learned so far about writing applications in Java: a trivia game that asks the user a series of questions and keeps track of the score.

Create a new java class named `TriviaNight` that performs the following tasks:

- It should ask the user a series of multiple-choice questions and determine whether the user's answer is correct for each question. We recommend a minimum of three questions.

- The program should keep a running tally of the number of correct answers so that it can display a final count after the user has answered all the questions.

- After the user has answered all questions, the program displays the final score along with a message that is appropriate for the score. For example, the programs should not say "Awesome!" if the user did not answer any of the questions correctly.

- **BONUS:** Include output for each question that tells the user whether the answer was correct along with their current score and the number of questions remaining.

The code and wording are completely up to you. Here is an example of what the program might look like without the bonus step:

```
It's TRIVIA NIGHT! Are you ready?!

FIRST QUESTION!
What is the lowest-level programming language?
1) Source code
2) Assembly language
```

```
3) C#
4) Machine code

YOUR ANSWER: 4

SECOND QUESTION!
Website security CAPTCHA forms are descended from the work of?
1) Grace Hopper
2) Alan Turing
3) Charles Babbage
4) Larry Page

YOUR ANSWER: 2

LAST QUESTION!
Which of these sci-fi ships was once slated for a full-size replica in
Las Vegas?
1) Serenity
2) The Battlestar Galactica
3) The USS Enterprise
4) The Millennium Falcon

YOUR ANSWER: 3

Nice job - you got 3 correct!
```

Exercise 5: Space Rustlers

This exercise will help you practice working with the if-else structure. Enter the code in
Exercise Listing 7.5 in a new file named SpaceRustlers. Make sure that the code works
before you make changes to it. Before running the code, look through what it is supposed to do. Can you predict what the output will be with the original values?

EXERCISE LISTING 7.5

SpaceRustlers.java

```java
public class SpaceRustlers {

    public static void main(String[] args) {

        int spaceships = 10;
        int aliens = 25;
        int cows = 100;
```

```
        if(aliens > spaceships){
            System.out.println("Vrroom, vroom! Let's get going!");
        } else{
            System.out.println("There aren't enough green guys to drive
these ships!");
        }

        if(cows == spaceships){
            System.out.println("Wow, way to plan ahead! JUST enough room for
all these walking hamburgers!");
        } else if (cows > spaceships){
            System.out.println("Dang it! I don't how we're going to fit all
these cows in here!");
        } else {
            System.out.println("Too many ships! Not enough cows.");
        }
    }
}
```

When you run this code, you should see the following:

```
Vrroom, vroom! Let's get going!
Dang it! I don't how we're going to fit all these cows in here!
Oh no! The herds got restless and took over! Looks like _we're_
hamburger now!!
```

After you get the original code to work correctly, look at the following, and update the code as necessary. Remember to test and run the code after each update to make sure it works as expected.

- What do else-if and if do? (Answer in a comment.)

- If you remove else from the else-if statement, what does *that* do?

- Add in another if-else block that prints out Hurrah, we've got the grub! Hamburger party on Alpha Centauri! if the aliens outnumber the cows. If the cows equal or outnumber the aliens, print Oh no! The herds got restless and took over! Looks like we're hamburger now!!.

Exercise 6: Picky Eater

- This exercise will help you practice using the conditional ANDs and ORs. Write a new program named *PickyEater* to help someone figure out whether their particularly picky-eater kid will eat the food that they have described.

Here are the rules:

- If the food has any spinach in it or a funny name, print `There's no way he'll eat that!`
- If the food has been fried more than two times but less than four and it is covered in chocolate, print `Oh, it's like a deep-fried Snickers. That'll be a hit!`
- If it has been fried twice and is covered in cheese, print `Mmm. Yeah, he'll eat fried cheesy doodles.`
- If it is broccoli, has more than six pats of butter on top, and is covered in cheese, print `As long as the green is hidden by cheddar, it'll happen!`
- But otherwise, if it is broccoli, print `Oh, green stuff like that might as well go in the bin.`

Exercise Listing 7.6 shows part of the code to get you started.

EXERCISE LISTING 7.6

PickyEater.java

```java
import java.util.Scanner;

public class PickyEater {

    public static void main(String[] args) {
        Scanner userInput = new Scanner(System.in);

        System.out.print("How many times has it been fried? (#) ");
        int timesFried = Integer.parseInt(userInput.nextLine());

        System.out.print("Does it have any spinach in it? (y/n) ");
        String hasSpinach = userInput.nextLine();

        System.out.print("Is it covered in cheese? (y/n) ");
        String cheeseCovered = userInput.nextLine();

        System.out.print("How many pats of butter are on top? (#) ");
        int butterPats = Integer.parseInt(userInput.nextLine());

        System.out.print("Is it covered in chocolate? (y/n) ");
        String chocolatedCovered = userInput.nextLine();
```

```
        System.out.print("Does it have a funny name? (y/n) ");
        String funnyName = userInput.nextLine();

        System.out.print("Is it broccoli? (y/n) ");
        String isBroccoli = userInput.nextLine();

        // Conditionals should go here! Here's the first one for FREE!

        if (hasSpinach.equals("y") || funnyName.equals("y")) {
            System.out.println("There's no way he'll eat that!");
        }
    }
}
```

The rest of the conditionals are up to you. Here is an example of what the output might look like:

```
How many times has it been fried? (#) 4
Does it have any spinach in it? (y/n) y
Is it covered in cheese? (y/n) y
How many pats of butter are on top? (#) 8
Is it covered in chocolate? (y/n) n
Does it have a funny name? (y/n) y
Is it broccoli? (y/n) n
There is no way he'll eat that...
```

Exercise 7: Field Day

For this exercise, you will practice using the compareTo() function of Strings. Start by creating a new program called FieldDay.

Your company has organized a morale event. They are hosting a picnic and field day in the park, and of course, they want to play team games and team-building games.

To do that, they want to assign all the people who show up to certain teams based on their last name—they've already figured out the distribution. All they need you to do is to write the program that can sort them. For example, it should take a last name as input and use that to output the team name.

Here are the specs:

- If a person's name falls before Baggins, then they are on the team Red Dragons.

- If the name is Baggins or if it falls after Baggins but before Dresden, they are on the team Dark Wizards.

- If the name is Dresden or if it falls after Dresden but before Howl, they are on the team Moving Castles.

- If the name is Howl or if it falls after Howl but before Potter, they are on the team Golden Snitches.

- If the name is Potter or if it falls after Potter but before Vimes, they are on the team Night Guards.

- If the name is Vimes or if it falls after Vimes, they are on the team Black Holes.

When you run your program, you should see something like the following:

```
What's your last name? Weasley
Aha! You're on the team "Black Holes"!
Good luck in the games!
```

Looping Program Flow

In this lesson, we continue to learn how to control the flow of a program. In Lesson 7, "Controlling Program Flow," we learned how to control flow through making decisions. In this lesson, we'll expand upon that to learn how we can use our code to repeat ourselves using looping expressions.

LEARNING OBJECTIVES

By the end of this lesson, you will be able to:
- Use loops to repeat the execution of code blocks
- Learn the different types of looping commands you can use
- Understand how to change conditions for keeping a loop going
- Discover how to break out of loops

LOOPS

In the previous lesson, you learned about controlling program flow using conditions. These conditions allowed you to branch your code flow based on decisions made within the code. In today's lesson we continue learning about how to control the flow of our programs by using loops.

Loops are absolutely critical in any nontrivial program. They allow you to repeat a sequence as many times as you need, or sometimes you want to just keep going until a condition is met.

Should your phone ring five times before it goes to voicemail? There's a loop for that. Want to process payroll checks for all employees? You just keep going until there are no more employees. Well, there is a loop for that, too. The two examples shown in Figure 8.1 encapsulate the key question we need to ask before creating a loop:

Do I know in advance how many times to loop?

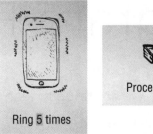
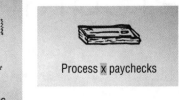

Process x paychecks

Ring 5 times

Figure 8.1 How many times to loop?

In the case of the phone ringing, we know that it should ring five times before it goes to voicemail. In the case of the payroll checks for employees, however, we might not know in advance how many times we need to repeat the process. You just want to simply start at the beginning of the pile and keep going until the pile runs out.

The kind of loop we use depends a lot on the answer to this question. Though you can often use many different types of loops in any particular situation, there is often a best choice. In the rest of this lesson, we will give you an overview of while loops, do/while loops, for loops, and special keywords called *jump statements* that we can use inside loops.

> **NOTE** *Loops* allow us to repeat the execution of a code block as long as some condition is true. There are three looping constructs in Java: while loops, do/while loops, for loops.

USING WHILE LOOPS

When you're a programmer, you can make the computer do some of the work for you. No one wants to write the same code over and over and over again. The first loops we'll discuss will be while loops. The basic syntax looks like this:

```
while(condition)
{
    // Code to be repeated
}
```

In a while loop, a condition is evaluated before each execution of a code block, including the first one. The code block will continue to be executed over and over, until the condition is evaluated to be false. So, the while loop checks the condition, and if it is true, then the code is executed, and the condition is checked again. If the condition is found to be false, then the code block is skipped, and program flow continues with the statement after the while code block.

Listing 8.1 presents a basic while loop that counts from 1 to 5. As you type this listing, notice the condition and code block that are being used.

LISTING 8.1

Using while to Count to 5

```
public class CountingNumbers {

    public static void main(String[] args) {

        int counter = 1;  // initializing our variable

        while (counter <= 5)
        {
            System.out.println( "Counting: " + counter );
            counter++;
        }

        System.out.println("...Done!");
    }
}
```

This is a short listing, but it illustrates the power of the while loop. When you run this program, you should see the following output:

```
Counting: 1
Counting: 2
Counting: 3
Counting: 4
Counting: 5
...Done!
```

When we look at this listing, you can see that a single variable is being created called counter. It is important to note that we are *initializing* this variable to 1. This will get our counting started. With our variable initialized, the next Java statement we get to is the new while statement. As you can see, we have the while followed by a condition that evaluates to either true or false. In this case, we know we just set counter to 1, and we know that 1 is less than or equal to 5, so our condition evaluates to true. That means the code block associated with the while statement will be executed.

In our code block we do two things. First, we print a message; we print a little text followed by the value of counter. After doing the work of our code block, we do the next statement, which is to increment counter by 1. The ++ operator adds 1 to the current variable. It is equivalent to doing the following:

```
counter = counter + 1;
```

So, in this case, counter goes from being 1 to being 2. With the end of the while code block reached, program flow goes back to the top, back to the while condition. The check is done again. This time counter equals 2, and 2 is less than or equal to 5, so the condition evaluates to true, and the while code block is executed again.

This continues to happen until counter++ sets counter equal to 6. At that point, program flow again goes to the while condition; however, when the counter value of 6 is checked, we find that 6 is not less than or equal to 5, so the condition resolves to false. Because the condition is false, program flow goes to the first statement after the while code block, which in this case is a line of code to print out the ...Done! message.

NOTE When doing Java coding, most lines of code end with a semicolon. Note that with the while command, there is not always a semicolon after the line with a while condition. The following is most likely an error:

```
while (counter <= 5);
```

The semicolon ends the while statement, which means any code block that follows will be considered as separate code and not part of the while command.

NOTE It is also worth noting that although we've shown a block of code after a while condition in curly brackets ({}), they are not required if the code to be executed is a single statement nor do pieces of the while statement have to be on separate lines. The following two while statements are valid:

```
while (counter <= 5)
    System.out.println( "Counting: " + counter++ );

while (counter <= 5) System.out.println( "Counting again: " + counter++ );
```

Initializing the while Loop

Looking at Listing 8.1, what would happen if we had initially set the value of counter to a
number greater than 5? Change the line of code where we declare and initialize counter
to the following:

```
int counter = 6;  // initializing our variable
```

Now when you compile and run the program, the output shows the following:

```
...Done!
```

As you can see, the code block within the while statement never executed. This is
because when the while statement checked the condition, it looked to see whether
the value of counter, which was 6, was less than or equal to 5. Since the value of 6 is not
less than 5, the condition evaluated to false, and the block was skipped without ever
being executed.

Incrementing the while Loop

What would happen if we left out the line to increment the counter? Try removing the
counter++ command. Compile and rerun the program. What happens? If we do this and
run the program, we are likely to see the following:

```
Counting: 1
Counting: 1
Counting: 1
Counting: 1
Counting: 1
Counting: 1
Counting: 1
Counting: 1
...
```

The program will continue to print the count of 1 forever. Because the condition will
always be true, the loop will run forever. We've created an infinite loop.

Breaking a Loop

Sometimes when we're learning things, we have to go beyond our comfort level. But we always have to make sure we are self-aware enough to know when to stop and take a break.

Along with this life lesson, we get to learn more about loops because loops can stop when a programmer tells them to take a break. Literally. To stop a loop, use the break keyword!

Here's an example:

```
while(condition)
{
    if(othercondition)
    {
        break;
    }
}
```

While the loop would normally continue until the condition changed to false, now there is another way to bail out—if the othercondition ever evaluates to true, we can use the break statement to stop the loop. The break statement will send control to the next line following the current loop.

Let's write a program to practice the new break statement. In Listing 8.2 is a new program named *BewareTheKraken*. In this program, we pretend we are diving in the ocean. We're going to keep going down, deeper and deeper, until the fish and everything gets too creepy and we have to stop.

LISTING 8.2

BewareTheKraken.java

```java
public class BewareTheKraken {

    public static void main(String[] args) {

        System.out.println("Get those flippers and wetsuit on - we're going diving!");
        System.out.println("Here we goooOOooOooo.....! *SPLASH*");

        int depthDivedInFt = 0;

        // Turns out the ocean is only so deep, 36200 at the deepest survey,
        // so if we reach the bottom ... we should probably stop.
        while(depthDivedInFt < 36200){
            System.out.println("So far, we've swum " + depthDivedInFt + " feet");
```

```
        if(depthDivedInFt >= 20000){
            System.out.println("Uhhh, I think I see a Kraken, guys....");
            System.out.println("TIME TO GO!");
            break;
        }

        // I can swim, really fast! 500ft at a time!
        depthDivedInFt += 1000;
    }
    System.out.println("");
    System.out.println("We ended up swimming " + depthDivedInFt +
" feet down.");
    System.out.println("I bet we can do better next time!");
  }
}
```

When we run the program in Listing 8.2, we should see the following:

```
Get those flippers and wetsuit on - we're going diving!
Here we gooo00oo0ooo.....! *SPLASH*
So far, we've swum 0 feet
So far, we've swum 1000 feet
So far, we've swum 2000 feet
So far, we've swum 3000 feet
So far, we've swum 4000 feet
So far, we've swum 5000 feet
So far, we've swum 6000 feet
So far, we've swum 7000 feet
So far, we've swum 8000 feet
So far, we've swum 9000 feet
So far, we've swum 10000 feet
So far, we've swum 11000 feet
So far, we've swum 12000 feet
So far, we've swum 13000 feet
So far, we've swum 14000 feet
So far, we've swum 15000 feet
So far, we've swum 16000 feet
So far, we've swum 17000 feet
So far, we've swum 18000 feet
So far, we've swum 19000 feet
So far, we've swum 20000 feet
Uhhh, I think I see a Kraken, guys....
TIME TO GO!

We ended up swimming 20000 feet down.
I bet we can do better next time!
```

Listing 8.2 might look longer than many we've seen before, but a lot of the code is for printing messages and comments. We can see that a while loop is created that will keep printing messages until a certain number is reached—in this case, a depth of greater than 36,200. In the body of the loop, however, there is a check to see whether the depth has reached 20,000. If it has, a break statement is executed, and the program flow jumps to the next command after the loop's code body.

This listing is a little arbitrary in that you could have simply had the while loop condition check for 20,000 feet instead of 36,200. In an exercise at the end of this lesson, you are asked to change this listing so that with each iteration of the loop, you are to ask the user if they want to continue to dive deeper. If they do not, then you will want to break out of the loop.

USING DO-WHILE LOOPS

There is another variant of the while loop, called the do-while. A do-while loop is almost identical to a while loop, except that do-whiles get straight to business—executing their code block first and checking the condition to see whether they should do it again only *after* it has been run once.

The syntax looks like this:

```
do
{
    // code to be repeated
} while (condition);
```

The best way to see the do-while loop in action is to show code. In Listing 8.3, we count to 5 with the do-while loop. This listing shows that we can do the same thing with the do-while loop that we can do with a while loop.

LISTING 8.3

Using do-while to Count to 5

```
public class CountingNumbers {

  public static void main(String[] args) {

      int counter = 1;  // initializing our variable

      do {
```

```
        System.out.println( "Counting: " + counter );
        counter++;
    } while (counter <= 5);

    System.out.println("...Done!");
  }
}
```

When you compile and run this listing, we should see the same output we saw from Listing 8.1.

```
Counting: 1
Counting: 2
Counting: 3
Counting: 4
Counting: 5
...Done!
```

When we look at Listing 8.3, we can see that a lot of the code is remarkably similar to what was done with the while loop. We start our listing by declaring our counter outside of the loop at the beginning of our program. As you can see, we create a counter called counter and initialize it to our starting number of 1.

Next we have the do command. The do command indicates the start of our code block for our loop. It will contain the code that is to be executed *while* our *condition* is true.

What do we do in the body of the loop? First, just like before, we want to print out the value of our counter, so we do that quickly. Then, just like the while loop, we have to do something inside our loop's body to change our condition for ending the loop. In this case, we will increment our counter by 1 by again using counter++. Remember that if we enter the loop and don't change any of the conditions, we will stay in that loop forever. In this case, just like in Listing 8.1, we simply increment our counter.

NOTE In our loop, we could count by a number other than one. Instead of using counter++, we could use something like this:

```
counter = counter + 2;
```

This would cause our listing to count by twos. We also don't have change our increment using addition. We could multiply, decrement, or do any other command that changes our initial value.

After the code block, we have the second half of the do-while statement, the `while` command followed by the condition that will determine whether our loop continues. In this case, our `while` condition is doing the same check of determining whether our counter is less than or equal to 5. After the condition, the entire do-while statement ends with a semicolon.

> **NOTE** It is important to notice that after the condition, there is a semicolon. This differs from the standard `while` command where you generally do not want a semicolon after the condition!

The big thing to remember is that with a do-while loop, rather than having the condition at the top, we have the condition at the bottom. This means that we're guaranteed to run this loop at least one time.

Making do-while Shine

While counting is nice for creating a simple illustration of how code works, it isn't a great use of a do-while loop. Let's get into an example where the do-while loop really shines!

One of the places where it really shines is when we're asking the user for input. A good example is a program that asks a user to input a number between 1 and 20. The program will keep asking for a number until the user enters one that is within this range. If the user's number is within the range, then the program can print a thank-you message and quit. The thank-you message can include the number that the user typed in.

For this program, we will have to do some setup. Because we are going to get input from the user, you'll need to use a `Scanner` object. This means we need to import the scanner code as we have done before.

```
import java.util.Scanner;
```

With the import in place, we will need to create a `Scanner` object within our class and let the scanner know where we want to read from. In this case, we want to read from `System.in`, which is the standard input or, in this case, the command line. The final code for creating and initializing our `Scanner` object called `sc` should look like the following:

```
Scanner sc = new Scanner(System.in);
```

> **NOTE** As a reminder, we print to `System.out`, which is the command line, and we read from `System.in`, which is the input from the command line.

Now that we have our scanner, we need to create two variables. The first one is going to be the user's number, which we'll call userNumber. The second variable is the string version of that number. Remember, we recommended that everything from the console be read as a string. We read the number as a string, and then we convert it from the string into a number. Our two variable declarations should look like this:

```
int userNumber;
String userNumberString;
```

You might notice that we declared our variables, but we didn't initialize them as we have done in previous listings. While we could initialize them at the same time we declare them, for this listing, we are going to do the initialization in the do-while loop's code block.

With our variable declared, we are ready to jump into the loop. The loop starts with the do keyword, followed by the block, and then the condition that will determine when our loop should end. In writing the code, we can set up the condition code before writing the code block.

Our block is going to keep executing as long as the user enters a number that is out of bounds. We decided earlier that our bounds is between 1 and 20. So if the user's number is less than 1 or greater than 20, then we don't have what we want, and we need to return to our loop and ask for another number to be entered. Our looping code would be like this:

```
do {
    // Ask for a number
} while ( userNumber < 1 || userNumber > 20);
```

If the entered number is between 1 and 20 inclusive, then our condition becomes false, and we stop the loop.

> **NOTE** You want to be careful in coding your condition statements. If you had used an AND (&&) operator instead of the OR (||), then your loop is going to keep going infinitely since a number can't be both less than 0 and greater than 20.

With our condition in place, the next step is to set up the code block of our loop, where we are going to get the number from the user. We'll start by printing out a message as we've done many times before.

```
System.out.println( "Please enter a number between 1 and 20: ");
```

This line of code is going to prompt the user. Following the pattern that we've seen before, the next thing we will do is wait for that input to come from the user. We'll use the nextLine feature of the scanner to get a string. We will then convert the string by hand using the Integer.parseInt method we learned about in Lesson 5. This final code should look familiar for getting the string and converting it. It should look like this:

```
userNumberString = sc.nextLine();
userNumber  = Integer.parseInt(userNumberString);    .
```

With this code, we're in good shape as far as the loop goes. We ask for a number between 1 and 20, we get a string value, and then we convert the string into a number. This should complete our do-while loop, which should now look like this:

```
do {
    System.out.println( "Please enter a number between 1 and 20: ");
    userNumberString = sc.nextLine();
    userNumber  = Integer.parseInt(userNumberString);
} while ( userNumber < 1 || userNumber > 20 );
```

If the user's number is out of bounds, our condition will send the program flow right back up to the top where we ask the user to enter a number once again. If the number entered is within our range, then we are going to quit our do-while loop and do any final wrap-up code. In our case, the wrap-up code will display a message that says "thank you" along with the number that they entered. Listing 8.4 pulls all these pieces together into a completed listing.

LISTING 8.4

Using do-while to Get a Number in Range

```
import java.util.Scanner;

public class CompareStrings {

  public static void main(String[] args) {

    Scanner sc = new Scanner(System.in);
    int userNumber = 0;
    String userNumberString;

    do {
        System.out.println( "Please enter a number between 1 and 20: ");
        userNumberString = sc.nextLine();
```

```
        userNumber = Integer.parseInt(userNumberString);
    } while ( userNumber < 1 || userNumber > 20 );

    System.out.println("Thank you!!! Your number was: " + userNumber);
    }
}
```

Go ahead and run the listing. Enter numbers less than 1 and higher than 20. The following is an example of what output you could see if you enter 0, then −4, then 22, and finally a number within the range, 5:

```
Please enter a number between 1 and 20:
0
Please enter a number between 1 and 20:
-4
Please enter a number between 1 and 20:
22
Please enter a number between 1 and 20:
5
Thank you!!! Your number was: 5
```

Run the program a few times with different values. As you can see, unlike while loops, because the condition is at the end of the do–while, the loop's code will always execute at least one time.

USING FOR LOOPS

In addition to the while and do–while loops, there is a third looping statement called for. The for loop allows you to iterate over a range of values. for loops are a bit different from while loops in that they generally define their beginning and ending points and incremental jumps. That makes for loops really good at iterating along set ranges.

The basic form of the for loop is as follows:

```
for (initialization; termination; increment) {
    // code I want to repeat a given number of times
}
```

It is worth looking at each of the pieces of this statement. The initialization statement runs only once as the loop execution begins. This code can be used to initialize any variables or do anything that needs to happen only once before the looping begins.

The termination expression is evaluated at the beginning of each loop; when it evaluates as false, the loop terminates. This is exactly like the condition in a while loop, which is checked prior to the code block being executed.

The increment expression is evaluated after each loop iteration; we can increment or decrement values in this expression. When you did a while loop or a do-while loop, you tended to do the incrementing within your loop's code block. As we can see, with a for loop, there is a special location for incrementing.

Each of these statements is optional in a for loop. The resulting for loops might look funny but work fine:

```
for(;;);  // infinite loop!
```

We saw how to count from 1 to 5 with using while and do-while. Listing 8.5 presents the code to accomplish this with a for loop.

> **NOTE** It is worth noting here that while we are counting from 1 to 5 using a for loop, many times for loops will start at zero. You will see the importance of this later in this course when we discuss topics such as arrays.

LISTING 8.5

Using for to Count to 5

```
public class CountingNumbers {

  public static void main(String[] args) {

    int counter;

    for ( counter = 1; counter <= 5; counter++ )
    {
        System.out.println( "Counting: " + counter );
    }

    System.out.println("...Done!");
  }
}
```

When we run this, we see the following output, which is becoming extremely familiar:

```
Counting: 1
Counting: 2
Counting: 3
Counting: 4
Counting: 5
...Done!
```

The pieces of this code should all be familiar based on what we've seen in the previous listings. Even so, it is worth looking at a couple of pieces closer.

Initializing the for Loop

In Listing 8.5, we initialized `counter` to 1. We could actually assign a value to initialize the counter to any value we would like. In fact, you could initialize it to a number such as 7.

```
for ( counter = 7; counter <= 5; counter++ )
```

Make this change to Listing 8.5. When we run the program now, the output looks like the following:

```
...Done!
```

No numbers are printed. This is because the termination condition is evaluated before the loop's code block is executed. In this case, because 7 is not less than or equal to 5, the condition evaluates to `false`, and program flow jumps to the statement after the `for` loop. The loop's code block is never executed!

Terminating the for Loop

In the middle of the `for` loop is a conditional statement. This statement is generally used to determine whether the `for` loop should be terminated or should continue. This statement works just like the conditional statements for the `while` and `do-while` loops.

In Listing 8.5, you saw the following conditional statement:

```
counter <= 5
```

Before the first iteration of the loop and after each subsequent iteration, this condition is checked. If it evaluates to true, the `for` loop's code block is executed. If it evaluates to false, then the program flow jumps to the first statement after the `for` statement.

Incrementing a for Loop

In Listing 8.5, we started with the number 1 and counted to 5 with our incrementor, adding 1 each time the loop cycled. We've seen that you can change the initialized value. You can also change what you are using to increment.

In Listing 8.6, we modify the listing so that it can start at 1 and continue to print numbers as long as our number is less than 21. The difference in this listing, however, is that we only want to print odd numbers. While there are a couple of ways we could do this, we'll change the increment expression to do the work. We can do this by incrementing our counter by 2 instead of by 1.

LISTING 8.6

Using for to Display Odd Numbers

```java
public class CountingNumbers {

  public static void main(String[] args) {

    int counter;

    for ( counter = 1; counter < 21; counter = counter + 2 )
    {
        System.out.println( counter );
    }

    System.out.println("...Done!");
  }
}
```

Take a look at Listing 8.6. You can see that we changed the terminating condition to be counter < 21 as we said we would. To the right of that, you can see a complete assignment expression where we take counter and we add 2 to its value and then assign it back to itself.

```java
counter = counter + 2
```

This shows that we can use any complete Java expression to do the incrementing. When we run this listing, we see the following output:

```
1
3
5
7
9
11
13
15
17
19
...Done!
```

This shows that the counter started at 1. It was incremented by 2 each time. When it got to a value that was no longer less than 21, our for loop exited and program flow went to the next statement after the for loop.

If we wanted to change this listing to print even numbers, what would we need to change? We could simply change the initialized value to start with 2 and again count by twos.

```
for ( counter = 2; counter < 21; counter = counter + 2 )
```

Now when we run this listing, the output is as follows:

```
2
4
6
8
10
12
14
16
18
20
...Done!
```

To count by fives, we can again change the incrementor. This time we would add 5 each time instead of adding 2.

```
for ( counter = 2; counter < 21; counter = counter + 5 )
```

If we change the code and run it again, we will see output that counts by 5 like this:

```
2
7
12
17
...Done!
```

Of course, if we expected the output to show the numbers 5, 10, 15, and 20, then we see that there is a mistake. The code starts with a value of 2 and then adds 5 each time. If we want the first number printed to be 5, then we'll need to change the initial value to be 5.

As we can see, the for loop gives us a lot of control. It is generally the best looping command to use if we want to iterate through a specific number of items.

> **NOTE** for loops are particularly useful in iterating over arrays or collections of items. We'll explore that more when we cover these data structures.

SUMMARY

In this lesson, we covered core features, and more specifically, you learned how to repeat code multiple times using three different looping constructs.

- `do-while`
- `while`
- `for`

We now have a richer vocabulary, which means that we can create more complicated programs. Our programs were pretty simple when all we could do was execute on one statement after another in order. We now have the ability to do much more complex programs. Now that we can make decisions and repeat ourselves, we need a way to describe our programs. In the next lesson, that is exactly what we will do. We will learn to use simple flowcharts to describe our solutions.

EXERCISES

This section includes coding exercises to introduce flow control. With the ability to now repeat pieces of code, you'll find that you can do even more with your code. The following exercises help to make sure you understand what you learned in the lessons. The best way to make sure you are learning and understanding the lesson is to apply it. Because understanding looping in your programs is critical, there are more exercises in this lesson for you to work with.

Exercise 1: Surfacing in BewareTheKraken.java

Exercise 2: Do or Do Not

Exercise 3: Guess Me Finally

Exercise 4: for and Twenty Blackbirds

Exercise 5: Spring Forward, Fall Back

Exercise 6: for Times

Exercise 7: for Times for

Exercise 8: Nesting for Loops

Exercise 9: Traditional Fizz Buzz

Exercise 1: Surfacing in BewareTheKraken.java

Modify Listing 8.2 on your own. In each iteration of the loop, ask the user if they want to stop. If they do, surface! Hint: You will need to add another break statement to the listing.

Exercise 2: Do or Do Not

Write a program to practice the do-while syntax. Create a new program named *DoOrDoNot* using the code in Exercise Listing 8.2. As you type it, read the code carefully and figure out what each line does.

EXERCISE LISTING 8.2

DoOrDoNot.java

```java
import java.util.Scanner;

public class DoOrDoNot {

  public static void main(String[] args) {

    Scanner input = new Scanner(System.in);
    System.out.print("Should I do it? (y/n) ");
    boolean doIt;

    if (input.next().equals("y")) {
      doIt = true; // DO IT!
    } else {
      doIt = false; // DONT YOU DARE!
    }

    boolean iDidIt = false;

    do {
      iDidIt = true;
      break;
    } while (doIt);

    if (doIt && iDidIt) {
      System.out.println("I did it!");
    } else if (!doIt && iDidIt) {
      System.out.println("I know you said not to ... but I totally did anyways.");
```

```
    } else {
        System.out.println("Don't look at me, I didn't do anything!");
    }
  }
}
```

Now look more closely at the code and experiment a bit.

- What does it print out if you tell it to do it?
- What if you tell it not to?
- Comment out the do-while loop and write a while loop that checks the same condition and executes the same loop code.
- When you just have a while loop, what prints out when you tell it to do it?
- What about when you tell it not to?

Exercise 3: Guess Me Finally

Always improving—that's software for you. Create a new program named *GuessMeFinally* that starts with your original guessing game from Lesson 7's exercises. For this version, make the following changes:

- Instead of letting the user try only once more if they get it wrong, let them keep going until they get it right.
- If they get it on the first try, print Wow, nice guess! That was it!. Otherwise, print Finally! It's about time you got it!.

When the user runs the program, they should see something like the following:

```
I've chosen a number between -100 and 100. Betcha can't guess it!
Your guess: 44

Ha, nice try - too low! Try again!
Your guess: 99

Too bad, way too high. Try again!
Your guess: 74

Ha, nice try - too low! Try again!
Your guess: 82

Finally! It's about time you got it!
```

Exercise 4: for and Twenty Blackbirds

Practice for loops with a new program about blackbirds. Create a new program named *ForAndTwentyBlackbirds* using the code in Exercise Listing 8.4. Make sure it works as expected and then answer the questions that follow.

EXERCISE LISTING 8.4

ForAndTwentyBlackbirds.java

```java
public class ForAndTwentyBlackbirds {

    public static void main(String[] args) {
        int birdsInPie = 0;
        for (int i = 0; i < 20; i++) {
            System.out.println("Blackbird #" + i + " goes into the pie!");
            birdsInPie++;
        }

        System.out.println("There are " + birdsInPie + " birds in there!");
        System.out.println("Quite the pie full!");
    }
}
```

When you run this program, you should see the following:

```
Blackbird #0 goes into the pie!
Blackbird #1 goes into the pie!
Blackbird #2 goes into the pie!
Blackbird #3 goes into the pie!
Blackbird #4 goes into the pie!
Blackbird #5 goes into the pie!
Blackbird #6 goes into the pie!
Blackbird #7 goes into the pie!
Blackbird #8 goes into the pie!
Blackbird #9 goes into the pie!
Blackbird #10 goes into the pie!
Blackbird #11 goes into the pie!
Blackbird #12 goes into the pie!
Blackbird #13 goes into the pie!
Blackbird #14 goes into the pie!
Blackbird #15 goes into the pie!
Blackbird #16 goes into the pie!
Blackbird #17 goes into the pie!
Blackbird #18 goes into the pie!
```

```
Blackbird #19 goes into the pie!
There are 20 birds in there!
Quite the pie full!
```

Once you have the original version working as expected, make the following changes:

- Change the listing so that the loop counts to the more traditional 24 birds.

- Also update the bird number printouts so the count is from 1 to 24. What did you change?

Exercise 5: Spring Forward, Fall Back

Practice different ways to set up the parts of a for loop. Create a new project named *SpringForwardFallBack* using the code in Exercise Listing 8.5, paying attention to each line of code so that you know what it's supposed to do. Once you have the code working, answer the questions that follow.

EXERCISE LISTING 8.5

SpringForwardFallBack.java

```java
public class SpringForwardFallBack {

    public static void main(String[] args) {

        System.out.println("It's Spring...!");
        for (int i = 0; i < 10; i++) {
            System.out.print(i + ", ");
        }

        System.out.println("\nOh no, it's fall...");
        for (int i = 10; i > 0; i--) {
            System.out.print(i + ", ");
        }
    }
}
```

Now consider the following questions.

- What are the start/stop ranges of output for both loops?

- How can you update the first loop so that it prints out the same range as the second loop, changing only the start point or the stopping point?

- How can we fix the code so the comma doesn't get printed on the last iteration of the loop?

NOTE We learned that the ++ operator increments a variable by 1. The −− operator decreases a variable by 1.

Exercise 6: for Times

Write a program named *ForTimes* that helps you remember your times tables. Ask the user for a number and then print out the 1 to 15 times tables of that number. Use a for loop. When you run the program, you should see something like the following:

```
Which times table shall I recite? 7
1 * 7 is: 7
2 * 7 is: 14
3 * 7 is: 21
4 * 7 is: 28
5 * 7 is: 35
6 * 7 is: 42
7 * 7 is: 49
8 * 7 is: 56
9 * 7 is: 63
10 * 7 is: 70
11 * 7 is: 77
12 * 7 is: 84
13 * 7 is: 91
14 * 7 is: 98
15 * 7 is: 105
```

Exercise 7: for Times for

Refactor your times table program from the previous exercise so that instead of just "reciting" a times table, the program prints out each "times" as a question and waits for an answer. If the user answers correctly, then they get a point! If not, the program gives them the correct answer.

Print the total number of points at the end. As a bonus, print out a message that they should study more if they get less than 50 percent correct. If they get more than 90 percent correct, then give them a congratulatory message!

Here is an example of what the program might look like:

```
Which times table shall I recite? 5
1 * 5 is: 5
Correct!
2 * 5 is: 10
Correct!
3 * 5 is: 13
```

```
Sorry no, the answer is: 15
4 * 5 is: 20
Correct!
5 * 5 is: 25
Correct!
6 * 5 is: 22
Sorry no, the answer is: 30
7 * 5 is: 35
Correct!
8 * 5 is: 40
Correct!
9 * 5 is: 45
Correct!
10 * 5 is: 11
Sorry no, the answer is: 50
11 * 5 is: 23
Sorry no, the answer is: 55
12 * 5 is: 44
Sorry no, the answer is: 60
13 * 5 is: 65
Correct!
14 * 5 is: 70
Correct!
15 * 5 is: 75
Correct!
You got 10 correct.
```

Exercise 8: Nesting for Loops

for loops are great. But loops *within* loops can be even better. This is called *nesting*, and with a couple of small loops we can execute lots of code. In this exercise, use nested for loops to make some ASCII art.

Create a new program named *ForByFor* using the code in Exercise Listing 8.8. Once you have the original code working, change the code so that the middle column is made of $, the middle row is made of @, and the very center is made of #.

EXERCISE LISTING 8.8

ForByFor.java

```java
public class ForByFor {

    public static void main(String[] args) {
```

```
    for (int i = 0; i < 3; i++) {
        System.out.print("|");

        for (int j = 0; j < 3; j++) {
            for (int k = 0; k < 3; k++) {
                System.out.print("*");
            }
            System.out.print("|");
        }
        System.out.println("");
    }
  }
}
```

The first time you run this, you should see the following:

```
|***|***|***|
|***|***|***|
|***|***|***|
```

One you've made the changes suggested, you should see the new output as shown:

```
|***|$$$|***|
|@@@|###|@@@|
|***|$$$|***|
```

Exercise 9: Traditional Fizz Buzz

Fizz Buzz is a common programming challenge. It counts numbers, replacing the factors of 3 or 5 with *fizz* and *buzz*. Create a new program named *FizzBuzz* that performs the following tasks:

- Ask the user for a number.
- Use a for loop to count from zero, replacing every multiple of 3 with *fizz* and every multiple of 5 with *buzz*. Multiples of both should print out fizz buzz.
- Every time you print out fizz, buzz, or fizz buzz, keep track. When you've reached the number received from the user, stop.
- Finish it all up with a large, all-caps printout of TRADITION!!!!!.

Here's an example of what the program might look like when it runs:

```
How many units of fizzing and buzzing do you need in your life? 7
0
1
```

Lesson 8: Looping Program Flow   191

```
2
fizz
4
buzz
fizz
7
8
fizz
buzz
11
fizz
13
14
fizz buzz
TRADITION!!!!!
```

Lesson 9

Understanding Flowcharts and Algorithms

Flowcharts allow us to visualize how the application will flow from one instruction to the next, from start to finish. Building a flowchart before we start to code a program helps ensure that we don't skip any steps in the program itself, as well as giving us a tool to easily communicate those steps to others.

LEARNING OBJECTIVES

By the end of this lesson, you will be able to:
- Explain what an algorithm is
- Describe how developers use flowcharts as part of the software development process
- Identify basic shapes in a flowchart
- Map an algorithm to a flowchart

FLOWCHART BASICS

One of the interesting things about programming is how surprisingly simplistic computers and programs really are. Even though we can create massive-scale programs that perform complex tasks, there are really only three things a program can do.

- **Sequence**: Execute a series of statements in order
- **Branch**: Follow a specific path based on a defined condition
- **Loop**: Repeat a series of instructions until a condition is met

We use the term *flow of control* to define the path that a program takes from one instruction to the next, and we use a flowchart to visualize the flow of control.

Another important term is *algorithm*. While TV shows and movies make algorithms sound like very technical things that only a software developer could understand, the term *algorithm* is really just a well-defined set of instructions that a computer or similar machine can follow to reach a desired output. In other words, we use flowcharts to diagram algorithms.

Sequences

By default, the simplest path in an algorithm is to move sequentially from one statement to the next. Our "Hello, World!" application is an example of this. As shown in Figure 9.1, it includes two statements that are executed one after the other, and then the program ends. This control structure is called a *sequence*.

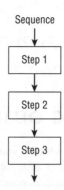

Figure 9.1 Flowcharting the "Hello, World!" sequence

Sequences are the easiest control structure to understand because they simply execute statements in the order in which they are given. The computer reads the code left to right, top to bottom, just like reading a book.

Ultimately, the instructions of a program that actually do the work required will be organized into sequences. A sequence can become quite large as methods can call other methods and objects may need to sub some of their work out to other objects.

As an example, consider the workflow of checking out on an e-commerce website. When you hit the checkout button, the program will complete a series of steps that need to be done across multiple objects. The top object generally controls the workflow of the checkout process, but subsequences could include the following:

1. Logging in

2. Entering payment information

3. Sending payment information to the payment processor/bank

4. Notifying the warehouse of the order

5. Notifying the shipping company to pick up the order

6. Emailing the customer a confirmation

And so on.

A skilled developer will lay out each of these processes in detail before they begin to write code. They will separate the code into methods and objects that group related things together, while keeping in mind ease of maintenance and testability. So, each step in a sequence may end up calling other sequences.

Branches

In a *branch* situation, the program reaches a point where there are two or more possible next steps, and it must evaluate a condition to determine which path to take. Branches are always based on a question that can be answered as either true or false, and in most instances, the true case determines the sequence that the program will follow. However, there can also be a false case where a different sequence can be followed.

A branch case can be as simple as logging into a website. As shown in Figure 9.2, in a branching flowchart, a diamond represents the condition that will determine which

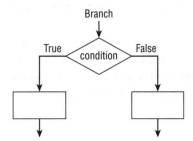

Figure 9.2 A branching flowchart

branch the flow of control will follow, for example, "Is the username and password correct?" If the condition is true, then the program takes the user to the home page. If it is false, the program will display an error and prompt the user to try again.

Loops

In a looping situation, we continue to run a sequence of instructions until some condition is met. We do this frequently in our day-to-day lives. When washing our hands, our condition is, "Are my hands clean yet?" If not, then we will keep scrubbing until they are clean.

There are several different varieties of loops in software development. Some loops will run a specific number of times, such as looping through the number of characters in a string of text. If we know how many characters are in the string, we know how many times we want to loop.

In other cases, we don't know in advance how many times we will need to loop. In the previous website example, the user may enter their username and password correctly the first time, but because humans are imperfect creatures, they may not enter the information correctly until the second time or the tenth time. In these cases, we would want to structure the loop to continue until they get it right.

A loop includes a branch, but the sequence following the branch returns to the branch similar to what is shown in Figure 9.3.

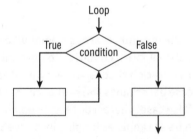

Figure 9.3 A looping flowchart

A loop will continue until a specified condition is met. Once the condition is met, the loop ends, and the flow of control moves to the next block of instructions in the program.

One thing that developers must watch out for is endless (or infinite) loops. It is quite possible to define a loop's condition such that the condition can never be met (such as defining a login loop to require both a username and password but failing to ask the user to enter the password). In that case, the loop will run indefinitely until something else stops it.

FLOWCHARTING

Using our flow of control structures and branch statements, we can come up with some interesting algorithms. In fact, as we pointed out earlier, even the most complex scenarios must ultimately break down into these three structures.

While there are many symbols available in flowcharting, the most common include the following:

- **Oval**: Indicates the start and end points of an algorithm
- **Rectangle**: Indicates an instruction that the computer must complete
- **Parallelogram** (a tilted rectangle): Indicates input and output
- **Diamond**: Indicates a condition

We also use one-sided arrows to indicate the order in which the steps will be completed. Technically, a flowchart can be oriented in any way because the arrows define the order in which the steps will be completed, but they are most commonly oriented from top to bottom (so the program starts at the top and ends at the bottom) or left to right. Larger flowcharts can include a combination of top-to-bottom and left-to-right orientation.

Flowcharts can certainly be written out by hand, although it's often best to use a pencil or another erasable medium to make corrections easier. There are also several software options, including Draw.io (a free online diagramming tool) and LucidChart (a paid program that includes a free option). Microsoft Office products (including Visio, Word, and PowerPoint) also include flowchart tools, as does Drawings in Google Drive.

NOTE

- Draw.io can be found in your operating system's app store or at `drawio.com` and `app.diagrams.net`.
- LucidChart can be found online at `www.lucidchart.com`.
- Google Drawings can be found in the Google Chrome store.

FLOWCHART EXAMPLE

Now let's look at how we might use a flowchart to diagram a simple algorithm. Consider a method that requires the user to enter an odd number. The steps for this might include the following:

1. Declare variables to store the keyboard input and parsed number.
2. Start the loop.

1. Prompt the user to enter an odd number.

2. Read the input from the keyboard.

3. If the input is a number

   - If the number is odd

     - Exit loop

   - If the number is not odd

     - Inform the user that the number is not odd

     - Restart the loop

4. If the input is not a number, do the following:

   - Inform the user that the input is not a number

   - Restart the loop

3. Return the number.

So, we have a loop that should run until an odd number is entered. Checking for an odd number requires two checks: first that it is a numeric entry and second that the parsed number is odd.

The previous list is a form of *pseudocode*, which can be used to supplement (or even replace) flowcharts in early development processes. Pseudocode sounds technical (like *algorithm*), but it really refers to the process of writing out a program's steps using a more natural human language that anyone could understand. We can then translate the pseudocode into the programming language of choice (such as C#, Java, or Python) once we are sure we have identified all the required steps.

In the pseudocode, each indentation in the text represents a code block, and each of those blocks will be a shape in the flowchart. A flowchart representing the steps in this algorithm might look Figure 9.4.

NOTE You now have the pseudocode for a program as well as a flowchart. As an exercise for this lesson, write the code for this program.

SUMMARY

Flowcharts are a powerful tool for visualizing how the logic in your program will flow and for communicating that to others. With what we have learned in this lesson, we can construct readable flowcharts to help us write better code.

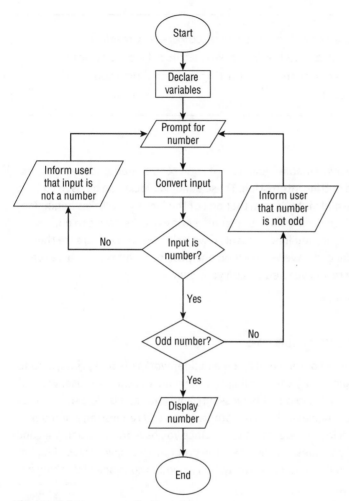

Figure 9.4 An example flowchart

We recommend that you start any program you write by sketching a flowchart or writing out the steps in pseudocode (if not both) even before you open your IDE to create the program.

The bottom line is that if you can't solve a problem on paper or on a whiteboard, then you can't solve it in code. Making sure you can explain in plain English what your program is trying to do, at least to yourself, is an essential first step in thinking through the coding logic. It's worth spending the time up front to plan things. It will save lots of pain and frustration later.

> **TIP** In construction, they say, "Measure twice, cut once." Creating a flowchart is like measuring, and coding is like cutting. It's a lot easier to make adjustments when you are flowcharting or measuring than it is when you are cutting code.

EXERCISES

Now that we understand types, variables, and flow of control statements such as `if` statements and loops, things are getting interesting. These building blocks can be used to build more complex code. We learned in this lesson that one of the biggest mistakes beginning coders make is diving right into coding without planning just what they want to do.

As an exercise for this lesson, you'll be presented with a game. You will create the flowchart and then write the code. We've provided one possible solution for this exercise, so don't look ahead until you've tried this on your own.

Exercise 1: A Guessing Game

Exercise 1: A Guessing Game

Just as a good writer creates an outline and a home builder works off blueprints, a good programmer plans their logic before they begin programming. For this exercise, you will write out the steps you need to map out the guessing game and then build a flowchart.

In this version of the guessing game, have the program start by requesting a number from the first player in a specified range, say, 1 to 20. Once you have this number, a second player should be asked to try to guess the number. The program then gives clues of higher or lower until player 2 eventually guesses correctly. You'll need to consider a few things:

- What pieces of data do we need to track?
- We need to have a process for player 1 to enter the number and for player 2 to guess.
- How many times does the user need to guess? It won't necessarily be the same from game to game.
- We'll need to prompt the user for an input.
- We'll need to read the user's input from the keyboard.
- Did the user guess the right number? What if they guessed wrong?
- Did the user even guess within the right range?

- If the guess was in the range, was it correct? Is the guess higher than the answer? Is it lower?
- Do we need to display a message?
- Do we need to have them enter another guess?

Consider all these questions and create a flowchart.

NOTE Focus on the flowcharting of this game. If you think about writing the code, you might notice a flaw in how this game operates.

If player 2 can see the prompt and answer that player 1 entered, then it is going to be extremely easy to guess the solution. In the next lesson, we'll learn how to update this program to have the computer randomly generate the number to be guessed.

A Possible Flowcharting Solution

Don't read any further or peek at the following until you've created your flowchart. Here are the details for one possible flowcharting solution along with the code for this exercise.

The Guessing Game Flowchart

Starting our flowchart, we first need to figure out what pieces of data we need to keep track of. We need a variable for the answer. We will also need one for the user input, which we'll refer to as the *guess*. Finally, we need a scanner to read input from the console. So, in terms of our process, the first three things we need to do is declare these three variables.

Next, we need to have a process to prompt player 1 to enter the number to be guessed. After prompting, we'll want to read their input from the keyboard. This is an input/output process, so we'll use the parallelogram to represent getting that number. We'll store that value in our answer variable. This is shown in section 1 of Figure 9.5.

NOTE Note that we didn't do any error checking to make sure that the number entered is within the range we set. This is something you can add to the flowchart on your own.

Player 2 can now start taking guesses. How many times player 2 takes a guess is going to depend on how lucky the player is. The number of guesses won't necessarily be the same from game to game. This sounds like a job for a `while` loop.

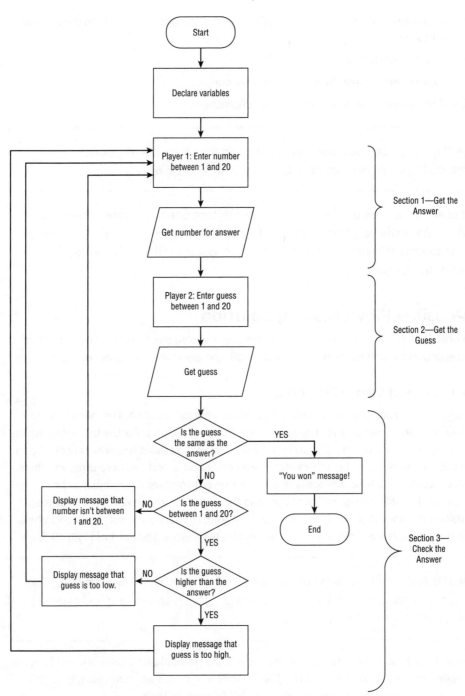

Figure 9.5 The guessing game flowchart

In the loop, we'll prompt the player for input (their guess) and again read their input from the keyboard. This is shown in section 2 of the flowchart in Figure 9.5.

The first thing we want to know after receiving the inputs is if the user guessed right. If the player did enter the correct guess, we can show a victory message and end the program.

What if they guessed wrong? Then we'll need to execute our false condition. At this point, we'll then want to see whether they guessed in the given range. In our case, that range was between 1 and 20. If the user didn't guess in that range, we'll display a message, and then we'll go back to the input prompt.

If the guess was in the range, we can see if the guess was higher than the answer. If it was, then we'll print a message telling them to guess lower, and then we'll go back to prompt them to guess again.

Lastly, if the guess isn't equal to the answer and is in the range and it's not higher than the answer, then the only possible option is that the guess was too low, and we need to print a message to tell the player to guess a higher number before sending them back to the prompt asking them to enter a guess.

The Guessing Game Code

At this point, we have a pretty good understanding of how the guessing game works, and we've accounted for the basic needs and possibilities of it. Now it's your turn to translate your flowchart to code. Do this on your own before reading further.

When we translate a flowchart to code, the first thing we need to do is to declare our variables and set them to initial values. As you learned in an earlier lesson, do this with the proper types of Scanner, int, and int to declare your scanner, answer, and guess, respectively.

```
int answer = 0;
int guess = 0;
Scanner myScanner = new Scanner(System.in);
```

Next, you need to get the answer from the user and put it into the answer variable. You learned in an earlier lesson that this can be done in a couple of ways. Let's use System.out.println and the nextInt method to do that.

```
System.out.println("Player 1: Please enter a number between 1 and 20:");
answer = myScanner.nextInt();
```

Once we have the answer, we start our loop. We want to loop until player 2 guesses the right answer. This can be done by creating an infinite loop to break out of, so we'll use the "while true" trick.

```
while (true) {
    // program code that will need a break to exit!
}
```

With a loop started, it's time to prompt player 2 for a guess from the console. We can do this the same way we asked for the answer.

```
System.out.println("Please guess a number between 1 and 20: ");
guess = myScanner.nextInt();
```

Now let's look at what we do with the number entered. First, we check to see whether the guess is equal to the answer. If they guessed right, we want to leave the loop. We can do this with the break keyword. If they didn't answer correctly, then we can continue with the program. Our program can determine which part of the flowchart to follow.

```
if ( guess == answer )
{
    break; // they've solved the problem, so exit loop!
}
else
{
    // continue with program
}
```

Let's follow the victory logic. In this case, using break, we hop out of the while loop and tell the user that they guessed right. At that point, the program is complete and can end.

If the guess isn't the answer, then per the flowchart, we see if they guessed between 1 and 20. If the guess is less than 1 or greater than 20, then we know it is not in the range we want, so we'll give a message to the player and use the continue keyword to restart the loop and prompt the user to again enter a guess. If it is in the range, we'll keep going.

```
if (guess < 1 || guess > 20)
{
    System.out.println("Enter a guess between 1 and 20.");
    continue;
}
```

At this point, we have a guess in range, so we can see if the guess is bigger than the answer. If it is, then they need to guess lower, so we tell them that. And then we go back to the top using the continue keyword again.

```
if (guess > answer)
{
```

```
    System.out.println("Guess is too high. Pick a lower number!");
    continue;
}
```

If none of the previous conditions was true, then we can print a message saying they need to guess higher and let the loop go back to the top. Note that no continue is necessary here, because we're already at the bottom of the loop, and it's going to go back up to the top no matter what.

As you can see, each piece of the coding fits with each part of the flowchart. Having a logical map to follow like our flowchart makes the writing of the application much easier and less error prone. You can compare the complete code in Exercise Listing 9.1 with the flowchart presented in Figure 9.5 and see that they line up.

TIP When you're a professional programmer, you'll want to create not only flowcharts, but also object diagrams that list all your fields and methods, and even mockups of your frontend screens. This will not only help you organize your thoughts, but also shed light on your logic and flow to other developers, who may be called upon to review and edit your code later.

EXERCISE LISTING 9.1

The GuessingGame.java

```
import java.util.Scanner;

class GuessingGame

  public static void main(String[] args) {
    // declare the number variables and initialize to 0
    int answer = 0;
    int guess = 0;
    // declare and initialize a Scanner object
    Scanner myScanner = new Scanner(System.in);

    // ask player 1 to enter a number from 1 to 20
    System.out.println(
           "Player 1: Please enter a number between 1 and 20:");
    // now wait until a number is entered
    answer = myScanner.nextInt();
    // Note that there should be error checking here!
```

```java
// Now start getting guesses!
while( true )
{
    // Get a guess!
    System.out.println("Please guess a number between 1 and 20: ");
    guess = myScanner.nextInt();

    // Does the guess equal the answer?
    if ( guess == answer)
    {
        break; // they've solved the problem!
    }
    else if (guess < 1 || guess > 20)
    {
        System.out.println("Enter a guess between 1 and 20.");
        continue;
    }

    if (guess > answer)
    {
        System.out.println("Guess is too high. Pick a lower number!");
        continue;
    }
    System.out.println("Guess is too low. Pick a higher number!");
}

System.out.println("You got it! The answer was: " + answer );

}
}
```

Lesson 10
Adding Randomness to Your Programs

We often want the ability to produce unpredictable behavior in our applications: to simulate rolling a die or flipping a coin in a game, for example. In this lesson, we will examine the use of the Random class to do just that.

LEARNING OBJECTIVES

By the end of this lesson, you will be able to:
- Initialize a Random object
- Use a Random object to generate random integers from any minimum to any maximum
- Employ random integers to select a value from an array
- Generate double values from any minimum to any maximum using a Random object
- Apply random values to a coin flip (or model any other probability) as a boolean value

INITIALIZING THE RANDOM OBJECT

Doing things in the same way every time is important at times, but every now and again a bit of unpredictably is needed. In those situations, we use Random, a class whose entire job is to mix things up.

We have to construct Random before we can use it, but afterward, we've got a whole virtual box of crazy, random options. Let's look at a couple of the interesting things you can do with Random.

Including the Random Class

By including an import of the Java Random utility package, you can use a Random class in your programs. This package is included by adding an import statement to the top of your listing with the name of the package. This is similar to what you did to include Scanner in a previous lesson.

```
import java.util.Random;
```

The Random class provides useful methods for automatically generating random numbers. However, a computer's behavior is designed to be deterministic, meaning that we expect the same behavior every time. So how is randomness accomplished? It isn't.

In fact, what we are producing are *pseudorandom* numbers. However, this will be sufficient for our purposes.

Seeding Random Numbers

When we create a Random object that will generate our random numbers, there are two possible constructors we can use.

```
Random fixedSeed = new Random(112358);
Random timedSeed = new Random();
```

> **NOTE** We haven't really talked much about constructors. These will become clearer when we cover classes in more specific detail. For now, know that a constructor is what creates an object we create from our class.

The first constructor uses a *seed value* that we specify ahead of time. This means that every time the application runs, that Random object will produce the same sequence of random numbers. If we were to pick a different integer, a different sequence would be generated, but the sequence would still be the same every time we run the application.

In general, this is not what we want (since "random" behavior that never changes is fairly easy to predict). Instead, we should typically use the second constructor, which automatically generates a seed value based on the date and time that the application is run. As a result, every run of this application will produce a different random seed, and therefore the Random object will generate a completely different sequence of random numbers.

NOTE You can get more information about the Random class from the Java documentation at docs.oracle.com/en/java/javase/11/docs/api/java.base/java/util/Random.html.

TIP It is good practice to create a single Random object in your application and use that repeatedly. Creating multiple Random objects and generating only the first number in the sequence (particularly in a loop) ruins the pseudorandom nature of the generator. It also adds a lot of performance overhead to your application.

GENERATING RANDOM INTEGERS

The first method of generating random numbers we'll learn about creates random numbers from 0 up to any maximum number you specify, exclusive. *Exclusive* means that the maximum you specify will be excluded from possible outcomes, so you want to specify a value that is one *more* than the highest value you want Random to generate. For example, if you want to generate integers from 0 to 9, you must specify an upper range of 10.

This may seem slightly confusing, but there are some nice benefits we get as a result that we will see in a minute. First, let's take a look at generating random numbers from 0 to 9 (inclusive).

```
Random rng = new Random();
// generate 10 numbers, each between 0 and 9 inclusive
for (int i=0; i<= 10; i++) {
    int randomNumber = rng.nextInt(10);
    System.out.println(randomNumber);
}
```

Here, we can see that although we have specified a maximum of 10, since that maximum is exclusive, we will only produce numbers from 0 to 9. To get a range from 1 to 10, we need to add a + 1 after the nextInt() method. The new code line would look like this:

```
int randomNumber = rng.nextInt(10) + 1;
```

> **NOTE** You might be wondering why we couldn't have simply changed the call to nextInt() to nextInt(11). If we did that, we would get from 0 to 10 rather than from 1 to 10.

So, how can we make use of this? In programming, we often must work with indices that are numbered starting at 0 and that must stop *before* the length of the collection we're using. This is especially true when working with arrays, which you will learn about in Lesson 13, "Organizing with Arrays." The indexes in arrays start with 0. Based on this, the following is a snippet of code that randomly selects a name from an array of names:

```
Random rng = new Random();

String[] names = new String[] { "Alice", "Bob", "Clarice", "David", "Elizabeth" };
int randomIndex = rng.nextInt( names.length );
String randomName = names[randomIndex];
```

Here we define an array with five names and select one name at random, but nowhere in this code do we hard-code the number 5. Instead, we reference the length of the array. As a result, we can add or remove names to this array as we like, and it will still work as expected.

GENERATING RANDOM DOUBLES

Now that we've seen how to generate random integers, let's look at generating random numbers with a fractional component.

Often (especially if we're dealing with probabilities) we need the ability to generate random numbers from a continuous (rather than discrete) range. The Random class provides a fairly straightforward method for doing so called nextDouble(). The nextDouble() method will generate a random number between 0.0 (inclusive) and 1.0 (exclusive). Although the upper bound of 1.0 is exclusive, that is less significant than in the case of integers; while it will not produce the value 1.0, it *will* produce numbers just slightly under it, like 0.999999999998. The following code makes use of that method:

```
Random rng = new Random();

// this will generate a random double value from 0.0 (inclusive)
```

```
// to 1.0 (exclusive)

double randomValue = rng.nextDouble();
```

What can we do with this? Quite a bit!

Any time we have a probability we want to sample against, we can generate a number between 0.0 (0 percent) and 1.0 (100 percent) and see which side of it we end up on. For example, the following code simulates a coin flip and stores the result in a boolean variable:

```
Random rng = new Random();

double randomValue = rng.nextDouble();
boolean coinIsHeads = randomValue < 0.5;
```

So far, so good, but what if we want to generate numbers outside the range of 0.0 to 1.0? Unlike integers, Random does not provide an overload to specify a different minimum or maximum, so we'll have to do it ourselves.

The process for adjusting the output of the nextDouble() method involves two steps, which must be done in order.

1. Adjust the range to fit the range of our desired outputs. In this case, *range* means the maximum minus the minimum.

2. Shift the (now correctly sized) range to the right place.

Figure 10.1 illustrates this process.

Figure 10.1 Process for generating a number between a minimum and maximum

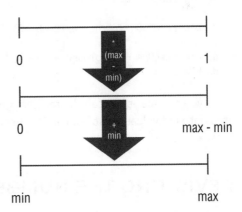

Each step must be considered in terms of its impact on both the minimum and the maximum.

- In the first step, we multiply by the range (the maximum minus the minimum), which will make the set of possible values wide enough to capture all of the outputs we care about, but the minimum is still zero.

- We fix that in the second step by adding the minimum (and again, since that could affect any number in that range, we have to consider the impact to both the minimum and the maximum).

Now let's look at this process in code. For this example, we'll generate numbers from 7.5 to 13.2:

```
Random rng = new Random();

// maximum is 13.2
// minimum is 7.5
double desiredOutput = rng.nextDouble() * (13.2 - 7.5) + 7.5;
```

This may look a little confusing, so let's break each of these steps into their own variables and see what that code looks like.

```
Random rng = new Random();

double min = 7.5;
double max = 13.2;

double range = max - min;

double zeroToOne = rng.nextDouble();

double stepOne = zeroToOne * range; // adjusting the range
double stepTwo = stepOne + min;     // shifting the range
```

As you can see, it is often clearer (though slightly longer) to place computation steps into individual variables. This is especially true when you are learning how to use these concepts.

REVISITING THE NUMBER GUESSING GAME

In the exercise in the previous lesson, you created a flowchart and code for a guessing game where a player tries to guess a number between 1 and 20, inclusively. The code was provided for you in Listing 9.1; however, the program had a flaw. The number to be guessed had to be entered, which made it visible to the person playing the game. Using the Random class, we can make the guessing game much more fun. Listing 10.1 presents an updated listing that adds what we learned about generating a random number.

LISTING 10.1

GuessingGame.java

```java
import java.util.Random;
import java.util.Scanner;

class GuessingGame {

  public static void main(String[] args) {
    // declare the number variables and initialize to 0
    int answer = 0;
    int guess = 0;
    Random rng = new Random(); // set up our random range variable

    // declare and initialize a Scanner object
    Scanner myScanner = new Scanner(System.in);

    // Generate a random number between 1 and 20
    answer = rng.nextInt(20) + 1;

    // Now start getting guesses!
    while( true )
    {
      // Get a guess!
      System.out.println("Please guess a number between 1 and 20: ");
      guess = myScanner.nextInt();

      // Does the guess equal the answer?
      if ( guess == answer)
        break; // they've solved the problem!

      else if (guess < 1 || guess > 20)
      {
        System.out.println("Enter a guess between 1 and 20.");
        continue;
      }

      if (guess > answer)
      {
```

```
        System.out.println("Guess is too high. Pick a lower number!");
        continue;
    }
    System.out.println("Guess is too low. Pick a higher number!");
}

System.out.println("You got it! The answer was: " + answer );

}
}
```

There are three primary changes to this listing. First, the import statement was added to include the Random package.

```
import java.util.Random;
```

Second, a new variable was declared and initialized to set a random seed for our random number.

```
Random rng = new Random(); // set up our random range variable
```

In this case, no value is passed to the initializer, Random(), so a random seed value is created based on the date and time the program is run.

For the third change, you can see that instead of prompting a user and doing a call to the Scanner object we now create a random integer value that we store in answer.

```
answer = rng.nextInt(20) + 1;
```

Because we want a number between 1 and 20, we can call the Random class's nextInt() method with 20 to get one of twenty values ranging from 0 to 19. We then need to add 1 to go from 1 to 20.

If you run this program, you will see something similar to the following. Of course, the number you are guessing is likely to be different, and the number of times it takes you to guess the number also might be different!

```
Please guess a number between 1 and 20:
10
Guess is too low. Pick a higher number!
Please guess a number between 1 and 20:
15
Guess is too high. Pick a lower number!
Please guess a number between 1 and 20:
13
You got it! The answer was: 13
```

Running it a second time shows that the number is different and random.

```
Please guess a number between 1 and 20:
10
Guess is too low. Pick a higher number!
Please guess a number between 1 and 20:
15
Guess is too low. Pick a higher number!
Please guess a number between 1 and 20:
18
You got it! The answer was: 18
```

OTHER RANDOM OPTIONS

It is worth noting that there are often multiple ways to do things when programming. This is true when trying to generate randomness as well. One option that is similar to the Random class covered in this lesson is Math.random(), which is a method provided as part of a Math class in the JDK.

Other options can be found with the ThreadLocalRandom and SecureRandom classes. These are advanced classes that take into account threading and provide a much more performant solution for generating random numbers.

SUMMARY

We've now seen how randomness can be added to an application and how to use those random values to model real-world things such as flipping a coin or selecting a value from a list. This has many real-world applications including statistical modeling, games, and similar applications.

This can also have other consequences for your application down the line, however. Randomness makes things like debugging trickier, if only because the program behavior will not be the same from one run to the next. In another lesson, we'll consider how to use random values sensibly and safely.

EXERCISES

This section includes coding exercises using random numbers. For each of the exercises in this activity, you should create a new Java class with the appropriate name.

Exercise 1: A Little Chaos

Let's create a program to practice using Random. Create a new class named ALittleChaos using the code in Exercise Listing 10.1. Make sure it works before you start playing with the code.

You should note that a couple of new things are introduced in this list. You should be able to guess what they are doing. First, you'll see that the method nextBoolean() is being called on our random variable. As expected, this will return a random boolean value, true or false.

The second thing you'll see that might be new is that instead of a string being passed to the System.out.print() method, we are passing a call to our random method to get a new random value. That random value is then being printed out along with a concatenation to a short string.

EXERCISE LISTING 10.1

ALittleChaos.java

```java
import java.util.Random;

public class ALittleChaos {

    public static void main(String[] args) {

        Random randomizer = new Random();

        System.out.println("Random can make integers: " + randomizer.nextInt());
        System.out.println("Or a double: " + randomizer.nextDouble());
        System.out.println("Or even a boolean: " + randomizer.nextBoolean());

        int num = randomizer.nextInt(100);
```

```
        System.out.println("You can store a randomized result: " + num);
        System.out.println("And use it over and over again: " + num + ", " + num);
        System.out.println("Or just keep generating new values");
        System.out.println("Here's a bunch of numbers from 0 - 100: ");

        System.out.print(randomizer.nextInt(101) + ", ");
        System.out.print(randomizer.nextInt(101) + ", ");
        System.out.print(randomizer.nextInt(101) + ", ");
        System.out.print(randomizer.nextInt(101) + ", ");
        System.out.print(randomizer.nextInt(101) + ", ");
        System.out.println(randomizer.nextInt(101));
    }
}
```

Here's an example of the output. Remember that we are using random values, so you should see values that are completely different from the ones shown here.

```
>Random can make integers: -1990223926
Or a double: 0.19256054969742875
Or even a boolean: false
You can store a randomized result: 66
And use it over and over again: 66, 66
Or just keep generating new values
Here's a bunch of numbers from 0 - 100:
66, 64, 49, 43, 8, 36
```

Once the starting code works, play around with it a bit. Here are some examples:

- What happens if you change `randomizer.nextInt(101)` to `randomizer.nextInt(51) + 50`?

- Can you include random numbers in a math statement?

- Experiment with different number types to see what the outcomes look like.

Exercise 2: Opinionator—Making Random Choices

Ever had a hard time making up your mind? Don't worry—Random is here to save you! All you have to do is write down all the options (`if` statements are good for this) and then have Random choose between them.

To put this in action, write a simple practice program to choose your favorite animal. Add the code in Exercise Listing 10.2 to a new class named Opinionator. Note that while this code will run without error (if it's keyed correctly), it includes a bug that your IDE might not find. See whether you can find it and fix it. You should see whether you can find the error before entering this into your IDE.

EXERCISE LISTING 10.2

Opinionator.java

```java
import java.util.Random;

public class Opinionator {

    public static void main(String[] args) {
        Random randomizer = new Random();
        System.out.println("I can't decide what animal I like the best.");
        System.out.println("I know! Random can decide FOR ME!");

        int x = randomizer.nextInt(5);

        System.out.println("The number we chose was: " + x);

        switch (x) {
          case 0:
            System.out.println("Llamas are the best!");
            break;
          case 1:
            System.out.println("Dodos are the best!");
            break;
          case 2:
            System.out.println("Woolly mammoths are DEFINITELY the best!");
            break;
          case 3:
            System.out.println("Sharks are the greatest, they have their
own week!");
            break;
          case 4:
            System.out.println("Cockatoos are just so awesomme!");
            break;
          case 5:
            System.out.println("Have you ever met a naked mole-rat?
They're GREAT!");
            break;
        }

        System.out.println("Thanks Random, maybe YOU'RE the best!");
```

```
        }
}
```

Here is one possible outcome:

```
I can't decide what animal I like the best.
I know! Random can decide FOR ME!
The number we chose was: 3
Sharks are the greatest, they have their own week!
Thanks Random, maybe YOU'RE the best!
```

Exercise 3: High Roller

One fun way to use random numbers is to simulate rolling dice or flipping coins. Use the code in Exercise Listing 10.3 to create a new program named *HighRoller* that rolls a six-sided die. Make sure that the initial version of the program works correctly before experimenting with the code.

EXERCISE LISTING 10.3

HighRoller.java

```java
import java.util.Random;

public class HighRoller {

    public static void main(String[] args) {

        Random diceRoller = new Random();

        int rollResult = diceRoller.nextInt(6) + 1;

        System.out.println("TIME TO ROOOOOOLL THE DIE!");
        System.out.println("I rolled a " + rollResult);

        if (rollResult == 1) {
            System.out.println("You rolled a critical failure!");
        }
    }
}
```

Here is a sample output for this program:

```
TIME TO ROOOOOOLL THE DIE!
I rolled a 6
```

Once you have verified that the base code works as expected, make the program more interactive.

- Ask the user to tell you the number of sides a single die has.
- Roll the die to generate a number between 1 and # sides.
- Add in a conditional that prints the following:
  - `You rolled an even number!` if it rolled an even number.
  - `You rolled a critical! Nice job!` if it rolled the max.

Exercise 4: Coin Flipper

Flip a coin programmatically. This exercise is for you to do on your own. Write a program named *CoinFlipper* that simulates a random coin toss, but without using `nextInt()`. When your program runs, you should see output similar to the following:

```
Ready, Set, Flip....!!
You got TAILS!
```

Exercise 5: Guess Me More

Improving and refactoring programs is often a constant process. Take the number guessing program from Exercise Listing 9.1 and improve it. Save the new version under a new class called `GuessMeMore`. With your update, add the following changes:

- Make the number chosen be a random number between −100 and 100.
- Add a variable to track the number of times the player guesses. Print this number when the player finishes the game.

Here is an example of what you should see:

```
Please guess a number between −100 and 100:
−35
Guess is too low. Pick a higher number!
Please guess a number between −100 and 100:
45
Guess is too low. Pick a higher number!
```

```
Please guess a number between -100 and 100:
71
You got it! The answer was: 71
Number of guesses: 3
```

Exercise 6: Fortune Cookie

This exercise is for you to do on your own. Write a program to print a random quote. You can create a program named *FortuneCookie* that randomly prints a quote to the screen. Use the following list to inspire you, but you can use your own favorite quotes for your program to randomly choose among for your display:

```
"Those aren't the droids you're looking for."
"Never go in against a Sicilian when death is on the line!"
"Goonies never say die."
"With great power, there must also come great responsibility."
"Never argue with the data."
"Try not. Do, or do not. There is no try."
"You are a leaf on the wind, watch how you soar."
"Do absolutely nothing, and it will be everything that you thought it
could be."
"Kneel before Zod."
"Make it so."
```

The code and other output are up to you. Here is an example of a possible outcome using the previous quotes:

```
Your Geek Fortune: Try not. Do, or do not. There is no try.
```

Here is the random output from a second running of the program:

```
Your Geek Fortune: Those aren't the droids you're looking for.
```

Debugging

In this lesson, we will build on what we learned in Lesson 3 and take a closer look at how to debug a program. Using the code from the original WindowMaster program, we'll review how to set breakpoints and learn more about how to debug, including how to execute the program in debug mode, step through the program, and examine the values of variables while the program is executing.

LEARNING OBJECTIVES

By the end of this lesson, you will be able to:
- Execute a program in debug mode
- Set breakpoints in code
- Step through code
- Examine variables at set points in code

CREATING A FILE TO DEBUG

In this lesson, we are going to look a little deeper into the debugger and how it works. It is worth emphasizing that the debugger is a really valuable tool. When people are starting out in development, they often overlook this fact. But it is one of the most important tools in our toolbox. It is one of the ways that the IDE, whether it be NetBeans or another program, can help pinpoint the problems that you are having in your code.

When we write code, we believe we know what it is doing because we believe we wrote it the right way, so it can be frustrating when it is not doing what we want it to do. Always keep in mind that the computer only does what we tell it to do. Generally speaking, if our program isn't working right, it's nearly always due to something that we wrote.

A small percentage of the time, an error is in somebody else's code that we are using. If you have the mindset that bugs (coding errors) are going to happen, then you can lower your stress, and finding and fixing them just becomes a kind of puzzle.

When a program has an error or doesn't run like we expect, then we have to figure out where we went wrong and go back to fix it. That is where a debugger can really help us.

Let's get started. If you have the original code for WindowMaster from Lesson 6, open the project and make sure that it compiles and runs correctly. If you don't have that code anymore, create a new project called WindowMasterDebug using the code in Listing 11.1. Once that is done, save the file and make sure that the program runs correctly.

> **NOTE** Listing 11.1 is the same WindowMaster that was presented
> in Listing 6.3 with the name of the class and Java file changed to
> `WindowMasterDebug` and `WindowMasterDebug.java`, respectively.

LISTING 11.1

`WindowMasterDebug.java`: The `WindowMaster` Listing

```java
import java.util.Scanner;

public class WindowMasterDebug {

  public static void main(String [] args) {
    // declare variables for height and width
    float height;
    float width;

    // declare String variables to hold the user's height and
    // width input
    String stringHeight;
    String stringWidth;
```

```
        // declare other variables
        float areaOfWindow;
        float cost;
        float perimeterOfWindow;

        // declare and initialize the Scanner
        Scanner myScanner = new Scanner(System.in);

        // get input from the user
        System.out.println("Please enter window height:");
        stringHeight = myScanner.nextLine();
        System.out.println("Please enter window width:");
        stringWidth = myScanner.nextLine();

        // convert String values of height and width to float values
        height = Float.parseFloat(stringHeight);
        width = Float.parseFloat(stringWidth);

        // calculate the area of the window
        areaOfWindow = height * width;

        // calculate the perimeter of the window
        perimeterOfWindow = 2 * (height + width);

        // calculate the total cost - use a hard-coded value
        // for material cost
        cost = ((3.50f * areaOfWindow) + (2.25f * perimeterOfWindow));

        // display the results to the user
        System.out.println("Window height = " + stringHeight);
        System.out.println("Window width = " + stringWidth);
        System.out.println("Window area = " + areaOfWindow);
        System.out.println("Window perimeter = " + perimeterOfWindow);
        System.out.println("Total Cost =   " + cost);
    }
}
```

When you run this in the NetBeans IDE and enter **10** for the height and **10** for the width, you should see output like that shown in Figure 11.1.

SETTING BREAKPOINTS

As a reminder, breakpoints are just places in the program where we are telling the debugger to stop execution so we can make sure things look the way we believe they should look.

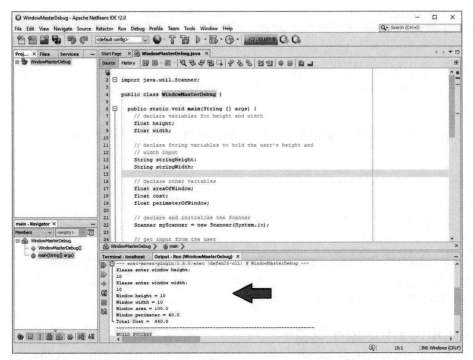

Figure 11.1 The WindowMaster output

As you saw in Lesson 3, setting breakpoints in NetBeans is easy: just click in the *leftmost margin* of the code window *on the line number* where you want to put the breakpoint. Setting a breakpoint allows you to stop execution of your code at that location when running in debug mode. To show the debugger working, we'll put breakpoints on three lines. We'll add one on the line where we are setting up our scanner. We'll add a second one on the line where we are converting our string height into the actual number so we can use the number for our calculation. We'll add a third and final breakpoint to the line where we calculate the cost. Again, you can left-click the line number to set the breakpoint. Clicking a second time will remove the breakpoint. Figure 11.2 shows the three breakpoints set in the WindowMaster program.

> **NOTE** The line numbers marked in Figure 11.2 are 24, 33, and 44; however, based on comments and spacing you have in your listing, your numbers could be different.

```
23        // declare and initialize the Scanner
□         Scanner myScanner = new Scanner(System.in);
25
26        // get input from the user
27        System.out.println("Please enter window height:");
28        stringHeight = myScanner.nextLine();
29        System.out.println("Please enter window width:");
30        stringWidth = myScanner.nextLine();
31
32        // convert String values of height and width to float values
□         height = Float.parseFloat(stringHeight);
34        width = Float.parseFloat(stringWidth);
35
36        // calculate the area of the window
37        areaOfWindow = height * width;
38
39        // calculate the perimeter of the window
40        perimeterOfWindow = 2 * (height + width);
41
42        // calculate the total cost - use a hard-coded value
43        // for material cost
□         cost = ((3.50f * areaOfWindow) + (2.25f * perimeterOfWindow));
45
```

Figure 11.2 WindowMaster breakpoints

Stepping through Code

Once breakpoints are set, we are ready to start debugging. To do this, you must execute your program in Debug Mode, which is done by clicking the *Debug Project* button ( ) in the toolbar. The project will begin execution and then pause at your first breakpoint. Your first breakpoint will change from pink to green, like what you see in Figure 11.3.

It is important to note the difference between running in regular mode and running in debug mode. When running in debug mode, you can see that within the NetBeans IDE, at the bottom, there is an additional tab displayed. Instead of the normal Output tab dialog being displayed, we are likely seeing a tab labeled as *Variables*. To see the output and respond to any prompts, you'll need to click the *Output* tab.

You might notice in the Variable tab that even though we have declared several variables in our program, none of them is yet visible. The variables from our program will become visible as values are assigned to them.

Running the Debugger

When we clicked the *Debug Project* button, the code was executed up until the first breakpoint on line 24. We know the code is paused at line 24 because it is green.

With the code paused, we have several options. These two are worth focusing on:

- Step Over (F8)
- Continue

The Step Over option lets us step through a statement. It basically says, execute this line of code, go to the next line of code, and then stop. You can Step Over by pressing F8 or by selecting *Step Over* from the NetBeans Debug menu. This will allow the code on line 24 to execute, and then execution will pause again on the next executable statement (line 27). The breakpoint on line 24 will turn pink again, and line 27 will turn green (indicating that this is where execution has halted); you will now see the Scanner variable myScanner in the Variables window, as shown in Figure 11.4.

Figure 11.3 Execution paused at first breakpoint

If you were to continue pressing F8 or selecting to Step Over commands, you could progress through the listing; however, let's continue program execution by pressing F5. This is the Continue debugging command that should allow the program to execute until the next breakpoint, which for the listing here is in line 33. This allows the program to run until either it hits another breakpoint or it completes.

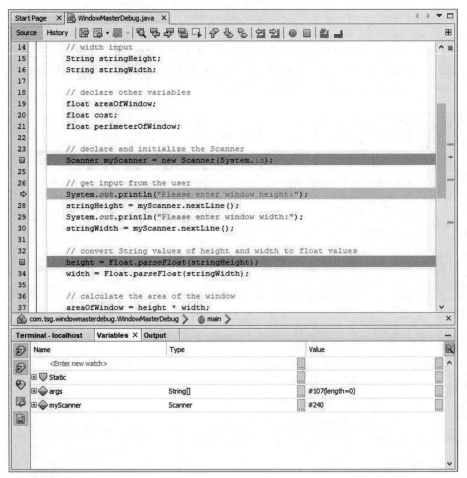

Figure 11.4 Execution paused at line 27

You will notice that nothing seems to happen after you press F5. This is because your program is waiting for user input (see line 28) in Figure 11.4. Provide input by clicking the *Output* window tab and then typing the requested values. After you have typed in the second value, execution will halt on our next breakpoint, which is line 33, as shown in Figure 11.5.

Figure 11.5 Execution paused at the second breakpoint

> **NOTE** As mentioned, when we look at the debug window, if we have a line that's green, it indicates where the execution of the code has paused.

Examining Variables

With the code stopped at line 33, it is worth looking at the Variables window again at the bottom of the IDE. In Figure 11.5, you can see that the Output window is selected at the bottom of the IDE. If we select the *Variables* tab, we should see something like Figure 11.6.

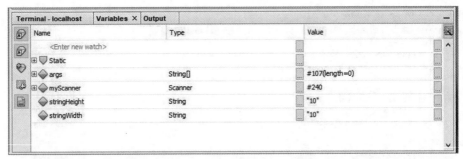

Figure 11.6 The Variables tab

In looking at the Variables window, we see that things have changed. Now, there are two new variables showing, `stringHeight` and `stringWidth`, along with the values you entered in the Output window. These variables are now showing because we ran the code that initializes them. These were lines 28 and 30 in Figure 11.5.

What's more important than just seeing these values, however, is that you also have the ability to change these values within the Value column of the Variables window. Currently, you can see in Figure 11.6 that both variables contain a string value of "10". We can change these to a different value such as 20 by typing in a 2 and 0 (or 20). The value will be changed to a string, as shown in Figure 11.7.

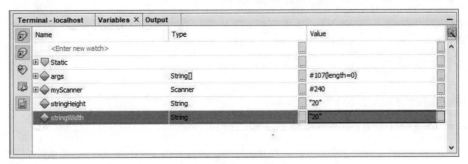

Figure 11.7 Updating values in the Variables window

We can continue the execution of the next line of our program by pressing F8. This will execute line 33 where we had placed our breakpoint. The code on line 33 takes the string for height and turns it into a number for us.

```
height = Float.parseFloat(stringHeight);
```

Our number is converted into a float. After pressing F8 to step over the line, we end up with line 34 highlighted in green, and our Variables window is updated again, as shown in Figure 11.8.

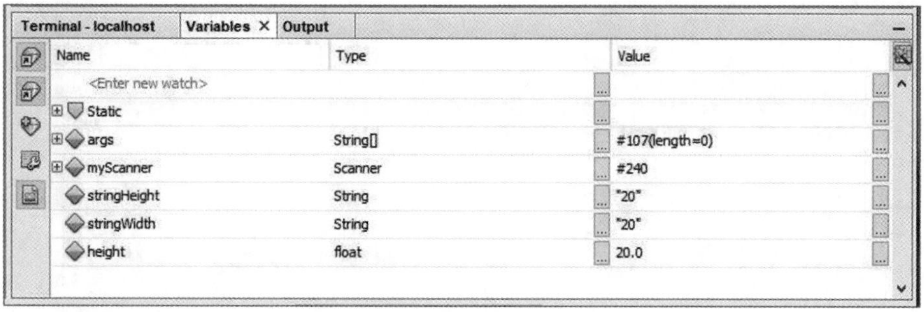

Figure 11.8 Variables window now shows height

Notice that we moved down to line 34, and our height variable became visible in our Variables window because it is now initialized. More importantly, we can see that the string 20 was converted into the float 20.0. If we press F8 again, we'll execute the next line of code, which does the conversion for width.

As you can see, we are calling into the parseFloat method. It is converting these strings into floats, which we can see as they happen. Within the Variables window, we can see that we still have the strings that we entered into our string variables, and we also have our float values in the float variables we created.

If you press F8 one more time, we will execute an expression in line 38.

```
areaOfWindow = height * width;
```

Our expression here takes two operands, which are height and width, which are both floats. In this expression, we are going to multiply these two values together and put the result into areaOfWindow.

With this line having been executed, if you look at the Variables window, you will see that the area of the window has been calculated, and it's 400.0, which is exactly what we should expect. Figure 11.9 shows the current status of the debugger.

If you press F8 two more times, you'll execute lines 40 and 44, which you can see in Figure 11.9. These are the additional two calculations. You'll also see that perimeterOf-Window and cost will be added to the Variables window.

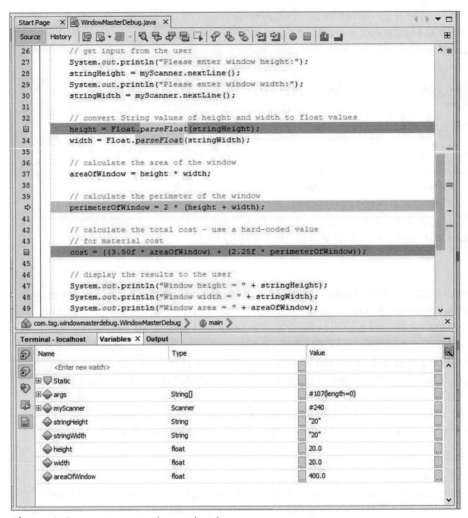

Figure 11.9 areaOfWindow determined

The Console and the Debugger

If you've been following along, then you know we are now at the line of code where we start printing information to the console window. If you look at the console window now, you will see that it shows the input we've entered, but none of the output has yet to be shown. Press F8 one more time, and you'll run the next line of code, line 47, as shown in Figure 11.10.

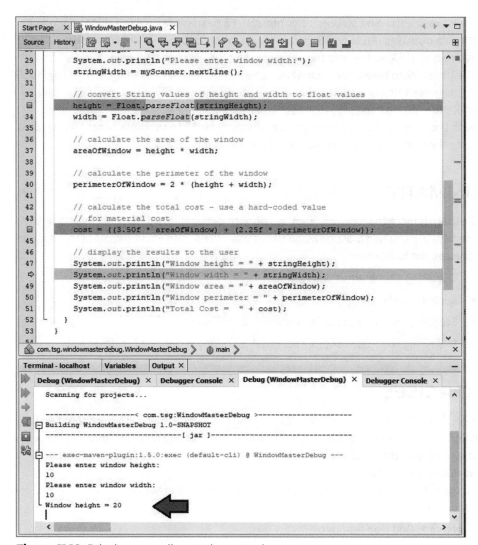

```
29        System.out.println("Please enter window width:");
30        stringWidth = myScanner.nextLine();
31
32        // convert String values of height and width to float values
          height = Float.parseFloat(stringHeight);
34        width = Float.parseFloat(stringWidth);
35
36        // calculate the area of the window
37        areaOfWindow = height * width;
38
39        // calculate the perimeter of the window
40        perimeterOfWindow = 2 * (height + width);
41
42        // calculate the total cost - use a hard-coded value
43        // for material cost
          cost = ((3.50f * areaOfWindow) + (2.25f * perimeterOfWindow));
45
46        // display the results to the user
47        System.out.println("Window height = " + stringHeight);
          System.out.println("Window width = " + stringWidth);
49        System.out.println("Window area = " + areaOfWindow);
50        System.out.println("Window perimeter = " + perimeterOfWindow);
51        System.out.println("Total Cost =  " + cost);
52    }
53  }
```

com.tsg.windowmasterdebug.WindowMasterDebug > main >

Terminal - localhost | Variables | Output ✕

Debug (WindowMasterDebug) ✕   Debugger Console ✕   Debug (WindowMasterDebug) ✕   Debugger Console ✕

```
Scanning for projects...

---------------------< com.tsg:WindowMasterDebug >---------------------
Building WindowMasterDebug 1.0-SNAPSHOT
--------------------------------[ jar ]---------------------------------

--- exec-maven-plugin:1.5.0:exec (default-cli) @ WindowMasterDebug ---
Please enter window height:
10
Please enter window width:
10
Window height = 20
```

Figure 11.10 Printing out a line to the console

You can see in Figure 11.10 that we've run the first call to println. The second call to println is highlighted in green, so it has not yet been executed. In Figure 11.10, the Output tab is selected. You can see that only the first line of output is being displayed. In this case, it is the height of the window.

If we execute the next statement by pressing F8 to step over, we see that the window width gets displayed. Pressing F8 one more time prints out the area of the window. Two more presses of F8, and we see the perimeter and the cost get displayed.

The key point to take away from what we've just done is to note that we were able to look at the execution of each individual line of code and see its results. You were able to control the execution and see what each line was doing.

With the program near the end, you can simply press F5 to continue. What this will do is execute the rest of the program until it's done and exit normally.

SUMMARY

While there is more that you can learn and do with debugging, what you learned in this lesson will help you find most common issues you will run into when coding. In this lesson, we covered the following:

- Executing a program in debug mode
- Setting breakpoints
- Stepping through a program statement by statement
- Examining the values of program variables during program execution

EXERCISES

This section includes coding exercises to help you get comfortable with the debugger. In addition to what is presented here, you should use the debugger to step through the programs you create throughout this book to see when and how variables are assigned and what values they contain.

For now, here are the exercises to provide you with more experience using the debugger:

Exercise 1: Odd Odd Numbers

Exercise 2: A Simple Question of If

Exercise 1: Odd Odd Numbers

Exercise Listing 11.1 should look familiar. This listing was presented in Lesson 8 when you learned about the looping statements. Enter this listing again as presented here and then run it.

EXERCISE LISTING 11.1

Using for to Display Odd Numbers

```
public class CountingNumbers {

  public static void main(String[] args) {

    int counter;

    for ( counter = 0; counter < 21; counter = counter + 2 )
    {
        System.out.println( counter );
    }

    System.out.println("...Done!");
  }
}
```

When you run this listing, you'll see that the numbers printed are not odd, which might seem odd. While you should be able to easily find and fix the issue without the debugger, that's not the purpose of this exercise.

Rather, set a breakpoint on the following line:

```
System.out.println( counter );
```

When you run the program in debug mode, what happens? You have a single breakpoint, but how many times does the program pause?

Run the program again in debug mode with the same breakpoint. Using the Variables window in the debugger, change the value of counter so that odd numbers are printed correctly.

Exercise 2: A Simple Question of If

Enter Exercise Listing 11.2 as presented.

EXERCISE LISTING 11.2

Looper.java: A Simple Question of If

```
public class Looper {

    public static void main(String[] args) {
```

```
        int counter = 10;

        for (int looper = 1; looper < 10; looper++) {
            if (counter < 10) {
                // put a break point on the following line.
                System.out.println("Counter is less than 10!");
            } else {
                System.out.println("Counter is greater or equal to 10!");
            }

            System.out.println(counter);
        }
    }
}
```

Put a breakpoint on the following line, and then compile and execute the listing in debug mode:

```
System.out.println("Counter is less than 10!");
```

How many times does the listing pause at the breakpoint? Is this what you expected? Experiment with moving the breakpoint and note the number of times the breakpoint pauses the execution of the program.

Lesson 12
Adding Methods

Do you like to repeat yourself unnecessarily? Do you like to leverage technology and/or techniques to reduce the amount of work you need to do? Have you ever been called lazy—as a compliment?

In this lesson, we'll look at methods. Methods allow us to better organize our code so that it can be used in multiple places. This, of course, means less work. Good coders are lazy coders—well, smart and lazy.

LEARNING OBJECTIVES

By the end of this lesson, you will be able to:
- Explain the DRY principle
- Define a method
- Explain the parts of the method signature
- Use proper naming conventions for methods
- Explain return values
- Use input parameters
- Refactor code
- Explain the concept of scope as it applies to code
- Learn about stepping into code with the debugger

WHY METHODS?

One of the important concepts in writing good code is the DRY principle: Don't Repeat Yourself. When given a task, we want to do it well, and we only want to do it once. Methods allow us to write a bit of code, give it a name, and then use that code over and over again anywhere in our program. Methods give us two new tools for designing and writing solid code:

- We can reuse code that we've written.
- We can use methods to break down large, complex tasks into simpler steps.

Methods don't add any features to the language itself. They are an organizational tool. A large component of writing good software consists of good code organization.

DEFINING METHODS

A method is defined by a *method declaration*, which is made up of the following parts:

```
<access modifier> static <return type> <method name> (<parameter list>)
<exception list> {
    <method body>
}
```

The following describes each of these parts:

- **Access modifier**: For now, we'll use `public`. Other values are possible, and we'll cover them in a later lesson.
- **The `static` keyword**: This is optional, but for now, we'll always use it. We'll learn more about the `static` keyword later.
- **Return type**: This indicates the data type of the value returned by the method; use `void` if the method does not return a value.
- **Method name**: This is the name for the method. The rules for identifiers apply here, but there are additional conventions we'll cover in more detail in this lesson.
- **Parameter list**: This is a comma-delimited list of input parameters. Each parameter consists of a data type followed by an identifier. The parameter list must be enclosed in parentheses; if the method has no parameters, we must use empty parentheses.
- **Exception list**: We'll cover this later. Leave it blank for now.
- **Method body**: The method body is the code block for this method.

Figure 12.1 is a basic method called add that illustrates many of the method parts. The following sections will expand on method declarations by introducing you to the important concept of method signatures as well as providing a deeper look at method naming conventions, working with returned values, and understanding input parameters.

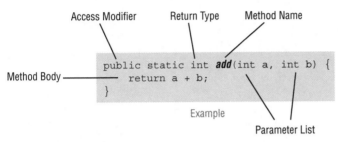

Figure 12.1 An example of a method declaration

Method Signature

While we identified a lot of terms related to methods and method declarations in the previous section, there is one more definition that we need to cover here, and it is for *method signature*. The method signature is related to method declaration, but it's a little bit narrower.

The method signature consists of the following:

- The method name
- The parameter list

We'll talk more about method signatures when we get to the object-oriented features of Java in a later lesson. For now, know that this is an important definition.

> **NOTE** Knowing the definition of a method signature is a common interview question for Java developers, so make sure you memorize it!

Method Naming Conventions

Each of your methods will be named. Technically, a method name can be any legal identifier. We learned about identifiers in Lesson 4 if you need a review of what is legal. There are, however, additional conventions that further restrict method names in practice. Method names should

- Begin with a lowercase letter
- Be a verb (if a single word name)
- Begin with a verb (if a multiword name) followed by other words
- Be in camel case (i.e., the first letter of the second and following words should be capitalized)

Here are some examples:

- `calculateTotal`
- `processOrders`
- `storeUserData`
- `getFullname`
- `checkCardValidity`

> **NOTE** The compiler won't yell at you if the first letter of a method name is not lowercase; however, other Java programmers probably will yell at you.

Return Values

Methods can return values to the caller, but they don't have to. In the programs we have created previously in this course, we have seen examples of both.

- `System.out.println("Hello")` does not return a value to the caller; it simply prints a value to the console.
- The `Scanner` method `nextLine()` does return a value to the caller; it returns the string of characters that the user typed into the console. We put that value into a variable (see the WindowMaster program in Lesson 6).
- `Float.parseFloat("5.32")` does return a value to the caller; it converts the string data type input parameter into a float data type and returns it. We put that value into a variable and then use it to perform math calculations (see WindowMaster).

Whether or not your method returns a value, you must indicate the return type of your method when declaring the method. If your method does not return a value, the return type is `void`; otherwise, it is the data type of whatever value the method returns. In the following example, we have a function called `printHiYa` that does not return a value, so its return type is `void`:

```
public static void printHiYa() {
    System.out.println("HiYa");
}
```

In this second example, we have method called `calculcatePi` that returns a number, specifically a double, so its return type is `double`:

```
public static double calculatePi() {
    return 22/7;    // approximately PI
}
```

> **NOTE** If we want to know what type a method is a returning, we just have to look at the piece of code right before the method's declaration (name). If we want to know the value being returned, it appears in the method's code, proceeded by the return keyword.

Using Return Values

Let's take a look at a listing to get a closer view of how return values can be used within our code. Listing 12.1 is a fun program that has a main method as well as three other methods that we'll use to review how return types can be used.

LISTING 12.1

Working with Return Values

```
public class getNumbers {

    public static void main(String[] args) {

        get2();

        int num = get3();
        System.out.println(num);

        System.out.println( get4() );
    }
```

```
    public static int get2() {
        return 2;
    }
    public static int get3() {
        return 3;
    }
    public static int get4() {
        return 4;
    }
}
```

When we run this listing, we will see the following output:

```
3
4
```

When we're calling a method, we can use a return value in many different ways. In the code in Listing 12.1, we can see that three methods have been created called get2, get3, and get4. Each returns a simple number as an integer. We will use each of these three methods to show three things we can do with the returned values.

The first thing we can do with a returned value is ignore it. If you look at the main method, you'll see that it does a call to get2(). The get2() method returns an integer with the value of 2; however, it does nothing with it. We simply ignore it, and that's fine.

The second thing we can do is put the value returned into a variable and then use that variable in some way. In looking at the main method, you can see that we call get3(). The value returned from get3() is placed in an integer that we've created called num. We can then use the num integer in the rest of our program. In this case, we simply print it to the console.

The third way we can use the return type is to actually just pass the call to the method into another method, such as System.out.println(). When this happens, the method we are passing will be evaluated, and the value returned will be used. In Listing 12.1, we pass the get4() method as a parameter to the System.out.println() method. The returned value of 4 from get4() is passed into println() and just printed to the console.

Input Parameters

Methods can have zero or more input parameters. *Input parameters* are simply place-holders for values (declarations for the variables) that will be "passed in" as data for the method to use. Methods without parameters are useful because we can reuse the code contained in the method in many places. However, methods get really powerful when we can pass parameter values into them.

Here's a somewhat contrived example: say we wanted to write some reusable code that added two numbers together. Further, let's assume that we don't know how to use parameters. If this were the case, we'd have to write a separate method for each number pair we wanted to add.

```
public static int add1And1() {
    return 1 + 1;
}

public static int add1And2() {
    return 1 + 2;
}

public static int add1And3() {
    return 1 + 3;
}
```

And so on...

This is not a good situation. To be able to add any two numbers, we would have to write an infinite number of these methods.

Each equation applies to only one situation; while the equation is true, it is not general.

```
1 + 1 = 2
1 + 2 = 3
1 + 3 = 4
```
And so on...

What we really want is the general equation for adding two numbers together.

```
a + b = y
```

We want to be able to supply the values for a and b and have the method calculate y for us. We'll use input parameters to help us here.

```
public static int add(int a, int b) {
    return a + b;
}
```

Now we have a method that will take any two numbers and will calculate the sum. Note that for each parameter, we included an identifier and an associated data type. In fact, we have declared each parameter similar to a variable declaration. In this case, both parameters are of type int.

Matching Number of Parameters

It is worth repeating that the number of parameters and their data types *must* match the type and number defined by the method; otherwise, the code for the method call won't compile. For example, if the method definition looks like this:

```
public void sayHello(String a, String b){
    // Code here
}
```

then the method call will have to look like this:

```
sayHello("Bob", "Sue");
```

or like this:

```
String a = "Bob";
String b = "Sue";
methodName(a, b);
```

Listing 12.2 pulls this into a listing we can enter and execute.

LISTING 12.2

A Method with Two Parameters

```
public class MethodForms {

    public static void main(String[] args) {
        sayHello( "Bob", "Sue");
    }

    public static void sayHello( String a, String b ){
        System.out.println("Hello " + a + " and " + b );
    }
}
```

When we run this program, we can see that the two values passed are received by the sayHello() method, which uses them to display a message as such:

```
Hello Bob and Sue
```

What happens when you modify the code to what is shown in Listing 12.3 where we pass only one parameter when two are expected?

LISTING 12.3

A Method Receiving Only One of Two Parameters

```
// This listing causes an error!
public class MethodForms {

    public static void main(String[] args) {
        sayHello( "Bob" );
    }

    public static void sayHello( String a, String b ){
        System.out.println("Hello " + a + " and " + b );
    }
}
```

If you compile and run this listing, you will get an error. Similarly, if you pass more than two parameters:

```
sayHello( "Bob", "Sue", "John" );
```

you will also get an error. As you can see, it is critical that you pass values that match with your method's parameters.

Matching Parameter Types

In addition to making sure the number of items you send to your method is the same as the number of parameters in your method definition, you also must make sure the types of each value you send match the type listed in the method definition. Just as with sending the wrong number of parameters, if you send a wrong type for a parameter, you will also get an error when you run your program. Listing 12.4 is a modification of Listing 12.2 where a numeric value is being sent when a String is expected.

LISTING 12.4

Calling a Method with a Wrong Parameter Type

```
// This listing causes an error!
public class MethodForms {
```

```
public static void main(String[] args) {
    sayHello( "Bob", 10 );
}

public static void sayHello( String a, String b ){
    System.out.println("Hello " + a + " and " + b );
}
}
```

Looking at the code, you can see that the numeric value of 10 is being sent as the second parameter. Because sayHello( ) is expecting the second parameter (b) to be a String, you will get an error when you try to run this.

> **NOTE** A parameter passed to a method can be a literal, a variable, or as you saw earlier, even another method. As long as the item being passed evaluates to the appropriate data type, it can be used.

Passing Parameters

Let's step back and look more closely at what is happening when you pass a value to a method. Look at Listing 12.5.

LISTING 12.5

MathFun with Parameters

```
public class MethodFun() {
    public static void main(String[] args) {
        int num = 42;
        silly(num);
    )

    public static void silly(int x) {
        System.out.println("My parameter is: " + x);
    }
}
```

This program creates a variable called num, which is passed to a method called silly( ). The method then prints out a message with our variable so that the final output looks like the following:

```
My parameter is: 42
```

Let's dig into what is happening here. You can see that we create a variable called num and assign the value of 42. This is nothing new. We then use the num variable as a parameter and pass it to `silly`. Here is what is important. What is happening behind the scenes is that the value of num is actually being copied into the variable x in `silly`'s parameter list. So when `silly` is running, it is using a copy of what was in num. When the `silly` method ends, x goes away; however, the original num in `main` still exists and still retains its original value.

> **NOTE** Note that num and x are two different variables and are stored in two different places by the program. What is happening is we are passing the value from one to the other, which is often referred to as *passing by value*.

In Listing 12.5, `silly()` is passed a variable of the appropriate type. We can also pass other items as long as what is passed is the correct type. We saw passing a variable. A second thing we could pass is a literal.

```
silly(42);
```

Third, as you saw earlier, we can also pass another method that resolves to the right type. A fourth option is to pass any valid expression that resolves to the right type. The following are all valid calls to our `silly()` method:

```
silly( 4 + 3);               // same as passing 7
silly( 100 /4 );             // same as passing 25
silly( 10 - 3 + 12 / 3 * 10 + 3);   // same as passing 50
silly( num + 3 );            // same as passing 45 if num is 42
```

> **NOTE** You might have noticed something a bit odd about how we've been using `System.out.println()`. We've passed it numbers, `Strings`, and other things and it worked! That is a bit different from what has just been described. In Lesson 15, you'll learn what is happening to allow `println()` to be so adaptive to different types!

METHOD FORMS

Now that you've seen the parts of a method and seen how parameters work, we will take a look at some of the forms that methods can take. Given the rules discussed, there are four forms that a method can take.

- No return value, no parameters
- Return value, no parameters
- No return value, one or more parameters
- Return value, one or more parameters

It is worth reviewing each of these to see how they differ.

No Return Value, No Parameters

The first example of a method form we will examine is a method that has no return value and takes no parameters.

```
public static void doit() {
    System.out.println("Hello");
    return;
}
```

Because no value is returned, the return type of our method called doit is set to void. Because there are no parameters, there is nothing in the parentheses.

> **NOTE** It is worth noting that we included the return keyword in this code; however, because the end of the method was reached, it was not required. The method would have returned regardless.

Return Value, No Parameters

The second example of a method form is one that has a return value but takes no parameters.

```
public static int get5() {
    return 5;
}
```

This method returns a value, so there is a return type, which in this example is an `int`. Because there are no parameters, there is nothing in the parentheses.

No Return Value, One or More Parameters

The third example of a method form is one that does not have a return value, but does have one or more parameters.

```
public static void silly(int i) {
    System.out.println("My parameter is: " + i );
}
```

Because no value is returned, the return type is set to `void`. There is a parameter being passed to this method. The parameter is called `i` and is of type `int`.

Return Value, One or More Parameters

The fourth example of a method form is one that has a return value and takes one or more parameters.

```
public static int add(int a, int b) {
    return a + b;
}
```

This method returns a value, so there is a return type, which in this example is an `int`. There are parameters being passed to this method as we can see by looking at the identifiers between the parentheses. In this case, there is an integer called `a` and an integer called `b` being passed to the method.

NOTE `System.out.println(...)` is not a return value.

One fairly common point of confusion for beginning programmers is the difference between returning a value from a method and printing something to the console. Returning a value from a method requires the `return` keyword, as shown in the previous examples.

The `static` Keyword

We are always using the `static` keyword for our method definitions in this part of the course. Don't worry about the meaning right now—we'll cover it in detail when we learn about the object-oriented features of Java in the next unit. Once we learn what the `static` keyword means, we'll use it much less frequently. For now, just remember to include it with your method definition. If you forget it, your code might not compile.

PULLING IT ALL TOGETHER

Let's put all of this newfound knowledge about methods to work for us by creating a method that we can use in one of our programs.

So far, the WindowMaster program we've used in previous lessons is in good shape, but we are repeating ourselves in at least one place. We're going to clean that up by creating a reusable method. Listing 12.6 presents the current code from WindowMaster with some redundant code highlighted.

LISTING 12.6

`WindowMaster.java`: The WindowMaster Listing

```java
import java.util.Scanner;

public class WindowMaster {

  public static void main(String [] args) {
    // declare variables for height and width
    float height;
    float width;

    // declare String variables to hold the user's height and
    // width input
    String stringHeight;
    String stringWidth;

    // declare other variables
    float areaOfWindow;
    float cost;
    float perimeterOfWindow;

    // declare and initialize the Scanner
    Scanner myScanner = new Scanner(System.in);

    // get input from the user
    System.out.println("Please enter window height:");
```

```
    stringHeight = myScanner.nextLine();
    System.out.println("Please enter window width:");
    stringWidth = myScanner.nextLine();

    // convert String values of height and width to float values
    height = Float.parseFloat(stringHeight);
    width = Float.parseFloat(stringWidth);

    // calculate the area of the window
    areaOfWindow = height * width;

    // calculate the perimeter of the window
    perimeterOfWindow = 2 * (height + width);

    // calculate the total cost - use a hard-coded value
    // for material cost
    cost = ((3.50f * areaOfWindow) + (2.25f * perimeterOfWindow));

    // display the results to the user
    System.out.println("Window height = " + stringHeight);
    System.out.println("Window width = " + stringWidth);
    System.out.println("Window area = " + areaOfWindow);
    System.out.println("Window perimeter = " + perimeterOfWindow);
    System.out.println("Total Cost =  " + cost);
  }
}
```

The first two highlighted lines look similar to the third and fourth lines.

```
System.out.println("Please enter window height:");
stringHeight = myScanner.nextLine();

System.out.println("Please enter window width:");
stringWidth = myScanner.nextLine();
```

The following two lines are almost identical as well:

```
height = Float.parseFloat(stringHeight);
width = Float.parseFloat(stringWidth);
```

This presents a great opportunity for refactoring this code into a reusable method. Refactoring is simply the process of reorganizing and/or cleaning up your code without adding, subtracting, or changing functionality. After refactoring, the code still does the same thing it did before, but it is now more readable and maintainable.

The first step in refactoring code into a method is to divide out the similarities and the differences of the repeated code. The similarities of the code will represent the main body of the new method. The differences can be factored out into input parameters and/or return types for the method. We'll follow a process similar to the one we followed with the add method in the earlier "Parameters" section.

Identifying the Similarities

What are the similarities in our code example? For each input value that we request from the user, we do the following:

1. Print a message to the console to let the user know what type of value we're asking for.
2. Wait for the user to provide the value, read the value, and store it in a variable.
3. Convert the string value read from the console into a float value that we can use for mathematical operations later in the program.

Identifying the Differences

We also need to determine the differences. What are the differences in the repeated code?

- The message printed to the console is different for each value requested.
- We store the user-provided values in different variables.

Creating the Method

Armed with this knowledge of similarities and differences, we can now create our new method. We'll need to do the following:

1. Decide on a name.
2. Decide whether the method needs input parameters. If so, how many and of what type?
3. Decide whether the method needs to return a value. If so, what type?
4. Write the code for the body of the method.

Setting the Name

You learned earlier the characteristics of creating a method name. Using that, we'll call our new method `readValue` since it is reading a value.

Determining Parameters

For the decision regarding input parameters, we need to look at our list of differences. What needs to vary each time we run the method?

According to our list, the message changes, and the variable in which we store the user value changes. We will need to provide a message each time—this sounds like an input parameter. Putting the user value into a variable sounds like a return type, so we'll handle that next. It looks like we'll have one input parameter that will represent the message we want to print to the console to prompt the user for a value.

What type should this be?

To answer this, we look at the existing code. In the existing code, the user prompt message is represented by a string literal that is passed to `System.out.println()`, which means that our input parameter should be a string as well.

Setting a Return Type

Now for the return type. In the existing code, we store both string and float representations of the values entered by the user. If you look closely, however, you will notice that we really only care about the float representation of these values — the string representations are only needed because the console doesn't understand numbers. We want to prompt the user to input a value and then get the float representation of the value; we do not want to deal with strings. This indicates that the return type of the method should be float.

> **NOTE** You could set the return type to be a string; however, you would then end up doing a similar conversion each time you've gotten a response from your new method. There is no point doing something over and over if you can put it into a method and have it done in one place.

Our Basic Definition

At this point, we've determined all the pieces to be able to create our method definition. This is what we have so far:

```
public static float readValue (String prompt) {
    // method body TBD
}
```

Note that for now we are making our methods `public` and `static`. We then have the return type we determined, which is float. This is followed by our new method name, `readValue`. Finally, we have our parameter, which is a string. Since this parameter is a textual prompt, we'll name our parameter `prompt`.

Our Method Body

With a definition in place, we now need to make our method do something useful. Our method needs to do the following:

1. Print the provided prompt to the console.

2. Wait for the user to input a value.

3. Read the value.

4. Convert the value into a float data type.

5. Return the converted value.

We need a Scanner variable to read the value in from the console. You may wonder why we can't use the one in `main`. This has to do with *scoping rules*, which we will cover in the next section. For now, just go with it. Listing 12.7 presents our method.

LISTING 12.7

The New readValue() Method

```
public static float readValue(String prompt) {

    // declare and initialize a Scanner variable
    Scanner myScanner = new Scanner(System.in);

    // print prompt to Console
    System.out.println(prompt);

    // read value into String data type
    String input = myScanner.nextLine();

    // convert the String to a float
    float floatVal = Float.parseFloat(input);

    // return the float value
    return floatVal;
}
```

Using the Method

The final step in our refactoring adventure is to replace the repeated code in our example with calls to our new method. We will replace the lines highlighted in Listing 12.4 with just two lines (each line will be a call to our new method).

You'll notice also that we no longer need the variables `stringHeight` or `stringWidth`, which means we can remove the lines on which they are declared. However, removing these variables causes a compilation problem. Why? Well, we are still printing out the value of `stringHeight` and `stringWidth` to the console. Now that they are gone, we have a problem. To fix this, we'll simply print out the float values (`height`, `width`) instead. After making all these changes, WindowMaster looks like Listing 12.8.

LISTING 12.8

The Refactored WindowMaster Program

```
import java.util.Scanner;

public class WindowMaster {

  public static void main(String [] args) {
    // declare variables for height and width
    float height;
    float width;

    // declare other variables
    float areaOfWindow;
    float cost;
    float perimeterOfWindow;

    // declare and initialize the Scanner
    Scanner myScanner = new Scanner(System.in);

    // get input from user
    height = readValue("Please enter window height:");
    width = readValue("Please enter window width:");

    // calculate the area of the window
    areaOfWindow = height * width;

    // calculate the perimeter of the window
    perimeterOfWindow = 2 * (height + width);
```

```java
        // calculate the total cost - use a hard-coded value
        // for material cost
        cost = ((3.50f * areaOfWindow) + (2.25f * perimeterOfWindow));

        // display the results to the user
        System.out.println("Window height = " + height);
        System.out.println("Window width = " + width);
        System.out.println("Window area = " + areaOfWindow);
        System.out.println("Window perimeter = " + perimeterOfWindow);
        System.out.println("Total Cost =  " + cost);
    }

    public static float readValue(String prompt) {

        // declare and initialize a Scanner variable
        Scanner myScanner = new Scanner(System.in);

        // print prompt to console
        System.out.println(prompt);

        // read value into String data type
        String input = myScanner.nextLine();

        // convert the String to a float
        float floatVal = Float.parseFloat(input);

        // return the float value
        return floatVal;
    }
}
```

When you run our newly refactored WindowMaster program, you will see output that looks just like what you've seen before.

```
Please enter window height:
10
Please enter window width:
10
Window height = 10.0
Window width = 10.0
Window area = 100.0
Window perimeter = 40.0
Total Cost =  440.0
```

> **NOTE** We can have as many methods as we want in a class. Any additional methods we are creating get declared outside the main method, but inside the code.

SCOPE

Now, we return to the questions regarding scope. Looking at our code, we have a variable called `myScanner` of type Scanner that is declared and initialized in the main method. We also have a variable called `myScanner` of type Scanner that is declared and initialed in the `readValue` method. This raises some questions.

- Do we need both? Why?
- How can we have two different variables with the same name? How can the compiler tell them apart?

The answers to these questions have to do with the concept of scope. As we've seen, a Java program consists of blocks of code. These blocks are marked by curly braces, {}. We have also seen that these blocks can be nested; for example, the `WindowMaster` class block contains both the `main` method block and the `readValue` method block. Method blocks can contain other blocks of code such as `if` statement blocks, `while` loop blocks, etc.

The Java language allows us to define variables inside a block of code. These variables are said to be local to that block of code. Variables declared in outer blocks can be accessed by code inside nested code blocks, but the reverse is not true. Code in outer blocks cannot "see into" nested blocks. Listing 12.9 presents some examples of this.

LISTING 12.9

A Look at Scope

```
public static void main(String[] args) {
    int age = 42;

    for (int i = 0; i < 5; i++) {
        // this is ok - the nested block can access the variables
        // in the outer block
        System.out.println(age);
    }

    if (age < 18) {
        // this is ok - the nested block can access the variables
```

```
        // in the outer block
        int yearsToWait = 18 - age;
    }

    // NOT ok - outer block cannot access variables declared inside
    // inner blocks
    System.out.println(yearsToWait);
}
```

If you are using other Java IDEs or the command line, then this listing likely will not compile or run. If you are using NetBeans, then while the program might compile, when you run it, you will get an error. You might see the following:

```
42
42
42
42
42
Exception in thread "main"
```

While the program ran in NetBeans, it has an error. If we look at the NetBeans IDE in Figure 12.2, we see that line 24 shows an error. This error occurs with the last call to System.out.println(). The variable yearsToWait was declared within the code block of the previous if statement, so it has limited scope to just the if statement's block of code. Once the if statement's block of code ended, the variable was no longer available, so the program couldn't access it and gave an error.

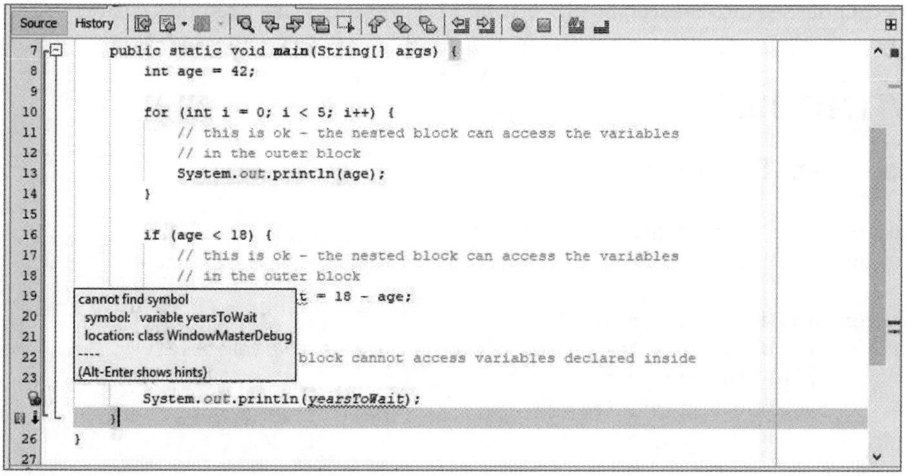

Figure 12.2 Error in NetBeans

DEBUGGING AND STEP INTO

We will now step back for a moment and take another look at debugging to review what is happening with program flow and to learn a new feature within the NetBeans debugger. Listing 12.10 is a simple listing we will use.

LISTING 12.10

MethodFun Program for Debugging

```
public class MethodFun {

    public static void main(String[] args) {
        int num = 42;
        doIt(num);
        doIt(num);
        doIt(num);
    }

    public static void doIt(int x) {
        System.out.println("My number: " + x);
    }
}
```

This listing is simple and straightforward. An integer is created called num, which is assigned the value of 42. The doIt() method is then called three times with the value of num passed each time. Within the doIt() method, the value of num is accepted in a variable called x, and it is simply printed with a message to the screen. The final output looks like the following:

```
My number: 42
My number: 42
My number: 42
```

Enter this listing into NetBeans and make sure it works cleanly. Once it is working, there are two things we want to explore. The first is how we can set a breakpoint inside a method and have it go to that breakpoint every time even though we're executing inside the main method. The second is how we can step into something.

Setting a Breakpoint in a Method

First, let's set a breakpoint at line 22, as shown in Figure 12.3.

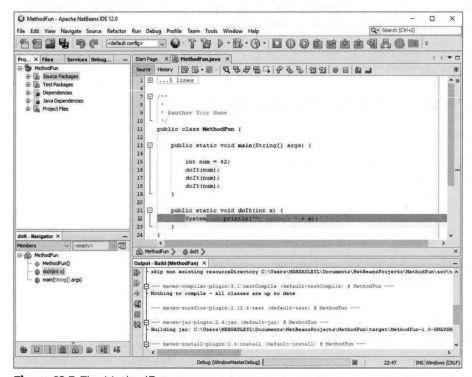

Figure 12.3 The MethodFun program

NOTE In case you've forgotten how to set a breakpoint, you can click the line number or click the line of code and press Ctrl+F8. See Lesson 11 if you need a refresher on basic debugging.

As we can see in the figure, the breakpoint has been set *in* the doIt( ) method and not in the main method. If you press the button to run in debug mode (or press Ctrl+F5), the program will start and run until it hits our breakpoint.

When the listing breaks, you will notice that we are in our doIt() method. The coding window has highlighted a line in green, as shown in Figure 12.4, so we know that is where we've stopped.

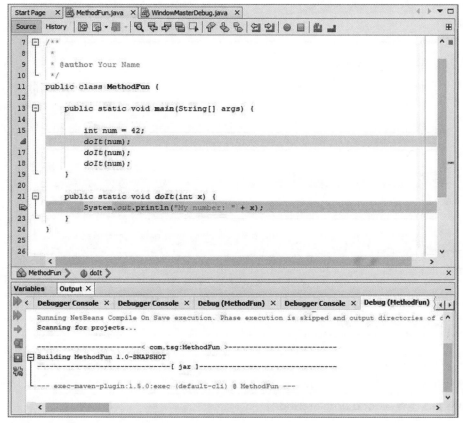

Figure 12.4 The first time through

We can also see that the first doIt() line is gray. That is because we've entered that method. If we click the *Output* window, we will notice that no output is displayed. That is because we have not yet run the System.Out.println() call.

If we continue (or press F5), the program will run until we hit the breakpoint again with the next call of doIt(). In Figure 12.5, we can see that once again we are back at the System.Out.println() line, which is highlighted in green. We can also see that second call to doIt() is now highlighted. Additionally, we can see in the Output window that 42 has been printed once from the previous execution of the method.

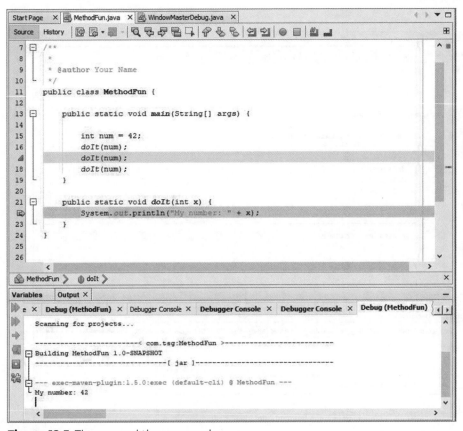

Figure 12.5 The second time around

If we continue again, the code will run to the next breakpoint, which is again in a doIt() method. The output will show another 42 printed. A final press of *Continue*, and the program runs to the end with our output showing the complete list of 42 three times.

Stepping into Code

We've just seen how a breakpoint can be set within a method. Now we are going to move our breakpoint to show how we can step into code. Place your breakpoint on the first call to doIt(). This is line 16 in Figure 12.5 but might be a different line in your listing.

With the breakpoint set, let's debug our program. The program should run until it reaches our first doIt() call with the breakpoint, as shown in Figure 12.6.

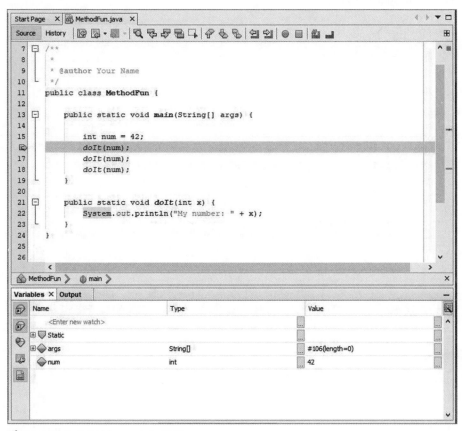

Figure 12.6 Breaking on doIt()

With the cursor now at line 16, no output has happened yet. The Output window will show no numbers. This is because we stopped before calling doIt(). Up to this point, we've seen Step Over, and we've seen Continue. If we choose to step over the next line, we will end up running doIt(), and the following doIt() method will be highlighted. What would be more useful is to be able to go *into* doIt(). That's where Step Into helps us.

If we look at the Debug menu, we see there is another option called Step Into. This option can also be accessed with F7 or the Step Into button ( ). Pressing this button takes us into the code that is highlighted instead of taking us to the line that follows it.

Let's dive into whatever this is doing. With the code stopped on line 16 in Figure 12.5, selecting to Step Into will go from that line to line 22. Do this and the result should be what we see in Figure 12.7.

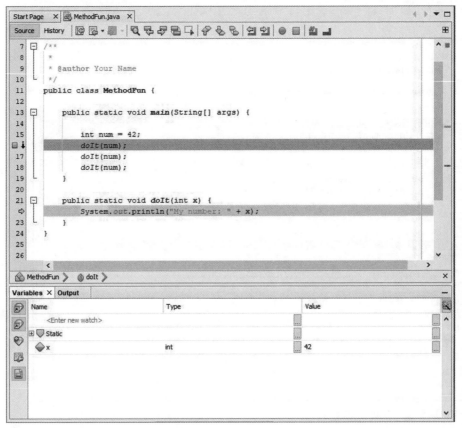

Figure 12.7 Stepping into doIt( )

This will let us shift program flow into the doIt( ) method, where we can then see what it is doing. If we choose to continue, then once we've stepped through the doIt( ) code, we'll be popped back to the main method to continue.

> **NOTE** If you are on the System.out.println( )line and press Step Into, then the debugger is going to take you into the code for the println( ) method. If this happens, you can either step through the code or hit Continue in the debugger to finish running the program.

Debugging and Scope

We've seen setting a breakpoint in a method, and we've seen how to use Step Into. There is something else worth noticing in what we just did. This is related to program scope.

In Figure 12.6, we saw what the IDE looked like when our program control was in the main method. More importantly, if you look at the Variables window in the lower half of the debugger window, you can see that we have access to our args variable and our num variable. What you don't see is variable x that is also in our program. That is because x is not part of the main method.

When we step into the doIt() method, as shown in Figure 12.7, what is displayed in the Variable window changes. We now see the x variable that is part of our doIt() method. This variable was created for doIt() and initialized with the value passed. In this case, a copy of what was in num is used to initialize x. Once program control returns to the main method, the Variable window will no longer show x as being available and will be back to showing num. Only the variable that is in scope and available is shown in the Variable window.

SUMMARY

In this lesson, we covered a lot by learning all about methods. Here's some of what we covered:

- Why methods are important
- How to define methods
- What a method signature is
- The different forms a method can take
- How to create a useful method by refactoring code
- Java scoping rules
- How to step into the code in methods when using a debugger

EXERCISES

Most people learn best by doing, so this section includes a couple of coding exercises using static method definition and execution to help you confirm you've learned this lesson. The exercises are as follows:

Exercise 1: Method to the Madness

Exercise 2: Return to Sender

EXERCISE 1: METHOD TO THE MADNESS

Write a program called *MethodToTheMadness*, as shown in the code in Exercise Listing 12.1. After making sure it works, add the second method call needed to print the rest of the code.

EXERCISE LISTING 12.1

MethodToTheMadness.java

```
public class MethodToTheMadness {
    public static void main(String[] args) {
        eatMe();
        System.out.println("\n – Lewis Carroll, Alice in Wonderland");
    }

    static void eatMe(){
        System.out.println(" 'But I don't want to go among mad people,' Alice
remarked.");
        System.out.println(" 'Oh, you can't help that,' said the Cat.");
        System.out.print(" 'We're all mad here. I'm mad. You're mad.'");
    }

    static void drinkMe(){
        System.out.println(" 'How do you know I'm mad?' said Alice.");
        System.out.println(" 'You must be,' said the Cat, 'or you wouldn't
have come here.' ");
    }
}
```

After you add the second method call, you should see the following when you run the program:

```
'But I don't want to go among mad people,' Alice remarked.
 'Oh, you can't help that,' said the Cat.
 'We're all mad here. I'm mad. You're mad.' 'How do you know I'm mad?'
said Alice.
 'You must be,' said the Cat, 'or you wouldn't have come here.'
 – Lewis Carroll, Alice in Wonderland
```

Exercise 2: Return to Sender

In this exercise, you will match return types to variables by using the ReturnToSender program shown in Exercise Listing 12.2. You should enter the listing and then fix the type definitions so that they match the return types of the called methods. Once everything matches correctly, compile and run it.

EXERCISE LISTING 12.2

ReturnToSender.java

```java
public class ReturnToSender {
    public static void main(String[] args) {

        ??? aMystery = mystery();
        ??? totallyUnexpected = unexpected();
        ??? aSurprise = surprise();
        ??? itsClassified = classified();
        ??? aSecret = secret();

        System.out.println("The methods have returned! Their results...\n");
        System.out.println("Mysterious: " + aMystery);
        System.out.println("    Secret: " + aSecret);
        System.out.println("Surprising: " + aSurprise);
        System.out.println("Classified: " + itsClassified);
        System.out.println("Unexpected: " + totallyUnexpected);

    }

    public static int secret(){
        return 42;
    }

    public static double surprise(){
        return 3.14;
    }

    public static char mystery(){
        return 'X';
    }

    public static boolean classified(){
        return true;
    }
}
```

```
        public static String unexpected(){
            return "Spanish Inquisition";
        }
    }
```

When you run the completed listing, you should see the following:

```
The methods have returned! Their results...
```

```
Mysterious: X
Secret: 42
Surprising: 3.14
Classified: true
Unexpected: Spanish Inquisition
```

Exercise 3: MatchWork

In this exercise, you will practice using parameters. Create a new program using the code in Exercise Listing 12.3. Fix the method call by changing the ??? to the correct number of literal values. When everything matches correctly, compile and run it.

EXERCISE LISTING 12.3

MatchWork.java

```java
public class MatchWork {
    public static void main(String[] args) {

        System.out.println(" The word Cart should come before Horse
alphabetically : " + comesBefore(???));
        System.out.println(" Half of 42 = " + halfOf(???));
        System.out.println(" (short) Pi = " + pi(???));
        System.out.println(" The first letter of the word Llama is: " +
firstLetter(???));
        System.out.println(" 1337 x 1337 = " + times1337(???));

    }

    public static double pi(){
        return 3.14;
    }
```

```java
    public static int times1337(int x){
        return x * 1337;
    }

    public static double halfOf(double y){
        return y / 2;
    }

    public static String firstLetter(String word){
        return word.substring(0, 1);
    }

    public static boolean comesBefore(String a, String b){
        return a.compareToIgnoreCase(b) < 0;
    }
}
```

When you run this program, you should see the following output:

```
The word Cart should come before Horse alphabetically : true
Half of 42 = 21.0
(short) Pi = 3.14
The first letter of the word Llama is: L
1337 x 1337 = 1787569
```

Exercise 4: Barely Controlled Chaos

We usually write methods to capture functionality that we plan to use over and over again. That way we don't have to keep writing the same code. Instead, we can write it once (make sure it's perfect!) and then call that example whenever we need it.

Let's use what we've learned so far to encapsulate a couple of methods we'll use to generate a random mini-sentence (like a micro Mad Lib) over and over again. Write a program called *BarelyControlledChaos* starting with the code in Exercise Listing 12.4.

After you enter that code, add what is needed to complete the listing.

- Write a method that returns a randomly chosen color (have it choose from at least five different colors).

- Write a method that returns a randomly chosen animal (have it choose from at least five different animals).

- Write another method that returns a random integer chosen from a range (min/max) that can be either of the two numbers or anything between.

When you're done defining and implementing these methods, replace the ??? in the main method with a call to the appropriate type.

EXERCISE LISTING 12.4

BarelyControlledChaos.java

```java
public class BarelyControlledChaos {

    public static void main(String[] args) {

        ??? color = ???; // call color method here
        ??? animal = ???; // call animal method again here
        ??? colorAgain = ???; // call color method again here
        ??? weight = ???; // call number method,
            // with a range between 5 - 200
        ??? distance = ???; // call number method,
            // with a range between 10 - 20
        ??? number = ???; // call number method,
            // with a range between 10000 - 20000
        ??? time = ???; // call number method,
            // with a range between 2 - 6

        System.out.println("Once, when I was very small...");

        System.out.println("I was chased by a " + color + ", "
            + weight + "lb " + " miniature " + animal
            + " for over " + distance + " miles!!");

        System.out.println("I had to hide in a field of over "
            + number + " " + colorAgain + " poppies for nearly "
            + time + " hours until it left me alone!");

        System.out.println("\nIt was QUITE the experience, "
            + "let me tell you!");
    }

    // ??? Method 1 ???
    // ??? Method 2 ???
    // ??? Method 3 ???
}
```

When you complete this listing and run it, you should see something similar to the following (but with your random values and information):

```
Once, when I was very small...
I was chased by a magenta, 80lb miniature mammoth for over 12 miles!!
I had to hide in a field of over 4593 periwinkle poppies for nearly 3 hours
until it left me alone!

It was QUITE the experience, let me tell you!
```

Lesson 13

Organizing with Arrays

Arrays are the first collection type that we are going to learn about. It is the most fundamental of the collection types, and many of the other collection types we will learn later use the array structure under the covers in creative ways to yield interesting effects.

When we mention that a type is a collection, we mean that it can hold multiple simple or complex data values inside it.

LEARNING OBJECTIVES

By the time you finish this lesson, you will be able to:

- Differentiate between elements of an array and the indexes of those elements
- Explain one-dimensional, multidimensional (including two-dimensional), and jagged arrays
- Instantiate different ranks and lengths of arrays
- Access elements in an array
- Deal with errors that occur when attempting to access an array

WHAT IS AN ARRAY?

We have covered a lot of Java basics up to this point. We understand variable types, and we can use flow of control statements to branch and loop our code blocks. We also learned how to group repeatable blocks of code into methods. The next piece we need to understand is how to store and work with collections of items.

Consider a situation where we want to store a list of five integers. Without collections like arrays, we would have to declare five variables. That's maybe not a big deal when we are talking about five variables, but what if you had to store 10,000 variables? This is where arrays help us.

An array is a set of uniform data elements that can be accessed using indexes.

- An *element* is a single item in an array.

- *Uniform* means that all elements in a given array must have the same data type.

- The *index* of an element refers to its position in the array. (Array indexes start at 0!)

We can visualize an array like lockers at an amusement park. Arrays always start at index 0 and count up from there. In our previous reference to storing a list of five values, we could get an array of length 5, which would have the indexes from 0 to 4, as shown in Figure 13.1.

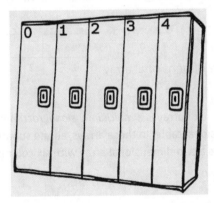

Figure 13.1 An array of lockers

Arrays can have any number of *dimensions*. A one-dimensional array is a vector, a two-dimensional array is a table, and a three-dimensional array is a cube. We use the term *rank* to describe the number of dimensions in an array.

Each dimension in an array has a *length*, which describes the number of positions in that direction. For example, in the case of a two-dimensional table with two rows and six columns, one dimension would be of length 2 and the other would be of length 6, as shown in Figure 13.2.

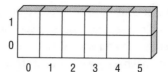

Figure 13.2 A two-dimensional array

The total length of the array itself is the total number of elements in all dimensions. So, our table shown in Figure 13.2 would have an array length of 12 (6 rows * 2 columns).

The *index* of each element in array is an integer that refers to a specific element space in the array. Indexes in most modern programming languages start with 0. For example, in our two-dimensional table, the element in the second row and third column would be located at index [1][2].

Types of Arrays

We can create three types of arrays. The first type is the *one-dimensional array*, as shown in Figure 13.3. This can be thought of as a single line or, in math terms, a *vector* of elements.

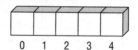

Figure 13.3 One-dimensional array

The second type of array is a *multidimensional rectangular array*, which is structured like a two-dimensional table. In these arrays, all the subarrays have the same length. Figure 13.4 shows a two-dimensional array with six columns and three rows.

Figure 13.4 A two-dimensional multidimensional array

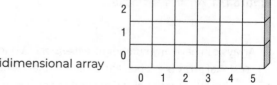

If we add another subarray to this array, we end up with a three-dimensional array, as shown in Figure 13.5.

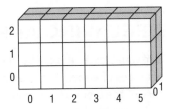

Figure 13.5 A three-dimensional multidimensional array

The third and last type of array is the *multidimensional jagged array* in which each sub-array is a single independent array and, as such, can have different lengths, as shown in Figure 13.6.

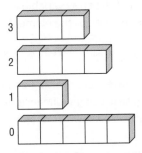

Figure 13.6 A multidimensional jagged array

Unlike some languages (such as JavaScript), array size is *fixed* in Java. This means that after you instantiate an array and specify its dimension and lengths, those lengths cannot be changed. Additionally, while you can go beyond three-dimensional arrays, this is typically unnecessary and gets confusing. As a result, we generally err on the side of simpler data structures.

Element vs. Index

As indicated earlier, it is important to be able to distinguish between the data stored in the array (the *elements* of the array) and the integers that define *where* that data is stored (the *indexes* of the array).

One metaphor that can help you keep the distinction in mind is that of houses on a street. Each house has a numeric address on the street, but the house is not the same thing as the address (and similarly, the address is not the same thing as the house). The address (index) allows us to go to the right part of the street (array) and view the house (element) at that location.

DECLARING ARRAYS

Like variables, arrays can be declared, initialized, and then used. Because there are different types of arrays, in this lesson we will look at the process for initializing and declaring for each of the types before pulling things together with accessing array elements.

The syntax for declaring an array variable depends on the shape of the array to be created. Let's look at each of the different shapes independently.

Single-Dimensional Arrays

The declaration of the array variable is simplest for a single-dimensional array. You must simply provide the type of the elements to be stored, followed by square brackets.

```
int[] arrayOfInts;  //creates a single-dimensional array
```

In this case, we have created a single-dimensional array of integers called `arrayOfInts`. It is worth noting that a single-dimensional array has one dimension. As such, single-dimensional arrays are also known as one-dimensional arrays.

> **NOTE** Whenever you see something followed by square brackets in Java, it is a good indicator that you are dealing with an array.

Rectangular Arrays

Rectangular arrays are also relatively simple. To add another dimension to the array, you simply add another set of square brackets to the declaration. Each set of brackets will determine the dimension of the array: [ ] for one dimension, [ ][ ] for two dimensions, and so on.

The following is an example of creating a multidimensional array of integers called `my2DArray` that has two dimensions:

```
int[][] my2DArray = new int[4][4];
```

It is worth noting that in addition to declaring this two-dimensional array, it is being set to hold 4 by 4 elements, or 16 total elements.

The following declaration creates a multidimensional array that has three dimensions. It is being initialized so that all three dimensions have five elements. This means the array can hold up to 5 × 5 × 5, or 125 float values.

```
float[][][] my3DArray = new float [5][5][5];
```

> **NOTE** Newer Java programmers often try to put the square brackets after the name of the array instead of after the type when declaring the array. While this will work, the brackets should go after the type when declaring and then later after the name when using the array.

Jagged Arrays

Both a rectangular and a jagged array can be considered to be an array *of* arrays. As such, the syntax for declaring variables of that type will involve multiple square brackets to indicate the nesting of arrays. You can declare a jagged array similar to a multidimensional array.

```
int[][] myArray = new int[2][];
```

In this case, you are declaring an array of integers; however, on the right you can see a difference. While this is set to have two rows, the number of columns has not been stated. That will be determined when the array is initialized.

INITIALIZING ARRAYS

In simple terms, arrays are blocks of memory, just like any other variable. This means we can initialize an empty array and add elements to it later, or we can initialize an array that already includes the elements we want the array to hold.

If we initialize an empty array, we specify the number of elements we want to allocate space for without providing the data to be stored immediately. Depending on the data type, default values will be placed at each location in the array.

In the other method of initialization, we can provide data right away, and the size of the array will be inferred and set to exactly the size required for that data.

Keep in mind that you cannot change the size of an array after it has been initialized. This means you must define the size correctly when you initialize an array, even if the elements themselves are initially empty.

NOTE Because array sizes are set when initialized, it is worth taking time to plan out an array on paper before coding it.

Initializing a Single-Dimensional Array

As with declaration, initialization is simplest with single-dimensional arrays. Initializing the array requires setting up the memory area for the values to be stored. To set this up, we use the new keyword. This keyword is followed by what is being set up and initialized. For example, consider the following code:

```
int[] numbers = new int[4];
```

Looking to the left of the equal sign, you can see that this code declares a single-dimensional array called numbers. Looking to the right, you can see that the new keyword is being used to initialize this array. It is being created as an array of four integers. Because no values are indicated, each of the four elements in the array will be implicitly set to a default value for integers, which is 0.

The following is a declaration for the same array. This time, however, the values are explicitly being set to zero.

```
int[] numbers = { 0, 0, 0, 0 };
```

As you can see to the right of the equal sign, curly braces are being used to enclose the block of default values. Because there are four values, this single-dimensional array will be set to have four elements. If we were to visualize this array after any of these statements has been executed, it would look like Figure 13.7.

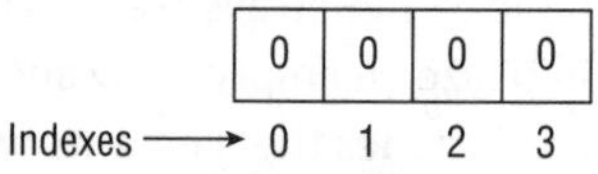

Figure 13.7 Our initialized single-dimensional array   Indexes ⟶

0	0	0	0
0	1	2	3

While we set the value to zero, we could have used any valid integer value when declaring and initializing the array.

```
int[] numbers = { 20, 33, 44444, 123 };
```

Initializing a Rectangular Array

If we want a tabular data structure (a rectangular array, which is also a two-dimensional array), instead of putting a single number like the 4 earlier, we declare it as an `int[][]` (with brackets to define the dimension of the array), and then we put both dimensions in the brackets when we initialize it. The following code would create an array with 2 rows and 3 columns:

```
int rows = 2;
int columns = 3;
int[][] table = new int[rows] [columns];
```

Instead of using literals to initialize this array, variables were used. This is perfectly acceptable. The previous code is equivalent to having written the following:

```
int[][] table = new int [2][3];
```

This would produce an array of default `int` values, as shown in Figure 13.8.

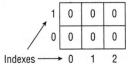

Figure 13.8 Declaring and initializing a two-dimensional array

As with single-dimensional arrays, multidimensional arrays can be auto-initialized. The following code creates the same two-dimensional array, but with values in each element:

```
//                  row 0        row 1
int[][] autoInitTable = { { 5, 3, 1 }, { 2, 4, 6 } };
```

Figure 13.9 shows these values can be visualized.

In this setup, each "row" in the array is a separate subarray, and each subarray includes the same number of elements.

> **NOTE** The designation of the first dimension as a "row" and the second as a "column" is arbitrary. Arrays don't have a spatial layout: they're just memory locations with numeric addresses. We could have just as easily made the first dimension the "column" and the second the "row." However, when you work with multidimensional arrays, it will be critical for you to establish and maintain consistent conventions across your application.

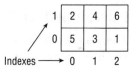

Figure 13.9 Initializing a two-dimensional array with values   Indexes ──────➤ 0   1   2

Initializing a Jagged Array

Unlike the rectangular array described earlier, a jagged array includes multiple arrays of varying lengths. As a result, jagged arrays do not have a regular shape, and initialization is slightly trickier.

You saw the declaration of a jagged array earlier, as well as part of the initialization. The following is an initialization of another jagged array that has three rows:

```
int[][] jagged = new int[3][];
```

To initialize these rows, you then need to set each of the rows to an array.

```
jagged[0] = new int[] { 1, 2 };
jagged[1] = new int[] { 3, 4, 5, 6 };
jagged[2] = new int[] { 7, 8, 9 };
```

You can see that the first row is initialized to two values. The second row is set to four values. Finally, the third row is set to three values. If you were to visualize the result of this jagged array, it would look similar to Figure 13.10.

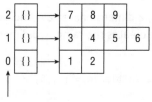

Figure 13.10 Our initialized jagged array   Indexes

NOTE If you were to have more than two dimensions in a jagged array, it is recommended that only the last dimension should be jagged.

ACCESSING ARRAY ELEMENTS

Now that we have arrays declared and initialized, it is time to get to the important information: accessing the array elements. To access an individual element, we simply use the index of the element we want to work with inside square brackets. Let's look at how to access each of the types of arrays.

> **NOTE** The trickiest part for beginners is remembering that indexes start at zero. So, if you want the first element, it is at index zero [0].

Accessing Elements in a Single-Dimensional Array

As mentioned, you access array elements using an index number within square brackets. As an example, let's consider our one-dimensional array example.

```
int[] numbers = new int[] { 3, 5, 2, 0 };
```

It's important to remember that the index is the position in the array starting with zero, and the value is what is stored in the element at the index's position. For example, the second element in the numbers array we just created and initialized has the index 1 and the value 5. This is illustrated in Figure 13.11.

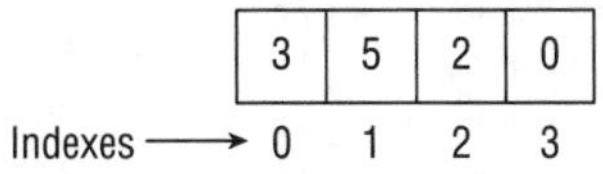

Figure 13.11 Index vs. value

In this array, in the second slot is the value of 5. If we wanted to replace the 5 with a 7, we would do the following:

```
numbers[1] = 9;
```

As you can see, we are using the name of the array along with square brackets that contain the index of the item we want. We can then treat this (numbers[1]) like any other integer variable. In this case, we are simply assigning a new value of 9 to it. Similarly, we could print the value of the second position:

```
System.out.println(numbers[1]);
```

This would print the value we just assigned, which is 9. The following would print the value of 2:

```
System.out.println(numbers[2]);
```

To print the first value of 3, we would use an index of 0, so the code would be as follows:

```
System.out.println(numbers[0]);
```

Listing 13.1 provides a working sample of code that illustrates this in action, plus a little more.

LISTING 13.1

Using a One-Dimensional Array

```
public class ArrayFun {

    public static void main(String[] args) {

        int ourNumber = 0;
        int[] numbers = new int[]{3, 5, 2, 0};

        System.out.println("Our Numbers: ");
        System.out.println(numbers[0]);
        System.out.println(numbers[1]);
        System.out.println(numbers[2]);
        System.out.println(numbers[3]);
        System.out.println("ourNumber: " + ourNumber);

        numbers[1] = 9;
        ourNumber = numbers[0];

        System.out.println("Our Numbers Now: ");
        System.out.println(numbers[0]);
        System.out.println(numbers[1]);
        System.out.println(numbers[2]);
        System.out.println(numbers[3]);
        System.out.println("ourNumber: " + ourNumber);
    }
}
```

When this is executed, the following output should be generated:

```
Our Numbers:
3
5
2
0
ourNumber: 0
Our Numbers Now:
3
9
2
0
ourNumber: 3
```

Most of what is in this listing matches what we mentioned before. The main new action is that we can also see that an element from our array (number[0]) is being assigned to the variable ourNumber.

NOTE Don't confuse the *index* of an element with its *value*.

Accessing Elements in a Multidimensional Array

As we increase the number of dimensions in the array, simply place the index in a bracket for each dimension. Figure 13.12 shows a 2 × 3 array that has each element filled with a value.

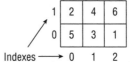

Figure 13.12 Elements in a multidimensional array

If we wanted to assign number to a variable from the first row and second column this array, we could do the following:

```
int gottenNumber = autoTable[0][1];
```

This assumes the table name is autoTable. Looking at Figure 13.12, you can see that the value assigned to gottenNumber would be 3. If we wanted to assign the item in the second row and third column to a variable, we could do the following:

```
int anotherNumber = autoTable[1][2];
```

In this case, anotherNumber is assigned the value of 6.

Accessing Elements in a Jagged Array

A jagged array is accessed in the same way as a multidimensional array; however, we need to be aware of how many items are in the columns. Figure 13.13 shows an example of a jagged array.

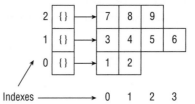

Figure 13.13 Elements in a jagged array

In looking at the figure, if we wanted to get the second element from the third array, we would do the following:

```
int eight = jagged[2][1];
```

If we wanted to replace the value in the second position of the first array, which is currently 2, we could do that as follows:

```
jagged[0][1] = 42;
```

In this case, we are replacing the 2 with the value of 42.

ITERATING THROUGH ARRAYS

Now that we have seen how to set up and access arrays, it is time to take our learning to the next level. Arrays and loops go hand in hand. Any time you want to read through multiple elements of an array, in particular when the incoming arrays could have different lengths, you will need to "loop" through it.

Depending on the type of loop, this means *either* looping through the valid *indexes* of the array and using the indexes as shown earlier to access the elements at those locations *or* iterating through the *elements* directly.

When performing the second kind of loop, we will not know what index we're on at any given time. We don't typically need to know the index, but there are cases when we do need this information.

In sections that follow, we will walk through a series of examples of some of the techniques for iterating through arrays. We'll walk through summing elements, changing looping direction, and printing pairs of elements. Before we jump into those techniques, let's start by simply iterating through a simple single-dimensional array, as shown in Listing 13.2. We will use the same array we used in Listing 13.1.

LISTING 13.2

Iterating through a Single-Dimensional Array

```
public class ArrayFun2 {

    public static void main(String[] args) {

        int [] numbers = new int[]{3, 5, 2, 0};

        System.out.println("Starting....");
        for (int ctr = 0; ctr < numbers.length; ctr++) {
            System.out.println("ctr = " + ctr + " Numbers = " + numbers[ctr]);
        }
        System.out.println("....Done!");
    }
}
```

Running Listing 13.2 results in output that should not surprise you.

```
Starting....
ctr = 0 Numbers = 3
ctr = 1 Numbers = 5
ctr = 2 Numbers = 2
ctr = 3 Numbers = 0
....Done!
```

There is only one new thing in this listing. The rest should look familiar based on what has been taught up to this point. The listing starts by creating and initializing our array of numbers called numbers. This is just like we saw in the previous listing. The interesting things, however, start happening with our `for` loop. In this case, we are going to use our counter as the index into our array. As such, we start by setting our counter, `ctr`, to an initial value of 0.

We want to then step through the array until we get to the end. This is where something new is happening. We can use the length of the array to determine the number of times we loop through the array. It is important to remember that the length refers to the number of elements in the array, so an array's length is always 1 less than the highest index in the array. As can be seen in the listing, we are comparing value of `ctr` to the value of `numbers.length`. We can simply iterate our counter each time until we reach the length!

Iterating through Multidimensional and Jagged Arrays

Iterating through multidimensional and jagged arrays can be done similarly. Both are relatively straightforward once the length of the array is known. Let's start by looking at Listing 13.3, which iterates through a two-dimensional array and prints its values.

LISTING 13.3

Iterating through a Two-Dimensional Array

```java
public class ArrayFun3 {

    public static void main(String[] args) {
        String[][] words = {{"One", "Two", "three"},
        {"red", "white", "blue"},
        {"cat", "rabbit", "cow"}};

        System.out.println("Starting....");
        for (int i = 0; i < words.length; i++) {
            for (int j = 0; j < words[i].length; j++) {
                System.out.println("i = " + i + " j = " + j + " is "
+ words[i][j]);
            }
            System.out.println("-----");
        }
    }
}
```

When we run this listing, we get the following output:

```
Starting....
i = 0 j = 0 is One
i = 0 j = 1 is Two
i = 0 j = 2 is three
-----
i = 1 j = 0 is red
i = 1 j = 1 is white
i = 1 j = 2 is blue
-----
i = 2 j = 0 is cat
i = 2 j = 1 is rabbit
i = 2 j = 2 is cow
-----
```

Taking a look, you can see that this time, instead of using integers, we've switched to creating an array of Strings. Regardless of the data type being used, the array will be used in the same way. You can see that we create a two-dimensional string called words and then load it with words. In this case, we are creating a 3 × 3 array based on the three groups of values being initialized.

Once the data is initialized, then just like with a one-dimensional array, we use a for loop to iterate through each dimension of the array. With multiple dimensions, however, we nest the for loops. In the first for loop, you'll see that we check for the length of words.

```
for (int i = 0; i < words.length; i++) {
```

This gives us the number of elements in the first dimension. Within that for loop, we then check the length of each item within that dimension.

```
for (int j = 0; j < words[i].length; j++) {
```

If you were doing a jagged array, your process would be exactly the same. Add a few words to the code in Listing 13.3 in the initialization and run the code again. For example, if we change the initialization to the following:

```
public static void main(String[] args) {
    String[][] words = {{"One", "Two", "three", "four", "five"},
    {"red", "white", "blue"},
    {"cat", "rabbit"}};
```

Making this change and rerunning the program creates the following output:

```
Starting....
i = 0 j = 0 is One
```

```
i = 0 j = 1 is Two
i = 0 j = 2 is three
i = 0 j = 3 is four
i = 0 j = 4 is five
-----
i = 1 j = 0 is red
i = 1 j = 1 is white
i = 1 j = 2 is blue
-----
i = 2 j = 0 is cat
i = 2 j = 1 is rabbit
-----
```

As you can see, nothing else in the code had to be changed.

Sum the Elements of an Array

Let's go back to Listing 13.2 and take it a little bit further by using the values in the elements rather than just displaying them. Listing 13.3 iterates through a new array. This time, in addition to displaying the output, we are also determining the sum of all the numbers. Listing 13.4 presents the new code.

LISTING 13.4

Summing Values in an Array

```java
public class ArrayFun4 {

    public static void main(String[] args) {

        int[] numbers = {3, 5, 2, 1, 10, 42 };
        int sum = 0; // keep running total
        for (int ctr = 0; ctr < numbers.length; ctr++) {
            sum += numbers[ctr];
            System.out.println("ctr = " + ctr + " current sum = " + sum);
        }
        System.out.println("Final sum: " + sum);
    }
}
```

When we run the program, we should see the following:

```
ctr = 0 current sum = 3
```

```
ctr = 1 current sum = 8
ctr = 2 current sum = 10
ctr = 3 current sum = 11
ctr = 4 current sum = 21
ctr = 5 current sum = 63
Final sum: 63
```

> **NOTE** For fun, change the values used to initialize the array and run the program again.

Looping Back to Front, with a Twist

In Java, a `for` loop can count up or down, so we can also loop through an array from back to front if we want. In fact, let's go from back to front and print only the elements that are in odd-numbered indexes. Enter and run Listing 13.5 to see this in action.

LISTING 13.5

Going Backward in an Array

```
public class ArrayFun5 {

    public static void main(String[] args) {

        int[] numbers = {3, 5, 2, 1, 10, 42};
        // start at last index, go to first (0)
        for (int ctr = numbers.length - 1; ctr >= 0; ctr--) {
            if (ctr % 2 == 1) {
                System.out.println("index " + ctr + " - " + numbers[ctr]);
            }
        }
    }
}
```

The output of this code would be as follows:

```
index 5 - 42
index 3 - 1
index 1 - 5
```

If we review this listing, everything should look familiar. You can see that instead of starting with zero and going to the length of the array, we are instead starting with the length and working toward zero. Instead of adding to our counter, we subtract from it. This is all done within the for loop. To only display the values in the odd index locations, we simply use the modulus operator (%). If we have a remainder, then we know the index is odd.

Printing Pairs of Elements

For this example, let's consider that we want to print pairs of elements, skipping one number in between each pair. So, if we have an array with numbers 1, 2, 3, 4, 5, 6, we want to print 1, 2 and then 4, 5. This is exactly what Listing 13.6 is doing.

LISTING 13.6

Printing Pairs of Elements and More

```
public class ArrayFun6 {

    public static void main(String[] args) {

        int[] numbers = {1, 2, 3, 4, 5, 6};

        for (int i = 0; i < numbers.length - 2; i += 3) {
            System.out.println("Pair: (" + numbers[i] + ", " +
numbers[i + 1] + ")");
        }
    }
}
```

When we run this, we can confirm that the output is as follows:

```
Pair: (1, 2)
Pair: (4, 5)
```

In this listing, there are three key ideas being demonstrated. The first is that for each printout, we include two numbers and skip one number. This means using three elements in each loop. Thus, our increment for the loop needs to be i += 3.

The second relates to the check for the length of the array that we have used in previous listings. Since we are reading three elements in, we need to stop earlier than length. We can use i < numbers.length for one element at a time, but since we have 3, we need to subtract the difference (3 − 1 = 2).

Finally, this listing illustrates that we can use an expression as an index. So `[i + 1]` is the index next to the current element `i`.

NOTE As always, be sure to write pseudocode, flowchart the process, or simply write the steps of the process out with sample data before attempting to code. The majority of times when new programmers have an array issues, it is because they have not solved the problem on paper before writing code.

CHANGING THE SIZE OF AN ARRAY

As mentioned earlier, we cannot change the size of an array once it is initialized. What we *can* do is initialize a new, larger array and copy all the elements over to it, as shown in Listing 13.7.

LISTING 13.7

Changing an Array's Size

```
public class ArrayFun7 {

    public static void main(String[] args) {

        int[] numbers = {3, 5, 2, 1};
        for (int i = 0; i < numbers.length; i++) {
            System.out.println("ctr = " + i + " current sum = " + numbers[i]);
        }
        System.out.println("Number of items: " + numbers.length);

        numbers = growArray(numbers, 5);

        for (int i = 0; i < numbers.length; i++) {
            System.out.println("i = " + i + " current value = " + numbers[i]);
        }
        System.out.println("Number of items: " + numbers.length);
    }
```

```java
public static int[] growArray(int[] original, int howManyMoreElements) {
    int[] newArray = new int[original.length + howManyMoreElements];

    for (int i = 0; i < original.length; i++) {
        // copy the element at the current index
        // from original to newArray
        newArray[i] = original[i];
    }

    return newArray;
}
}
```

In this listing, we are creating an array of numbers that contains four numbers. We iterate through the array and print out each number followed by printing out the number of items in the array.

Once we have done this, we do a call to a new method we have created called growArray. Notice that we pass the name of our array to this method along with an integer indicating how many more elements we want added. This method returns to our listing a new bigger array that we assign back to the array we had created. Once we have done this, we again iterate through our array and show the elements to confirm that we do indeed have a bigger array. The final output is shown here:

```
ctr = 0 current sum = 3
ctr = 1 current sum = 5
ctr = 2 current sum = 2
ctr = 3 current sum = 1
Number of items: 4
i = 0 current value = 3
i = 1 current value = 5
i = 2 current value = 2
i = 3 current value = 1
i = 4 current value = 0
i = 5 current value = 0
i = 6 current value = 0
i = 7 current value = 0
i = 8 current value = 0
Number of items: 9
```

If you look at the growArray() method we created, you will see that the code is similar to what we've seen. In this case, the method is returning a type of int[], which is simply an array of integers. For parameters, it is taking our original integer array as well as an integer indicating the number of elements to add.

```
public static int[] growArray(int[] original, int howManyMoreElements) {
```

The method simply creates a new array. It then uses a `for` loop to iterate through the elements of the original array and use the original indexes to map the elements to the same locations in the new array. Once we have completed this, we return the newly created array back to the calling method.

DEALING WITH ERRORS

Index out-of-range exceptions are the most common exceptions you encounter when dealing with arrays. Simply put, this error occurs when we try to access an element of an array that does not exist. Consider the following array:

```
int[] numbers = {1, 2, 3, 4, 5, 6}
```

There are only six elements in this array, so the max index is 5. What happens if we try to execute the following line of code?

```
System.out.println(numbers[52]);
```

If we do this, we will get an exception, or more specifically an array index out-of-bounds exception. This error only occurs at run time.

If you get this error when iterating through an array, the error usually means that your loop's conditional expression (such as `i < {expression}`) is incorrect.

In our previous example of growing an array in Listing 13.6, if the `howManyMoreElements` had been negative, when our `for` loop was set to loop for each element in the original array, it would have had more indexes than the `newArray`. As a result, it would throw the `ArrayIndexOutOfBoundsException` once the loop progressed past the last element of `newArray`.

SUMMARY

Arrays are a fundamental construct of collections and a common topic in technical interviews, especially in coding challenges in interviews. In practice, most developers prefer to use more robust collection structures such as List, Set, and Map; however, many other languages use the array structure heavily. Additionally, the array being a core piece of the more robust collection structures requires us as developers to be comfortable with it if we are to understand how those structures are implemented and create our own more complicated collections.

In this lesson, we learned all about single-dimensional (also called one-dimensional), multidimensional, and jagged arrays. We saw how to declare, initialize, and use arrays in a variety of ways.

At this point, we have learned the basic building blocks of the Java programming language. It's now time to shift the focus toward applying Java to object-oriented concepts.

EXERCISES

Below are additional coding exercises to help you practice what you are learning about the Java programming language. These are to do on your own, so most will not always include answers. Many of the exercises cover accepting user input via Scanner. There are several exercises for you to apply what you learned in this lesson:

Exercise 1: A Rainbow

Exercise 2: Still Positive

Exercise 3: Fruit Basket

Exercise 4: Simple Combination

Exercise 5: Hidden Nuts

Exercise 6: Summative Sums

Important!
Type all code yourself so that you better understand the code and you learn how to handle mistakes on your own.

Exercise 1: A Rainbow

Practice using arrays by making a text rainbow. Create a new program using the code in Exercise Listing 13.1. In the listing, you will type out the code to create and print a String[]. You should notice that something doesn't quite match up. Fix the code to print out the colors in true ROYGBIV order!

EXERCISE LISTING 13.1

ARainbow.java

```java
public class ARainbow {
    public static void main(String[] args) {
        String[] colors = {"Red", "Orange", "Yellow", "Green", "Blue",
"Indigo", "Violet"};

        System.out.println(colors[5]);
        System.out.println(colors[3]);
        System.out.println(colors[2]);
        System.out.println(colors[1]);
        System.out.println(colors[4]);
        System.out.println(colors[0]);
        System.out.println(colors[6]);

    }
}
```

What you should see after you have updated this listing is the following:

```
Red
Orange
Yellow
Green
Blue
Indigo
Violet
```

Exercise 2: Still Positive

In this exercise, practice using arrays with conditionals. Start by creating a program called StillPositive.java that determines all the positive numbers and prints them. Use the following array of numbers:

```
int[] numbers = { 389, -447, 26, -485, 712, -884, 94, -64, 868, -776, 227,
-744, 422, -109, 259, -500, 278, -219, 799, -311};
```

When you run your program, you should see the following output:

```
Gotta stay positive ...!
389 26 712 94 868 227 422 259 278 799
```

Exercise 3: Fruit Basket

Use the code in Exercise Listing 13.3 to create a program that iterates through the array of fruit and prints out a count of the number of apples, the number of oranges, the number of other fruit, and the total amount of fruit in our basket.

EXERCISE LISTING 13.3

FruitBasket.java

```java
public class FruitBasket {

    public static void main(String[] args) {
        String[] fruitBasket = {"Orange", "Apple", "Orange", "Apple", "Orange",
            "Apple", "Orange", "Apple", "Orange", "Orange", "Orange", "Apple",
            "Orange", "Orange", "Apple", "Orange", "Orange", "Apple", "Apple",
            "Orange", "Apple", "Apple", "Orange", "Orange", "Apple", "Apple",
            "Apple", "Banana", "Apple", "Orange", "Orange", "Apple", "Apple",
            "Orange", "Orange", "Orange", "Orange", "Apple", "Apple", "Apple",
            "Apple", "Orange", "Orange", "PawPaw", "Apple", "Orange", "Orange",
            "Apple", "Orange", "Apple", "Kiwi", "Orange", "Apple", "Orange",
            "Apple", "Orange", "Orange", "Apple", "Apple", "Orange", "Orange",
            "Apple", "Orange", "Apple", "Kiwi", "Orange", "Apple", "Orange",
            "Dragonfruit", "Apple", "Orange", "Orange"};

        int numOranges = 0;
        int numApples = 0;
        int numOtherFruit = 0;

        // Fruit counting code goes here!

        // Print The Results!

    }
}
```

Here is the initial output:

```
Total# of Fruit in Basket: 65
Number of Apples: 28
Number of Oranges: 33
Number of Other Fruit: 4
```

Exercise 4: Simple Combination

Practice combining arrays into one array. Combine the following two arrays into one large array and then print out the whole new array. Exercise Listing 13.4 gives you the code to start with.

EXERCISE LISTING 13.4

SimpleCombination.java

```java
public class SimpleCombination {
    public static void main(String[] args) {
        int[] firstHalf = {3, 7, 9, 10, 16, 19, 20, 34, 35, 45, 47, 49};
// 12 numbers
        int[] secondHalf = {51, 54, 68, 71, 75, 78, 82, 84, 85, 89, 91, 100};
// also 12!

        int[] wholeNumbers = new int[24];

        // Combining code should go here!

        // Printing code should go here

    }
}
```

When you run the program, you should see the following output from your one array:

```
All together now!:
3 7 9 10 16 19 20 34 35 45 47 49 51 54 68 71 75 78 82 84 85 89 91 100
```

Exercise 5: Hidden Nuts

Squirrels like to hide their nuts, but they're not always good about finding them again. Using the code snippet in Exercise Listing 13.5 as a base, iterate through the hiding spaces and find out where the squirrel put his nut and print the results to the screen.

EXERCISE LISTING 13.5

HiddenNuts.java

```java
import java.util.Random;

public class HiddenNuts {

    public static void main(String[] args) {

        String[] hidingSpots = new String[100];
        Random squirrel = new Random();
        hidingSpots[squirrel.nextInt(hidingSpots.length)] = "Nut";
        System.out.println("The nut has been hidden ...");

        // Nut finding code should go here!
    }
}
```

When you run this program, you should see code similar to the following; however, your nuts should end up in different locations!

```
The nut has been hidden ...
Found it! It's in spot# 42
```

Exercise 6: Summative Sums

Write a static method that takes in an array of integers, adds them together, and returns the result. Call your new method inside a main method and print out the results. You can use the following three example arrays with your program:

```
{ 1, 90, -33, -55, 67, -16, 28, -55, 15 }
{ 999, -60, -77, 14, 160, 301 }
{ 10, 20, 30, 40, 50, 60, 70, 80, 90, 100, 110, 120, 130,
140, 150, 160, 170, 180, 190, 200, -99 }
```

Using these three arrays, here is what you should see for results:

```
#1 Array Sum: 42
#2 Array Sum: 1337
#3 Array Sum: 2001
```

PART III

Fundamentals of Classes and Objects

Lesson 14
Object-Oriented Concepts

In this lesson, we are going to look at some general object-oriented concepts. We will explore different ways of abstracting problems, define object orientation (one way to abstract problems), describe the characteristics of an object-oriented language, and discuss the concept of public interface vs. private implementation.

LEARNING OBJECTIVES

By the end of this lesson, you will be able to:

- Differentiate between various types of computer programming languages
- Define the five things that make a language object-oriented
- Explain what a type is and how it is used in Java
- Explain how public interface and private implementation work together
- Describe loose coupling
- Explain the single responsibility principle and cohesion
- Explain the concept of delegation
- Relate delegation to encapsulation

ABSTRACTION

There are many ways to approach a particular problem that you are trying to solve. One approach is to start with the model of the solution space and then attempt to map the problem into it. This is the approach of many languages.

Assembly language closely matches the underlying computer mechanics. If you want to solve a particular problem, you must think in terms of how the computer works first and then figure out how to map the problem into that paradigm. This means that you must think about problems in terms of binary numbers, registers, addition, and subtraction. This requires you to understand how to do things like move data into registers, decrement the value in a register, and use various processor operations. Solving a problem with assembly language requires a thorough knowledge of the actual processor being used.

Functional languages model everything as mathematical functions and immutable data structures. Here, everything is a function that takes inputs and produces values or does work. This means you must think about the problem in terms of mathematical functions, inputs, outputs, and data structures.

Logic programming languages model all problems as relations, facts, and rules. These languages are based on formal logic and require the programmer to map the problem domain into facts and rules in these languages.

Object-oriented languages take a different approach in that they represent concepts in both the solution space and the problem space as objects. Since the real world is essentially full of objects, this is very convenient. Take a car, for example—it can be described as a collection of properties (weight, color, number of doors, etc.) and behaviors (drive, turn, roll up window, turn on radio, etc.). This is how we model objects in an object-oriented language: via properties and behaviors. Less translation is needed to map a car into one of these objects than is needed to map a car into some of the approaches taken by non-object-oriented languages.

OBJECT ORIENTATION

What makes a language object-oriented? Object orientation can be summarized like this:

- Everything is an object.
- A program is just a collection of objects that tell each other what to do by sending messages (in Java's case, these messages are method calls).
- Each object can be made up of or composed of other objects (this is called *composition* in Java).
- Every object has a type.

- All objects of a particular type can receive the same messages (in Java, this means that they all have the same methods).

Grady Booch put it more simply: "An object has state, behavior, and identity."
Let's break this down:

State: This means that the properties of an object have certain values at certain times. For example, a car might have a velocity of 50 miles per hour right now, but 0 miles per hour in 10 seconds. The combination of these values at a given point in time describes the object's state.

Behavior: This means that an object has some capacity to do something. In Java, these capabilities are represented as methods. Many times, these methods change the state of the object.

Identity: Here we are talking about the ability to distinguish one object from another even when the objects are the same type. For example, I can differentiate the shade tree in my front yard from the one in my backyard.

TYPES

Every object in Java has a type. A *type* is a classification that defines the structure and range of values for the type and the associated operations allowed on those values. On the one hand, there are native or intrinsic Java types that we have already learned about such as int, float, and boolean, but we are also free to create our own types in Java. In fact, every time we define a new Java class, we define a new type.

We have also used a few non-native types that are not part of the Java language itself, such as Random and Scanner. In later lessons, we'll look at the details of how to create our own data types and how to create programs that contain several data types cooperating to solve problems.

> **NOTE** While Java is considered an object-oriented language, not everything in Java is an object. As an example, the primitive types such as int, float, and double are not objects.

PUBLIC INTERFACE/PRIVATE IMPLEMENTATION

Every class should have a *public interface* that defines how the outside world can interact with it. Behind this public contact should be a *private implementation*. This allows us to separate "what" an object does from "how" it does it. Calling code (the code from other parts of the program that use the object) should not be concerned with how an object fulfills the contract and should in no way ever rely on the specifics of the implementation (or side effects of a particular implementation) when using the object. The implementer of the object reserves the right to change the implementation details at their discretion.

Let's look at an example from our everyday lives that illustrates why this concept is so important: the fast-food drive-through. The public interface at a drive-through is familiar to all of us. They can vary somewhat, but the basic interface follows four steps. First, there is a menu displaying items and prices; next, there is a speaker where we place our order; next, there is a window where we pay; and finally, there is a window where we get our food. As a customer of the restaurant (and user of drive-through public interface), I have no idea about how my order is processed, how and when the ingredients are delivered, how the food is cooked, or how many cooks are in the kitchen—and frankly, I really don't care. I just want to order my food, pay for it, and enjoy my meal. The restaurant is free to upgrade its ordering system, get new stoves, hire more cooks, or make any other changes to their system, and as long as the drive-through works as it did before and the food tastes the same, I'm a happy customer.

ENCAPSULATION AND DATA HIDING

One way to help facilitate the notion of public interface and private implementation is through *encapsulation* and *data hiding*. Well-designed classes prevent direct access to their properties by calling code (remember, calling code is code from other parts of the program that use the object). Instead, they force this access through getter and setter methods. This prevents the calling code from being aware of the internal details of the object. This allows the internal representation of the properties to change without the knowledge of the calling code. This technique leads to *loose coupling* between the calling code and the object.

SINGLE RESPONSIBILITY PRINCIPLE AND COHESION

A well-designed class has a well-defined area of responsibility. Generally speaking, this means the class does one thing, does it completely, and does it well, so a class is *cohesive* and follows the *single responsibility principle*. The class should fully contain all aspects of its area of responsibility. The public interface of the class must be defined so that its function is crystal clear (even though how it is implemented is hidden).

Let's return to our drive-through example. If the drive-through interface (i.e., the menu, order speaker, payment window, and pickup window) is to be cohesive, it must allow us to do everything involved in ordering, paying for, and picking up our meal. For example, the interface would not be cohesive if at the payment window, I had to get out of my car, walk over to the bank, transfer funds from my account to the restaurant, and then return to my car. On the other hand, the drive-through should be limited to just ordering and paying for food. For example, I shouldn't have the option of renewing my driver's license at the payment window. This is clearly outside the scope of what a fast-food drive-through should do.

Although this is just an example, you can see how cohesive interfaces make sense. These principles apply to objects just as they apply to drive-through restaurants.

DELEGATION

The concept of delegation is complementary to encapsulation. If our class is well-encapsulated, it will only handle tasks that are within its well-defined area of responsibility. If one or more of the tasks within the class's area of responsibility require a subtask that is outside the class's main area of responsibility, the class must *delegate* that task to another class. We have already seen examples of this in our code—we delegate to System.out for writing to the console and to the Scanner object for reading from the console.

For example, a drive-through that does not specialize in baking bread "delegates" this responsibility to a bakery that bakes the buns and delivers them to the restaurant. As the consumer of the restaurant interface, I do not care whether the buns are baked on site or at a bakery and delivered. As long as the buns are fresh, taste good, and have the correct nutritional content, I am a happy customer. The restaurant specializes in putting together the finished hamburger. They delegate things such as baking the buns and processing the meat to other companies.

SUMMARY

This was a quick introduction to some of the big concepts of object-oriented programming. The remaining lessons in this section cover these topics in detail and will set you on the path to becoming an object-oriented programmer.

Creating Classes and Types

I n this lesson, we'll look at how we define and create new types in Java and what comprises these new types.

LEARNING OBJECTIVES

By the end of this lesson, you will be able to:

- Create new types
- Differentiate between classes and objects
- Explain the use of accessors and mutators (or getters and setters)
- Use the dot operator to access object public properties or methods
- Use the `this` keyword
- Instantiate an object
- Invoke a method
- Relate constructors to methods
- Apply the `static` keyword to methods and constants

CREATING NEW TYPES

Every time we define a new class in Java, we are defining a new type. As discussed earlier in the course, there are two categories of data types in Java: primitive types and reference types. New classes fall into the latter category.

Types (classes) in Java simply consist of *fields* (or *properties*) and *behaviors* (or *methods*). Fields and behaviors are sometimes referred to as *members*. You have already used several user-defined types, including Scanner and String.

Listing 15.1 presents a new class called Dog. We could also say that Listing 15.1 is presenting a new type called Dog!

LISTING 15.1

A New Class/Type Called Dog

```java
public class Dog {

    private String name;
    private double weight;

    public String getName() {
        return name;
    }

    public void setName(String name) {
        this.name = name;
    }

    public double getWeight() {
        return weight;
    }

    public void setWeight(double weight) {
        this.weight = weight;
    }

    public void bark() {
        System.out.println("WOOF!");
    }

    public void sit() {
        System.out.println("Sitting...");
    }

}
```

In looking at the Dog class, we can see that it contains a couple of properties and several methods. The properties are name and weight. The methods are getName(), setName(), getWeight(), setWeight(), bark(), and sit().

CLASSES VS. OBJECTS

A *class* is a definition, like the blueprint of a house. A blueprint is a detailed model of a building. It may show you how to build your house, but you can't live in a blueprint. As illustrated in Figure 15.1, you have to build the house, following the plan in the blueprint, before you can move in. Similarly, you must instantiate an object, based on the definition contained in the class, before you can use it.

Figure 15.1 Blueprints versus the actual house

Another way to approach this is to think of a class as an idea and an object as the instantiation of that idea. For example, a class is like the idea of a German shepherd, whereas an object is my German shepherd named Buster. You can pet Buster, but you cannot pet the idea of a German shepherd.

PROPERTIES, ACCESSORS, AND MUTATORS

In the previous lesson, we talked about encapsulation and data hiding. A common technique used to achieve data hiding in Java is the use of *accessors* and *mutators* (these are also known as *getters* and *setters* in Java). Accessors and mutators are simply methods that get and set (respectively) the values of the properties (or fields) on an object.

The process of using getters and setters for a field is to declare the field as private and then create methods that start with get... and set.... For example, the following declares a private field called name:

```
private String name;
```

The getter and setter for name would be public methods that could look like this:

```
public String getName() {
    return name;
}

public void setName(String name) {
    this.name = name;  // we'll talk about 'this' later in this lesson!
}
```

So, why would we go to all the trouble to create these methods when we could simply let clients access and change the values of our class's properties directly? As mentioned, it is desirable for code that uses an object to have no idea how the properties are stored or calculated. This code should just know what each getter and setter does. By doing so, we create self-governing objects. That is, any changes made to the state of the object (changes to properties) are made only by the object's methods.

For example, a Student class might have a property called ID, which represents the student ID. This student ID is typically generated by the school and cannot be changed by anyone else. In this case, it is best to have the ID property as private and then implement a getter to return the ID of the student (and in this case, we can skip implementing a setter for the ID property since we don't want any entity to change it).

DOT OPERATOR

The *dot operator* (.) is used to access visible properties or methods of an object. The dot operator is used for static and nonstatic properties and methods. On the left side of the dot operator is the class name (for static fields and methods) or the variable name of the instance (for nonstatic fields or methods). On the right side of the dot operator is the method or field we want to access.

We have seen many examples of the dot operator.

- `SimpleMath.add(...)`: **Static**
- `System.out.println(...)`: **Static**
- `myDog.bark()`: **Nonstatic**
- `currentStudent.getGradePointAverage()`: **Nonstatic**

this KEYWORD

In Listing 15.1, you saw the use of the this keyword. The this keyword is used to refer to the instance of the class in which the code is currently executing. It is used in conjunction with the dot operator to access properties and methods of the containing class. Optionally, you don't need the this keyword unless there is a name collision. It is common to see the this keyword used in accessors, mutators, and constructors (as with both the Dog and Student examples earlier). Additionally, static methods and variables should not be referred to with the this keyword.

> **NOTE** The this keyword cannot exist outside constructors and instance methods of a class.

METHODS/BEHAVIORS

In addition to properties (and their corresponding getters and setters), classes can have behaviors. The behaviors of a class are implemented as *methods*. As we saw earlier in the course, methods are simply named blocks of code that can be *invoked* (or called) by other code in the program to accomplish some purpose. Methods are always contained inside a class definition—they cannot stand on their own.

In the example shown in Listing 15.1, there were both regular methods—bark() and sit()—and getter/setter methods for the name and weight properties.

If your class is well designed, the methods in the class will match the purpose of the class. In other words, they must be cohesive. For example, in the previous Dog class, it would not make any sense to have a method called meow().

> **NOTE** You might have noticed that the methods on the Dog class are not marked static. Up until this point, we have marked all methods static, so this is something new. Nonstatic methods are known as *instance methods*. We look at object instantiation and how to invoke instance methods on an object later in this lesson. We will also take a detailed look at the static keyword and its use at the end of this lesson.

CONSTRUCTORS

A *constructor* is a special method that is called when you create an instance of your class. Constructors are usually used to initialize the properties of a newly instantiated (*newly created*) object. Although constructors are methods, there are some special rules that must be followed when creating a constructor.

- A constructor must have the same name as the class that it is a part of. For example, the constructor for a class called Dog would be Dog().
- Constructors never have a return type, not even void.
- Constructors can have parameters but don't have to.
- There can be more than one constructor in a given class.
- You don't have to create a constructor for your class as long as the superclass has no-arg constructors. If you don't create one, the compiler will supply one called the *default constructor*. The default constructor has no parameters and appears to have an empty method body. Such a constructor is the default constructor whether you write it or the compiler provides it.

Let's take another look at the Dog class, as shown in Listing 15.2. This time with a default constructor and one that takes name and weight parameters.

LISTING 15.2

The Dog Class with Constructors Included

```java
public class Dog {

    private String name;
    private double weight;

    public Dog() {

    }

    public Dog(String nameIn, double weightIn) {
        this.name = nameIn;
        this.weight = weightIn;
    }

    public String getName() {
        return name;
    }

    public void setName(String name) {
        this.name = name;
    }
```

```
    public double getWeight() {
        return weight;
    }

    public void setWeight(double weight) {
        this.weight = weight;
    }

    public void bark() {
        System.out.println("WOOF!");
    }

    public void sit() {
        System.out.println("Sitting...");
    }

}
```

OBJECT INSTANTIATION AND METHOD INVOCATION

Because the Dog class in Listing 15.2 has two constructors, we now have two options for creating a new Dog object. We can create a Dog using the default constructor that we wrote (i.e., the one that has no arguments), or we can use the constructor that has two parameters.

First, let's look at creating a Dog object using its default constructor. We will start by creating a class called App. We will include a main method from which we'll instantiate our Dog object.

```
public class App {

    public static void main(String[] args) {

        Dog myDog = new Dog();

    }
}
```

If no values are explicitly set on the fields of a class when it is instantiated, the fields get initialized to their default values: null for reference types, 0 for primitive numbers, and false for booleans. Since we used the constructor with no arguments, the fields in our new Dog (myDog) were initialized to their default values: null for name and 0.0 for weight.

To set values for name and weight, we must invoke the setter methods for these two properties. As mentioned, we do this with the dot operator:

```
public class App {

    public static void main(String[] args) {

        Dog myDog = new Dog();
        myDog.setName("Spot");
        myDog.setWeight(34.0);

    }
}
```

Now myDog has the name Spot and weighs 34 pounds.

Because we have the second constructor, we can create a new Dog with values of our choosing for name and weight when we instantiate the object, as in the following example:

```
public class App {

    public static void main(String[] args) {

        Dog anotherDog = new Dog("Buster", 23.5);

    }
}
```

The variable anotherDog is instantiated with the name Buster and a weight of 23.5 pounds.

> **NOTE** To recap, if we have variables of local scope, then we must initialize them before they can be used, and we must do that ourselves. But when we instantiate a class, any of the fields in the class that are not initialized in the constructor will get their default values. For all primitive types, that means the numbers go to 0 and booleans go to false. Reference types get initialized to null.

static KEYWORD

Now that we know a little bit more about classes and objects, let's revisit the static keyword to learn where and when it is appropriate to use it for fields and methods. First, let's look at some facts about the static keyword.

- *If a field or method is marked as static, it means that it is associated with the class and not with any particular instantiation of the class.* This means that there is only ever one copy of a field or method that is marked static. This one copy exists whether zero or 97 instances of the class are created. For example, if name on our Dog class were static, all Dog objects would share the same name.

- *Static fields and methods can be accessed without creating an instance of the class.* This follows from the previous item. The one and only copy of a static field or method exists even if no instances of the class have been instantiated.

- *Nonstatic properties and methods are associated with a particular instance of the class, which means that they are accessible only through that particular instance of that object.* This also means that nonstatic fields and methods do not exist until one or more instances of the class have been created.

Given this curious set of properties, when is it appropriate or desirable to mark a method or property static? There are four common use cases for the static keyword:

- Main method
- Constant values
- Utility methods
- Factory pattern

static and the Main Method

We have seen this example of the static keyword from the first program we wrote: HelloWorld. The main method is the *entry point* of our program—this is where the program kicks off. Since this is the first thing that is going to be run in the program (even before any objects are instantiated), it has to be static. There is no way for the JVM to create our object and then call main—where would that code live? Instead, the JVM locates our class and then calls main to begin execution.

static and Constant Values

Constants are another place where it is appropriate to use the static keyword. We can define a constant value (for example, a constant for the value of pi) as a static field on a class. This means that there will only ever be one copy of that constant in our program. The value can't be changed, so there is no reason to have a copy of the value associated with every instance of the class. The example in Listing 15.3 shows what this looks like.

static **and Utility Methods**

Utility methods such as those performing math operations are great candidates for using the static keyword. Methods that are marked static must not attempt to change the state of the class with which they are associated. Again, math operations are perfect examples of this. They take inputs, operate on those inputs, and produce outputs. In fact, all the methods and constants on the Math class in Java are marked static.

Listing 15.3 is a simple class that shows what a static constant and static methods look like.

LISTING 15.3

Using Static Contants and Methods

```
public class SimpleMath {

    public static final double PI = 3.14;
    public static int add(int a, int b) {
        return a + b;
    }

    public static int subtract(int a, int b) {
        return a - b;
    }
}
```

As you can see, we have declared PI as a public static final double field, and we have two methods, add() and subtract(), that are also marked static.

We have discussed why marking these fields and methods as static makes sense, but we haven't discussed how this will affect how other code interacts with this field and these methods. Marking these members static means that we can access them without first instantiating an instance of the SimpleMath class. In some occurrences, we must first instantiate an object before we can access its methods. One example is Scanner, which requires that we declare and instantiate a Scanner before we can call a method on our new instance, like this:

```
Scanner myScanner = new Scanner(System.in);
myScanner.nextLine();
```

When using static methods or fields, we do not have to first instantiate the object; we can use it directly from the class. This is because static members are associated with the class itself, rather than with a particular instantiation of the class.

```
SimpleMath.add(5, 3);
```

PULLING IT ALL TOGETHER

A lot has been covered in this lesson, so let's step back and use NetBeans to walk through creating a simple project to create an application and a separate class. The application we create will be called Adder and will have static constants and methods. We will walk through NetBeans and see a feature or two that it provides to help us pull this together.

Create a new application in NetBeans. In NetBeans, select File ➢ New Project to open the New Project dialog. Just as we suggested in the first part of this course, select Maven as the category and Java Application for Projects. Then click the *Next* button.

In the New Java Application dialog, give the project a name. We can use the name *ObjectInstantiation* since we will be creating an object. We can leave the rest of the values and click the *Finish* button to create our project.

Within the project now displayed, right-click the package name and select New ➢ Java Class, as shown in Figure 15.2, to create a new class.

Give the class a name of App. Giving your first class the name of App is a pattern you can use throughout the rest of this book as you create applications with multiple classes. The App class will be the one that holds your main method. For other classes that are created, we will name them based on what they do. With our App class created, our project should look similar to Figure 15.3.

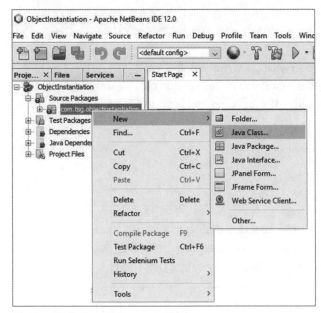

Figure 15.2 Creating a new class

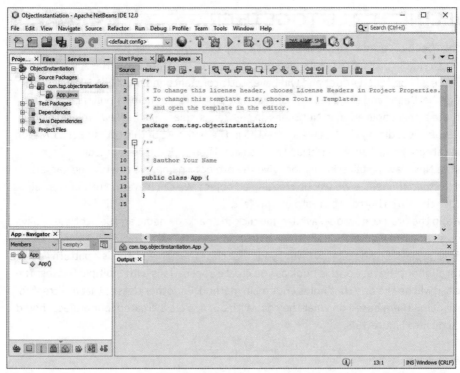

Figure 15.3 Our App class in NetBeans

We'll set up our App class similar to what we've been doing. We'll start by creating a main method. Since we are using NetBeans, you can use a shortcut to enter the declaration for main. Type **psvm** on a line within the App class and press the Tab key. This should expand out to the following:

```
public static void main(String[] args) {

}
```

> **NOTE** A program is nothing but objects sending messages back and forth cooperating with each other to solve a task. In Java, the way that we send those messages back and forth is by calling methods.

Creating a New Class

With our main method in place, we are ready to add some functionality to our program. We are going to create a new class that will provide some math functionality. To keep it simple, our new class will start with just a single method for adding two numbers. To add the new class, once again right-click our class's package name and select New ➢ Java Class (as shown in Figure 15.2). This time call the new class Adder, since our class will be adding numbers. The new class should be displayed in NetBeans similar to what is in Figure 15.4.

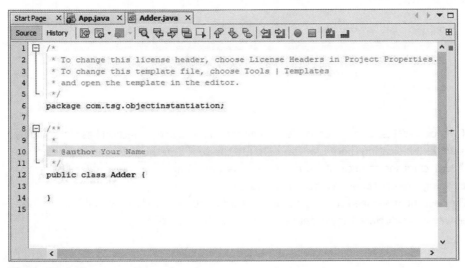

Figure 15.4 The new Adder class

Within this class, we are going to add an add() method that will be used to simply add two integers and return the result. The code to add to your Adder class is as follows:

```
public int add(int a, int b) {
    return a + b;
}
```

It is worth noting that our Adder class does not have a main method. As we have mentioned before, we need only one main method in our program, and we've already set that up within our App class.

With this add() method added to the Adder class, click the tab to pull up the code for your App.java class. Within the main method of our App class, we want to call our add() method. What we had done in the past with a method was to simply call it and save the value returned. We generally would then print out the value. Code to do this would look something like Listing 15.4.

> **TIP** Another NetBeans shortcut is that you can type sout on a new line and press tab. This will expand to System.out.println("");.

LISTING 15.4

App Code to Add Two Numbers

```
public class App {

    public static void main(String[] args) {

        int sum = add(5, 4);
        System.out.println("The sum is " + sum);
    }
}
```

If we look at this code in NetBeans, we will see that the add() method has red squiggly lines under it indicating there is an issue. To use the add() method, we need to instantiate the Adder class and then call it from our main method. That means our code in Listing 15.4 is not going to work for us. We need to replace it.

The first thing we need to do is get an instance of our Adder class. We will do this the same way we've declared any other variable, but with a type of Adder.

```
Adder myAdder = new Adder();
```

We have seen declarations like this in the past. When we created scanners and some other things, we did it this same way. In this case, Adder is a user-defined type that we created.

Let's take a look at this code a little bit. The first part should be familiar in that we have the type, Adder, and the name of the variable, myAdder, that will hold our object of this type. We are then setting our variable equal to a new Adder object by calling new and the Adder constructor, Adder(). If you recall, the only method we put in our Adder class was the add() method. We did not supply a constructor in Adder. So, the compiler will actually supply a constructor for us that has no arguments.

> **NOTE** What we're doing is telling the Java Runtime to create a new object based on this Adder template and hand this back a reference.

Now that we have a reference, we can get to the add() method. Within our main method, we can now define an integer to hold our sum and then use our object. Update the App code to look like Listing 15.5.

LISTING 15.5

Creating an Adder Object

```java
public class App {

    public static void main(String[] args) {

        Adder myAdder = new Adder();

        int sum = myAdder.add(4, 5);
        System.out.println("The sum is " + sum);
    }
}
```

You can see that our declaration has been added; then in the following line we create the sum variable to hold the result of adding two numbers using the myAdder object we created. When you enter this code in NetBeans, you will notice that after typing myAdder and then the dot, as such:

```java
int sum = myAdder.
```

NetBeans will pop up a dialog similar to Figure 15.5. This is a dialog that shows all the methods the myAdder object contains.

You might notice that there are all kinds of other items such as methods listed in addition to our add( ) method. For now, just ignore this stuff. We will cover it in more detail when we talk about inheritance in a later lesson. For now, you can either continue typing or simply select the add( ) method from the list.

Go ahead and pass 4 and 5 to the add( ) method, as shown in Listing 15.5. With the listing completed, run the program. You should see that the add( ) method works and our output is shown as follows:

```
The sum is: 9
```

At this point, we've created a new class (type), created an instance, and used it in our listing to call a method in that class. But we aren't done.

> **NOTE** What is happening behind the scenes is that the App class is passing messages to the Adder class. Specifically, it is passing a 4 and a 5 to a method in the Adder class. The Adder class then has a method that is returning a message to the App class with the result of 9.

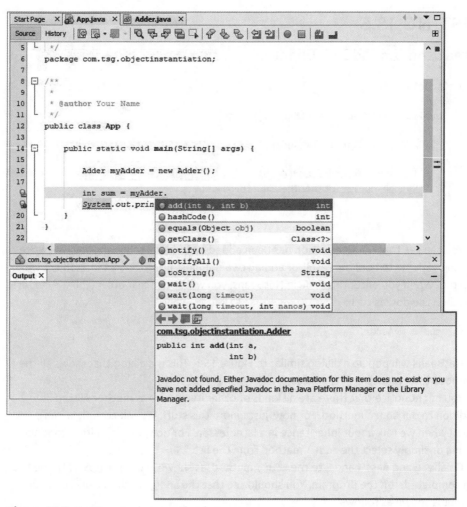

Figure 15.5 NetBeans class method pop-up

> **NOTE** In a program that has more than one class, only one of the classes will have a main method. We recommend you call the class with the main method App.

Going Static

With our Adder class in place, what would happen if we added the static keyword to the add() method we created? It is worth backing up a little bit and talking about a couple of things related to static.

One of the things we said earlier was that the `static` keyword could be used to associate a method or field with the class instead of with a particular object created from the class. In Listing 15.5, we did not use the `static` keyword with the add( ) method, so to use the method, we had to instantiate a new `Adder` class to create a reference.

The `static` keyword associates the add( ) method with the class. What that means is that we don't have to instantiate the `Adder` class; this method just exists when our program starts up. Let's change the code in our `Adder` class to include the `static` keyword. Your new method should look like this:

```
public static int add( int a, int b) {
    return a + b;
}
```

There is something within NetBeans worth noting at this point. As you can see in Figure 15.6, when we added the `static` keyword into the listing, NetBeans changed add to be italicized. This lets us easily identify static methods because they are italicized.

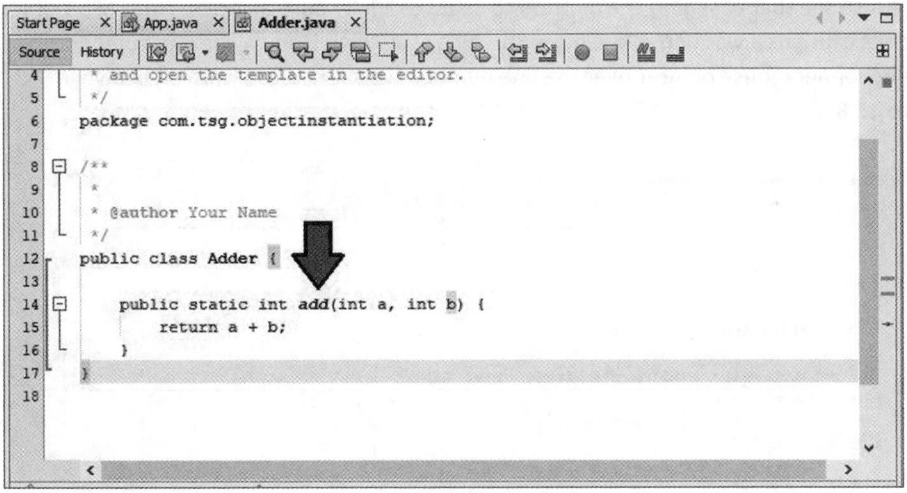

Figure 15.6 NetBeans italicizes static method names.

With `static` added to our add( ) method, we can look back at the App class in NetBeans. There are a couple things that have changed in NetBeans in this class.

First, in Figure 15.7, we can see that the call to the add class is now italicized in the App class as well. This again indicates that the class is static.

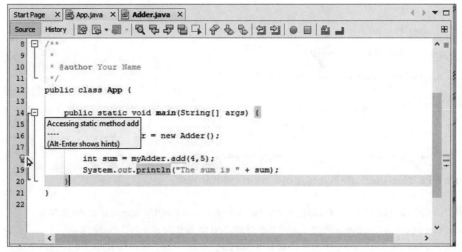

Figure 15.7 Back in the App class after making add( ) static

We also see that changing the method to static didn't cause an error in our App class but does cause us a warning. We can see this by the warning icon on the line number. If we hover our mouse pointer over the line number, we will see the warning shown in Figure 15.8.

Figure 15.8 Accessing static method warning

The warning is telling us that we are accessing a static method while using an instance of the class. What we've done is instantiate Adder to create a specific instance; then we've called add( ) on that particular instance. Doing this no longer makes sense because add( ) is a static method. In this case, we don't need to define an instance. We can make a couple of changes to our Adder class in Listing 15.5.

First, we no longer need to declare an instance. As such, we can remove the following line:

```
Adder myAdder = new Adder();
```

Because we no longer have myAdder, we need to also change the code line that follows. As you learned earlier in the "static KEYWORD" section, we know the static method is associated with the class, not any instance of the class. So, instead of putting the name of a variable of type Adder, we put the class name.

```
int sum = Adder.add(4, 5);
```

Listing 15.6 shows the resulting updated code for the App class.

LISTING 15.6

Updated App Class Using static Method in Adder

```
public class App {

    public static void main(String[] args) {

        int sum = Adder.add(4, 5);
        System.out.println("The sum is " + sum);
    }
}
```

When you run the updated listing, you should get the output showing that the sum still results in 9, as shown in Figure 15.9.

When to Go Static

So, the real question is, why would we use something like this, right? Why don't we make everything static? Why are some things instance variables whereas some things aren't?

There are a couple of cases where static is necessary. One place where it is necessary is on our main method. All our main methods have to be static.

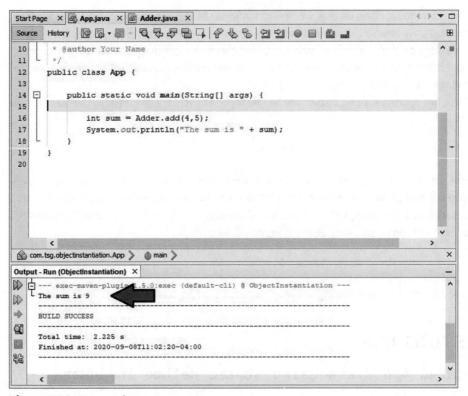

Figure 15.9 Output from our app

The other place where static methods are really good is when we have constants. With constants we don't really need multiple copies. For example, we would need only one copy of a constant such as PI. In fact, if we wanted, we could put a constant for PI into our Adder class. To do that, we could add an additional line of code to our Adder class, as shown in Listing 15.7.

LISTING 15.7

Our Adder Class with Static PI Added

```
public class Adder {

    public static final double PI = 3.14;

    public static int add(int a, int b) {
```

```
        return a + b;
    }
}
```

With the additional line of code, our `Adder` class now has a constant static value for PI that we can use. We could then use PI from other places by just calling `Adder.PI`.

Existing Static Methods

As we just saw in our example, constants make great static values. Methods that take consistent input and always return the same output are also good candidates for static. For example, if we give our `add()` method the same two inputs, it always gives us the same output no matter what. It doesn't matter how many times we call it, we get the same results. The method is not really keeping track of any state. It just takes the inputs, computes the output, and gives it back. Methods like this are great candidates for the `static` keyword.

As Java developers, we can put these types of static methods together in classes, and those classes can be a library of classes. In fact, one such library of classes already exists called the `Math` class.

The `Math` class provides a variety of uses including calculating sine, cosine, tangent, or arctangent. It also has functions such as `abs()` for calculating the absolute value as well as a number of defined constants, such as E and PI.

To see what is available in the `Math` class, within your `App` class, you can type `Math.` (`Math` followed by a dot) and get a pop-up similar to what you saw earlier with `Adder`. Figure 15.10 shows part of the list of items you can access.

These math functions can be used without the need to instantiate a `Math` object; we can use just these functions. We don't have to write them ourselves, and we don't have to instantiate an object.

SUMMARY

In this lesson, we took a closer look at what makes up a class, how to define new types, some of the properties of constructors, how to instantiate objects, and when and where to use the `static` keyword. These are all important tools that will help us create well-designed object-oriented software. In the next lesson, we'll look at how the JVM manages all of these objects in memory.

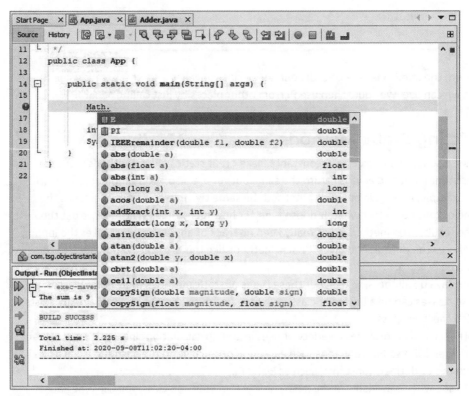

Figure 15.10 The Math class

EXERCISES

The following are additional coding exercises to help you practice what you are learning about the Java programming language. These are to do on your own, so most will not always include answers. Many of the exercises cover accepting user input via Scanner. There are several exercises for you to apply what you learned in this lesson:

Exercise 1: Class Modeling

Exercise 2: Refactoring

Exercise 3: A Multiclass Problem

Exercise 1: Class Modeling

Create a new NetBeans project called ClassModeling. You are given two different scenarios for modeling each of these real-world objects. Consider the important properties and methods needed for each scenario and each model and then create a Java class for each of the following:

- House
  - Model a house as if the class were to be part of a GPS mapping system.
  - Model a house as if the class were to be part of a 3D design system.
- Airplane
  - Model an airplane as if the class were to be part of an air traffic control system.
  - Model an airplane as if the class were to be part of a flight simulator.
- Car
  - Model a car as if the class were to be part of an inventory system for a car dealership.
  - Model a car as if the class were to be part of a video game.
- Ice cream
  - Model ice cream as if the class were to be part of the control system at the dairy that makes the ice cream.
  - Model ice cream as if the class were to be part of the stocking system at a grocery store.
- Book
  - Model a book as if the class were to be part of a publishing system that the author uses to write the book.
  - Model a book as if the class were to be part of a library cataloging system.

Do the following for each class:

- Define properties, determining which will be read/write and which will be read-only.
- Implement setters and getters (as appropriate) for each property.

- Implement a constructor to initialize some or all of the property values.

- Determine what behaviors the class should have and then define (do not implement) the methods associated with each behavior.

Exercise 2: Refactoring

So far, all the code that we've written in previous lessons has resided in one class. The objective of this exercise is to practice modeling and packaging code into classes and to instantiate and call methods on a class from another class.

In this exercise, you will refactor code you wrote in previous exercises from previous lessons. Move all the code for each lab into a new class with no main method. Write code for the main method in a separate class that instantiates your new class and executes a method that runs the program.

Refactor the following exercises:

- Lesson 7: Birthstones

- Lesson 10: Opinionator

- Lesson 10: Coin Flipper

- Lesson 10: Guess Me More

- Lesson 12: Method to Madness

Use the following example as a pattern for refactoring your labs. In the example, a HelloWorld program is refactored so that it consists of two classes instead of just one. Here is the original program:

```
public class HelloWorld {

    public static void main(String[] args) {
        System.out.println("Hello, World!");
    }
}
```

The first step in refactoring the program is to move the functionality that is currently contained in the main method to a new nonstatic method. We'll call the new method sayHello:

```
public class HelloWorld {

    public static void main(String[] args) {

    }
```

```
    public void sayHello() {
        System.out.println("Hello, World!");
    }
}
```

Next, we'll remove the main method from the `HelloWorld` class:

```
public class HelloWorld {

    public void sayHello() {
        System.out.println("Hello, World!");
    }
}
```

The `HelloWorld` class is now how we want it to be, but we are left with a problem: our program no longer has a class with a main method in it, so there is no way to run it. The next step is to create a new class called `App` and to implement a main method within that class.

```
public class App {

    public static void main(String[] args) {

    }
}
```

This is okay; our program will now run, but it won't do anything because the main method is empty. The final step in refactoring our program is to add code to `main` that instantiates a `HelloWorld` object and then calls the `sayHello()` method,

```
public class App {

    public static void main(String[] args) {

        HelloWorld myHelloWorld = new HelloWorld();
        myHelloWorld.sayHello();

    }
}
```

The refactoring is now complete.

Exercise 3: A Multiclass Problem

The objective of this exercise is to practice designing and implementing programs that have more than one class.

- Design a class (no main method) called `SimpleCalculator` that performs basic math operations (addition, subtraction, multiplication, division) on two operands.

- Create another class called `App` that presents a simple console calculator UI to the user. This second class should handle all user input and console output and must use the first class to perform all the math operations.

  - The UI should give the user a choice of operations. One of the choices should be to exit the program.

  - After the user selects an operation, the UI should ask the user for two operands and then display the result of the calculation.

  - The UI should then display the menu of choices again.

  - When the user chooses to exit the program, the UI should print a thank-you message.

- Before coding, create a flowchart for your program.

Managing Storage and Memory

In this lesson, we'll look at how and where data is stored and managed in memory and how objects are referenced.

LEARNING OBJECTIVES

By the end of this lesson, you will be able to:

- Compare and contrast stack and heap memory in a running program
- Explain object references
- Explain how the new keyword works with constructors to create objects in memory
- Compare and contrast manual memory management and garbage collection
- Explain why Java is a pass-by-value language

PROGRAMS AND MEMORY

When your program is running, its data must be stored in memory. There are two main areas of memory that the JVM uses to store the data associated with our programs: the stack and the heap. As our program runs, each method (including main) gets some memory on the stack. The memory that each method gets is called a *stack frame*. Any new object created by our program will get some memory on the heap. We'll look at the details of what ends up on the stack and heap and why things end up on one or the other in this lesson.

The Stack

The *stack* is a memory structure that is managed by the JVM. The stack is a last-in, first-out (LIFO) data structure. In a stack data structure, new items are added to the top—this is known as *pushing* the item onto the stack. Items are also removed from the top of the stack—this is known as *popping* the item off the stack. This means that the last thing we pushed onto the stack will be the first thing to get popped off, which is why this data structure is described as last-in, first-out.

For a visual reference, think of the stack of plates at a restaurant buffet. As the plates are added, they pile up on the previously added plates, as shown in Figure 16.1. When you get to the buffet, you take the plate that is on top, which was the last one that was added.

Figure 16.1 A stack in programming is like a stack of plates

Rather than adding plates to a stack at the buffet, the JVM adds a stack frame for each method that gets executed in the program. The first stack frame for our program always contains the information for our main method.

The stack frame contains the following information:

- Values of all primitive type variables declared in the method
- The heap location of any nonprimitive types declared in the method
- Values of the parameters passed into the method
- JVM bookkeeping information about the method

The good news is that the JVM takes care of all the stack manipulation, so we do not have to do anything with it in our code. However, the workings of the stack and heap are common interview questions. In addition, knowing the basic functionality is a foundation for learning more advanced concepts and will give you a better understanding of how programs interact with the JVM and operating system and how code can be optimized.

Let's take a look at an example. Consider the following method:

```
public void method(int parameter) {
    int x = 5;
    int y = parameter;
}
```

Now let's suppose we call this method with a parameter of 10, like this:

```
method(10);
```

Here we have a method that takes an `int` parameter and then creates two more integers. The calling code invokes the method, passing a value of 10 to the `parameter` variable. Because these are primitive types, the data and the variable name are stored on the stack. The `method()` entry on the stack represents the bookkeeping information the JVM needs to keep track of the execution environment. The four values beneath the `Stack` label in Figure 16.2 represent the stack frame for `method()`.

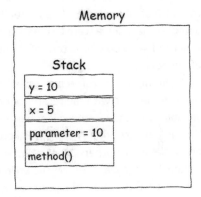

Figure 16.2 The stack once `method(10)` is called

When `method()` is done executing, the memory on the stack will be popped off it, which will cause `y`, `x`, `parameter`, and `method()` to be deleted from memory.

If `method()` is invoked again later in the program, the JVM will build a new stack frame and push it onto the stack. In this case, for primitive types such as `int`, notice that the data value is physically copied to the new memory space. If we were to change the value of `parameter`, it would not affect the value of `y` because `y` and `parameter` are contained in two separate memory spaces in the stack frame.

The Heap

The *heap* is an area where chunks of memory are allocated to store reference types. Unlike the stack, things can be removed from and added to the heap in any order. Whereas the items on the stack, particularly primitive types, are stored in a single segment of memory, the heap requires two segments of memory.

- On the heap is the actual data, which is some type of object.

- On the stack is a pointer to the actual data. The value of this pointer is the address location in memory where the data on the heap can be found.

This concept can be confusing to the beginning developer: why not have only a stack? The main reason is efficiency. While a simple type, such as int, only requires a single piece of data, we have already seen that classes can contain many members and different pieces of data.

When we pass something small, like an int, between methods, it is fine to just make a copy of that data, but what if you had a customer object that also contained invoice history and other pieces of information? What if you had a list of all the customer objects in the state of Ohio? You could potentially have tens of thousands of pieces of data inside a single object. If we were to create a complete copy of all this data every time we called a method, we would have tens of thousands more calls, and our computer could run out of memory.

So, in the case of reference types such as classes, it is more efficient to store the object once on the heap with the reference on the stack. When you pass a class object to another variable, only the reference is copied—not the object itself. Thus, all variables that point to the same object on the heap are linked. So, if you make a change to the heap object using one variable, the others, being pointers to the same object, also "see" the update.

Consider the class Person shown in Listing 16.1. It has two data fields, name and age. This class will be a blueprint to create as many Person objects as we may need in our program.

LISTING 16.1

A Simple Person Class

```
public class Person {
    private String name;
    private int age;

    public String getName() {
        return name;
    }
```

```
public void setName(String name) {
    this.name = name;
}

public int getAge() {
    return age;
}

public void setAge(int age) {
    this.age = age;
}
}
```

Let's go ahead and create one:

```
Person p = new Person();
```

We have already discussed constructors a bit, and we saw that they are just special methods that are called when we create new objects of a type. When the new keyword and one of the constructors of a class are used together, the JVM creates a new object of that particular type on the heap and hands us back a reference to this object. Because name and age are fields, they will be auto-initialized. name is a String, which is not a primitive type, so it will receive a null value. age is an int, which has a default value of 0.

Right now, the stack and heap look like what is shown in Figure 16.3.

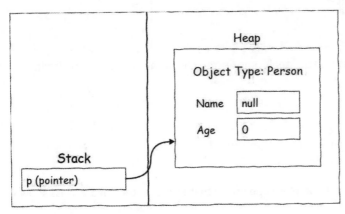

Figure 16.3 The stack and heap with a constructed Person

The variable p is simply a reference to the actual Person object on the heap. The value stored in p is the heap location of the newly created Person object.

Now, what happens if we were to define a second variable and assign the value of p to it like this:

```
Person p2 = p;
```

In this case, the JVM would only copy the pointer; it would not create a second object on the heap. After the statement is executed, the stack would look like what is shown in Figure 16.4. Notice that p and p2 point to the same Person object on the heap.

At this point, if we were to assign a value to name using the p variable and a value to age using the p2 variable, because they are pointing to one single object, they would both see the data updates, as shown in Figure 16.4.

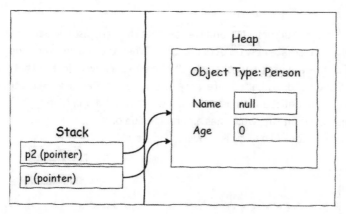

Figure 16.4 Two variables on the stack pointing to the same object on the heap

```
p.setName("Mary");
p2.setAge(19);

System.out.println(p.getAge()); // prints 19
System.out.println(p2.getName()); // prints Mary
```

Listing 16.2 adds this code to a complete app listing that also uses the Person class shown in Listing 16.2.

LISTING 16.2

Modifying Data on the Heap

```java
public class App {
    public static void main(String[] args) {

    Person p = new Person();
    Person p2 = p;

    p.setName("Mary");
    p2.setAge(19);

    System.out.println("Person p: ");
    System.out.println(p.getAge());
    System.out.println(p.getName());

    System.out.println("Person p2: ");
    System.out.println(p2.getAge());
    System.out.println(p2.getName());
    }
}
```

If you look at this listing, you can see that a name is added to p, but not an age. Similarly, an age was added to p2, but not a name. When the code is executed, the output confirms that the information was changed in both (see Figure 16.5).

```
Person p:
19
Mary
Person p2:
19
Mary
```

To recap, the difference between user-defined (reference) types and primitive types can be summarized as follows:

- Primitive types are stored on the stack. When data is passed by value, a copy of the data is made, such that changes to the value do not affect the other copies.

- User-defined types are stored on the heap with only a reference stored on the stack. When a reference is passed to a method, a copy of the reference is made. This means the object on the heap now has one more reference pointing to it and that changes to the data made through any reference to that object are seen by all other references to that object.

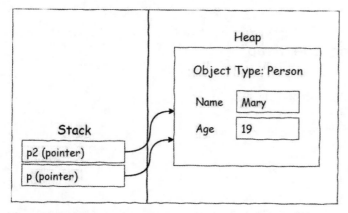

Figure 16.5 The stack and heap after the update

It is worth remembering that Java is a *pass-by-value language*. This means that a copy is made of any value passed into a method. In the case of primitive types, the actual value of the variable (for example, 5 if the variable is an `int`) is copied into a new memory location on the stack. In the case of user-defined types, a copy of the reference value is made and stored into a new memory location on the stack.

> **NOTE** While knowing how the stack and heap work doesn't really get used in your day-to-day job, knowing how memory allocation works and how the stack and heap do their jobs is something that can come up in an interview for Java programmers.

GARBAGE COLLECTION

As we have discussed, Java is a managed language. This means that the programmer is not responsible for allocating and releasing memory manually. In Java, we simply create objects and/or native data types as we need them in our programs, and the JVM takes care of releasing all memory as appropriate. As discussed previously, all memory allocated on the stack is automatically released when a method completes, and its associated stack frame is destroyed.

Memory used by objects on the heap is eligible for garbage collection when there are no more references to the object. We can explicitly take a reference away from an object on the heap by setting the reference to null. Because the reference variables are stored on the stack, they will go away when their respective stack frames go away (i.e., when their enclosing method returns), which also removes the references from the object to which they point. This process is called *garbage collection*, and the component responsible for doing this is called the *garbage collector*. Periodically, the garbage collector will sift through the objects on the heap and check to see whether they are still being referenced on the stack. If they are not, they will be marked for cleanup and might be removed from memory.

Garbage collection is one of the key features of managed languages and is a reason why you would choose a language like Java or C# over, say, C++. In unmanaged languages, the developer is responsible for managing memory allocation and deallocation (deletion). If a developer fails to do this properly, it can cause significant issues such as memory corruption, application crashes, and memory leaks. A memory leak occurs when objects continue to be added to memory but not properly cleaned up.

Potential Interview Question

What are some reasons you would choose a managed language like Java or C# over an unmanaged language like C++?

REFERENCE AND NULL VALUES

It is important to look at objects a little more closely to fully understand how they are initialized and used. Understanding this can help prevent possible errors in your code.

As mentioned earlier, primitive data types are considered value types. When created, they are given default values. We learned that numerical values default to zero and booleans to false. When using user-defined types, which we've referred to as reference types as well, default values are set to null. Let's take a look at Listing 16.3, which is a new App class that uses the Person class we created earlier.

LISTING 16.3

Defaulting References to Null

```
public class App {

    public static void main(String[] args) {

        Person person = new Person();
        person.setAge(35);

        System.out.println("Age = " + person.getAge());
```

```
        System.out.println("Name = " + person.getName());
    }
}
```

There is not a lot happening in this listing. It creates a Person object using the default constructor and then sets the age to 35. The name within the Person object is not set to a value, so it is left to the default. If you look at the following output from the listing, you see that the default for name is null:

```
Age = 35
Name = null
```

With initialization, all user-defined types get a value of null. You see this in the Person class here. It is also true of other reference types such as String.

What is null? It is a special value in Java that indicates we have a user-defined type that is not associated to any object on the heap. So, we have an object, but it's not pointing to anything.

What happens if we set our object to null, as shown in Listing 16.4?

LISTING 16.4

Setting an Object to Null: Error Alert!

```
public class App {

    public static void main(String[] args) {

        Person person = new Person();
        person.setAge(35);
        person.setName("Eric");

        person = null;

        System.out.println("Age = " + person.getAge());
        System.out.println("Name = " + person.getName());
    }
}
```

You can see in Listing 16.4 that we are still instantiating our person object on the heap. We then initialize both the age and name in our person object this time. We then decide we no longer want this person object, so we set person to null, thus removing its reference from the object. In short, person no longer points to anything.

What is the impact of this on our program? The program will compile; however, when you try to run it, things go wrong.

```
Exception in thread "main" java.lang.NullPointerException
        at App.main(App.java:21)
```

We are now getting an error. As you can see, the program says we have an exception in the main thread. The type of the exception is a `NullPointerException`.

In Java a `NullPointerException` is an error in the code. If we have a reference to a person object, it is an error to try to operate on it if it's not actually pointing to something on the heap. It's a reference, so it needs to reference something.

A good analogy as to what is happening is a television remote control. Having a reference variable that points to nothing (null) is in a lot of ways like having a remote control, but not having the television. You can press the buttons on the remote, but nothing is going to happen, because there is no television associated to it.

In our code, we create an object that is pointing to a `Person` object on the heap, and everything is fine. When we assign `null` to person, it is like we removed the TV and now just have the remote, which is useless.

What we have learned is that if we try to operate on a reference to an object that's null, we are going to get a `NullPointerException`. The way to fix this is to make sure that we have instantiated our reference and that we are pointing to a real object on the heap.

> **NOTE** You will learn about handling exceptions like `NullPointerException` in your code using error handling. This will be covered in Lesson 23.

SUMMARY

It is impossible to build any sort of significant application without using variables. Understanding the types of variables, how they are managed in memory, and the scope in which their data is available is a key foundation that must be understood before learning more complicated topics.

Memory management is handled automatically in the majority of Java programming, but understanding how it works will make you a better developer and better at optimizing code for performance. Memory management, although not a typical focus in day-to-day coding, is a popular topic in software developer job interviews, so you should work to gain confidence in describing its workings with examples before interviewing.

This lesson wrapped up discussing how reference types default to null and how you can get a `NullPointerException` if your reference type does not point to an object on the heap.

Lesson 17

Exploring Interfaces, Composition, and Inheritance

In this lesson, we will overview three more language features that help us write good software: interfaces, composition, and inheritance.

Proper use of these features can help us create well-designed object-oriented programs, and you will use them throughout your career. In this lesson, we discuss each of these features and look at the kinds of problems each can address. Think of this lesson as your guide to what these features are and why and when to use them. The implementation details of each of these features will be covered in more detail in the next few lessons as well as throughout the rest of the course. We will learn where these tools are appropriate and how to use them in projects. For now, just concentrate on the big concepts associated with each of these features.

LEARNING OBJECTIVES:

By the end of this lesson, you will be able to:

- Explain how interfaces, composition, and inheritance help you write code
- Explain how interfaces work with classes to implement capabilities in the classes' methods
- Explain how composition and inheritance work together for code reuse
- Determine when to use an interface, composition, and/or inheritance within code

HOW DO THESE TOOLS HELP?

Interfaces, composition, and inheritance can help us write better, more maintainable software by doing the following:

- Allowing us to control how other code interacts with our objects
- Allowing us to define relationships between the objects in our programs
- Helping us keep our implementations private
- Helping us integrate code from several teams or vendors
- Allowing us to develop different pieces of large applications in a distributed manner
- Helping us to follow the Don't Repeat Yourself (DRY) principle

None of these language features is a "silver bullet"; they each have an appropriate time and place. Part of becoming a good software developer involves developing good judgment to know where and when a particular feature or technique is or isn't appropriate; this good judgment comes with practice. You will have plenty of practice (and guidance from us) with these concepts throughout the rest of this course.

INTERFACES

Java developers use the term *interface* in at least two different ways. We used this term earlier in a general or conceptual way to describe the capabilities that a class advertises or makes available to other code: the public interface versus the private implementation. In this lesson, we introduce a more specific use of the term. Here, *interface* refers to a specific feature of the Java language.

You can think of a Java *interface* as a contract. We can create Java classes that promise to implement (or fulfill) all the capabilities described in the interface. In practical terms, a Java interface is a list of methods that must be implemented by any class that claims to fulfill that interface. An introduction to what this looks like in code will be covered in a specific interface write-up in Lesson 18. Additionally, interfaces will be covered throughout the course as we apply them in listings and exercises.

Interfaces are good at expressing a loosely coupled, contract-based relationship. These types of relationships are especially good at enabling interoperability, and they give us a mechanism to protect our private implementation. Contract-based relationships are also useful in helping to integrate code from different teams or vendors. Once everyone agrees on the interface, each team is free to develop their private implementations in any way they want without affecting other parts of the program.

Let's look at an example where an interface is used to enable interoperability and integration. Suppose that we are on a team that works for a car company. We have expertise in building cars, and we want to make all the vehicles in our lineup self-driving. Although we know how to create vehicles, we have no expertise in creating the software and hardware systems that control our vehicles. Rather than develop this capability in-house, we would like to incorporate self-driving technology from someone like Google or Tesla.

One way to do this would be to work with Google or Tesla to integrate their software with each of the vehicles in our lineup, one by one. We could start with the compact cars, move to mid- and full-size, and end with our pickups and SUVs. If we take this approach, we might have to write custom software to integrate with each of the different vehicles in our lineup, which would be a lot of work.

On the other hand, we could create a single navigation interface that each of the vehicles in our lineup would implement. Each underlying implementation would be different, but the interface describing how to control and navigate our vehicles would be the same. As far as the self-driving system is concerned, all of the vehicles would look exactly the same. This means that we would have to write the code that integrated the self-driving system with the vehicles only one time.

This arrangement gives us the freedom to change the implementation details about the car without affecting the self-driving system. Further, the self-driving system doesn't have to worry about the differences in the actual implementation of a sedan or a pickup, because it treats everything as a vehicle.

NOTE A class may implement as many interfaces as it needs.

COMPOSITION AND INHERITANCE

Composition and inheritance allow us to express relationships between objects and to reuse code. Although they are similar in some ways, they take different approaches and express different types of relationships. This means you must first determine the type of relationship you want to express before you can decide if you want to use composition or inheritance. Once you determine this, the code follows naturally.

Composition

Composition is a feature of just about every programming language—it is not unique to object-oriented languages. In object-oriented languages like Java and C#, *composition* is the mechanism that allows objects to be made up of other objects. Composition allows us to express a *has-a* relationship. It allows us to reuse code by creating fields in our objects that are other objects. We then delegate to the contained object when we want to take advantage of the capabilities of that object.

We see composition around us in the real world every day. Let's go back to the fast-food drive-through example we used in Lesson 14 and look at how the restaurant is put together behind the scenes. We can assume that the restaurant will need a stove of some kind to prepare the food, a point-of-sale system, a freezer, a drink dispenser, and so on. When designing the restaurant, the architect doesn't design the stove, freezer, point-of-sale system, or drink dispensers. Instead, they create a space for these things in the overall restaurant design. When it comes time to build the restaurant, the contractor won't build these components from scratch but will instead order them from a supplier and install them into the restaurant. At this point, the restaurant *has a* stove, *has a* freezer, *has a* point-of-sale system, and *has a* drink dispenser. Cooking, freezing, sales, and drink dispensing capabilities are then delegated to these pieces of equipment.

Composition is great at these kinds of relationships where you need the capabilities of another object, but that is as far as the relationship goes. It is important to point out that the restaurant *has a* stove, but no one would ever say that the restaurant *is a* stove. This brings us to the next feature, inheritance.

> **NOTE** We'll go deeper into composition in Lesson 19.

Inheritance

Inheritance is a core feature of object-oriented languages like Java and C#. In fact, without this feature, a language can be object-based but cannot be object-oriented. *Inheritance* allows us to express an *is-a* relationship between two types. These types of relationships express a hierarchical relationship or taxonomy. We use inheritance when we want to create a class that is just like another class but with just a few more features or capabilities. It expresses a true inheritance or specialization relationship.

To illustrate this concept, let's look at another example from the real world: motorcycles. All motorcycles have two wheels, a motor, handlebars, brakes, and a throttle (among other things—we'll keep it simple for this illustration).

Now let's look at a dirt bike. A dirt bike has all the characteristics of a motorcycle plus knobby off-road tires and a high-performance suspension. In other words, a dirt bike is a specialized version of a motorcycle. We want to inherit all the features of a motorcycle and then add in the special features of the dirt bike.

Next, let's look at a street bike. Like the dirt bike, it has all the features of a motorcycle, plus a headlight, a taillight, turn signals, and a license plate. And just like the dirt bike, it inherits all the features from a motorcycle and adds in its special parts—it is a specialized motorcycle.

Both a dirt bike and a street bike have an *is-a* relationship with a motorcycle. A dirt bike *is a* motorcycle, and a street bike *is a* motorcycle. No one would ever say that a dirt bike *has a* motorcycle—it actually is a motorcycle.

In object-oriented terms, motorcycle is the *parent* of both dirt bike and street bike. Both dirt bike and street bike are said to *extend* motorcycle. We'll see what all this looks like in code in a separate, inheritance-specific write-up in Lesson 20.

USING INTERFACES, COMPOSITION, AND INHERITANCE

As you gain experience as a software developer, it will become easier to know when to use interfaces, composition, and inheritance. As you see more situations and work on more projects, patterns will emerge that will help you decide which of these tools to use. You will certainly make mistakes along the way and choose the wrong one from time to time, which is okay because this is where we really learn.

There are, however, some rules of thumb that you should follow to start off on the right foot. First, you will find that we almost exclusively use interfaces and composition in the software we write for this course and in web application development in general. That doesn't mean that inheritance is bad—far from it. It just means that it is not the right tool to express the kinds of relationships we model when building web applications.

Even though we will not be writing much code that uses inheritance, the code we write will use classes that have inheritance relationships all the time. In fact, every class you create will have an implicit inheritance relationship with a class called Object. Inheritance is often used in the frameworks and libraries that we will use to build our applications. If it is done well, we don't notice these relationships unless we look at the source code.

> **NOTE** We'll see the details of how every class implicitly inherits from the Object class when we go into more detail on inheritance in Lesson 20.

SUMMARY

In this short lesson, we discussed three powerful language features: interfaces, composition, and inheritance. At this point, you should have a good understanding of the kinds of relationships between objects that each can model and have a good mental framework for what these features look like from various analogies from the real world.

We'll begin to see what these features look like in code in the next several lessons as we dig deeper into understanding the concepts by using them in more complex programs throughout the rest of this course. We'll start by looking at the basic code for each of these in the next three lessons.

> **NOTE** Throughout the rest of the course, we'll point out situations where we are using interfaces, composition, and inheritance. We'll explain the benefits and show you what it looks like in code. Make sure you pay attention to these situations and that you truly gain an understanding of why we are applying these language features in the ways presented to you.

Lesson 18
Diving into Interfaces

In this lesson, we will look at how interfaces are created and used. Interfaces can help us integrate code from different teams and allow us to express loosely coupled, contract-based relationships between components. Here, we will cover declaration, implementation, and extension of interfaces. We will also look at the restrictions on interfaces and how interfaces work with polymorphism.

This is not an exhaustive treatment of interfaces. We're just going to cover the basics. As you start creating more advanced programs, you will learn how to apply interfaces in increasingly sophisticated situations, so this is just the beginning of our journey with interfaces.

LEARNING OBJECTIVES

By the end of this lesson, you will be able to:

- Declare an interface
- Implement an interface
- Implement multiple interfaces
- Discuss interface restrictions
- Extend an interface
- Relate polymorphism to interfaces

WHAT IS AN INTERFACE?

An *interface* is a reference type, just like classes and enums. The big difference is that interfaces are never instantiated. That is to say, you cannot do this:

```
new SomeInterface()
```

What an interface does is define a set of methods that provide standard behaviors that any type that *implements* the interface must provide.

DECLARING AN INTERFACE

Declaring an interface is similar to declaring a class. Just as with a class, the interface must reside in a file with the same name as the interface and a .java extension. For example, the interface in Listing 18.1 must reside in a file called Vehicle.java.

LISTING 18.1

The Vehicle Interface

```
public interface Vehicle {

    public void moveForward(int milesPerHour);
    public void moveBackward(int milesPerHour);
    public void stop();
    public void turnLeft();
    public void turnRight();
    public void engineOn();
    public void engineOff();
}
```

Compared to class declarations, the key differences when declaring interfaces are as follows:

- The `interface` keyword is used instead of the `class` keyword.
- An interface can have abstract methods, default methods, and static methods.
- Abstract methods are methods that are declared without an implementation.
- A semicolon is placed after each method definition.
- In the previous example, none of the defined methods has implementations because they are abstract methods (we can use the `abstract` keyword, but it's implicit).
- Default, static, and private methods can have implementations in an interface.
- All abstract, default, and static methods in an interface are implicitly public.

Interfaces can include method declarations. In fact, all types of methods can be declared in an interface: with or without return types, with or without parameters, and in any combination. In the examples that follow, methods are declared with no return types just to simplify the examples.

IMPLEMENTING AN INTERFACE

To have an interface do anything useful, we must create a class that promises to fulfill the contract defined by the interface. When we do this, we say that a class *implements* the interface.

This is necessary because you cannot instantiate a standard interface on its own. It must have an implementing class. This requires two things.

- The class must declare that it implements a given interface.
- The class must provide implementations for each of the methods defined in the interface.

Listing 18.2 shows an example of a class called `MidsizeSedan` that implements the `Vehicle` interface that we defined in Listing 18.1.

LISTING 18.2

The `MidsizeSedan` Class

```
public class MidSizeSedan implements Vehicle {
```

```java
    @Override
    public void moveForward(int milesPerHour) {
        // implementation code here...
    }

    @Override
    public void moveBackward(int milesPerHour) {
        // implementation code here...
    }

    @Override
    public void stop() {
        // implementation code here...
    }

    @Override
    public void turnLeft() {
        // implementation code here...
    }

    @Override
    public void turnRight() {
        // implementation code here...
    }

    @Override
    public void engineOn() {
        // implementation code here...
    }

    @Override
    public void engineOff() {
        // implementation code here...
    }

}
```

You can see that the MidsizeSedan class has methods that align with those in the interface. Keep in mind that the code is not shown in this listing to simplify the example and
allow you to focus on the fact that the methods match up.

The @Override symbol is an annotation. *Annotations* are a form of metadata that help
describe the program but are not part of the program itself. They can be used in
different ways.

- The compiler can use annotations to help detect errors.
- Code generation tools can use annotations.
- Some annotations are available to be inspected at runtime.

In this case, the `@Override` annotation indicates that the methods in our class (`MidsizeSedan`) were defined in the interface (`Vehicle`), and this class is providing an implementation.

INTERFACE RESTRICTIONS

Because interfaces are meant to be contracts, Java imposes restrictions on them.

- Interfaces cannot have member fields (but they may define constants).
- None of the methods can have implementations. From Java 8 onward, however, interfaces are allowed to have default implementations of methods, which can be useful in certain contexts. For reverse compatibility, adding methods to an interface does not cause your implementer's code to need to be recompiled.

> **NOTE** We will not be using default implementations in this course. Versions prior to Java 8 did not allow this.

IMPLEMENTING MULTIPLE INTERFACES

A class may implement more than one interface. Such a class must simply list all the interfaces that it implements and then provide implementations of all the methods of each interface.

For example, suppose we create an interface called `Trackable`. The purpose of this interface is to allow someone to locate or track vehicles in their fleet. The interface might look like Listing 18.3.

LISTING 18.3

A Trackable Interface

```
public interface Trackable {

    public void sendCurrentLocation();
    public void beaconOn();
    public void beaconOff();
}
```

Now we can have our `MidsizeSedan` from earlier implement both `Vehicle` and `Trackable`, as shown in Listing 18.4.

LISTING 18.4

MidsizeSedan Implementing Two Interfaces

```java
public class MidSizeSedan implements Vehicle, Trackable {

    @Override
    public void moveForward(int milesPerHour) {
        // implementation code here...
    }

    @Override
    public void moveBackward(int milesPerHour) {
        // implementation code here...
    }

    @Override
    public void stop() {
        // implementation code here...
    }

    @Override
    public void turnLeft() {
        // implementation code here...
    }

    @Override
    public void turnRight() {
        // implementation code here...
    }

    @Override
    public void engineOn() {
        // implementation code here...
    }

    @Override
    public void engineOff() {
        // implementation code here...
    }

    @Override
    public void sendCurrentLocation() {
```

```
        // implementation code here...
    }

    @Override
    public void beaconOn() {
        // implementation code here...
    }

    @Override
    public void beaconOff() {
        // implementation code here...
    }

}
```

EXTENDING AN INTERFACE

There are times when you might want to define an interface that has the same capabilities as an existing interface but with one or more additional methods. In this case, we can
extend an existing interface. The new interface declares that it extends the existing interface and then defines only its new methods.

For example, say we have a new line of business that takes some of our existing vehicles
and turns them into emergency vehicles (such as police cruisers or ambulances). The interface for these vehicles must include the capabilities of our existing Vehicle interface, but
we also need the ability to control sirens and flashers. For this situation, our new interface
might look something like Listing 18.5.

LISTING 18.5

Extending an Interface

```
public interface EmergencyVehicle extends Vehicle {

    public void flashersOn();
    public void flashersOff();
    public void sirenOn();
    public void sirenOff();

}
```

Any class that implements EmergencyVehicle must provide implementations for the
methods defined in EmergencyVehicle and for all the methods defined in Vehicle. For
example, an Ambulance class might look like Listing 18.6.

LISTING 18.6

An Ambulance Class

```java
public class Ambulance implements EmergencyVehicle {

    @Override
    public void flashersOn() {
        // implementation code here...
    }

    @Override
    public void flashersOff() {
        // implementation code here...
    }

    @Override
    public void sirenOn() {
        // implementation code here...
    }

    @Override
    public void sirenOff() {
        // implementation code here...
    }

    @Override
    public void moveForward(int milesPerHour) {
        // implementation code here...
    }

    @Override
    public void moveBackward(int milesPerHour) {
        // implementation code here...
    }

    @Override
    public void stop() {
        // implementation code here...
    }

    @Override
    public void turnLeft() {
        // implementation code here...
    }
```

```
@Override
public void turnRight() {
    // implementation code here...
}

@Override
public void engineOn() {
    // implementation code here...
}

@Override
public void engineOff() {
    // implementation code here...
}

}
```

INTERFACES AND POLYMORPHISM

Polymorphism is a pillar of object-oriented design. *Polymorphism* means "many-formed," and the key idea is that an object can take more than one form. Objects can be treated polymorphically when they implement an interface or when they use inheritance to extend another class. For now, we will restrict our discussion to polymorphism and interfaces. To illustrate this concept, let's look at the MidsizeSedan class shown earlier.

In its last incarnation, MidsizeSedan implements two interfaces: Vehicle and Trackable. This means that a MidsizeSedan object can be treated as any one of these three types:

- MidsizeSedan
- Vehicle
- Trackable

Let's see what this looks like in code:

```
MidSizeSedan car = new MidSizeSedan();
```

In this first example, we simply create a new MidsizeSedan object on the heap and point to it with a MidsizeSedan reference. This is straightforward: this is how we have been instantiating and referring to objects so far in the course. Our reference variable (car) has access to all the methods on MidsizeSedan.

Here is our next example:

```
Vehicle vehicle = new MidSizeSedan();
```

In this example, we create a new MidsizeSedan object on the heap, but this time we point to it with a Vehicle reference. In this case, a complete MidsizeSedan object is created on the heap, just like the previous example. However, since we have chosen to treat the MidsizeSedan as Vehicle by referring to the MidsizeSedan object with a Vehicle reference, we only have access to the methods on the MidsizeSedan that are defined in the Vehicle interface. As far as we are concerned, the object we've created is just a Vehicle and nothing more.

Finally, here is our last example:

```
Trackable trackable = new MidSizeSedan();
```

In this example, we create a new MidsizeSedan object on the heap, but this time we point to it with a Trackable reference. In this case, a complete MidsizeSedan object is created on the heap, just like in the previous two examples. However, since we have chosen to treat the MidsizeSedan as a Trackable by referring to it with a Trackable reference, we only have access to the methods that are defined in the Trackable interface. As far as we are concerned, the object we created is just a Trackable and nothing more.

In each of the previous examples, a new, complete MidsizeSedan object is created on the heap. The difference is that we refer to the newly created object with different reference types. The reference types, in turn, determine how the newly created object looks to us—a MidsizeSedan, a Vehicle, or a Trackable object.

SUMMARY

In this document, we looked at the basics of implementing interfaces in code. The following are the important points:

- How to declare an interface
- How to implement an interface
- How to extend an interface
- How to implement more than one interface
- How polymorphism works with interfaces

Remember that we just covered the basics of interfaces here. Throughout the rest of the course, you will learn how to use this language feature effectively in the projects and examples.

Lesson 19

Diving into Composition

In this very short lesson, we'll take an initial look at what composition looks like in Java code. In Lesson 17, we discussed how composition can be used to model a *has-a* relationship between objects. In this lesson, we will look at a simple example of composition.

Later in this part of the course, we'll explore the power of composition after we learn about the List and Maps data structures in Lessons 21 and 22. We'll use these data structures and composition to create components later in this course.

LEARNING OBJECTIVES

By the time you finish this lesson, you will be able to:

- Define composition
- Compare projects built with composition to projects without composition

WHAT IS COMPOSITION?

One of the main characteristics of an object-oriented language is that objects can be made up of other objects. This is done through *composition*. From a coding standpoint, this means that one or more of the fields in an object are other objects rather than primitive types or strings.

To illustrate this point, look at two examples of modeling a book in Java. In each model, we want to keep track of the following:

- Book title
- Book ISBN
- Book author, including contact information
- Book publisher, including contact information

Book without Composition

Let's start with an example that does not use composition, which we'll call BadBook. In the BadBook class, we will model all the information about the book using strings. It might look something like Listing 19.1; however, note that the getters and setters for the fields are not shown in order to make the example easier to read.

LISTING 19.1

The BadBook Class

```
public class BadBook {
    private String title;
    private String isbn;
    private String authorName;
    private String authorStreet;
    private String authorCity;
    private String authorState;
    private String authorZip;
    private String publisherName;
    private String publisherStreet;
    private String publisherCity;
    private String publisherState;
    private String publisherZip;
    private String publisherPhone;
}
```

This class keeps track of the minimum data required, but it feels messy. All the information is in separate fields, and there is nothing to tie the author or publisher information together.

Should a book really have a field called `publisherCity`? Shouldn't a publisher be a separate entity? The same is true about the author. An `authorCity` field feels sloppy. What if a book has more than one author? How do we handle that?

Book with Composition

Let's see how we can approach this problem using composition. First, let's look at the entities we have to keep track of:

- Book
- Author
- Publisher
- Address

The first three are probably obvious to you, but the fourth one might not be. We're choosing to model an address as an entity because both authors and publishers have an address, and, in this example, all addresses have the same format.

Let's model these objects and then see how they relate to each other. We'll start with `Address`, as shown in Listing 19.2. We will keep things simple with our `Address` class by having just a street, city, state, and zip.

LISTING 19.2

An Address Class

```
public class Address {
    private String street;
    private String city;
    private String state;
    private String zip;
}
```

Next, the `Author` class can be created as shown in Listing 19.3. Again, we'll keep things simple by having just a first name, last name, and address.

LISTING 19.3

An Author Class

```
public class Author {
    private String firstName;
    private String lastName;
    private Address address;
}
```

Now we are using composition. The Author class *has-an* address. We put the street, city, state, and zip information in the Address object and create a field in the Author class of type Address to hold that information for us. This is nice because it puts all the address information in a single container.

The Publisher class in Listing 19.4 looks similar to the Author class, except that publishers have fields for name and phone instead of fields for first and last name.

LISTING 19.4

A Publisher Class

```
public class Publisher {
    private String name;
    private Address address;
    private String phone;
}
```

Here, again, we are using composition. We can see that the Publisher class *has-an* address.

Finally, let's look at the Book class. Things get more interesting here. We need to keep track of the title, ISBN, publisher, and all authors. To account for the possibility of having more than one author, we will create a field that is an array of Author objects. Listing 19.5 shows what our Book class looks like.

LISTING 19.5

The Book Class

```
public class Book {
    private String title;
    private String isbn;
```

```
    private Author[] authors;
    private Publisher publisher;
}
```

We're now using composition on two levels: the Book class *has-a* publisher and *has-an* array of authors, and the Publisher and Author classes each *have-an* address. Further, we are using an array to hold the Author objects for our book.

This is a much cleaner design. Each set of related information—address, publisher, author, and book—is in its own class. We are using composition to build objects that contain other objects.

SUMMARY

Composition is a powerful tool that you will use frequently in the rest of this course and throughout your career. We looked at a simple example of composition, but this is just the beginning and only introduced the general syntax of using composition. As the course goes on, we will show you how to use composition to create well-designed applications.

EXERCISES

The following are some additional exercises to help you practice what you are learning about composition. These are to do on your own. The exercises include the following:

Exercise 1: Classroom Composition
Exercise 2: Cookbook

Exercise 1: Classroom Composition

Put composition into practice. Take the Classroom class in Exercise Listing 19.1 and break it down into classes. Consider what things a classroom has versus what things describe a classroom. For example, a classroom has a teacher.

EXERCISE LISTING 19.1

The Classroom Class

```
public class Classroom {
    private String className;
    private int    classGradeLevel;
```

```
    private String teacherFirstname;
    private String teacherLastname;
    private String student1Firstname;
    private String student1Lastname;
    private int    student1Grade;
    private String student2Firstname;
    private String student2Lastname;
    private int    student2Grade;
    private String student3Firstname;
    private String student3Lastname;
    private int    student3Grade;
    private int    maximumNumberStudents;
}
```

Hint
A classroom generally has a teacher and students.

Exercise 2: Cookbook

A cookbook is often full of recipes. Exercise Listing 19.2 is a class to hold a cookbook. Use composition to simplify the Cookbook class.

As a note, this is a pretty bad cookbook, but you can make it better. Most cookbooks have more than two recipes, and most recipes have more than three ingredients. As you refactor this listing so that it uses composition, your result should allow it to use as many recipes and ingredients as needed by the users of your new classes.

EXERCISE LISTING 19.2

The Cookbook Class

```
public class Cookbook {

    String title;
    String authorFirstname;
    String authorLastname;
    Double price;
    int yearPublished;
    String recipe1Name;
    String recipe1AuthorFirstname;
    String recipe1AuthorLastname;
```

```java
        String recipe1Ingredient1;
        Double recipe1Ingredient1Amount;   // ie. 1.25
        String recipe1Ingredient1MeasurementType; // ie. Tablespoon
        String recipe1Ingredient2;
        Double recipe1Ingredient2Amount;
        String recipe1Ingredient2MeasurementType;
        String recipe1Ingredient3;
        Double recipe1Ingredient3Amount;
        String recipe1Ingredient3MeasurementType;
        String recipe1MixingInstructions;
        String recipe1CaloriesPerServing;
        String recipe1Servings;
        String recipe2Name;
        String recipe2AuthorFirstname;
        String recipe2AuthorLastname;
        String recipe2Ingredient1;
        Double recipe2Ingredient1Amount;   // ie. 1.25
        String recipe2Ingredient1MeasurementType; // ie. Tablespoon
        String recipe2Ingredient2;
        Double recipe2Ingredient2Amount;
        String recipe2Ingredient2MeasurementType;
        String recipe2Ingredient3;
        Double recipe2Ingredient3Amount;
        String recipe2Ingredient3MeasurementType;
        String recipe2MixingInstructions;
        String recipe2CaloriesPerServing;
        String recipe2Servings;
    }
```

Lesson 20
Diving into Inheritance

In this part of our lesson, we will look at specialization and inheritance. In Lesson 17, we discussed how inheritance can be used to model an *is-a* relationship between objects. These relationships are hierarchical in nature and express a true inheritance, or parent-child, relationship between objects. In this lesson, we will cover extension of classes, method overloading, method overriding, access control, and how polymorphism works with inheritance.

As mentioned earlier in this lesson, you won't explicitly use inheritance often in the rest of this course or in web application development, but you will implicitly use inheritance all the time. Inheritance is a foundational concept of object-oriented programming, and you must have a good understanding of this concept to be a successful object-oriented developer.

LEARNING OBJECTIVES

By the end of this lesson, you will be able to:
- Explain how everything extends object
- Explain what a parent class is, including synonyms
- Explain what a child class is, including synonyms
- Use access control to extend objects
- Explain is-a versus has-a relationships
- Discuss the benefits of a well-designed inheritance hierarchy
- Reuse code with inheritance
- Overload a method
- Explain the use of constructors with derived and base classes
- Use polymorphism with inheritance
- Relate an abstract base class to a base class and an interface

EVERYTHING EXTENDS OBJECT

The `Object` class is the parent of every class in Java; it is at the root of the class hierarchy. In other words, everything starts here. You do not have to do anything explicit to create this relationship. It happens automatically when you define a class.

The `Object` class has 12 methods, which means that every class ever created in Java implements these 12 methods. It is fairly common practice to replace the default implementation of `equals`, `hashCode`, and `toString` with versions specific to your class by *overriding* them. We will take a closer look at overriding methods later in this document, and then we'll look at how to override `equals`, `hashCode`, and `toString` specifically in a later lesson.

TERMINOLOGY

Before we dig into the details of implementing inheritance relationships, we need to discuss some terminology. Inheritance is one area of object-oriented languages where terminology can be a bit confusing for newcomers. There are several ways of expressing the relationship between a parent class and the classes that extend it.

- Parent class
  - Also referred to as *superclass* or *base class.*

- When classes extend a parent class, they inherit the properties and behaviors of the parent class.
- Child class
  - Also referred to as the *subclass*, *extended class*, or *derived class*.
  - This class inherits the properties and behaviors of the base class when it extends the base class.
  - This class can add properties and behaviors to those of the base class.
  - This class can override (i.e., provide its own implementation of) properties and behaviors of the base class. We'll look at overriding in this lesson.
  - We say this this class specializes the base class.

Unfortunately for the newcomer, all these terms are in common use and are used fluidly and interchangeably by developers. For example, a developer might refer to a parent class as a *parent class*, a *base class*, and a *superclass* in the same conversation. Make sure that you understand these terms and know how to use them properly.

ACCESS CONTROL

So far, we have seen public and private access to properties and methods. We now look at a new keyword: `protected`. If we mark a property or method of a base class `protected`, it means that property or method can be seen by the base class, all derived classes, and other classes in the package, but it cannot be seen by any other class (in other words, it is as if that property or method were private with respect to other classes). If you think there is a good chance that a class will be extended in the future, it is good practice to mark the properties of the class protected instead of private. In general, you should use the most restrictive access level that makes sense for each member of your class.

Table 20.1 outlines what access is allowed by each of the modifiers.

Table 20.1 Access Allowed by Modifier

Modifier	Class Access?	Package Access?	Subclass Access?	World Access?
public	Yes	Yes	Yes	Yes
protected	Yes	Yes	Yes	No
no modifier	Yes	Yes	No*	No
private	Yes	No	No	No

* unless in the same package

INHERITANCE

There are times when we want to explicitly create an *is-a* relationship between two objects. In a previous lesson, we looked at this type of relationship between motorcycles, dirt bikes, and street bikes. Here, we'll talk about a fictional human resources (HR) system in which we need to have employees, managers, and summer interns.

A well-designed inheritance hierarchy is built so the parent class is the most general (i.e., it contains all the fields and methods common to its descendants) and the child classes *specialize* the parent. In our example, Employee will be the base class, and both Manager and SummerIntern will extend Employee.

Let's look at the Employee class first, as shown in Listing 20.1. Note that we make firstName and lastName protected so that the child classes will have access to these members.

LISTING 20.1

The Employee Class

```java
public class Employee {
    protected String firstName;
    protected String lastName;

    public void doWork() {
        // code to do work ...
    }

    public void createYearlyObjectives() {
        // code to create yearly objectives...
    }
```

```java
    public String getFirstName() {
        return firstName;
    }

    public void setFirstName(String firstName) {
        this.firstName = firstName;
    }

    public String getLastName() {
        return lastName;
    }

    public void setLastName(String lastName) {
        this.lastName = lastName;
    }
}
```

All employees have these capabilities whether they are accountants, software developers, managers, or even the CEO; however, many employees have additional capabilities and responsibilities. For example, a manager can hire and fire people and can give performance reviews. A manager is a special kind of employee—it inherits some common properties and behaviors, but it also extends the functionality of what an employee does with new and/or different properties and behaviors.

In Java, this specialization relationship is achieved via inheritance and is implemented using the extends keyword. Listing 20.2 shows a Manager class that extends the earlier Employee class.

LISTING 20.2

A Manager Class

```java
public class Manager extends Employee {
    public void hire() {
        // code to hire someone...
    }

    public void fire() {
        // code to fire someone...
    }

    public void givePerformanceReview() {
        // code to give performance review
    }
}
```

Even though only the additional Manager-specific methods are contained in the Manager class definition, all the members of Employee are included in Manager. To illustrate this, in NetBeans or your IDE, create classes with the Employee and Manager classes from the previous two listings. In a new App class, write the code to instantiate a new Manager object in NetBeans or your IDE.

```
Manager manager = new Manager();
manager.
```

When you type the dot after manager, you should see the editor's help pop-up showing the available members, as shown in Figure 20.1.

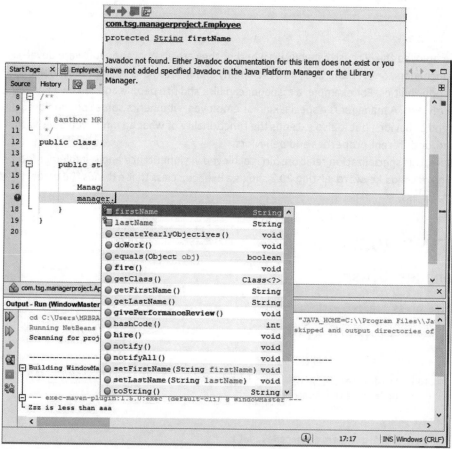

Figure 20.1 The members of the Manager class

You can see that in addition to hire(), fire(), and givePerformanceReview(), the Manager class has all the methods defined in Employee: doWork(), createYearlyObjectives(), and the getters and setters for firstName and lastName. You will also notice that Manager has all of the methods defined on Object. The Manager class gets all this functionality because it extends Employee.

CODE REUSE THROUGH INHERITANCE

The previous example illustrates how code can be reused through inheritance. If we have a group of objects (Employees, for example) that all have common properties and behaviors, we can put the common properties and behaviors into a base class and then extend it into particular subclasses (Manager, for example).

This means we only need to write the common code one time. These subclasses each get all the common code from the Employee class and are free to add properties and behaviors for their particular purposes. The subclasses are also free to override properties or behaviors of the base class. In this way, inheritance promotes code reuse and is a great tool to help organize our code.

METHOD OVERLOADING

Earlier in this course, we talked about method signatures and defined a method signature as the combination of the name of the method and its parameter list. In any given class, each method must have a unique signature. This brings us to a new term: *method overloading*. We can overload a method by creating methods in a class that share the same name but have different parameter lists.

For example, look at the class, Adder, in Listing 20.3.

LISTING 20.3

Overloaded add() Methods

```
public class Adder {

    public int add(int a, int b) {
        return a + b;
    }
}
```

```
    public float add(float a, float b) {
        return a + b;
    }

}
```

This class has two methods, both named add. The first takes two int parameters, and the second takes two float parameters. The compiler knows which one to call at runtime based on the types of the parameters passed in.

Similarly, Listing 20.4 shows another version of an Adder class also with two methods also called add. This time the add methods have different numbers of parameters, which is valid as well.

LISTING 20.4

Another Overloaded Set of add() Methods

```
public class Adder {

    public int add(int a, int b) {
        return a + b;
    }

    public float add(float a, float b, int c) {
        return a + b + c;
    }
}
```

Note that this listing is not very practical, but it does illustrate that you have a different number of parameters. In this case, if two int values are passed, the first add() method is called. If three ints are passed, the second is called. Ultimately, you can create as many overloaded add() methods in Adder as you want as long as each has something that is different to give them different signatures—one or more types and/or a different number of parameters.

> **NOTE** Technically, method overriding is not an inheritance topic; however, the related topic of method overriding, which is covered next, is associated to inheritance.

METHOD OVERRIDING

With inheritance comes the ability to override methods. This simply means that the child class will replace the implementation of a base class method with an implementation of its own.

For example, all Employees objects in our system have the ability to set objectives via the createYearlyObjectives() method. This method is implemented in the Employee base class and can be reused by all subclasses. This was demonstrated in the example in Listing 20.1.

It is possible that a manager would require a different implementation for createYearlyObjectives()—perhaps the manager must set their own objectives *and* must set goals for each of their direct reports, for example. If this were the case, we would simply implement createYearlyObjectives() in the Manager class, which would override (i.e., replace) the implementation contained in the Employee class.

NOTE Please note a key difference between overriding and overloading:

- When you *override* a method in a child class, it must have the same signature as the corresponding method in the parent class.
- When you *overload* a method, it must have a unique signature.

NOTE A common interview question might ask when overriding happens versus overloading. Overriding happens at runtime. Overloading happens when compiling.

We have two implementation options when overriding a method.

- We can completely replace the functionality of the parent class.
- We can add to the functionality of the parent class.

For the first option, we simply re-implement the method in the child class. This new implementation will replace the implementation in the parent class. For the second option, we re-implement the method in the child class, but at some point, we call the method in the parent class. If we do this, the parent method will run just like any method call made in code.

In Listing 20.5, the Manager class overrides the createYearlyObjectives() method but does not call the version of the method in Employee.

LISTING 20.5

Overriding a Method

```java
public class Manager extends Employee {
    public void hire() {
        // code to hire someone...
    }

    public void fire() {
        // code to fire someone...
    }

    public void givePerformanceReview() {
        // code to give performance review
    }

    @Override
    public void createYearlyObjectives() {
        // we're overriding the version of this method in Employee
        // put new code here...
    }
}
```

Looking at Listing 20.5, you see that the method is presented in the same manner with the exception of adding the following line of code before it:

```java
@Override
```

In the example in Listing 20.6, the `Manager` class again overrides the `createYear-lyObjectives()` method, but this time it calls the version in `Employee` and then adds its new code.

LISTING 20.6

Overriding and Extending a Method

```java
public class Manager extends Employee {
    public void hire() {
        // code to hire someone...
    }
```

```
public void fire() {
    // code to fire someone...
}

public void givePerformanceReview() {
    // code to give performance review
}

@Override
public void createYearlyObjectives() {
    // we're overriding the version of this method in Employee
    // put new code here...
    super.createYearlyObjectives();
    // put more new code here...
}
```

NOTE In Listing 20.6, you can call the parent's version of the method that you are overriding at any point in the method.

In this listing, you can see that we use the super keyword to reference the parent class. The keywords super and this are related. The super keyword always refers to the parent of the current class, and this always refers to the class itself.

CONSTRUCTORS

We know from past lessons that constructors are simply special methods that, when used in conjunction with the new keyword, get called when instantiating an object of a particular class. Thus far, we have had to deal with only one constructor because our classes have not extended a base class.

Things get more complicated with derived classes. With a derived class, we have the constructor of the derived (child) class and the constructor of the base (parent) class. Remember also that a derived class can extend a class that is itself a derived class, which means that we could be dealing with several constructors.

Knowing the order of constructor execution is important as the class hierarchy becomes more complicated. Remember that the first line of every constructor is either an explicit constructor call or an implicit call to super(). This helps to remember that the super class constructor always runs first

> **NOTE** We use derived and base class in this discussion. Child class could have been used synonymously with derived class, and parent class could have been used synonymously with base class. Developers often intermix these terms.

To help us with calling constructors and other objects of the immediate base class, we can use the keyword super. The super keyword is useful to explicitly call the constructor of the base class or when you need to access a method of the base class that has been overridden by the derived class.

Our focus now is on inheritance and, more specifically, constructors. The following are rules for dealing with constructors in derived classes (*you should memorize these rules*):

- The call to super(...) must be the *first statement* in the constructor.
- If you do not explicitly call super in the constructor of a derived class, the compiler will automatically call the base class default constructor. If one doesn't exist, a compilation error will occur.
- The base class constructor can be invoked in a derived class by calling super(...) where (...) is the parameter list that may be empty.
- You can call super(...) only from within the constructor of the derived class—*not from anywhere else.*
- The call to super must match the signature of a valid constructor in the base class.
- If your derived class does not define a constructor, the compiler provides the derived class with a default constructor that does nothing but call super, invoking the default constructor of the base class.
- You are allowed to call this(...) as the first line instead, which will call a different constructor in the derived class.
- Eventually, the super constructor will get called (before all other constructors).
- Calls to constructors in this() or super() must be first.
- Circular constructor references are disallowed by the compiler.

Listing 20.7 and Listing 20.8 show updated `Employee` and `Manager` classes with simple constructors added. These constructors print a simple message letting us know they've been executed.

LISTING 20.7

The Updated Employee Class

```java
public class Employee {

    protected String firstName;
    protected String lastName;

    Employee() {
        System.out.println("Employee Constructor");
    }
    public void doWork() {
        // code to do work ...
    }

    public void createYearlyObjectives() {
        // code to create yearly objectives...
    }

    public String getFirstName() {
        return firstName;
    }

    public void setFirstName(String firstName) {
        this.firstName = firstName;
    }

    public String getLastName() {
        return lastName;
    }

    public void setLastName(String lastName) {
        this.lastName = lastName;
    }
}
```

LISTING 20.8

The Updated Manager Class

```java
public class Manager extends Employee {

    Manager(){
        // super() is implicitly added here by the compiler
        // as the first statement of the constructor

        System.out.println("Manger Constructor");
    }

    Manager(int aValue ){
        // super() - without parameters - is implicity added here by the
        // complier as the first statement of the constructor
        System.out.println("Manager Constructor with argument");
    }

    public void hire() {
        // code to hire someone...
    }

    public void fire() {
        // code to fire someone...
    }

    public void givePerformanceReview() {
        // code to give performance review
    }
}
```

We see in Listing 20.8 that we've included comments where a call to the super()
constructor would implicitly occur. Listing 20.9 illustrates this.

LISTING 20.9

Watch the Constructors Work

```java
public class App {

    public static void main(String[] args) {
```

```
        System.out.println("Create an employee: ");
        Employee employee = new Employee();
        System.out.println("Create a manager: ");
        Manager manager = new Manager();
        System.out.println("Done");
    }
}
```

When we execute this listing with our classes, we get the following output:

```
Create an employee:
Employee Constructor
Create a manager:
Employee Constructor
Manager Constructor
Done
```

As we can see, the employee was instantiated, and its constructor was called. There should be no surprise there. When the Manager was instantiated, its constructor was called, but the constructor of the base class was also called first. This happens because an implicit call to super() was executed at the beginning of the Manager's constructor.

Listing 20.10 shows an updated Manager class with the super being (unnecessarily) included.

LISTING 20.10

Manager Class with super Added

```
public class Manager extends Employee {

    Manager(){
        super();
        System.out.println("Manager Constructor");
    }

    Manager(int aValue ){
        System.out.println("Manager Constructor with argument");
    }

    public void hire() {
        // code to hire someone...
    }
```

```
    public void fire() {
        // code to fire someone...
    }

    public void givePerformanceReview() {
        // code to give performance review
    }
}
```

When we execute Listing 20.9 again using this new `Manager` class, we get the same output.

```
Create an employee:
Employee Constructor
Create a manager:
Employee Constructor
Manager Constructor
Done
```

> **NOTE** They key piece of information to retain at this point is that we have access to the super keyword to access things in base classes and that by default constructors in derived classes will call the base class constructors first.

POLYMORPHISM

We introduced the concept of polymorphism when we discussed interfaces in Lesson 17. Polymorphism also applies to inheritance. The reason that an object can take more than one form stems from the idea discussed earlier: when an object extends another object, it creates an *is-a* relationship with the base class.

For example, a `Manager` *is an* `Employee`, which means that we can use an `Employee` object reference to point to a `Manager` object. In other words, we can treat the `Manager` object like an `Employee`. Please keep in mind that the reverse is not true. A `Manager` has all the capabilities and characteristics of an `Employee` (plus some), but not all `Employees` have the capabilities and characteristics of `Managers`. A real-world example of this would be the relationship between mammals and dogs. All dogs are mammals (and can be treated as such), but not all mammals are dogs.

Let's look at an example with Employee and Manager.

```
Manager manager = new Manager();
Employee employee = new Manager();
```

Here we are referencing a Manager object with a Manager reference and an Employee reference. Again, this is perfectly fine because a Manager *is-an* Employee.

If we use NetBeans, we can take a look at which methods are available to each reference. Figure 20.2 shows what is presented for the Manager reference.

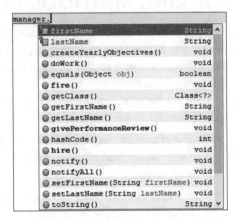

Figure 20.2 Methods available to the Manager reference

Here we see that all the Manager methods and all the Employee methods are available.

If we take a look at the Employee reference as shown in Figure 20.3, we see that the list shown isn't the same.

Here you can see that only the Employee methods are available to the Employee reference. The object that was created on the heap is actually a Manager object, but the Employee reference only gives us access to the methods defined in the Employee class.

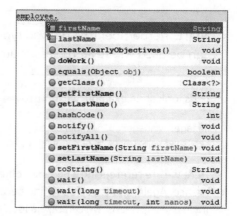

Figure 20.3 Methods available to the Employee reference

CALLING METHODS POLYMORPHICALLY

The fact that we can override superclass methods in a subclass, along with the fact that we can use a superclass reference to point to a subclass object, leads to some interesting questions as to which version of the method will be invoked—the superclass version or the subclass version?

Here are the rules, using Employee and Manager (and the createObjectives method) as an example:

- If you have an instance of Employee pointed to by an Employee reference, the Employee version of createObjectives is called (obviously, because no other version exists).

- If you have an instance of Manager that *has not* overridden the Employee version of createObjectives and is pointed to by a Manager reference, the Employee version of createObjectives is called (again, this is straightforward because there is no other version).

- If you have an instance of Manager (as in the previous bullet) but it is pointed to by an Employee reference, the Employee version of createObjectives is called (it is still the only version of the method).

- If you have an instance of Manager that *has* overridden the Employee version of createObjectives and is pointed to by a Manager reference, the Manager version of createObjectives is called (this is also intuitive).

- If you have an instance of Manager that *has* overridden the Employee version of createObjectives and is pointed to by an Employee reference, the Manager version of createObjectives is called (perhaps not what you would expect).

ABSTRACT BASE CLASSES

The final object-oriented code organization tool that we will talk about in this lesson is the abstract base class. An abstract base class has some properties of a regular base class and some characteristics of an interface.

- Like an interface, an abstract class cannot be instantiated—only subclasses of an abstract class can be instantiated.

- Like an interface, an abstract base class can define abstract methods (definition only—no implementation) and then force subclasses to provide an implementation.

- Like a regular base class, an abstract base class can provide fully implemented methods that get inherited by child classes. We call these fully implemented methods *concrete methods*.

- Like a regular base class, an abstract base class can contain fields that are visible to the child classes.

These features allow you to create classes that implement code common to potential subclasses (so the code can be reused), force subclasses to have certain behaviors (i.e., methods), and force subclasses to provide their own implementations of those behaviors.

SUMMARY

This was an overview of the most important features of inheritance. Remember that inheritance is a foundational concept in object-oriented programming, and it is something that you must be familiar with. Here are the key topics we covered in this lesson:

- Expressing an inheritance or *is-a* relationship between classes by extending classes using the extends keyword

- Method overloading

- Method overriding

- Controlling access to the members of your class

- Polymorphism and inheritance

EXERCISES

Most people learn best by doing, so this section includes an exercise using what you learned in this lesson.

Exercise 1: Working with Shape

Exercise 1: Working with Shape

Create a set of classes to represent a square, rectangle, triangle, and circle. Have these classes inherit from an abstract base class called Shape. Each class will implement at least two read-only fields, area and perimeter represented by their getters: getArea(), which will return the area of the shape; and getPerimeter(), which will return the perimeter of the shape.

Here's a tip if you need it: The abstract base class, Shape, will have a property called color and the two methods getArea() and getPerimeter(), but they will be empty. They are designed to be overridden by inherited shapes, so make sure that any shape that inherits from the base class implements their own versions of getArea() and getPerimeter() based on the type of shape it is. It is suggested you start with a square because this should be the easiest to implement. Create a Shape base class, inherit a square from it, and override the two methods. If you have done this correctly, it should give you the idea for the others.

NOTE If you are uncertain about read-only fields, revisit Lesson 15.

Lesson 21
Understanding Collections

This lesson is a look at the Java Collections Framework. Collections are data structures that allow you to store multiple values in a more flexible manner than simple arrays. We'll look at common Collections Framework classes and the relationship between interfaces and implementations in this context.

LEARNING OBJECTIVES

By the end of this lesson, you will be able to:
- Describe the Collections Framework
- Understand the difference between interface and implementation
- Understand the difference between lists, sets, and maps
- Know several commonly used collections of each type

COLLECTIONS IN JAVA

In the broadest sense, a *collection* is simply a data structure that groups multiple elements together into a single unit. Collections usually represent a group of related data such as a class of students, a group of addresses, or a list of classes in a school schedule. We make extensive use of collections in programming to manipulate groups of related data.

The Java Collections Framework is a library of code that allows programmers to manipulate groups of related objects. Because the Collections Framework is available to all Java programmers, we gain the benefit of not having to "reinvent the wheel" for collections manipulation. Because this framework is widely used, the implementation of these algorithms has been honed over time to be fast, efficient, and bug-free.

Another benefit of the framework is that there is one application programming interface (API) that is widely used by Java programmers. This means that you can easily read and understand someone else's Collections Framework code when working on new projects or when helping someone else with an issue.

JAVADOC

The best place to learn about the structure and capabilities of the Collections Framework and any of its specific implementations is the Javadoc. As mentioned earlier in this course, a Javadoc is an HTML-formatted code document that is generated from special Javadoc tags in the comments of code. All the code that comes with the JDK has extensive Javadocs available online. This should be the first place you look to see how a particular method or interface is supposed to work.

The official website for documentation of the Java Standard Edition Platform is at docs .oracle.com/javase. This web page will display the documentation homepage for the latest version of the Java platform. The Javadoc for the components of the Java platform can be found under the Specifications heading on the page and is called *API Documentation*. For example, the Java 15 API Documentation is available at docs.oracle.com/en/java/javase/15/docs/api/index.html. The API Documentation page looks like Figure 21.1.

> **NOTE** Java and the Java tools continue to be updated. Developers will often choose to use a version that is known to be tried and true, and thus stable, rather than using the most recently released version. Fortunately, documentation for multiple recent versions is available online. To see the API documentation for version 11 or 12, you can simply change the 15 in the mentioned URL to 11 or 12, respectively.

You can navigate all the packages and/or classes of the Java platform using the links within the page or the search bar in the upper right. Clicking a package or class will display the details of that package or class in the main window.

For example, Figure 21.2 shows the details for the List interface.

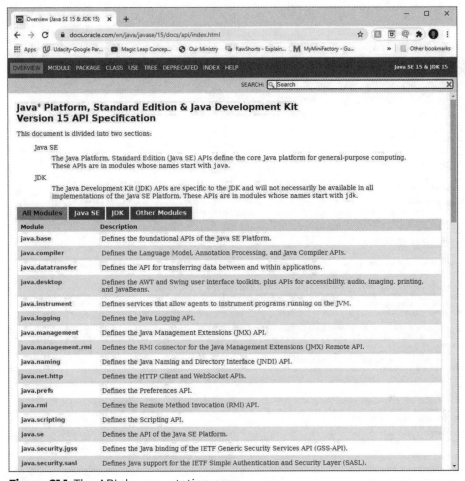

Figure 21.1 The API documentation page

COLLECTIONS FRAMEWORK STRUCTURE

You will do a complete examination of the Collections Framework Javadoc in an exercise, but there are a few things that you should know about the Collections Framework.

- The framework consists of several interfaces and several implementing classes. This is a great example of how interfaces are used in the real world.

- The underlying implementations have different characteristics. For example, Sets cannot have duplicate entries, but Lists can.

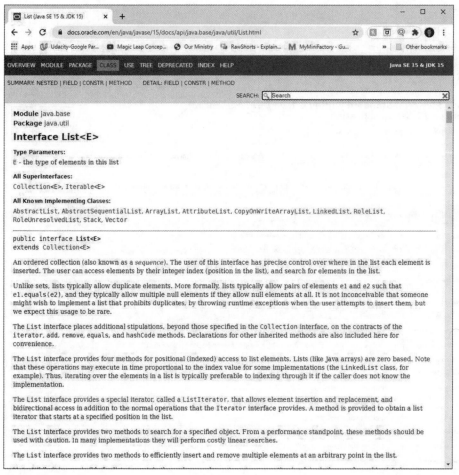

Figure 21.2 Details for the List interface

You should explore the Javadoc in detail to gain a full understanding of the Collections Framework, but we'll start by taking a closer look at the description of the Collection interface and its add method to get you familiar with reading Javadoc.

The Javadoc documentation has an excellent breakdown for the Collection interface itself. Note that the documentation of an interface or class always includes the name of the interface or class, type parameters (if applicable), superinterfaces (i.e., parent interfaces), subinterfaces (i.e., child interfaces), a list of all classes that implement the interface (or interfaces), a description of the interface or class, a note indicating the first version of Java where the interface or class was included, and a list of related interfaces or classes.

A lot of this verbiage may be intimidating to you at this point in your learning, but that is okay. You should always go to the Javadoc first, try to understand what it is saying about the interface or class, and then ask questions about things you don't understand.

> **NOTE** The Collection interface can be found here:
> `docs.oracle.com/en/java/javase/15/docs/api/java.base/java/util/`
> `Collection.html`

INTERFACE VS. IMPLEMENTATION

A common pattern we see when using collections is that we program to the *interface* but instantiate using the *implementation*. This means we end up with code like this:

```
List<String> strings = new ArrayList<>();
```

In this example, `List` is an interface, and `ArrayList` is an actual implementation of that interface. The interface defines all the behavior we expect of the collection, and the implementation decides how that behavior is actually performed behind the scenes.

Different implementations will do things sometimes differently behind the scenes, but they will all give you the methods the interface contains. One of the benefits of this is that if you decide to change the implementation, you only need to change what instantiates it; the rest of your code can stay the same. There will be no methods in your code that need to change.

Some implementations, like the Stack implementation of List, will give you extra methods: push (for adding things) and pop (for removing things) in this example. If you want to take advantage of those features, however, you cannot declare the variable with the interface, or those special features will not be available. In that situation, you declare the variable with the implementation you want to use.

```
Stack<String> stringStack = new Stack<>();
```

This is okay to do, but it does mean you are tied to that implementation of the collection. If we are using pop and push in our code, we cannot change it to an ArrayList without rewriting our code to stop using pop and push.

> **NOTE** This lesson is an overview. We will go into more detail on using collections such as Lists as well as using Maps in the next two lessons.

ITERATOR

An *iterator* is an object that allows you to visit each element in a collection individually. All iterators have a hasNext method that returns true if there are more elements to visit and a next method that retrieves the next element. Some iterators also implement the remove method, which is used to remove elements from the collection during iteration, but this method is not required. We will see examples of using an iterator to visit all the elements in a collection in the following sections.

> **NOTE** If you are removing items from a collection, you generally don't use an Iterator. For removing an item or iterating in a reverse order, you should use a traditional for loop.

COMMONLY USED INTERFACES IN THE COLLECTIONS FRAMEWORK

There are several commonly used interfaces in the Collections Framework. We will take a quick look at the following three interfaces:

- List
- Set
- Map

These are overviewed here; however, we will cover Lists in greater detail in Lesson 22, and Maps will be covered in greater detail in Lesson 23.

Quick Look at List

List is an interface that extends Collection. It is an ordered collection of items that may include duplicate elements. Two commonly used Lists are ArrayList and Stack.

ArrayList

The ArrayList is the List implementation we will use the most. Like any implementation of the List interface, the ArrayList has all the features of the Collection interface and all the features of the List interface.

One way to think about the ArrayList is like an array on steroids. The main convenience that ArrayLists have over arrays is that you can dynamically add and remove elements from an ArrayList and it will automatically resize for you.

> **NOTE** You can find ArrayList in the Javadocs at `docs.oracle.com/en/java/javase/15/docs/api/java.base/java/util/ArrayList.html`.

Stack

A Stack is another List implementation that adds in specialty methods to treat the List like a last in, first out (LIFO) stack. Those specialty methods are `push` to place an object on the top of the Stack, `pop` to remove an object from the top of the Stack, and peek to see what object is on the top of the Stack.

> **NOTE** You can find Stack in the Javadocs at `docs.oracle.com/en/java/javase/15/docs/api/java.base/java/util/Stack.html`.

Quick Look at Set

Set is another interface that extends Collection. Commonly used Sets include HashSet and TreeSet. There are two differences between a List and a Set:

- Each item in a Set must be unique: all duplicates are ignored. Lists do allow duplicate items. In this case, the equivalence between objects is based on the `equals` and `hashCode` methods.

- A Set does not maintain order, whereas a List will. This means that when you retrieve items from a Set, the items may appear in a different order each time.

HashSet

A HashSet is the type of Set we typically use. It determines whether an object is unique based on the `equals` method of the object.

> **NOTE** You can find HashSet in the Javadocs at `docs.oracle.com/en/java/javase/15/docs/api/java.base/java/util/HashSet.html`.

TreeSet

A TreeSet is a Set that does maintain an order. It will default to the natural order of the objects, such as numerical or alphabetical order. If the objects are more complex you can provide a Comparator that tells the TreeSet how to compare and order the objects.

> **NOTE** You can find TreeSet in the Javadocs at `docs.oracle.com/en/java/javase/15/docs/api/java.base/java/util/TreeSet.html`. You can find more on Comparator in the Javadocs at `docs.oracle.com/en/java/javase/15/docs/api/java.base/java/util/Comparator.html`.

Quick Look at Map

Maps are a part of the Collections Framework, but they do not extend Collection. A Map is an object that maps keys to values. We can retrieve collections of the keys or values in a Map, so they are tied to the Collections Framework.

All keys in a Map must be unique, while values can be duplicated. Because of that when we get all the keys, we get a Set; getting all the values gives us a List. Two common Maps are HashMap and TreeMap.

HashMap

A HashMap is the Map we use most often. Entries in the HashMap have no defined order and cannot guarantee that any order will remain consistent over time.

> **NOTE** You can find HashMap in the Javadocs at `docs.oracle.com/en/java/javase/15/docs/api/java.base/java/util/HashMap.html`.

TreeMap

A TreeMap is a Map that will maintain an order based on the keys. Similar to the TreeSet we talked about previously, it will use the natural order or a Comparator to determine the order.

> **NOTE** You can find TreeMap in the Javadocs at `docs.oracle.com/en/java/javase/15/docs/api/java.base/java/util/TreeMap.html`.

SUMMARY

In this lesson, you learned that the Java Collections Framework gives us a number of different ways to store multiple objects in memory. When using these collections, we typically program to the interface, while instantiating using a specific implementation. What our application needs should determine which implementation of the Collection or Map you use. There are several good implementations of each, so it is up to you to decide what makes the most sense in your code. In the next two lessons, we'll dig deeper into Lists and Maps.

Lesson 22

Introduction to Lists

This lesson is a quick introduction to Lists. Lists are a type of data structure that allows you to store values and objects in a more flexible manner than arrays.

LEARNING OBJECTIVES

By the end of this lesson, you will able to:

- Describe some of the different types of Lists available
- Explain how generic types work in Java
- Use Lists in your code
- Use enhanced `for` loops with Lists
- Create and use an Iterator

LIST

List is an interface that extends Collection. It is an ordered collection of items that may include duplicate elements. The List interface has quite a few methods, but the ones that you will be using most are the following:

- add
- get

- remove
- size

We include examples of using these methods in this lesson, but you should read the Javadoc associated with these methods to become familiar with how they work.

TYPES OF LISTS

There are several types of Lists that exist in the Java Collections Framework. Although we will focus on the ArrayList, we will also discuss the LinkedList and Stack so that you are prepared if a situation arises where your program can benefit from them. In addition to the ArrayList, let's take a quick look at the LinkedList and Stack.

ArrayList

Think of the ArrayList class as a supercharged array. Arrays are great data structures, but they have some limitations, especially that once defined, Arrays cannot shrink or grow. An ArrayList can automatically shrink and grow dynamically, so you can easily add or remove new elements whenever you like.

However, removing or inserting items in the middle of the ArrayList causes all the other elements to be shifted, which is slower than other operations. An ArrayList will also maintain the order in which things were inserted into it based on following first in, first out (FIFO). Modern Java developers prefer ArrayList to Array unless they are absolutely certain about the size of the data and trying to gain a very small performance boost.

> **NOTE** All the Collection interfaces provide a better API for manipulation and filtering arrays.

LinkedList

Another type of list is the LinkedList. The LinkedList class does not store elements in an array. You can think of the linked list as a chain of elements. A linked list has a *head*, which is the first element, and a *tail*, which is the last element. Each element in the list, often referred to as a *node*, contains the data object and a pointer to the next node. When each of the nodes just points to the next node, it is a *singly linked list*. Conceptually, it looks like Figure 22.1.

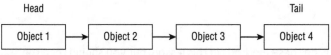

Figure 22.1 A conceptual look at a linked list

We also can have *doubly linked lists* where each node points to the next node and the previous, as shown in Figure 22.2. The LinkedList class in Java is a doubly linked list.

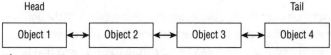

Figure 22.2 A doubly linked list

The main benefit to using the LinkedList over an array or ArrayList structure is that insertions and deletions from the middle do not require shifting elements. For example, to insert an item called Object 5 in between Objects 3 and 4 of the singly linked list shown in Figure 22.1, we would simply point the next node reference of Object 3 to Object 5 and set the next node reference of Object 5 to Object 4 as shown in Figure 22.3.

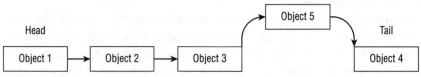

Figure 22.3 Inserting into a linked list

In the end, nothing shifts, and only the reference arrows are changed.

The trade-off for efficient insertions and deletions is that linked lists take up more memory, and unlike an array, which can navigate to an element directly by index, a linked list has to *traverse* the list, or walk node by node, until it finds a specific element.

> **NOTE** Developers tend to prefer the ArrayList to the LinkedList. However, in job interviews, being able to describe and create your own simple linked list data structure is a fairly common task. Knowing the trade-offs between the two is also a common interview question.

Stack

The Stack class is just like the memory stack examples we have seen in this course. The stack has basic methods of push( ) and pop( ) to place objects on top and remove from the top, as well as a peek( ) method, which allows you to examine the top object without removing it. The Stack class is a last-in, first-out (LIFO) structure.

An example of where you might use a Stack is with undo functionality in a word processor application. Hitting the shortcut for undo (Ctrl-Z) will undo your actions in reverse order, so if you were to store each action as a Stack, you could easily pop actions off last to first.

UNDERSTANDING GENERICS

Before we can dig into the details of lists, we need to discuss *generic types* (or simply *generics*) in Java. The definition of a generic type from Oracle is:

A generic class or interface that is parameterized over types.

So, what does that mean?

Java data structures like Lists are containers that hold other objects for us. They are generic (or parameterized) types. The generic type mechanism in Java allows us to specify the type of objects that a list can hold. It also allows a class to define what other type it can act on in a generic fashion.

For example, we could specify a list that holds strings. If we do this, we will encounter an error if we try to put anything other than strings into our list. Earlier versions of Java had no generic types, and you could put any type of object into a list. This meant that you had to check each time you retrieved a value from your list to ensure that it was the type you were expecting. You can still create a collection like this, but you will find that it is almost always advantageous to create containers that only accept a particular type. It makes your code cleaner, smaller, and easier to maintain, and it allows the compiler to ensure that you are not mistakenly putting the wrong type of object in your data structure. The following List examples all use generic types.

The way that we tell the compiler that we want a list of strings instead of a list of Student objects is with angle brackets. For example, this is how you would declare a list of strings:

```
List<String> myList;
```

Here is a declaration of a list of Student objects:

```
List<Student> studentList;
```

In the previous lesson, we referenced the Javadoc as a source of additional information. Note that the Javadoc documentation for Collection and List uses the placeholder E for the type of the Collection or List. This is done to signify that the method will accept a parameter of the type that the data structure is declared to hold.

> **NOTE** The angle brackets (`<>`) are also known as the *diamond operator*. When the angle brackets contain a value, such as `<int>`, then it is called the *type parameter*.

USING LISTS

As we have mentioned, the major advantage of using List over an array is that, unlike an array, a list can dynamically grow, so you can keep adding items without having to specify a size. While there are many available members in the List type, we will cover the most commonly used ones here. Let's take a look at using Lists by creating and instantiating a list and then adding items to it. We will follow this by seeing how to access, insert, and remove items from the list.

Instantiating a List

The List class is not static, so we use the `new` keyword to instantiate it. At the time of creation, you must identify the type of elements that you want to store in the List. It should be any class: `String`, `Person`, `BankAccount`, or any other nonprimitive type. You can even have a List of List if you wanted.

As an example, we will create a list of `String` types, which we will put into an ArrayList.

As a good programming habit, one of the things we should do is program to interfaces. Like the other classes in the Collections Framework, there are interfaces for List that can be used. Using interfaces helps us enforce encapsulation and other good programming practices. It will also provide flexibility for changing our implementations later if that becomes necessary.

> **NOTE** As you start creating more sophisticated programs, you will want to program to interfaces as well.

What we want to do, therefore, is declare a variable of type List. Because List is a generic (which we mentioned earlier), we can set our new list to hold a specific type, in this case only items that are of type String. To do this, we use the angle brackets and indicate the type.

```
List<String> strings
```

This creates a List for String objects called `strings`, which we can also instantiate as an object.

```
List<String> strings = new ArrayList<>();
```

Notice that in each example we declare the variable as a `List` type, but then in this instantiation we are saying it is a new `ArrayList<>()`. In this case, `ArrayList` is a concrete implementation of `List`. We typically want to create our lists this way, with the actual type of the `List` we are using on the right side of the expression.

You will also notice that we didn't include `String` in the diamond operator on the right of this instantiation. That is not necessary because it is implied to be a string based on what has been set up in the generic on the left. Finally, you see the parentheses. These are included because we are calling the constructor for the `ArrayList<>`, in this case with no parameters.

If you are entering this line of code into NetBeans, you'll notice that `List` and `Array-List` are flagged as having problems (red squiggly lines under them). The issue is that `List` and `ArrayList` can't be found because we haven't imported them into our class yet. If you are using NetBeans, you can click the line number with the red dot that shows the error. This displays a pop-up list of options for fixing our issue, as shown in Figure 22.4.

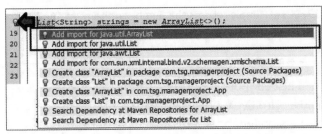

Figure 22.4 NetBeans help for fixing missing imports.

From the list, you can simply click the option *Add import for java.util.ArrayList* and then click *Add import for java.util.List*. This will add the following two import statements to your code:

```
import java.util.ArrayList;
import java.util.List;
```

Of course, we could have simply typed the import information into the IDE if we already knew it.

At this point, we have instantiated a new list. What we have, however, is an empty list of `Strings`. Listing 22.1 confirms that our list is empty by printing its size.

LISTING 22.1

The Size of strings

```
import java.util.ArrayList;
import java.util.List;

public class App {
    public static void main(String[] args) {

        List<String> strings = new ArrayList<>();

        System.out.println("List size: " + strings.size());
    }
}
```

When we execute this code, we see the following output:

```
List size: 0
```

The `size()` method on our `ArrayList` simply returns the number of items in our list, which in this case is zero. This should make sense, being that the list is empty.

NOTE The selected type for a List cannot be a primitive type (`int`, `boolean`, `char`, etc.). If you need to hold a primitive type in a List, you should instead use the corresponding class version (wrapper reference type): `Integer` or `Boolean` or `Character`. Each primitive type has a class version you can use in situations like this. These classes are also known as *wrapper classes*. For example, a list of `Integer` objects would look like this:

```
List<Integer> numbers = new ArrayList<>();
```

Adding Items to a List

With our ArrayList created, we are ready to add items to it. There is one main way to add things to a List: the add() method. Using our strings list from earlier, we can add new strings like this:

```
strings.add("A");
strings.add("B");
strings.add("C");
```

Listing 22.2 expands on the previous listing to add a couple of items.

LISTING 22.2

Adding Items to strings

```
import java.util.ArrayList;
import java.util.List;

public class App {

    public static void main(String[] args) {

        List<String> strings = new ArrayList<>();

        System.out.println("List size: " + strings.size());

        strings.add("The First String");
        strings.add("The Second String");
        strings.add("The Third String");
        System.out.println("List size: " + strings.size());
    }
}
```

As you can see, after printing the initial size of strings, the next three lines of code add new strings to our ArrayList using the add() method. After doing these additions, we again print the size of strings and see that it has been updated accordingly.

```
List size: 0
List size: 3
```

Accessing Items in a List

The List class is an *indexed* collection, which means that individual elements can be accessed via index just like an array, except we do so by using the get() method. In Listing 22.2, we used add() to add items to the strings list. The current state of that list is as follows:

Element	Index
The First String	0
The Second String	1
The Third String	2

Using the get() method along with the index of the element we want, we can retrieve a value. For example, if we were to run the statement strings.get(2), the output would be The Third String.

This also means we can loop through a List using a for loop. Something to be aware of is that while arrays have a length property we can use as a loop control, the List class has a size() method that we will want to use. Listing 22.3 expands on the previous listing to now print out the elements in strings.

LISTING 22.3

Getting Elements from a List

```
import java.util.ArrayList;
import java.util.List;

public class App {

    public static void main(String[] args) {

        List<String> strings = new ArrayList<>();

        System.out.println("List size: " + strings.size());

        strings.add("The First String");
        strings.add("The Second String");
        strings.add("The Third String");
        System.out.println("List size: " + strings.size());

        for (int i = 0; i < strings.size(); i++) {
            System.out.println(strings.get(i));
        }
    }
}
```

You can see that the output from executing this code is exactly what we would expect.

```
List size: 0
List size: 3
The First String
The Second String
The Third String
```

Inserting Items into a List

We can also use the add() method to place elements wherever you like in a list. There are two parameters in this use of the method to insert an item. The first is the index at which you want to insert the new item, and the second is the element you want to insert. Here's an example:

```
strings.add(1, "A New String");
```

Executing this line of code after creating the list in Listing 22.3 would result in a List that looks like this:

Element	Index
The First String	0
A New String	1
The Second String	2
The Third String	3

The new element, A New String, has been placed at position 1; consequently, the element formerly at position 1 and all elements after it have been shifted further into the list and their indexes changed.

> **NOTE** If you want to place an item at the beginning of the list, you can use an index of 0.

Removing Items from a List

There are several ways to remove items from a List. The first is to use the clear() method to remove all the items in the List. If you want to be more selective, you can use the remove() method in a couple of different ways.

Using `remove()` and passing in an object will scan the List, and when Java finds an item that matches the object, it will remove it from the List and stop.

For example, in Listing 22.4 we create a list that includes "Apple", "Banana", "Cherry", and "Date" and then remove "Banana".

LISTING 22.4

Removing an Element from a List

```
import java.util.ArrayList;
import java.util.List;

public class App {

    public static void main(String[] args) {

        List<String> strings = new ArrayList<>();

        strings.add("Apple");
        strings.add("Banana");
        strings.add("Cherry");
        strings.add("Date");
        System.out.println("List size: " + strings.size());

        for (int i = 0; i < strings.size(); i++) {
            System.out.println(strings.get(i));
        }

        strings.remove("Banana");

        System.out.println("List size: " + strings.size());

        for (int i = 0; i < strings.size(); i++) {
            System.out.println(strings.get(i));
        }
    }
}
```

This code is straightforward. Once again, we create our list of `Strings` called `strings`. We add the four elements as we did before and then print the size followed by printing each of the elements to confirm that they were added. We then call the `remove()` method and pass the value we want found and removed, in this case `Banana`. To confirm that this was removed, we print the size, which decreased by one, and then we loop through and print each element. When we look at the output, we can see that Banana is indeed gone.

```
List size: 4
Apple
Banana
Cherry
Date
List size: 3
Apple
Cherry
Date
```

It's worth noting that the remove() method will remove the first matching item it finds in the list. If we had added two Banana elements into Listing 22.4, then only the first one would have been removed.

We can also use remove() and pass in an index position. It will remove whatever item is at that position, while also returning the item in case it is to be used for anything. For example, the following would remove the item at position 1 of strings:

```
strings.remove(1);
```

> **NOTE** Remember, position 1 is the second item in the List. Indexes start at 0.

Again, as things are removed, the size of the List shrinks accordingly. When working with remove() and index positions, we need to be careful to make sure that we don't use an index value beyond the size of our List nor should we try to remove an item by index position if the List is empty. Doing so will cause an exception to be thrown which could crash our program if not handled correctly. Lesson 26 shows how to handle exceptions. In this case, you would be handling an IndexOutOfBoundsException.

ENHANCED APPROACHES TO ACCESS LIST ITEMS

There are two additional approaches for accessing items in a list. Because these alternative methods are used by Java developers for accessing items, it is important to be familiar with them. These include using enhanced for loops and using an Iterator.

The Enhanced for Loop and Lists

While we can use a normal for loop to iterate through a List, an easier way is to use the enhanced for loop that lets us visit each element in our List. We use it exactly the same way that we use it with a normal array; however, the format is simpler.

```
for( type Operand : List_name) {
}
```

The *type Operand* represents what we want to pull out of our list each time through the loop. On the other side of the colon, we include the List that we want to use to pull items from. Listing 22.5 shows this enhanced for loop in action.

LISTING 22.5

Using the Enhanced for Loop

```
import java.util.ArrayList;
import java.util.List;

public class App {

    public static void main(String[] args) {

        List<String> strings = new ArrayList<>();

        strings.add("Apple");
        strings.add("Banana");
        strings.add("Cherry");
        strings.add("Date");

        for (String currentString : strings) {
            System.out.println(currentString);
        }
    }
}
```

The for loop will iterate through each index and on each loop provide access to each element in strings using the operand (currentString) that you have created. You will see the expected output when you execute this listing:

```
Apple
Banana
```

Cherry
Date

NOTE Do not remove elements using the enhanced for loop.

Visiting Each Element: Iterators

The enhanced `for` loop is one way to work through the items in a List. There is another way, which is through the use of an iterator.

One of the things that Lists and Collections have is this thing called an *iterator*. An iterator is used to visit all the elements in a Collection exactly once. As was mentioned earlier, a List is an ordered Collection; it's like an array. A Collection can have slots that can come in any order. They start at index 0 and go to index 1, 2, 3, 4, or to whatever the last index is based on how big the Collection or List is. An iterator comes into play because not all Collections have an order. An iterator's job is to make sure each item in the Collection is visited one by one, and only once.

NOTE We don't know what the order is in there, but the guarantee of an iterator is that we will visit each one exactly one time and only one time. We do know in a list that items are in first in, first out (FIFO) order. A set does not maintain order.

Let's take a look at what it entails to create and use an iterator.

Creating an Iterator

The first thing we must do is to get the iterator out of our List. We will start by declaring a variable, like we do with any variable, and this is going to be an Iterator. Just like Lists and ArrayLists, an Iterator is a generic type, so our declaration will be similar to what we saw earlier with Lists. In this case, we'll create an Iterator that works with `Strings` and instantiate it from the `strings` ListArray we've been using in this lesson as such:

```
Iterator<String> iterator = strings.iterator();
```

In looking at this line of code, you can see that the `iterator()` method on `strings` takes no parameters and is just going to return an `Iterator` that holds `Strings`. This is exactly what we wanted to do to get an iterator that will work with our `strings` ArrayList.

Of course, if you are running this in NetBeans, you are going to see that the Iterator gives an error because it isn't defined! Just like with List and ArrayList, you will need to include an import.

```
import java.util.Iterator;
```

With this code, we have an Iterator ready to be used. Regardless of whether you are using a List, Set, or another kind of Collection, you'll be able to set up an Iterator this same way.

Using the Iterator

When we have defined an Iterator for a List, Set, or other kind of Collection, we are guaranteed that it knows how to visit all the elements in that particular collection of objects. The iterator takes care of the implementation of getting through the elements once. We don't have to know or care how it does what it does, which is a really good thing.

With our Iterator created, we are ready to use it. We are going to use the iterator to move through our list of strings that we created earlier. With the Iterator, we want to loop through the items until we don't have any more. To do this, we will focus on next() and hasNext(). Listing 22.6 presents a List that we created in Listing 22.5; however, this time we added an Iterator to loop through the elements as well.

LISTING 22.6

Using an Iterator

```
import java.util.ArrayList;
import java.util.Iterator;
import java.util.List;

public class App {

    public static void main(String[] args) {

        List<String> strings = new ArrayList<>();

        strings.add("Apple");
        strings.add("Banana");
        strings.add("Cherry");
        strings.add("Date");
```

```
    // Display List with an enhanced for loop
    for (String s : strings) {
        System.out.println(s);
    }

    // Display List with an Iterator
    Iterator<String> iterator = strings.iterator();
    while (iterator.hasNext()) {
        String currentString = iterator.next();
        System.out.println(currentString);
    }
  }
}
```

When we execute this listing, we see the list printed out twice.

```
Apple
Banana
Cherry
Date
Apple
Banana
Cherry
Date
```

The values are printed out the first time using the enhanced for loop we saw earlier. After that, an Iterator is created called iterator that is instantiated using our Array-List, strings. With that in place, we're ready to loop through strings. Because we don't necessarily know the number of items, we need to first check to see whether there is an item to be read. We can do this with the hasNext() method. If there is an item to be read, then we can get it by using the next() method on our Iterator (iterator).

With the item read, we can loop and do the check to see whether there is another item. When the iterator reaches the end of the ArrayList, hasNext() returns false, and our loop will end.

> **NOTE** It is worth noting that the enhanced for loop and the use of an iterator do basically the same thing. The use of the iterator simply breaks the work out into more steps. An iterator is, however, safer to use when removing items. Both approaches are commonly used in Java programs, so it is good to be aware of how both work.

SUMMARY

You will see Lists all over enterprise applications as lists of customers, invoices, billing information, and other types are returned from databases and passed around your code. The ArrayList class is the go-to List class for Java developers when they need to store a collection of related items.

As you saw in this lesson, Lists use generics to save time and overhead by declaring what class will be used in a List. This makes it so we don't have to check each item we pull out of the List before using it. Be aware that while the examples in this lesson used Strings in the List, other types such as Person could have been used in the same way.

EXERCISES

Most people learn best by doing, so this section includes exercises using what you learned in this lesson.

Exercise 1: Three Threes

Exercise 2: Mixed-Up Animals

Exercise 1: Three Threes

Use what you learned today to create an ArrayList and then add the following strings to it in the order listed:

```
One
Two
Three
Four
Five
Six
Three
Seven
Three
Eight
```

After adding the items, iterate through your ArrayList and display the strings. Then write the code so that you find and remove the second and third Three string. Don't remove the first Three! Iterate and print the remaining items. Your final list should look like this:

```
One
Two
```

```
Three
Four
Five
Six
Seven
Eight
```

> **NOTE** When removing items from your ArrayList, you should use an iterator. Don't use an enhanced for loop.

Exercise 2: Mixed-Up Animals

Create an ArrayList that will be used to hold the names of different animals that will be entered by the user. As you add each string to the ArrayList, insert it where it belongs alphabetically. Print the list out after each time the user enters a new value. For example, if the user entered **Mouse** and then **Cat**, your list would look like:

```
Cat
Mouse
```

If they then entered **Dog**, your list should print as follows:

```
Cat
Dog
Mouse
```

Have the user enter 10 different animals in a mixed-up order. When you print the final list, it should be ordered alphabetically without any added work.

Lesson 23
Exploring Maps

This lesson continues the discussion of using collections by exploring the Map data structure, which is used for saving key/value pairs. In the lesson, we will primarily focus on the HashMap implementation and how to work with it in your code.

LEARNING OBJECTIVES

By the end of this lesson, you will be able to:
- Describe the Map interface
- Understand the HashMap implementation of Map
- Work the HashMap in your code

MAP INTERFACE

A Map is an object that maps keys to values. In general, a map models the concept of a mathematical function. In a map, each *key* can map to one and only one *value*, so it cannot contain duplicate keys.

While Maps are part of the Java Collections Framework, the Map interface itself is not a Collection (i.e., it does not extend the Collection interface, and it is not iterable); however, we can get a Collection of either the keys or the values of a Map or a Collection of Entry objects (both Key and Value).

The Map interface has many methods. In this lesson, we will cover the most often used methods, which are as follows:

- `get`
- `put`
- `keySet`
- `size`
- `values`

> **NOTE** We cover a few examples using these methods in this lesson; however, it is recommended that you should read the Javadoc associated with each to become familiar with how they work. You can find the Map interface in the Javadocs at `docs.oracle.com/en/java/javase/15/docs/api/java.base/java/util/Map.html` for Version 15, or at `docs.oracle.com/en/java/javase/11/docs/api/java.base/java/util/Map.html` if you are using version 11.

HashMap

We will focus on the HashMap implementation of the Map interface for now. HashMap is the most commonly used implementation of the Map interface. In the following sections, we'll review a number of code snippets to see the features of the HashMap. As an example, we'll see how it can be used to hold the population of several countries.

CREATING AND ADDING ENTRIES TO A MAP

Working with Maps is similar to working with other collections. This includes creating, instantiating, and then adding to a Map.

Instantiating a Map

Like with any class, the first step to using a Map is to declare a variable and then instantiate a Map object. Like the List we saw before, a Map is a generic type, so we need to say what type of elements it will hold.

A Map will differ from a List. When we created a List, we provided a type to identify the type of values that would be stored. In a Map, a type for the value still needs to be provided, but a type for the keys must also be included.

As an example, we will store populations for countries. Each country will be unique in that there cannot be two countries with the same name, so the country name will be our key. The population would then be the values being stored.

```
Map<String, Integer> populations = new HashMap<>();
```

This declares a Map that has a key that is a String value that will be able to hold our country name and an Integer that will be able to hold our value, which will be the population. Similar to Lists, we create a reference to the interface. In this case, a Map is equal to a new HashMap, the concrete implementation.

As was the case when we used other collections, for Map and HashMap to be used in our code, we'll need to import them.

```
import java.util.HashMap;
import java.util.Map;
```

Adding Data to a Map

With an empty Map created, we are ready to add something to it. We add data to a Map using the put() method, passing in the key first and then the value. For example, if we wanted to add the population for the United States, then we could use USA for the key and then the population as an Integer type for the value.

```
populations.put("USA", 328000000);
```

Using put(), this adds the value of 328000000 to our populations HashMap using the key USA. We could add additional countries in the same manner.

```
populations.put("Canada", 37590000);
populations.put("United Kingdom", 66800000);
populations.put("Japan", 126000000);
```

> **NOTE** We are using Integer to store population; however, using a Long might be more appropriate since it is possible for a country such as China to have a population that won't fit in an Integer.

Listing 23.1 presents the instantiation and addition of items into a simple listing.

LISTING 23.1

Creating a HashMap

```java
import java.util.HashMap;
import java.util.Map;

public class MapsExample {

    public static void main(String[] args) {

        Map<String, Integer> populations = new HashMap<>();

        populations.put("USA", 328000000);
        populations.put("Canada", 37590000);
        populations.put("United Kingdom", 66800000);
        populations.put("Japan", 126000000);

        System.out.println("Map size is: " + populations.size());
    }
}
```

One additional line was added to this listing in which we print out the number of elements in the Map that was created. We get the number of elements using the size() method. When executed, our four population elements are added with their key values.

```
Map size is: 4
```

The listing tells us that the size of the populations Map is 4, which matches what we added.

MANIPULATING WITH ENTRIES IN A MAP

While it is great to add elements to a Map, for it to be useful, we need to be able to access those elements. Additionally, because nobody is perfect, it would also be good to know how to replace or delete Map elements.

Looking Up Values in a Map

We use the get() method to look up a Value in a Map, passing in the key for what we want to retrieve. For example, if we wanted to get the population of Japan from our populations HashMap and save it in a new variable, we would pass the key value of Japan to the get() method as follows:

```
Integer foundPopulation = populations.get("Japan");
```

If we use a key that is not in the Map, get() will return a value of null. Listing 23.2 expands on the previous listing to print the population of Japan, which is a key in our Map. It also prints the value returned when trying to use a key (ASDF) that hasn't been added to the populations Map.

LISTING 23.2

Getting Values from a Map

```java
import java.util.HashMap;
import java.util.Map;

public class MapsExample {

    public static void main(String[] args) {

        Map<String, Integer> populations = new HashMap<>();

        populations.put("USA", 328000000);
        populations.put("Canada", 37590000);
        populations.put("United Kingdom", 66800000);
        populations.put("Japan", 126000000);

        System.out.println("Map size is: " + populations.size());

        Integer japanPopulation = populations.get("Japan");
        System.out.println("The population of Japan is: " + japanPopulation);

        Integer ASDFPopulation = populations.get("ASDF");
        System.out.println("The population of ASDF is: " + ASDFPopulation);
    }
}
```

The output from executing this is as follows:

```
Map size is: 4
The population of Japan is: 126000000
The population of ASDF is: null
```

As expected, this output confirms that Japan was found and that ASDF wasn't.

Replacing Data in a Map

If we want to replace data in a Map, we simply use the put() method again with the same key. In maps, the keys must be unique, so when we use put() with an existing key, we overwrite the existing data. If we want to update the population of the United States, then we use the key USA and our new population.

```
populations.put("USA", 328000002);
```

Once this has been executed, the new value for USA will be updated to 328000002, which is an increase of 2.

Removing Values from a Map

There are times when we might need to completely remove a key and its associated value from a Map. We can do this by using the remove() method and pass in the key. If we wanted to remove Japan from our Map, we'd pass the following:

```
populations.remove("Japan");
```

When this line of code is executed, an entry with a key of Japan will be removed from the Map.

GETTING KEYS AND LISTING MAPPED VALUES IN A MAP

At this point we've manipulated the data in our Map, and we've been able to pull out a value when we knew the key. In the real world, we might not always know the keys or the values. We might get a Map from a data store, or we might read a file where we don't know what the keys are. As such, it would be good to know how to get the keys and then to use those keys to get the values.

Listing All the Keys

Remember, keys have to be unique. If keys aren't unique, then we wouldn't be able to use them to get a value because there could be more than one result. Of course, while keys must be unique, a Map can have as many keys as you want.

Because of the uniqueness of the keys, when we retrieve them from a Map, we get them back in a Set. If you remember, we learned in a previous lesson that Sets are unordered Lists and must have unique values. This aligns with what we've said about the keys in Maps as well.

If we want all the keys in our populations Map that we created earlier, then we can create a Set and then pull the keys into the Set. Because a Set is a generic type, we need to say the type it will hold. The keys in our populations Map were Strings, so we could declare a keys Set as follows:

```
Set<String> keys
```

To then get the keys from our Map, we would use the keySet() method. This method returns a set of keys from our populations Map.

```
Set<String> keys = populations.keySet();
```

Once done getting the keys, you can then use an enhanced for loop (or other loop) to cycle through them, as shown in Listing 23.3.

LISTING 23.3

Printing the Keys from a Map

```
import java.util.HashMap;
import java.util.Map;
import java.util.Set;

public class MapsExample {

    public static void main(String[] args) {

        Map<String, Integer> populations = new HashMap<>();

        populations.put("USA", 328000000);
        populations.put("Canada", 37590000);
        populations.put("United Kingdom", 66800000);
        populations.put("Japan", 126000000);

        System.out.println("Map size is: "+ populations.size());

        // Update the USA
        populations.put("USA", 328000002);
```

```
        // get the Set of keys from the map
        Set<String> keys = populations.keySet();

        // print the keys to the screen
        for (String k : keys) {
            System.out.println(k);
        }
    }
}
```

In this listing we add values to the Map just like before and then print the size. We follow this by doing a call to put() to update the population for the United States. We simply add 2 to that population. The code should look familiar to that point.

We then create our Set object called keys. We call keySet() on our populations Map to get the set of keys.

With that completed, we use the enhanced for loop to cycle through each of the items in the Set that was created. As a reminder, for an enhanced for loop, to the left of the colon we declare a variable of the type we are pulling from the Set. In this case, we are getting the keys from our populations Map, which are String values. So, we will define a variable (k) of type String. To the right of the colon we supply the Collection that contains our elements we are grabbing. In this case, we are getting the elements from the keys object we just created and filled using keySet().

Within the body of our enhanced loop, we will get each key in our keys Set one by one. Our listing then simply prints each of these key values. Looking at the output, we see the size and updated population for USA followed by the list of our keys, which is exactly what we wanted.

```
Map size is: 4
The population of USA is: 328000002
Canada
USA
Japan
United Kingdom
```

> **NOTE** We cannot necessarily predict the order of the keys in the Set we get using keySet(). Most Map types do not save their data in a specific order.

Listing All the Values Key by Key

If we want to print out all the values in our Map, one way is to use the keySet() method as we did in Listing 23.3 and then use the get() method with each of those keys.

In Listing 23.4, we create our Map with items and then again use the enhanced for loop to display the value. In this case, you can see that we use the get() key with the obtained value in k to pull the value from populations.

LISTING 23.4

Getting Each Value Using the Obtained Keys

```java
import java.util.HashMap;
import java.util.Map;
import java.util.Set;

public class MapsExample {

    public static void main(String[] args) {

        Map<String, Integer> populations = new HashMap<>();

        populations.put("USA", 328000000);
        populations.put("Canada", 37590000);
        populations.put("United Kingdom", 66800000);
        populations.put("Japan", 126000000);

        Set<Map.Entry<String,Integer>> entries = populations.entrySet();

                for (Map.Entry e : entries) {
                    System.out.println("The population of " + e.getKey()
                        + " is " + e.getValue());
                }
        }
    }
}
```

When you execute this listing, we get each of the keys along with the corresponding values.

```
The population of Canada is 37590000
The population of USA is 328000000
The population of Japan is 126000000
The population of United Kingdom is 66800000
```

> **NOTE** You might have noticed that in Listing 23.4, the output printed the list of elements in a different order than they were added. They were added as USA, Canada, United Kingdom, and Japan, but printed as Canada, USA, Japan, and United Kingdom. As mentioned, Sets are unordered, so you should not rely on a specific order to be maintained.

Listing All the Values: Value Collection

There are times when we might want to grab all the Values from a Map collection without really caring about the keys. For example, if we simply wanted to get the average population of all the countries in our Map, then we wouldn't need the keys; we'd simply need the values.

We can also use the `values()` method to get a Collection of all the values in our Map. In this case, we are going to get the values as a Collection instead of a Set. In looking at our `populations` Map, when we call `values()`, it will return a Collection of the values, which will be the Integers containing the population numbers.

```
Collection<Integer> popValues = populations.values();
```

> **NOTE** The reason we want to use a Collection instead of a Set is that while we cannot have a duplicate key, we could have a duplicate value. A Collection lets us have duplicates, whereas a Set will not.

Most of Listing 23.5 should look familiar.

LISTING 23.5

Using a Collection to Get All Values

```java
import java.util.Collection;
import java.util.HashMap;
import java.util.Map;
```

```java
public class MapsExample {

    public static void main(String[] args) {

        Map<String, Integer> populations = new HashMap<>();

        populations.put("USA", 328000000);
        populations.put("Canada", 37590000);
        populations.put("United Kingdom", 66800000);
        populations.put("Japan", 126000000);

        // get the Collection of values from the Map
        Collection<Integer> popValues = populations.values();

        // list all of the population values
        for (Integer currentPopulation : popValues) {
            System.out.println(currentPopulation);
        }
    }
}
```

In this listing, we are once again adding four countries to our `populations` Map as we have done before. We then create a `Collection` of `Integers` called `popValues` and fill it with the values from our Map using the `values()` method. An enhanced `for` loop then prints each of these values using the `Integer currentPopulation` that was defined.

When this code is executed, the populations from our Map collection are displayed.

```
37590000
328000000
126000000
66800000
```

Remember, however, that these could be retrieved in any order.

NOTE We do not have access to the key information for any of the values when we use the `values()` method, so it is not always an applicable method to use. In fact, it is a common interview question to ask how to tell all the keys that go to `value(x)`.

SUMMARY

Maps are an often-used collection type that relies on key/value pairs. They are most appropriate to use when you have a collection that requires fast lookups by a unique key. As you learned in this lesson, there are several different ways you can work with Maps, and it is up to you to decide when each way makes sense to use.

EXERCISES

Most people learn best by doing, so this section includes exercises using what you learned in this lesson about Maps and previously in this course.

Exercise 1: State Capitals

Exercise 2: A Reusable User I/O Class

Exercise 3: Student Quiz Scores

Exercise 1: State Capitals

In this exercise, write a simple program that holds all the states and their corresponding capitals in a HashMap. Your program should include the following features:

- Create a Java Console application called StateCapitals.

- Create a HashMap to hold the names of the states and their corresponding capital names. (State name is the key; capital name is the value.)

- Load the HashMap with each state/capital pair. This can be hard-coded.

- Print all the state names to the screen. Hint: Get the keys from the map and then print each state name one by one.

- Print all the capital names to the screen. Hint: Get the values from the map and then print each capital name to the screen one by one.

- Print each state along with its capital to the screen. Hint: Use keySet() to get each value from the map one by one and then print both the key and value as you go.

Your resulting output should look similar to the following, although your order might vary:

```
STATES:
=======
Alabama
Alaska
Arizona
```

```
Arkansas
...
...

CAPITALS:
=========
Montgomery
Juneau
Phoenix
Little Rock
...
...

STATE/CAPITAL PAIRS:
====================
Alabama - Montgomery
Alaska - Juneau
Arizona - Phoenix
Arkansas - Little Rock
```

Exercise 2: A Reusable User I/O Class

The objective of this exercise includes designing and implementing programs that have more than one class. As such, you will create a reusable user class.

> **NOTE** Before coding, you should create a flowchart for your program to help plan what it will do.

Design a class that has methods to ask for and retrieve keyboard input from the user and to print information out to the console. Your class will not have a `main` method. Your class must implement the interface in Exercise Listing 23.1.

EXERCISE LISTING 23.1

UserIO Interface

```
public interface UserIO {

    void print(String message);
```

```
    String readString(String prompt);

    int readInt(String prompt);

    int readInt(String prompt, int min, int max);

    double readDouble(String prompt);

    double readDouble(String prompt, double min, double max);

    float readFloat(String prompt);

    float readFloat(String prompt, float min, float max);

    long readLong(String prompt);

    long readLong(String prompt, long min, long max);

}
```

The methods that you implement must behave in the following manner:

- print
  - Print a given String to the console. The String value displayed should be passed in as a parameter.
- readString
  - Display a given message String to prompt the user to enter in a String; then read in the user response as a String and return that value. The prompt message should be passed in as a parameter, and the String value read in should be the return value of the method.
- readInt
  - Display a given message String to prompt the user to enter in an integer and then read in the user response and return that integer value. The prompt message value should be passed in as a parameter, and the value that is read in should be the return of the method.
  - Display a prompt to the user to enter an integer between a specified min and max range and read in an integer. If the user's number does not fall within the range, keep prompting the user for new input until it does. The prompt message and min and max values should be passed in as parameters. The value read in from the console should be the return of the method.

- `readDouble`
  - Display a given message `String` to prompt the user to enter in a double and then read in the user response and return that double value. The prompt message value should be passed in as a parameter and the value that is read in should be the return of the method.
  - Display a prompt to the user to enter a double between a specified min and max range and read in a double. If the user's number does not fall within the range, keep prompting the user for new input until it does. The prompt message and min and max values should be passed in as parameters. The value read in from the console should be the return of the method.
- `readFloat`
  - Display a given message `String` to prompt the user to enter in a float, then read in the user response and return that float value. The prompt message value should be passed in as a parameter and the value that is read in should be the return of the method.
  - Display a prompt to the user to enter a float between a specified min and max range and read in a float. If the user's number does not fall within the range, keep prompting the user for new input until it does. The prompt message and min and max values should be passed in as parameters. The value read in from the console should be the return of the method.
- `readLong`
  - Display a given message `String` to prompt the user to enter in a long; then read in the user response and return that long value. The prompt message value should be passed in as a parameter, and the value that is read in should be the return of the method.
  - Display a prompt to the user to enter a long between a specified min and max range and read in a long. If the user's number does not fall within the range, keep prompting the user for a new input until it does. The prompt message and min and max values should be passed in as parameters. The value read in from the console should be the return of the method.

These methods will be used by another class with a `main` method, and this class implementation will be taking over the job of handling all the I/O to the console. Therefore, its methods need to be general so that the program built on top of it can use it to collect or display user input for just about anything.

The example in Exercise Listing 23.2 should be possible if your implementing class was called `UserIOImpl`.

EXERCISE LISTING 23.2

Testing the UserIO Interface

```java
public class TestingUserIO {
    public static void main(String[] args) {
        UserIO userIO = new UserIOImpl();
        int smallNum = userIO.readInt("Give me a small number :");
        int bigNum = userIO.readInt("Now give me a much bigger number! :");
        if(bigNum < smallNum){
            userIO.print("Hey! " + smallNum +" is BIGGER than " + bigNum);
            userIO.print("I guess I can fix it.");
            int swapNum = bigNum;
            bigNum = smallNum;
            smallNum = swapNum;
        }
        int betweenNum = userIO.readInt("Now give me one in between! : ",
smallNum, bigNum);
        userIO.print("I like the number " + betweenNum + "!");
    }
}
```

You will use the result of this class in the following exercise.

Exercise 3: Student Quiz Scores

In this exercise you will write a program that stores quiz scores for each student in a class and calculates the average quiz score for each student on request. The user should be able to do the following:

- View a list of students in the system
- Add a student to the system
- Remove a student from the system
- View a list of quiz scores for a given student
- View the average quiz score for a given student

It is up to you to design and implement a reasonable user interface (UI) menu system. You should design the UI and make a program flow chart before you begin coding.

Your program should include the following features:

- This program will be a Java console application called StudentQuizGrades.
- The program should use the UserIO class created previously for all console input and output.

- The program must store student quiz data in a HashMap that has the student name as the key and an ArrayList of integers as the values.

Once you have the program working, you can do the following for an additional challenge:

1. Calculate the average quiz score for the entire class.
2. Find and list the student(s) with the highest quiz score.
3. Find and list the student(s) with the lowest quiz score.

Lesson 24
Using Simple File Input and Output

Up to this point, we have been dealing with data as variables (primitives and objects) in memory and occasionally reading values from the console (and then promptly storing these values in a variable). This has worked well, but all of our data disappears when the program completes. To write truly useful programs, we must be able to store data when program execution ends and read that data the next time we run our programs.

In this lesson, we will begin to explore data persistence and ways that we can translate data from variables (in memory) to files (on disk) for long-term storage and then reverse the process when we need to access the data later. We will concentrate on storing data in flat text files for now, but the principles of this lesson continue to be relevant when we start storing data in relational databases.

We will also take a look at one way we can do simple file input and output. For now, however, we'll cover the basics—just enough to get data into and out of files.

LEARNING OBJECTIVES

By the end of this lesson, you will be able to:

- Describe options for data storage
- Describe how related data is represented in object-oriented languages
- Define marshaling and unmarshaling
- Explain the characteristics of a file format
- Create a plan to write data to and read data from a file
- Write to a file using `PrintWriter`
- Use `Scanner` to read from a file

DATA STORAGE AND REPRESENTATION

We have two options available to us for data storage: we can store data in memory, which is volatile, or we can store the data on more permanent media such as a hard disk, flash drive, or optical drive. Java has libraries that allow us to write data to and read data from more permanent media whether connected locally, on a network, or in the cloud. This is convenient for us, but these libraries don't have much intelligence—they will simply write out the bits that we give them. It is up to us to decide how this data should be represented and translated.

A group of related data is generally represented by an object in object-oriented languages such as Java. The object itself represents the thing being modeled (e.g., a student) and the fields on the object represent properties of the thing being modeled (e.g., first name, last name, age). In past lessons, we have seen how to create these classes and instantiate them into objects. We have also seen how to set values for the properties on the objects and even how to store them in maps and lists. We have not had to do any translation or marshaling/unmarshaling of any of these values because everything has always been stored as objects in memory.

Now that we want to permanently store this data, we must decide how the data will be represented. As mentioned in the overview, for now, we will be storing our data in flat text files on a local hard drive. We must encode the objects we have in memory in some way so that we can store them. The process of translating data from an object in memory into another format and writing it to permanent storage is known as *marshaling*. The reverse process—reading the data from permanent storage and translating it into objects in memory—is known as *unmarshaling*.

Our choice of using flat text files as our storage format implies that our data (even numbers) will be stored as text. We must design a file format that allows us to easily read from and write to the file, and that allows us to easily tell where the data of one object ends and the next one begins. We must also keep track of which fields are text and which fields are numbers so that we can convert them properly when reading from the file.

FILE FORMAT, MARSHALING, AND UNMARSHALING

To illustrate file format, marshaling, and unmarshaling, we will use the example of storing a student class roster to a file. We will discuss the particulars of the file format here and cover the details of the implementation in Lesson 27. In that lesson, a complete solution will be coded along with the lessons.

The key characteristics of any file format we choose to implement are as follows:

- We must be able to easily tell where one student record ends and the next one begins.
- We must be able to easily tell where one property within a student record ends and the next begins.
- Malformed records should have little or no impact on our ability to properly read subsequent records.
- The format must make it straightforward to read from and write to the file. In other words, the format should be easy to parse.

Given these overall requirements, we will go with the following file format:

- Each line in the file represents one student. This satisfies the first, third, and fourth bulleted items.
- Each field in the student record will be separated with the token : :. This satisfies the second item in the previous list. This token acts as a boundary between each field and can be called a *delimiter*. Commas and tabs are often used as delimiters.

As a bonus, we can tell how many students are in the roster by the number of lines in the file.

Student Class

In Listing 24.1, you see a Student class. The Student class shows how student data is stored in memory.

LISTING 24.1

The Student Class

```java
public class Student {
    private String firstName;
    private String lastName;
    private String studentId;
    private String cohort; // Java cohort month/year

    public Student(String studentId) {
        this.studentId = studentId;
    }

    public String getFirstName() {
        return firstName;
    }

    public void setFirstName(String firstName) {
        this.firstName = firstName;
    }

    public String getLastName() {
        return lastName;
    }

    public void setLastName(String lastName) {
        this.lastName = lastName;
    }

    public String getStudentID() {
        return studentId;
    }

    public String getCohort() {
        return cohort;
    }
```

```
    public void setCohort(String cohort) {
        this.cohort = cohort;
    }
}
```

If we look closely at the Student class, we see that there is nothing new being presented. Our class has four fields, firstName, lastName, studentID, and cohort, that we will want to save.

File Format Example

When we save our data, we will want to know the order and the file format. The file format is simply how the data will be stored in the file. In the case of our Student data, the following file format will be used:

```
<student id>::<first name>::<last name>::<cohort>
```

Here's an example:

```
0001::John::Doe::Java - August 2021
0002::Sally::Smith::Java - April 2021
0003::John::Jones::.NET - Jan 2021
```

Marshaling and Unmarshaling Approach

Now that we know how our student data will be represented in memory and on the disk, we can write code that translates from one to the other. This process will include opening the file, working with each Student object, and then cleaning up or closing everything.

Here is the outline for writing student data to the file:

1. Open the file for writing.

2. Go through the collection of students one by one.

3. For each student, do the following:

   a. Create a string consisting of student ID, first name, last name, and cohort (in that order), separated by ::.

   b. Write the string to the output file.

   c. Get the next student (if one exists) and go back to step a.

   d. If there are no more students to process, then quit.

4. Close the file.

Here is the outline for reading student data from the file:

1. Open the file for reading.

2. For each line in the file, do the following:

   a. Read the line into a string variable.

   b. Split the string into chunks at the `::` delimiter.

   c. Create a new student object.

   d. Use the first value from the split string to set the student ID.

   e. Use the second value from the split string to set the student first name.

   f. Use the third value from the split string to set the student last name.

   g. User the fourth value from the split string to set the cohort value.

   h. Put the newly created and initialized student object into a collection or map.

   i. If there are more lines in the file, go to step a.

   j. If there are no more lines in the file, quit creating student objects.

3. Close the file.

This high-level marshaling/unmarshaling approach will continue to be useful even as we move from storing our data in flat files to storing data in relational databases. We will use different tools and libraries, but the general concepts will remain the same.

SIMPLE FILE I/O

Let's dig deeper and cover the basics of how to do simple file input and output. We'll add more elegant error processing code after we learn about handling exceptions in Lesson 26. We'll start by writing to a file using `PrintWriter`. We will follow this by seeing how to use the same `Scanner` class we've used previously to read from the file we create.

> **NOTE** There are lots of ways to read and write to files. This lesson is presenting one approach to do this so that you can see the process. The focus of the following is not to go into depth, but so that you have a simple way to read and write to files on your own.

Writing to a File

We will use a `PrintWriter` object to write to our files. There are several other approaches that you can use to write to files, but we will use `PrintWriter` because it is similar to writing output to the console, which we've been doing with the `System.out`.

Because we are writing to a file, we will pass `PrintWriter` a `FileWriter` object to take care of handling the writing of the characters to the file. When we create the `FileWriter` object, we will pass it a single parameter—the name of the file we want to write. This can be any valid filename.

Because both `PrintWriter` and `FileWriter` are existing classes, we will need to include their code. As we have learned, this is done by adding `import` statements to our code:

```
import java.io.PrintWriter;
import java.io.FileWriter;
```

With the `import` statements in place, we can create our `PrintWriter` object.

```
PrintWriter out = new PrintWriter(new FileWriter("OutFile.txt"));
```

In this case, we are creating a `PrintWriter` object called `out`. As mentioned, we are passing into it a new `FileWriter` object that is created using our filename, `OutFile.txt`. The end result of this call is that we've opened a stream that can be used to write to our file.

With our `PrintWriter` object created, we can use it to write information. Listing 24.2 pulls this process together into a complete.

LISTING 24.2

Writing to a File

```
import java.io.FileWriter;
import java.io.PrintWriter;

public class SimpleFileIO {

    public static void main(String[] args) throws Exception {
        try ( PrintWriter out = new PrintWriter(new
FileWriter("OutFile.txt"))) {
            out.println("this is a line in my file...");
            out.println("a second line in my file...");
```

```
                out.println("a third line in my file...");
                out.flush();
                out.close();
            }
        }
    }
```

Taking a look at the code in the listing, we can again see that the main method starts by declaring and initializing a PrintWriter called out to write to a file called OutFile.txt. If OutFile.txt does not exist, it will be created automatically. If it does exist, it will be overwritten.

Once out is created, we can use its println() method to write to our file. We use println() in the same manner that we used it with System.out to display information to the console. You can see that we write three lines to our file in this listing.

Writing to a file is different from writing to the console. When we write out to the console, it shows up on the console right away. Well, when we write to a file, it may or may not go right away. The system might save the items to be written and write them out to the file in a more efficient way. For example, if we have a lot of little items being written to the file, then the PrintWriter might bundle them and write them to the file at the same time. As such, once we've done our three calls to println(), we don't know if our lines have actually written. By calling the flush() method, we force everything to be written to the file. This process gives us a method for getting everything written without further delay.

The last thing we need to do is call the close() method, which closes the underlying stream that PrintWriter uses to write to the file. It is important to close resources such as streams.

> **NOTE** Even though we don't have to manually allocate/deallocate memory in Java, we can still have resource leaks if we don't properly clean up after ourselves. In Lesson 26, you will learn about exception handling and using throws and try. Writing items to a file is an area of your code where you will want to apply exception handling (and the use of the try command).

Exceptions

When you typed the code from Listing 24.2 into your program, you might have noticed that after the call to main is the added phrase throws Exception. If you remove throws Exception from the line of code, then NetBeans will highlight an issue for the line where the PrintWriter is declared and initialized, as shown in Figure 24.1.

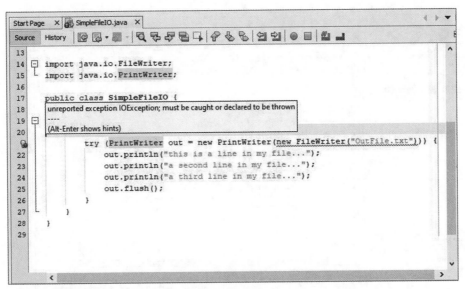

```
13
14  ⊟   import java.io.FileWriter;
15  └   import java.io.PrintWriter;
16
17      public class SimpleFileIO {
18          unreported exception IOException; must be caught or declared to be thrown
19  ⊟      ----
20          (Alt-Enter shows hints)
            try (PrintWriter out = new PrintWriter(new FileWriter("OutFile.txt"))) {
22              out.println("this is a line in my file...");
23              out.println("a second line in my file...");
24              out.println("a third line in my file...");
25              out.flush();
26          }
27      }
28  }
29
```

Figure 24.1 An exception that must be caught

Creating a new FileWriter can cause an exception called an IOException. When we encounter code that can throw an exception (as this code does), we should handle the error in some way.

One way to handle this situation is to put a label on our main method that indicates that the code contained in the main method may cause an exception to be thrown. In addition to that label, you will also see that the keyword try has been added. The use of PrintWriter has been placed within the try command's parentheses. The command that writes the information to the file has been placed in a code block for the try. This added code is the minimal code to handle an error should it happen.

For now, we are just going to label our code to indicate that it may cause an error and add a simple try command. We will learn about throw, try, and how to properly handle exceptions in Lesson 26 on exception handling. For now, you need to add these to your listing to fix the syntax error that will otherwise be identified by NetBeans.

The OutFile.txt File

When we run Listing 24.2, we don't see anything on the screen. That's because we didn't send anything to the screen. Rather, we sent it to the file OutFile.txt. You can find this file on your hard drive, or you can look at it from within NetBeans.

To find the file in NetBeans, start by clicking the Files tab in the Projects pane. This will show a different view of our project that lists all the files that we actually have on disk. As you can see in Figure 24.2, one of our files is the new OutFile.txt that we just created.

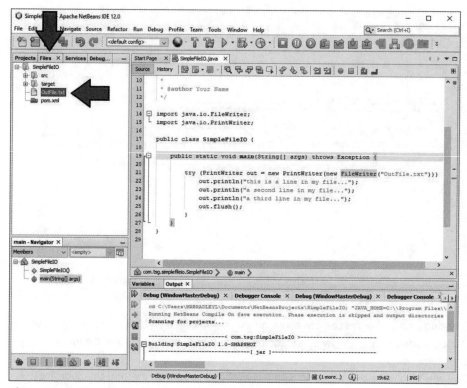

Figure 24.2 The Files tab

If you double-click OutFile.txt in the File tab, it will open the file, as shown in Figure 24.3.

As you can see, all three lines were written to our file. If you run the program again, it will overwrite these lines.

Reading from a File

We will use the Scanner object to read from our files. There are alternative approaches to reading from files, but we will use this one because it is similar to reading from the console. Listing 24.3 opens the file OutFile.txt, reads each line, and prints each line of the file to the screen.

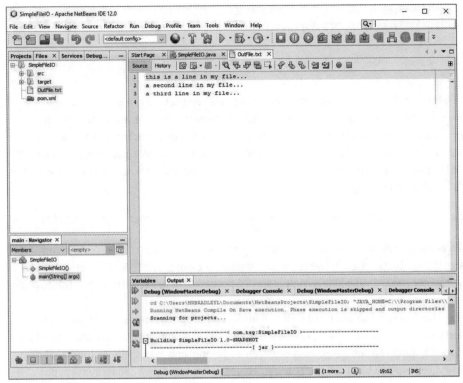

Figure 24.3 The OutFile.txt file

LISTING 24.3

Reading the OutFile.txt File

```java
import java.io.BufferedReader;
import java.io.FileReader;
import java.util.Scanner;

public class SimpleFileIO {

    public static void main(String[] args) throws Exception {

        Scanner sc = new Scanner(
                new BufferedReader(new FileReader("OutFile.txt")));

        // go through the file line by line
        while (sc.hasNextLine()) {
```

```
                String currentLine = sc.nextLine();
                System.out.println(currentLine);
            }
        }
    }
```

If we look at the `main()` method in our listing, we see that we are creating a new `Scanner`. We have created `Scanner`s in the past; however, this time we create it with a `BufferedReader` instead of `System.in`. The `BufferedReader` will require a new `FileReader` that includes the name of the file we want to read. We pass this filename (`OutFile.txt` in our case) to the `FileReader` constructor. This makes for a long line, but it opens our file for reading.

```
Scanner sc = new Scanner(new BufferedReader(new FileReader("OutFile.txt")));
```

Like working with the `FileWriter`, creating a new `FileReader` can cause an error. Specifically, if the file specified in the constructor does not exist, a `FileNotFoundException` will be thrown. Again, we will learn in Lesson 26 how to handle exceptions, but for now we added `throws Exception` to the `main()` method.

After the `Scanner` has been created and initialized properly, we use methods such as `hasNextLine()` and `nextLine()`, just as we do when reading from the console. The `hasNextLine()` checks to see whether there is an additional line in our file. As long as there is, the `while` loop will then call `nextLine()` to get it, followed by a call to `System.out.println()` to display it to the console.

```
this is a line in my file...
a second line in my file...
a third line in my file...
```

SUMMARY

In this lesson, you learned about the high-level marshaling/unmarshaling approach, which will be useful as you work with data, whether storing it in flat files or in databases. We then jumped into code to see a simple way to do file input and output. This lesson has just enough to get you started. We will look at some more complicated scenarios in future lessons.

EXERCISES

Most people learn best by doing, so this section includes exercises using what you learned in this lesson and previously in this course.

Exercise 1: Creating State Capitals

In this exercise, you write a program that creates a file called `StateCapitals.txt` that has a list of states and their capitals with a delimiter between them. The data to write to your file is as follows:

```
Alabama::Montgomery
Alaska::Juneau
Arizona::Phoenix
Arkansas::Little Rock
California::Sacramento
Colorado::Denver
Connecticut::Hartford
Delaware::Dover
Florida::Tallahassee
Georgia::Atlanta
Hawaii::Honolulu
Idaho::Boise
Illinois::Springfield
Indiana::Indianapolis
Iowa::Des Moines
Kansas::Topeka
Kentucky::Frankfort
Louisiana::Baton Rouge
Maine::Augusta
Maryland::Annapolis
Massachusetts::Boston
Michigan::Lansing
Minnesota::Saint Paul
Mississippi::Jackson
Missouri::Jefferson City
Montana::Helena
Nebraska::Lincoln
Nevada::Carson City
New Hampshire::Concord
New Jersey::Trenton
New Mexico::Santa Fe
New York::Albany
```

```
North Carolina::Raleigh
North Dakota::Bismarck
Ohio::Columbus
Oklahoma::Oklahoma City
Oregon::Salem
Pennsylvania::Harrisburg
Rhode Island::Providence
South Carolina::Columbia
South Dakota::Pierre
Tennessee::Nashville
Texas::Austin
Utah::Salt Lake City
Vermont::Montpelier
Virginia::Richmond
Washington::Olympia
West Virginia::Charleston
Wisconsin::Madison
Wyoming::Cheyenne
```

You will use this file for the following exercise.

> **NOTE** Keep it simple! You can write each of the lines of information just like you saw in Listing 24.2.

Exercise 2: Hashing the State Capitals

In this exercise, write a program that uses the file you created in Exercise 1 to load information into a HashMap. If you recall, you loaded state capitals into a HashMap in Exercise 1 of Lesson 23. This time, your program must do the following:

- Create a HashMap to hold the names of all the states and their corresponding capital names. (State name is still the key and the capital name is the value.)
- Load the HashMap with each state/capital pair using the StateCapitals.txt file you created in Exercise 1.
- After loading, print out how many state/capitals pairs are inside your map.
- Then print out all the state names to the screen.

Exercise 3: A State Guessing Game

Expand on Exercise 2. Create a small knowledge game. Choose a random state and prompt the user to input its capital. Let them know if they get it correct.

To take this exercise to the next level, make the following improvements:

- Ask them how many they want to guess and choose that many states. (Don't allow duplicates.)
- Give them a point for each correct guess and subtract one for each miss.
- Print out a total score at the end.

Here's some sample output (order may vary):

```
READY TO TEST YOUR KNOWLEDGE? WHAT IS THE CAPITAL OF 'Alaska'?
Juneau
NICE WORK! Juneau IS CORRECT!
```

Exercise 4: Objectifying States

This exercise is similar to the previous one, but you will create an object to hold information about the capital of each state. This object will be the value for each state/capital pair.

Also, instead of doing the exhaustive hand hard-coding of each capital's information, you should load in all the information from a given file. Your program must do the following:

- It will have a class called `Capital` with the following properties:
  - Name
  - Population
  - Square mileage
- It will have another class with your main method called `StateCapitalsApp`.
  - The main method should include a HashMap declared to map the name of a state to its corresponding `Capital` object. (The state name is the key; the `Capital` object is the value.)
  - Next, use your data unmarshaling strategy to use a file to create all appropriate `Capital` objects and store them under their appropriate state name in your HashMap. Use the data at the end of this exercise to create a file called `More-StateCapitals.txt` to be used.
- Print out a message detailing how many state capitals were loaded into your HashMap.
- Next, print out each state and its capital's name, population, and square mileage to the screen. (Hint: Use the key set to get each `Capital` object out of the map one by one and then print each field of the `Capital` object to the screen.)

- Prompt the user for a population limit, and print out all states and their capitals that have a population over that limit. (Hint: You will have to add code to ask the user for a minimum population. Once you have this value, go through each state/capital pair as you did for the previous step, but only print the information for capitals that have a population above the limit.)

- Finally, prompt the user for an area limit, and print out all states and capitals that have an area under that limit.

The following is sample output. The order of information may vary.

```
50 STATE/CAPITAL PAIRS LOADED.
================================
Alabama - Montgomery | Pop: 205000 | Area: 156 sq mi
Alaska - Juneau | Pop: 31000 | Area: 3255 sq mi
Arizona - Phoenix | 1445000 | Area: 517 sq mi
Arkansas - Little Rock | Pop: 193000 | Area: 116 sq mi
...

...


Please enter the lower limit for capital city population: 150000
150000

LISTING CAPITALS WITH POPULATIONS GREATER THAN 150000:

Alabama - Montgomery | Pop: 205000 | Area: 156 sq mi
Arizona - Phoenix | 1445000 | Area: 517 sq mi
Arkansas - Little Rock | Pop: 193000 | Area: 116 sq mi
...

...


Please enter the upper limit for capital city sq mileage:
150

LISTING CAPITALS WITH AREAS LESS THAN 150:
Arkansas - Little Rock | Pop: 193000 | Area: 116 sq mi
...

...
```

The following is the data you should have in your file. You can modify Exercise 1 to write this data instead of the data you used before:

```
Alabama::Montgomery::205764::155.4
Alaska::Juneau::31275::2716.7
Arizona::Phoenix::1445632::474.9
Arkansas::Little Rock::193524::116.2
```

```
California::Sacramento::466488::97.2
Colorado::Denver::600158::153.4
Connecticut::Hartford::124775::17.3
Delaware::Dover::36047::22.4
Florida::Tallahassee::181376::95.7
Georgia::Atlanta::420003::131.7
Hawaii::Honolulu::337256::85.7
Idaho::Boise City::205671::63.8
Illinois::Springfield::116250::54
Indiana::Indianapolis::820445::361.5
Iowa::Des Moines::203433::75.8
Kansas::Topeka::127473::56
Kentucky::Frankfort::25527::14.7
Louisiana::Baton Rouge::229493::76.8
Maine::Augusta::19136::55.4
Maryland::Annapolis::38394::6.73
Massachusetts::Boston::617594::48.4
Michigan::Lansing::114297::35
Minnesota::St. Paul::285068::52.8
Mississippi::Jackson::173514::104.9
Missouri::Jefferson City::43079::27.3
Montana::Helena::28190::14
Nebraska::Lincoln::258379::74.6
Nevada::Carson City::55274::143.4
New Hampshire::Concord::42695::64.3
New Jersey::Trenton::84913::7.66
New Mexico::Santa Fe::67947::37.3
New York::Albany::97856::21.4
North Carolina::Raleigh::403892::114.6
North Dakota::Bismarck::61272::26.9
Ohio::Columbus::787033::210.3
Oklahoma::Oklahoma City::579999::607
Oregon::Salem::154637::45.7
Pennsylvania::Harrisburg::49528::8.11
Rhode Island::Providence::178042::18.5
South Carolina::Columbia::129272::125.2
South Dakota::Pierre::13646::13
Tennessee::Nashville-Davidson::601222::473.3
Texas::Austin::790390::251.5
Utah::Salt Lake City::186440::109.1
Vermont::Montpelier::7855::10.2
Virginia::Richmond::204214::60.1
Washington::Olympia::46478::16.7
West Virginia::Charleston::51400::31.6
Wisconsin::Madison::233209::68.7
Wyoming::Cheyenne::59466::21.1
```

Lesson 25
Applying Application Design

In this lesson, we will step back from the code and focus on some foundational topics that are needed by master-level Java developers. We have seen that well-designed classes are cohesive and well encapsulated. As we start to write more complex applications—applications with multiple classes and a wide-ranging set of capabilities—we need additional tools and techniques to keep our code clean and easy to maintain. In this lesson, we will look at one of these techniques, tiered application design, and how we can apply it.

Additionally, we will discuss the software development lifecycle (SDLC). SDLC is a general term for the process or processes that we use to build software applications. There are many different approaches and schools of thought on this topic, but there are two main categories: waterfall and iterative. We will look at each approach and then outline the approach that we will use in the rest of the course.

LEARNING OBJECTIVES

By the end of this lesson, you will be able to:

- Define CRUD
- Explain how tiered design benefits application development
- Identify the basic tiers of tiered design
- Describe the different parts of the Model-View-Controller pattern
- Explain packages as they apply to coding development
- Understand what the software development lifecycle is
- Explain waterfall including its advantages and disadvantages
- Compare waterfall to iterative approaches to designing software
- Explain agile including its advantages and disadvantages

CRUD APPLICATIONS

CRUD stands for Create, Read, Update, and Delete. We use this to describe applications that are primarily concerned with managing, updating, and storing information. CRUD applications come in all shapes and sizes, for example:

- The contact manager on your phone

- Human resources (HR) and medical systems

- Amazon

- Facebook

Most business applications are CRUD applications to some degree. Because businesses depend on their data to run efficiently, CRUD applications are usually mission critical to a company. We will start building CRUD applications now using the design patterns and techniques that are used for building web applications. Many of these patterns and techniques are overkill for the small console applications we will be building in several of the next lessons, but we introduce these patterns to you now to help you prepare for building web applications.

Using a Tiered Design

Tiered application design allows us to ensure that our principles of separation of concerns, cohesion, and encapsulation are present in all parts of our applications. By keeping our concerns separated, we can reuse components in a variety of environments. In other words, our classes and layers are not tightly coupled to each other.

The Basic Tiers

CRUD applications have four basic layers:

- **Storage:** Files, databases, or other persistent storage
- **Data access:** Classes that handle retrieving and storing data
- **Business logic:** Classes that handle all logic specific to your problem domain (traditionally referred to as the *service layer*)
- **User interface:** Classes that handle all interaction with the user (traditionally referred to as the *presentation layer*)

In addition to these basic tiers, which are also shown in Figure 25.1, we have *data transfer objects* (DTOs). DTOs are used to move data from one tier to another in our applications. They are simply Java classes that have fields and getters/setters and no other methods. As the name implies, they are used to ferry data between the layers of our application.

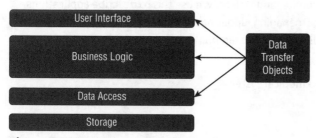

Figure 25.1 Basic tiers of an application

THE MODEL-VIEW-CONTROLLER PATTERN

We will use a specific tiered application design called the Model-View-Controller (MVC) pattern. MVC, which is shown in Figure 25.2, is one of many design patterns that software developers use to build applications. As the name implies, MVC applications consist of three main layers, or types, of components.

- **Model:** The model comprises all the components in the application that deal with representing and storing data. In our applications, this includes the storage layer, the data access layer, and the DTOs.

- **Controller:** The controller is the brain of the program. The controller orchestrates the actions of the other components in the application in a way that accomplishes the application's goals. You can think of a controller as a general contractor—it knows what needs to be done, when it needs to be done, and who can do it, but it never does the work itself. It uses other classes in the application to get the actual work done.

- **View:** The view is responsible for interacting with the user. No other component in the application is allowed to interact with the user. All of this must go through the view.

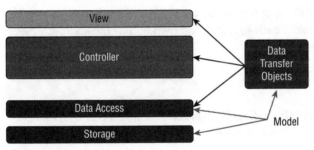

Figure 25.2 MVC model

Design Pattern

A *design pattern* is a general approach or template for solving a commonly occurring problem that can be applied in many different situations. Design patterns can be considered best practices that developers can apply to commonly occurring software design problems.

PACKAGES

There is a Java feature called *packages* that helps us further organize our code. Each package is essentially a folder into which we place related classes. We've been using packages in a nominal way already—the IDE automatically creates a package for each project that we create. Going forward, we will be more intentional about creating our packages.

Each of the basic tiers or types of classes has its own package. We recommend that you follow this pattern for all your projects in the remainder of the course:

- DTOs go in the dto package
- Data access objects (DAOs) go in the dao package
- Controller objects go in the controller package
- User interface objects go in the ui package

SOFTWARE DEVELOPMENT LIFECYCLE OVERVIEW

In addition to understanding the MVC pattern, it is also important to understand the SDLC, the process or processes that we use to build software applications. There are many different approaches and schools of thought on this topic, but there are two main categories: waterfall and iterative. We will look at each approach and then outline the approach that we will use in the rest of the course.

Waterfall

The *waterfall approach* to building software has been around a long time, and it is simple and intuitive. The main outline looks like an outline for approaching just about any project and consists of these parts:

1. There is an idea for a project.
2. All the requirements for the project are gathered, and a comprehensive specification is created.
3. The software is written according to the specification.
4. Testing is done against the specification.
5. Bugs are reported and fixed.
6. The project is shipped.

In a waterfall project, this sequence is done only once, which means that this process does not respond to change very well. It rests on the premise that all the requirements can be gathered and specified up front.

Despite its inflexible nature, the waterfall approach is well suited for certain types of projects. If you have a project where all the requirements are known up front and you know they won't change, this process is great. Generally, those types of projects involve systems that put people's lives on the line, such as avionics or medical equipment systems.

These types of systems must get it right the first time and must be verifiable against a stable specification because the price of a mistake is very high.

Iterative Development

Iterative software development takes a different approach. It embraces change because change is inevitable in most projects. Many of the steps in the iterative process are the same as those in the waterfall model, but the steps are repeated as many times as needed to complete the project. Each time through the process adds functionality and refines the project. It looks like this:

1. There is an idea for a project.
2. Initial requirements are gathered.
3. The next iteration is planned.
4. The features scheduled for that iteration are developed and tested.
5. The features scheduled for that iteration are delivered.
6. Wash, rinse, repeat steps 2–5 until the project is ready to ship.

This process rests on the premise that all requirements cannot be known up front and that even the requirements that are known up front are subject to change at any point. Steps 2 through 5 are repeated until the project is ready to ship. Each time step 2 is repeated, the team re-evaluates the overall requirements and makes sure that the project is still on course relative to the current situation.

The iterative approach is appropriate for almost all projects. It is especially appropriate for business applications because changes in the market or actions by competitors can drastically change the requirements of a project over time. The iterative approach expects those changes and mitigates the risk associated with those changes by delivering features a few at a time in each iteration and then frequently confirming that the project is on course to meet the current needs of the client.

AGILE DEVELOPMENT

We use a type of iterative development called *agile* in this course. There are many different approaches that call themselves agile, and each methodology has its own emphasis and terms for the concepts discussed here. Devotees of the different agile approaches can be a bit zealous and each company has its own take on agile development. We strive to show you these concepts in a method-agnostic manner. Having said that, we have to start with something, and we take concepts from the OpenUP and eXtreme Programming approaches.

Project Lifecycle

The big pattern that is repeated in the OpenUP approach consists of four phases.

- **Phase 1:** Inception
- **Phase 2:** Elaboration
- **Phase 3:** Construction
- **Phase 4:** Transition

This is the structure for the overall project as well as for each iteration within the project. The main idea is that as the project moves through the phases on a macro level, the team is adding value and reducing risk to the project. Value in an agile project equates to working, production-quality code that meets the current requirements of the project. The more working code the team has delivered, the greater the value of the project and the lower the risk to successful delivery.

Phase 1: Inception

Inception is the beginning of any project. To move on to the next overall phase of the project, the team must do the following:

- Agree on scope and objectives
- Understand what is to be built
- Identify key system functionality
- Determine at least one feasible solution
- Understand the high-level estimate for cost
- Understand the high-level schedule
- Understand the high-level risks to the project

In other words, all stakeholders must agree on what will be built, agree on the approximate cost (will it be $10,000 or $1,000,000?), agree on the time frame (will this take three months or three years?), and agree that a solution to the problem is feasible (for example, that the solution doesn't require time travel or some other impossibility).

Phase 2: Elaboration

Once all stakeholders agree to the criteria of the Inception phase, the project moves into Elaboration. In this phase, the stakeholders do the following:

- Gather more detailed requirements
- Design, implement, validate, and establish a baseline for the technical architecture of the project

- Mitigate essential risks
- Have a more accurate idea of costs and schedule

This phase is all about gaining a better understanding of the requirements and mitigating technical risk. The main deliverable of Elaboration is an *executable architecture*, which is a rudimentary working software proof-of-concept for the technically riskiest portions of the project. To the extent possible, the goal is to prove that a solution is possible. To move on to the next phase, all stakeholders must agree that the executable architecture represents the technical path forward. Everyone must also agree that the value delivered and remaining risks are acceptable.

Phase 3: Construction

Next, the project moves into the Construction phase. This is where the development team starts development of the features of the product. Features are delivered in an iterative manner—iteration lengths are short (usually from one to three weeks), and features are delivered at the end of each iteration. After each iteration, the team re-examines the requirements to make sure nothing has changed, corrects course if necessary, plans the features for the next iteration, and then develops the features for that iteration. Testing occurs constantly in this process. Features are tested as they are completed, and all bugs are fixed before the end of the iteration.

This process continues until the stakeholders determine that all the required features have been implemented and that it is time to switch focus to tuning, polishing, and deployment.

Phase 4: Transition

The Transition phase concentrates on getting the project ready for release. This phase includes beta testing to make sure that customer expectations are met and involves gathering information on lessons learned so that future projects can be improved.

Once all stakeholders agree that the software is ready for release, it is delivered, and the project comes to a close.

Iterations

The project lifecycle is measured in months and keeps its focus at the overall stakeholder level. The iteration lifecycle is measured in weeks and focuses on the team doing the planning and work for the iteration. Finally, the work item level is measured in days and is focused on the individual team member.

A few hours are spent at the beginning of each iteration planning the work to be done. Time is also spent here in verifying that all the project assumptions and requirements still hold. If requirements have changed, adjustments are made here. You can think of this as the Inception phase of the iteration.

After planning is complete, a few days are spent in up-front technical planning and architecture. This addresses any technical risks or concerns for the work to be done during the iteration. You can think of this as the Elaboration phase of the iteration.

After technical planning is completed, work on the features begins. Developers work on individual work items according to the iteration plan. Features are tested as they are delivered, and bugs are fixed as they are reported. The team strives to get a stable build at the end of each week. This is the Construction phase of the iteration.

As the iteration ends, all completed features are finalized and put into a final stable iteration build—this is the output of the iteration. A few hours are spent at the end of the iteration to gather lessons learned. This information is then used to make the next iteration better. This is the Transition phase of the iteration.

These iterations continue until all the required features of the application are complete. After that, the overall project moves into the Transition phase, and the entire project is delivered to the customer.

> **NOTE** Appendix C contains an agile approach checklist for console CRUD applications.

SUMMARY

Generally speaking, tiered design is overkill for console applications of the size we have been doing in this course so far. However, we are using this approach in preparation for moving our applications to the web. MVC is one of the most widely used patterns in web application development, and you will use it for all the web application projects and assignments.

This lesson also covered the software development lifecycle. The SDLC describes how we work in teams to deliver large applications to our customers. Understanding how this works and how you, as a developer, fit into the overall picture is important to your success as a professional software developer. You should follow the agile approach to development for your projects throughout the rest of this course.

Lesson 26
Handling Exceptions

I t is inevitable that your programs will sometimes have errors. These can be errors within your code such as dividing by zero, errors caused by bad data, or errors caused by numerous other reasons. Error conditions in Java are represented by exceptions. The Java mechanisms for handling exceptions are the try, catch, and finally constructs and the throws keyword.

One of the marks of a professional developer is that their programs handle exceptions and recover gracefully. This means that predictable error conditions are expected and do not crash the program because additional code is written to handle these runtime errors.

LEARNING OBJECTIVES

By the time you finish this lesson, you will be able to:

- Define an exception
- Differentiate between checked and unchecked exceptions
- Handle an exception with `try`, `catch`, and `finally`
- Throw an exception
- Explain exception translation and encapsulation

EXCEPTION HANDLING

There are two types of errors: runtime and compiletime. Compiletime errors must be fixed before you can compile and run your application. Runtime errors occur when your code is syntactically correct, but an unexpected issue occurs while running the application.

An example of a runtime exception is when your application attempts to access a file that isn't there or attempts to divide by zero. Opening a file and division are both valid code statements, so the application compiles fine. However, if a user enters a 0 denominator while the application is running or if an application attempts to read a missing file, you might encounter runtime errors.

Runtime errors fall into two categories: handled and unhandled. An unhandled runtime error will crash your program. At this point in the program, you have most likely seen a dialogue like this one:

```
Exception in thread "main" java.langArithmeticException: / by zero
    at com.sg.calculator.Calculate.divide(Calculate.java:30)
    at com.sg.caculator.App.main(App.java:59)
------------------------------------------------------------------
BUILD FAILURE
------------------------------------------------------------------
```

A runtime error occurred, and the application crashes and closes without allowing you to exit properly. What if this application was being used by your boss? How about a paying customer? What if they had unsaved information within the application? Would the information still be available in the application when they reopen it?

Listing 26.1 presents a simple piece of code that complies cleanly and runs. There should be no compile errors. This code is based on the Adder code you created in Lesson 5; however, instead of adding, this code is dividing.

LISTING 26.1

Dividing Two Numbers

```java
import java.util.Scanner;

public class Exceptions {

    public static void main(String[] args) {
        String input;

        double quotient = 0;
        int numerator = 0;
        int denominator = 0;

        Scanner myScanner = new Scanner(System.in);

        System.out.println("Please enter the numerator:");
        input = myScanner.nextLine();
        numerator = Integer.parseInt(input);

        System.out.println("Please enter the denominator:");
        input = myScanner.nextLine();
        denominator = Integer.parseInt(input);

        quotient = (double) numerator / denominator;

        System.out.println("The quotient is: " + quotient);
    }
}
```

---

[1] https://docs.oracle.com/javase/tutorial/essential/exceptions/definition.html

As mentioned, this code is a throwback to what you saw in early lessons but doing division instead of addition. The code prompts the user for two numbers: a numerator and a denominator. It grabs these as `Strings` from the console, converts them to numbers, calculates the quotient, and then displays the result.

As long as the user enters numbers and as long as the second number is not a zero, this listing works great. For example, the following output is from running the listing and entering 5 and 5:

```
Please enter the numerator:
5
Please enter the denominator:
5
The quotient is: 1.0
```

If you enter 5 and 0, you get an exception.

```
Please enter the numerator:
5
Please enter the denominator:
0
Exception in thread "main" java.lang.ArithmeticException: / by zero
        at Exceptions.main(Exceptions.java:32)
Command execution failed.
```

You also get an exception if you enter text instead of a number.

```
Please enter the numerator:
5
Please enter the denominator:
asdf
Exception in thread "main" java.lang.NumberFormatException: For input string:
"asdf"         at java.lang.NumberFormatException.forInputString(NumberFormat-
Exception.java:65)
        at java.lang.Integer.parseInt(Integer.java:580)
        at java.lang.Integer.parseInt(Integer.java:615)
        at Exceptions.main(Exceptions.java:30)
Command execution failed.
```

Clearly, we need to handle these problems to make a better, and more professional, experience for our users!

CATCH OR SPECIFY REQUIREMENT

If your code (or code that your code calls) can cause an exception to be thrown, you must either catch the exception or specify that your code might cause that error. *Catching* the exception means that you have written code to try to recover from the error or to simply report that the error occurred. *Specifying* the exception means marking your code to indicate that it may cause this error. In this case, you are not trying to recover from the error or report it. Your code simply throws the error and lets the calling code try to handle it.

EXCEPTION TYPES

There are two categories of exceptions: *checked* and *unchecked*. Checked exceptions are always subject to the "catch or specify" requirement, whereas unchecked exceptions are not. You are still free to handle (i.e., try to recover from) unchecked exceptions in your code, but you are not required to.

There are two types of unchecked exceptions: *errors* and *runtime exceptions*. Errors are abnormal conditions from which most programs should not attempt to recover, but there may be conditions under which you would want to attempt to recover from a runtime exception.

Anything that extends `Exception` (excluding `RuntimeException`) is a checked exception, and anything that extends `RuntimeException` is an unchecked exception. You can see this in the class hierarchy presented in Figure 26.1.

> **NOTE** In summary:
> - `RuntimeException` **extends** `Exception`.
> - **Both** `Exception` and `Error` **extend** `Throwable`.
> - `Throwable` **extends** `Object`.

HANDLING (CATCHING) EXCEPTIONS

We use the *try-catch-finally* construct to handle exceptions in Java. Let's look at each one of these.

try Block

When we identify code that we believe might cause an exception, we can surround it with a `try` block. This block can contain lines of the code that might cause different exception types, as well as lines of code that cannot cause an exception to occur. The `try` block marks the code you want to *try* to run.

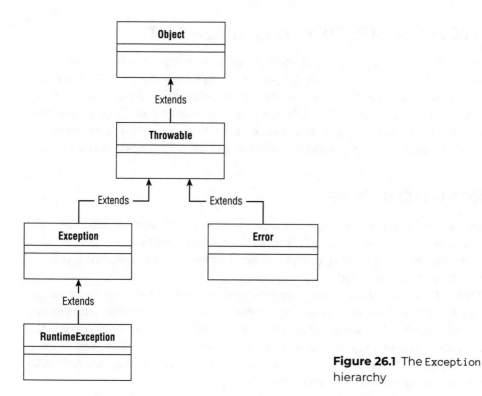

Figure 26.1 The Exception hierarchy

For example, in Listing 26.1, we had code to get input from the user. We could surround it with a try block as such:

```
try {
    input = myScanner.nextLine();
    numerator = Integer.parseInt(input);
}
```

We could also surround our division statement with a try block.

```
try {
    quotient = numerator / denominator;
}
```

catch Block

In general, each `try` block must be accompanied by at least one `catch` block. A `catch` block contains code that either attempts to recover from the exception or simply reports the error in some way (i.e., writes to a log file). In short, if a `try` block of code causes an exception, then the `catch` block tries to *catch* the error so that you can handle it without crashing your program.

If the `try` block contains code that throws more than one type of exception, you can have a separate `catch` block for each exception type so you can respond to each error in a different way. A `catch` block can also handle an entire class or family of exceptions, which is useful when you want to respond to all exceptions in the same way.

> **NOTE** As you can see, `catch` expects you to provide an exception type. While you could use the exception type of `Exception`, that doesn't give you much information about what issue occurred. In general, you can determine specific exceptions to catch by reviewing Java documentation or by looking at the exceptions your program causes when it is executed.

Expanding on our `try` block for entering a number, we can add a `catch` in case the user enters text instead of a number. That would look like this:

```
try {
    input = myScanner.nextLine();
    numerator = Integer.parseInt(input);
} catch (NumberFormatException ex) {
    System.out.println("You didn't enter a number!");
}
```

As you can see, the `catch` is followed by specifying the type that you want to catch and an identifier to store the exception into should it get caught. In this case, we are catching a `NumberFormatException` error. Any other exceptions will be not be caught and could still cause the program to terminate.

To prevent the division by zero from crashing the program, we would catch an error of type `ArithmeticException`.

```
try {
    quotient = numerator / denominator;
} catch (ArithmeticException ex) {
    System.out.println("Something went wrong: " + ex);
}
```

Starting with Java 7, exceptions could be combined if they were to be treated the same way. To do this *multi-catch* statement, you simply separated each possible exception with a |. For example, the following catches both an `ArrayIndexOutOfBoundsException` and an `ArithmeticException`:

```
try {
    // some code to try...
} catch(ArrayIndexOutOfBoundsException | ArithmeticException ex) {
    System.out.println("Something went wrong: " + ex);
}
```

This is equivalent to doing the following:

```
try {
    // some code to try...
} catch(ArrayIndexOutOfBoundsException ex) {
    System.out.println("Something went wrong: " + ex);
} catch(ArrayIndexOutOfBoundsException ex) {
    System.out.println("Something went wrong: " + ex);
}
```

finally Block

Each `try-catch` block combination may optionally be accompanied by a *finally* block. Code in the finally block will *always* run after the `try-catch` combination, whether an exception occurred or not.

finally blocks are well suited for code that cleans up resources. Without the finally block, the cleanup code would have to appear in both the `try` block and the `catch` block(s). The structure of the overall `try-catch-finally` block is as follows:

```
public static void myMethod() throws exception, another_Exception {
```

```
    try {
        //code that can cause an exception
        // goes here
    } catch (<exception type> identifier) {
        // code to handle this type
        // of exception
    } catch (<another_exception type> identifier) {
        // code to handle this type
        // of exception
    } finally {
        // code that runs whether an exception
        // occurred or not
    }
}
```

Listing 26.2 updates Listing 26.1 to include some exception handling. Note that while this handles exceptions, it is still not a great listing. To make the listing work better, you would want to add loops so that the user could get another chance to enter a number if they erroneously entered text.

LISTING 26.2

Dividing Two Numbers with Some Exception Handling

```
import java.util.Scanner;

public class Exceptions {

    public static void main(String[] args) {
        String input;

        double quotient = 0;
        int numerator = 0;
        int denominator = 0;

        Scanner myScanner = new Scanner(System.in);

        try {
            System.out.println("Please enter the numerator:");
            input = myScanner.nextLine();
            numerator = Integer.parseInt(input);
        } catch (NumberFormatException ex) {
            System.out.println("Input could not be parsed into an integer");
        }
```

```
    try {
        System.out.println("Please enter the denominator:");
        input = myScanner.nextLine();
        denominator = Integer.parseInt(input);
    } catch (NumberFormatException ex) {
        System.out.println("Input could not be parsed into an integer");
    }

    try {
        quotient = (double) numerator / denominator;
    } catch (ArithmeticException ex) {
        System.out.println("Something went wrong: " + ex);
    }

    System.out.println("The quotient is: " + quotient);
    }
}
```

SPECIFYING AND THROWING EXCEPTIONS

If you decide that your code should not attempt to catch (i.e., handle) the exceptions that may be thrown with the try-catch-finally construct, you must then specify that your code can cause those exceptions. This can be done using the throws keyword as part of your method definition. You simply add the throws keyword followed by a comma-delimited list of exception types that could be thrown to the method definition.

For example, the following method throws an IOException:

```
public static void myMethod() throws IOException {
    // method code goes here
}
```

You can also specify within the body of your method that it throws an exception. In this case, you would use throw instead of throws, and you would instantiate a new exception as shown in the following:

```
public static void myMethod(){
    // method code can go here
    throw new IOException();
}
```

As you can see, `throws` is used within the method signature, whereas `throw` is used within the method. The `throw` keyword is used to explicitly throw an exception, whereas the `throws` keyword is used to declare the exception.

EXCEPTION TRANSLATION AND ENCAPSULATION

There are times when you do not want your code to attempt to recover from an error, but you don't want to directly throw the exception that occurred either. Often, in these cases, you want to translate the exception from an implementation-specific exception (such as `FileNotFoundException` or `SQLException`) into a more general application exception (such as `ClassRosterDaoException`). These application-specific exceptions let the caller know that something went wrong in the DAO (for example, that some information could not be persisted), but it doesn't indicate anything about the underlying implementation.

This arrangement is known as *exception translation*, and it is an important technique in helping us maintain well-encapsulated classes and application layers. If we go through all the trouble of creating interfaces and keeping our implementations private only to have our errors tie us back to a specific implementation, we have failed. This is what is known as a *leaky abstraction*: the implementation details leak out to the caller through the implementation-specific exceptions. Developers commonly call this *exception wrapping*.

Fortunately, we can avoid this by doing exception translation. You simply put a `try-catch` around the code that can cause the exception, just as you would do if you were going to handle the exception. In the `catch` block, you create a new instance of the application-specific exception, passing in a message and the exception that got thrown as parameters to the constructor, as in the following example:

```
try {
    // code that can cause an exception
    // goes here
} catch (FileNotFoundException e) {
    throw new ClassRosterDaoException("Student data could not be read", e);
}
```

NOTE We'll see examples of exception translation and encapsulation in the Class Roster application in the next lesson.

SUMMARY

To write effective code, we should always remember the types and nature of errors that can be produced by the application. Implementing `try-catch-finally` and handling our exceptions is an important part of coding. Ensure that your application appropriately handles exceptions and gracefully exits from exceptions. Uncaught exceptions can definitely hinder user experiences and possibly make the application insecure.

When the user types in a letter when our program is expecting a number, our program blows up. This is because methods like `Integer.parseInt()` throw a runtime (unchecked) exception called `NumberFormatException` and methods like the `nextInt()` method on `Scanner` throw a runtime (unchecked) exception called `InputMismatchException`.

Now that we know about handling exceptions using the `try-catch` block, is there a way we can prevent our program from blowing up when the user types in some unexpected input? What kind of code would you have to add to your user input and output implementation to handle this situation? We'll take a deeper look at this in a later lesson, but this is a good topic to start thinking about now.

EXERCISES

The following are additional coding exercises to help you practice what you are learning about the Java programming language. These are to do on your own, so most will not always include answers. Many of the exercises cover accepting user input via `Scanner`. There are several exercises for you to apply what you learned in this lesson:

Exercise 1: Keep On Asking

Exercise 2: Arrays Gone Bad

Exercise 3: Exiting Gracefully

Exercise 1: Keep On Asking

Update Listing 26.2 using a `do-while` loop so that you keep prompting the user to enter a value until a number is entered. Also update the listing so that only positive numbers are entered.

Exercise 2: Arrays Gone Bad

Array indexes can cause problems for some developers. This can be the mistake of starting with an array index of 1 and inadvertently going up to the length of the array, which would be out of bounds, or it can be simply calling for an item in an array with an index that doesn't exist.

Exercise Listing 26.2 uses an array to allow a user to pick an animal based on a number. Because the number the user enters is used as the index for the array of animals, what happens if the user picks a number outside the array's index?

EXERCISE LISTING 26.2

A Bad Array

```
import java.util.Scanner;

public class Exceptions {

    public static void main(String[] args) {
        String input;
        int userPick = 0;
        String[] animals = {"cat", "dog", "squirrel",
            "frog", "fish", "hamster",
            "pig", "goat", "horse"};

        Scanner myScanner = new Scanner(System.in);

        // Display Animals
        for (int ctr = 0; ctr < animals.length; ctr++ )
        {
            System.out.println( (ctr+1) + " - " + animals[ctr]);
        }

        System.out.println("------------------------");
        System.out.println("Which pet would you like? ");
        System.out.println("Pick a pet number: " );

        // Get input from user!
        input = myScanner.nextLine();
        userPick = Integer.parseInt(input);

        // Display user's choice.
        System.out.println("You picked: " + animals[userPick]);
    }
}
```

Your job is to fix this listing so that the exception caused by using a bad index doesn't cause the program to blow up.

There is more than one way to fix the listing. One is to validate the user input to make sure it is within the range of the array's index values. The second is to check for an exception when using the value entered by the user. Because this is a lesson on exception handling, modify the code to use exception handling. While you are at it, add exception handling to the user input to make sure that it doesn't end if a whole number is not entered.

Some additional cleanup that you might want to do on this listing is to change the display so that the numbers go from 1 to 9 when listing the animals, instead of from 0 to 8.

```
1 - cat
2 - dog
3 - squirrel
4 - frog
5 - fish
6 - hamster
7 - pig
8 - goat
9 - horse
-------------------------
Which pet would you like?
Pick a number from 1 to 9 :
```

Exercise 3: Exiting Gracefully

In Lesson 24, you learned about creating and reading files. Rewrite Listings 24.2 and 24.5 to do exception handling. If an IOException or FileNotFoundException error is thrown, catch it, display a message saying there was a problem with the file, and exit the program gracefully.

Lesson 27

Pulling It All Together: Building the Class Roster App

In this lesson, we pull together everything you've learned to this point and put it into practice in an entire console application. The purpose of this code-along is to give you an example of how to design and build a console-based MVC CRUD application using all the tools and techniques you have learned so far. We'll build this project following the agile checklist in Appendix C and will organize it using tiered application design and MVC patterns demonstrated in this section.

PROGRAM OBJECTIVES

- Build a Class Roster program
- Include a menu of options that interacts with the user
- Add, view, and remove student information
- Include dependency injection in the application
- Handle exceptions within the application
- Persist the student data to a file

> **NOTE** You should use this lesson as a template for the exercises for building a DVD library.

APPLICATION REQUIREMENTS AND USE CASES

We will build an application that manages a roster of students. The user will be able to create, view, and delete students in the system, and all student data will be persisted to a file. Here are the use cases:

- Add Student
- View All Students
- View a Single Student
- Remove Student

Further, there is a requirement that the application store all the student data to a file so that student data persists between times the Class Roster application is run.

UNDERSTANDING THE APPLICATION STRUCTURE

Figure 27.1 is the UML class diagram of the Class Roster application. In this diagram, we introduce notation that represents interface, composition, and inheritance relationships.

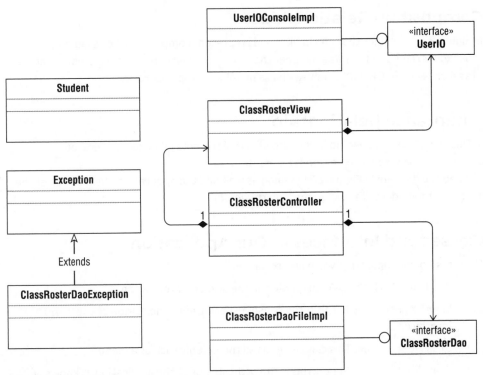

Figure 27.1 UML class diagram of Class Roster application

Interface Relationships

In Figure 27.1, the lines ending in circles show that a class implements a particular interface. For example, `ClassRosterDaoFileImpl` implements the `ClassRosterDao` interface in Figure 27.1. Our convention is to name the interface for the logical component that it represents—in this case, the `ClassRosterDao`. Each class that implements the interface will be named for the type of implementation that the class represents and always ends in `Impl` (for implementation). Here, our DAO is implemented using text files, so it is called `ClassRosterDaoFileImpl`. If we had an implementation that used a database instead, it might be called `ClassRosterDaoDatabaseImpl`.

> **NOTE** Different groups might adopt a different standard, so it is important to learn conventions when you join a new organization or team. Adding the `Impl` to the end of the name is just one convention. Another popular convention is to add an `I` at the beginning to indicate an interface, such as `IClassRosterDao` instead of `ClassRosterDaoImpl`.

Composition Relationships

In Figure 27.1, the lines that end in diamonds represent composition. For example, ClassRosterController has a member that is a ClassRosterDao and a member that is a ClassRosterView. ClassRosterView has a member of type UserIO.

Inheritance Relationships

In Figure 27.1, the line ending in the arrowhead represents inheritance. Here, our ClassRosterDaoException extends Exception.

Keep the diagram in Figure 27.1 in mind as we build the application. We'll see all of the implementation details as we go through this lesson.

Classes and Interfaces in Our Application

The Class Roster application will have six classes.

- Student: This is the DTO that holds all the student information.

- UserIOConsoleImpl: This is the console-specific implementation of the UserIO interface.

- ClassRosterView: This class handles all the UI logic such as a menu.

- ClassRosterController: This is the orchestrator of the application. It knows what needs to be done, when it needs to be done, and what component can do the job.

- ClassRosterDaoFileImpl: This is the text file–specific implementation of the ClassRosterDao interface.

- ClassRosterDaoException: This is the error class for our application. It extends Exception.

The application will also have two interfaces.

- ClassRosterDao: This interface defines the methods that must be implemented by any class that wants to play the role of DAO for class roster information in the application. We will implement a text file–based DAO in the code-along. You could imagine, however, an implementation that only stored student data in memory or one that stored student data in a database. Each class would be different, but all would implement that same interface, ensuring that they are all well encapsulated. Note that the ClassRosterController only uses this interface to reference the DAO. It is completely unaware of the implementation details.

- UserIO: This interface defines the methods that must be implemented by any class that wants to directly interact with the user interface technology. We will implement a console-based user interface in the code-along. You could imagine, however, an implementation that used a windowing system or some other technology. Again, each class would be different, but all would implement the same interface, ensuring that they are all well encapsulated. Note that ClassRosterView only uses this interface to interact with the user. It is completely unaware of the implementation details.

MVC Rules of the Game

We're about to start building the application, but before we do, we need to review the MVC rules of the game. Keep these in mind not only as we build this application but also as you build your other applications throughout the course.

- The controller is the "brains of the operation." It knows what needs to be done, when it needs to be done, and what component can do it. It acts like a general contractor, directing work but never doing the work itself.
- The view (and any helper classes) is responsible for all user interaction. No other component is allowed to interact with the user.
- The DAO is responsible for the persistence and retrieval of student data.
- The DTO is the container for student data. The DAO and DTO comprise the model.
- All components (model, view, and controller) can use DTOs.
- The controller can talk with both the view and the DAO.
- The DAO cannot access the view.
- The view cannot access the DAO.

Construction Approach

We will build the Class Roster application in the following steps:

1. Create the packages and empty classes and interfaces to create the shell of the program.
2. Create the menu system.
3. Implement each use case in order.

    a. Create Student
    b. Display All Students

c. Display a Single Student
d. Remove Student

We will build all functionality without file persistence first. After all the features are done, we will add persistence, which will require code to read from and write to files and handle/translate the associated exceptions.

NOTE These steps should be used as a guide when building the exercise applications in this course.

SETTING UP THE CLASS ROSTER APPLICATION SHELL

In this step, we will create the outline, or *shell*, of our program. This involves creating all the classes and interfaces (empty for now) in their correct packages so we have the overall structure of the program.

After creating a new project called ClassRoster, create the classes and interfaces shown in Figure 27.2.

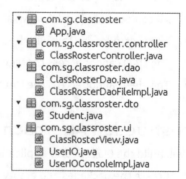

Figure 27.2 Class Roster classes and interfaces

The example uses the base package com.sg.classroster. Your base package may be different depending on what you specified when you created your project. Also, as indicated in Figure 27.2, ClassRosterDao.java and UserIO.java are interfaces, not classes.

> **NOTE** We strongly recommend that you match our naming convention throughout this code-along.

The first package listed Figure 27.2 is the `com.sg.classroster` package. To create this package, right-click *Source Packages* and select New ➢ Java Package, as shown in Figure 27.3.

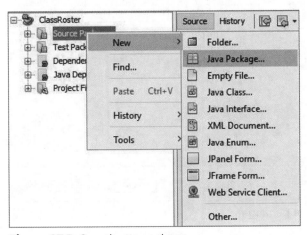

Figure 27.3 Creating a package

In the New Java Package window, type the name of the new package (**com.sg.classroster**) for Package Name, as in Figure 27.4. Click the *Finish* button when you are done.

You've created the new package. You can create the other packages shown in Figure 27.2 in the same manner.

Once the packages have been created, the Java classes and interfaces can then be created. You've created Java classes before. You create an interface in the same manner. To create the `ClassRosterDao` interface, in the package explorer, right-click the `com.sg.classroster.dao` package that you create by following the previous steps, and then select New ➢ Java Package, as shown in Figure 27.5.

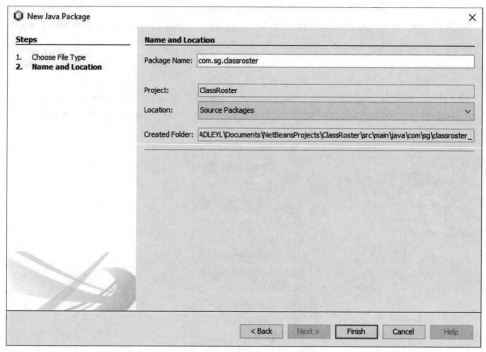

Figure 27.4 Naming the new Java package

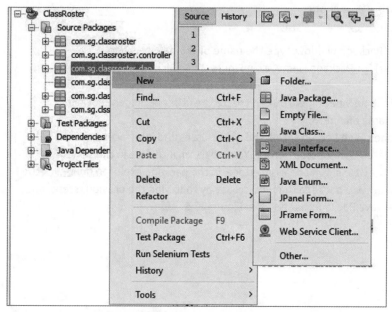

Figure 27.5 Adding an interface

When the New Java Interface dialog box appears, type **ClassRosterDao** into the Class Name text box, as shown in Figure 27.6. Click the *Finish* button when you are done.

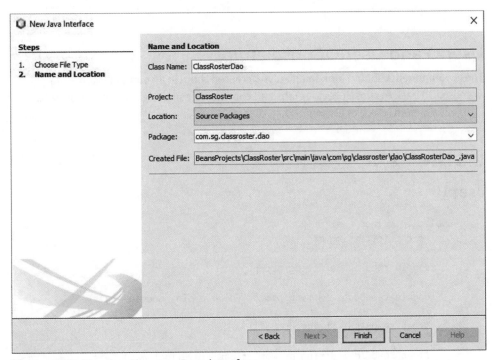

Figure 27.6 Naming the new Java interface

You can create the rest of the interfaces in the same manner. This will provide the shell of your application, which we will use throughout the rest of this lesson as we pull together the Class Roster program.

CREATING THE MENU SYSTEM

After the shell of the program is created, we can create the menu system, or user interface, for our application. The first version of our menu system won't be backed by any functionality, but it will allow the user to run the program and navigate through all the menu items.

This will involve working with the following files:

- App
- ClassRosterController

- ClassRosterView
- UserIO
- UserIOConsoleImpl

UserIO and UserIOConsoleImpl

These components should look familiar: you created them in an earlier lesson as an exercise. Go back to those previous labs and copy those components into this project.

UserIO should look like Listing 27.1.

LISTING 27.1

UserIO

```
public interface UserIO {
    void print(String msg);

    double readDouble(String prompt);

    double readDouble(String prompt, double min, double max);

    float readFloat(String prompt);

    float readFloat(String prompt, float min, float max);

    int readInt(String prompt);

    int readInt(String prompt, int min, int max);

    long readLong(String prompt);

    long readLong(String prompt, long min, long max);

    String readString(String prompt);

    public void close();
}
```

Take the implementation of UserIO that you completed in a previous lesson's exercises and copy it into UserIOConsoleImpl. Alternatively, you can use the code from Listing 27.2.

LISTING 27.2

UserIOConsoleImpl

```java
import java.util.Scanner;

public class UserIOConsoleImpl implements UserIO {

    final private Scanner console = new Scanner(System.in);

    @Override
    public void print(String msg) {
        System.out.println(msg);
    }

    @Override
    public String readString(String msgPrompt) {
        System.out.println(msgPrompt);
        return console.nextLine();
    }

    @Override
    public int readInt(String msgPrompt) {
        boolean invalidInput = true;
        int num = 0;
        while (invalidInput) {
            try {
                // print the message msgPrompt (ex: asking for the # of cats!)
                String stringValue = this.readString(msgPrompt);
                // Get the input line, and try and parse
                num = Integer.parseInt(stringValue); // if it's 'bob'
                                                     // it'll break
                invalidInput = false; // or you can use 'break;'
            } catch (NumberFormatException e) {
                // If it explodes, it'll go here and do this.
                this.print("Input error. Please try again.");
            }
        }
        return num;
    }
}
```

```java
@Override
public int readInt(String msgPrompt, int min, int max) {
    int result;
    do {
        result = readInt(msgPrompt);
    } while (result < min || result > max);

    return result;
}

@Override
public long readLong(String msgPrompt) {
    while (true) {
        try {
            return Long.parseLong(this.readString(msgPrompt));
        } catch (NumberFormatException e) {
            this.print("Input error. Please try again.");
        }
    }
}

@Override
public long readLong(String msgPrompt, long min, long max) {
    long result;
    do {
        result = readLong(msgPrompt);
    } while (result < min || result > max);

    return result;
}

@Override
public float readFloat(String msgPrompt) {
    while (true) {
        try {
            return Float.parseFloat(this.readString(msgPrompt));
        } catch (NumberFormatException e) {
            this.print("Input error. Please try again.");
        }
    }
}
```

```java
    @Override
    public float readFloat(String msgPrompt, float min, float max) {
        float result;
        do {
            result = readFloat(msgPrompt);
        } while (result < min || result > max);

        return result;
    }

    @Override
    public double readDouble(String msgPrompt) {
        while (true) {
            try {
                return Double.parseDouble(this.readString(msgPrompt));
            } catch (NumberFormatException e) {
                this.print("Input error. Please try again.");
            }
        }
    }

    @Override
    public double readDouble(String msgPrompt, double min, double max) {
        double result;
        do {
            result = readDouble(msgPrompt);
        } while (result < min || result > max);
        return result;
    }

@Override
    public void close(){
        this.console.close();
    }

}
```

NOTE If you find yourself with a missing or buggy `UserIOConsoleImpl`, you can download an official implementation to use instead: `www.wiley.com/go/ jobreadyjava` under the "Downloads" link.

ClassRosterController

Next, we'll start in the controller. Since this component is the "brains of the operation," it will control when the menu system is displayed. Our strategy here is to create a method that displays the menu, gets the user's menu choice, and then calls a method that performs an action based on the user's menu choice. Type the code in Listing 27.3 into your ClassRosterController.

LISTING 27.3

ClassRosterController

```java
public class ClassRosterController {

    private UserIO io = new UserIOConsoleImpl();

    public void run() {
        boolean keepGoing = true;
        int menuSelection = 0;
        while (keepGoing) {
            io.print("Main Menu");
            io.print("1. List Student IDs");
            io.print("2. Create New Student");
            io.print("3. View a Student");
            io.print("4. Remove a Student");
            io.print("5. Exit");

            menuSelection = io.readInt("Please select from the"
                    + " above choices.", 1, 5);

            switch (menuSelection) {
                case 1:
                    io.print("LIST STUDENTS");
                    break;
                case 2:
                    io.print("CREATE STUDENT");
                    break;
                case 3:
                    io.print("VIEW STUDENT");
                    break;
                case 4:
                    io.print("REMOVE STUDENT");
                    break;
```

```
            case 5:
                keepGoing = false;
                break;
            default:
                io.print("UNKNOWN COMMAND");
        }
    }
    io.print("GOOD BYE");
    io.close();
    }
}
```

App

Now we need to add the main method to the App class so we can test our menu system. In this method, we will instantiate our controller and call the run method. Add the code in Listing 27.4 to your App class.

LISTING 27.4

App Class

```
public class App {

    public static void main(String[] args) {
        ClassRosterController controller = new ClassRosterController();
        controller.run();
    }
}
```

Now run this code to make sure the menu is working. The output should look something like this:

```
Main Menu
1. List Student IDs
2. Create New Student
3. View a Student
4. Remove a Student
5. Exit
Please select from the above choices.
4
REMOVE STUDENT
1. List Student IDs
```

```
2. Create New Student
3. View a Student
4. Remove a Student
5. Exit
Please select from the above choices.
5
GOOD BYE
```

> **NOTE** You will need to add imports to your classes.

ClassRosterView

This initial version is okay for getting the structure of the run method, but it breaks the rule stating that the controller should only orchestrate work and shouldn't do any of the work itself. Although the controller is using the `UserIOConsoleImpl` class to interact with the user, the controller creates and determines the layout of the menu, which should be done by the view component instead.

Let's refactor this so the menu layout and rendering are in the view where it belongs. We'll do the following:

1. Move the functionality that prints the menu and gets the user's selection to `ClassRosterView`.

2. Have the controller use `ClassRosterView` instead of `UserIOConsoleImpl` for all the work involved in displaying the menu and getting the user's selection.

Add the code in Listing 27.5 to `ClassRosterView`.

LISTING 27.5

ClassRosterView

```java
public class ClassRosterView {

    private UserIO io = new UserIOConsoleImpl();

    public int printMenuAndGetSelection() {
        io.print("Main Menu");
        io.print("1. List Students");
```

```
            io.print("2. Create New Student");
            io.print("3. View a Student");
            io.print("4. Remove a Student");
            io.print("5. Exit");

            return io.readInt("Please select from the above choices.");
        }
    }
```

All we have done is move the functionality for printing the menu and getting the user's selection from the controller over to the view. Notice that we're using composition here—the ClassRosterView *has-a* UserIO member, and it uses UserIO to interact with the user. Remember that UserIO is an interface.

ClassRosterView uses the public interface, UserIO, and is unaware of the implementation details of the concrete implementation, UserIOConsoleImpl. In other words, ClassRosterView is unaware that it is writing to and reading from the console; it only knows that it is interacting with the user.

ClassRosterController

Now we need to return to the ClassRosterController. We'll add a member of type ClassRosterView, and we'll have the controller use it for displaying the menu and getting the user's selection. For now, we'll leave the UserIO member in our Controller and use it to print out the placeholder messages for each of the menu choices. As we implement each use case, we'll replace the calls to UserIO with calls to ClassRosterView. When we're done, there will be no calls to UserIO left in the controller; at that point, we will remove the UserIO member variable. Modify your controller to look like Listing 27.6.

LISTING 27.6

Modified ClassRosterController

```
public class ClassRosterController {

    private ClassRosterView view = new ClassRosterView();
    private UserIO io = new UserIOConsoleImpl();

    public void run() {
        boolean keepGoing = true;
        int menuSelection = 0;
        while (keepGoing) {
```

```java
        menuSelection = getMenuSelection();

        switch (menuSelection) {
            case 1:
                io.print("LIST STUDENTS");
                break;
            case 2:
                io.print("CREATE STUDENT");
                break;
            case 3:
                io.print("VIEW STUDENT");
                break;
            case 4:
                io.print("REMOVE STUDENT");
                break;
            case 5:
                keepGoing = false;
                break;
            default:
                io.print("UNKNOWN COMMAND");
        }

    }
    io.print("GOOD BYE");
}

private int getMenuSelection() {
    return view.printMenuAndGetSelection();
}

}
```

Here we have done two things.

- We created a new method called getMenuSelection() that we call to get the menuSelection in the run method.
- We made a call to printMenuAndGetSelection on the view member.

We'll use this pattern throughout the application. The run method will ask for the user selection and then route the request to a private controller method. These private controller methods will then orchestrate the work required to fulfill the user's requested action.

ADDING A STUDENT USE CASE

Now that we have the menu system in place, it is time to implement the first use case: Add Student.

The first use case is always the most work to implement because you only have a menu system at this point. Either you can start at the user interface and work your way back or you can start with the DTO and DAO and work toward the front. We'll start with the DTO and work our way toward the front.

Student (DTO)

The first thing we'll do is create the Student class. Enter the code from Listing 27.7 into your Student class.

LISTING 27.7

The Student Class

```
public class Student {
    private String firstName;
    private String lastName;
    final String studentId;
    // Programming Language + cohort month/year
    private String cohort;

    public Student(String studentId) {
        this.studentId = studentId;
    }

    public String getFirstName() {
        return firstName;
    }

    public void setFirstName(String firstName) {
        this.firstName = firstName;
    }

    public String getLastName() {
        return lastName;
    }
}
```

```
        public void setLastName(String lastName) {
            this.lastName = lastName;
        }

        public String getStudentId() {
            return studentId;
        }

        public String getCohort() {
            return cohort;
        }

        public void setCohort(String cohort) {
            this.cohort = cohort;
        }
    }
```

Notice that studentId is a read-only field. It is passed in as a parameter to the constructor, and there is no setter for this field. All other fields on the Student class are read/write and must be set manually after a Student object has been instantiated.

ClassRosterDao and ClassRosterDaoFileImpl

Now that we have our DTO, we need someplace to store it, so we'll create the initial versions of the ClassRosterDao interface and the ClassRosterDaoFileImpl class. Since we know all our user stories, we can define the complete ClassRosterDao interface here, but we'll only implement the functionality to create a new student at this time.

ClassRosterDao

The ClassRosterDao is pretty straightforward. We'll have one method for each use case. Add the code in Listing 27.8 to your ClassRosterDao file.

LISTING 27.8

ClassRosterDao

```
    public interface ClassRosterDao {

        /**
         * Adds the given Student to the roster and associates it with the given
```

```
 * student id. If there is already a student associated with the given
 * student id it will return that student object, otherwise it will
 * return null.
 *
 * @param studentId id with which student is to be associated
 * @param student student to be added to the roster
 * @return the Student object previously associated with the given
 * student id if it exists, null otherwise
 */
Student addStudent(String studentId, Student student);

/**
 * Returns a List of all students in the roster.
 *
 * @return List containing all students in the roster.
 */
List<Student> getAllStudents();

/**
 * Returns the student object associated with the given student id.
 * Returns null if no such student exists
 *
 * @param studentId ID of the student to retrieve
 * @return the Student object associated with the given student id,
 * null if no such student exists
 */
Student getStudent(String studentId);

/**
 * Removes from the roster the student associated with the given id.
 * Returns the student object that is being removed or null if
 * there is no student associated with the given id
 *
 * @param studentId id of student to be removed
 * @return Student object that was removed or null if no student
 * was associated with the given student id
 */
Student removeStudent(String studentId);
}
```

NOTE Again, you'll likely need to add imports, in this case for Student and List.

Notice that all the methods in the interface are commented with Javadoc comments. This not only provides great documentation in the source code but also allows you to run the Javadoc tool on your codebase to produce HTML documentation similar to what we looked at for Collection, List, and Map. It also populates information about your code when using the IDE's IntelliSense.

ClassRosterDaoFileImpl

For this use case, we'll create the initial version of ClassRosterDaoFileImpl and implement the addStudent() method.

Our first step is to make ClassRosterDaoFileImpl implement the ClassRosterDao interface. Add the implements keyword and the interface name, and then in NetBeans click the lightbulb icon to display the Implement all abstract methods option, as shown in Figure 27.7.

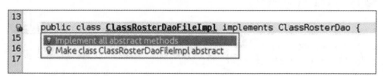

Figure 27.7 Implement all abstract methods option

After implementing all abstract methods, ClassRosterDaoFileImpl should look like Listing 27.9. You'll see that each method simply throws an UnsupportedOperationException for now, which is fine.

LISTING 27.9

After Implementing All Abstract Methods

```
public class ClassRosterDaoFileImpl implements ClassRosterDao {

    @Override
    public Student addStudent(String studentId, Student student) {
        throw new UnsupportedOperationException("Not supported yet.");
    }
```

```
@Override
public List<Student> getAllStudents() {
    throw new UnsupportedOperationException("Not supported yet.");
}

@Override
public Student getStudent(String studentId) {
    throw new UnsupportedOperationException("Not supported yet.");
}

@Override
public Student removeStudent(String studentId) {
    throw new UnsupportedOperationException("Not supported yet.");
}

}
```

As we mentioned earlier, the initial version of ClassRosterDaoFileImpl will hold all data in memory only. It won't read from or write to a file. We'll add the file persistence feature at the end. Even when we add the file persistence code, we'll need to have a data structure to hold all the student information. We're going to use a Map here because we need to look up students by ID, and this will be easy to do with a Map that uses student ID as the key.

Add the following private member to your ClassRosterDaoFileImpl along with the appropriate imports.

```
final Map<String, Student> students = new HashMap<>();
```

Now we are ready to implement the addStudent() method. This method is straightforward; we simply put the supplied student into our map using the supplied student ID as the key and we're done. Modify your addStudent() method to look like this:

```
@Override
public Student addStudent(String studentId, Student student) {

    return students.put(studentId, student);
}
```

ClassRosterView

We now have a DTO in which to carry student information, and we have a DAO in which we can store Student objects. Next, we need a way to get the information we need from the user to create a new Student object. For this, we'll go back to the ClassRosterView and add a method that does this for us. Add the method in Listing 27.10 to your ClassRosterView class.

LISTING 27.10

The getNewStudentInfo() Method

```
public Student getNewStudentInfo() {
        Student currentStudent = new Student(io.readString("Please enter
Student ID"));
        currentStudent.setFirstName(io.readString("Please enter First
Name"));
        currentStudent.setLastName(io.readString("Please enter Last
Name"));
        currentStudent.setCohort(io.readString("Please enter Cohort"));
        return currentStudent;
    }
```

This method prompts the user for the student ID, first name, last name, and cohort; gathers this information; creates a new Student object; and returns it to the caller.

We'll add two more methods to the view now. The first method simply displays a banner or heading to the UI indicating that the next interactions on the screen will be for creating a new student. The second method displays a message that the new student was successfully created and waits for the user to hit Enter to continue. Add the methods in Listing 27.11 to your ClassRosterView class.

LISTING 27.11

Additional ClassRosterView Methods

```
public void displayCreateStudentBanner() {
    io.print("=== Create Student ===");
}

public void displayCreateSuccessBanner() {
    io.readString(
            "Student successfully created.  Please hit enter to continue");
}
```

ClassRosterController

We now have all the individual parts: a DTO, a DAO with a method to store a Student DTO, and a view method that can gather student information from the user and create a new Student object. Our next step is to add code to the controller that coordinates all these parts so the user can choose to create a new student, enter all the information, and store the new student.

Before we write the logic to accomplish this task, we must create a ClassRosterDao member field in our Controller so we can have the DAO store the newly created Student object for us. Add the following line just after the ClassRosterView member field in your controller:

```
private ClassRosterDao dao = new ClassRosterDaoFileImpl();
```

Now we'll create a method in the Controller to orchestrate the creation of a new student. Our method will do the following:

- Display the Create Student banner
- Get all the student data from the user and create the new Student object
- Store the new Student object
- Display the Create Student Success banner

Of course, the Controller won't actually do any of this work. It will have the view and the DAO do all the heavy lifting. Add the following method to your controller:

```
private void createStudent() {
    view.displayCreateStudentBanner();
    Student newStudent = view.getNewStudentInfo();
    dao.addStudent(newStudent.getStudentId(), newStudent);
    view.displayCreateSuccessBanner();
}
```

Finally, we have to make a call to createStudent() in the run method when the user selects menu option 2. Update the switch statement in your run() method to look like this:

```
switch (menuSelection) {
    case 1:
        io.print("LIST STUDENTS");
        break;
```

```
        case 2:
            createStudent();
            break;
        case 3:
            io.print("VIEW STUDENT");
            break;
        case 4:
            io.print("REMOVE STUDENT");
            break;
        case 5:
            keepGoing = false;
            break;
        default:
            io.print("UNKNOWN COMMAND");
    }
```

At this point, you have implemented the Create Student use case. Of course, it is hard to see the results of our work because we can't view any of the students in the system yet. We'll fix that in the next step.

VIEWING ALL STUDENTS USE CASE

We'll follow the same pattern used in the Create Student use case for the View All Students use case.

1. Update the DAO implementation.

2. Update the view.

3. Update the controller.

This use case will be easier than Create Student because we don't have to start from scratch. We did a lot of the groundwork when we implemented the previous use case.

ClassRosterDaoFileImpl

Here we will implement the getAllStudents() method. Modify the getAllStudents() method so it looks like this:

```
@Override
public List<Student> getAllStudents() {
    return new ArrayList<Student>(students.values());
}
```

This code gets all the Student objects out of the students Map as a collection by calling the values() method. We pass that returned collection into the constructor for a new ArrayList. One of the constructors for ArrayList takes a collection as a parameter, which effectively allows us to convert the collection of Student objects into an ArrayList of Student objects that we can return from the method. Note that our method specifies that we'll return a List<Student>, but we create and return an ArrayList<Student>. This is perfectly fine because ArrayList implements the List interface so it can be treated as a List.

ClassRosterView

Next, we'll create a method that takes a list of Student objects as a parameter and displays the information for each student to the screen. After the list has been displayed, the method will pause and wait for the user to hit the Enter key. Add the method in Listing 27.12 to your ClassRosterView class.

LISTING 27.12

The displayStudentList() Method

```
public void displayStudentList(List<Student> studentList) {
    for (Student currentStudent : studentList) {
        String studentInfo = String.format("#%s : %s %s %s",
                currentStudent.getStudentId(),
                currentStudent.getFirstName(),
                currentStudent.getLastName(),
                currentStudent.getCohort());
        io.print(studentInfo);
    }
    io.readString("Please hit enter to continue.");
}
```

Now we will add the method to show the Display All Students banner. Add the following method to your ClassRosterView class:

```
public void displayDisplayAllBanner() {
    io.print("=== Display All Students ===");
}
```

ClassRosterController

We'll now add the code to our Controller to orchestrate the necessary activity to list all the students in the system. We'll create a method called listStudents() that will get a list of all Student objects in the system from the DAO and then hand that list to the view to display to the user. Add the following method to your controller:

```
private void listStudents() {
    view.displayDisplayAllBanner();
    List<Student> studentList = dao.getAllStudents();
    view.displayStudentList(studentList);
}
```

Finally, we have to make a call to listStudents() in the run method when the user selects menu option 1. Update the switch statement again in your run method to look like this:

```
switch (menuSelection) {
    case 1:
        listStudents();
        break;
    case 2:
        createStudent();
        break;
    case 3:
        io.print("VIEW STUDENT");
        break;
    case 4:
        io.print("REMOVE STUDENT");
        break;
    case 5:
        keepGoing = false;
        break;
    default:
        io.print("UNKNOWN COMMAND");
}
```

You should now be able to run the program, create a new student, and view the student's ID and name. Here is a sample run of the program:

```
Main Menu
1. List Student IDs
2. Create New Student
3. View a Student
```

```
4. Remove a Student
5. Exit
Please select from the above choices.
2
=== Create Student ===
Please enter Student ID
0001
Please enter First Name
Joe
Please enter Last Name
Cool
Please enter Cohort
Java Jan 2020
Student successfully created.  Please hit enter to continue.

Main Menu
1. List Student IDs
2. Create New Student
3. View a Student
4. Remove a Student
5. Exit
Please select from the above choices.
1
=== Display All Students ===
0001: Joe Cool Java Jan 2020
Please hit enter to continue.

Main Menu
1. List Student IDs
2. Create New Student
3. View a Student
4. Remove a Student
5. Exit
Please select from the above choices.
```

GETTING A STUDENT USE CASE

You have now completed the second use case. Next, we'll tackle viewing a single student.
Again, we'll follow the same pattern for this use case:

1. Update the DAO implementation.

2. Update the view.

3. Update the controller.

ClassRosterDaoFileImpl

Here we will implement the `getStudent()` method. This method is quite simple. We just ask the `students` `Map` for the `Student` object with the given ID and return it. Modify your `getStudent()` method to look like this:

```
@Override
public Student getStudent(String studentId) {
    return students.get(studentId);
}
```

ClassRosterView

We will implement three new methods in the view for this use case:

- `displayDisplayStudentBanner()` shows the Display Student banner.
- `getStudentIdChoice()` asks the user for the ID of the student to display.
- `displayStudent()` displays a student's information to the user.

Add the methods in Listing 27.13 to your view.

LISTING 27.13

Methods to Display a Student

```
public void displayDisplayStudentBanner () {
    io.print("=== Display Student ===");
}

public String getStudentIdChoice() {
    return io.readString("Please enter the Student ID.");
}

public void displayStudent(Student student) {
    if (student != null) {
        io.print(student.getStudentId());
        io.print(student.getFirstName() + " " + student.getLastName());
        io.print(student.getCohort());
        io.print("");
    } else {
        io.print("No such student.");
    }
    io.readString("Please hit enter to continue.");
}
```

ClassRosterController

Here we need to create the `viewStudent()` method. This method asks the view to display the View Student banner and get the student ID from the user. Then it asks the DAO for the student associated with the ID. Finally, it asks the view to display the student information. Add the method presented in Listing 27.14 to your controller.

LISTING 27.14

The `viewStudent()` Method

```
private void viewStudent() {
    view.displayDisplayStudentBanner();
    String studentId = view.getStudentIdChoice();
    Student student = dao.getStudent(studentId);
    view.displayStudent(student);
}
```

Finally, we have to make a call to `viewStudent()` in the run method when the user selects menu option 3. Update the `switch` statement in your run method to look like this:

```
switch (menuSelection) {
    case 1:
        listStudents();
        break;
    case 2:
        createStudent();
        break;
    case 3:
        viewStudent();
        break;
    case 4:
        io.print("REMOVE STUDENT");
        break;
    case 5:
        keepGoing = false;
        break;
    default:
        io.print("UNKNOWN COMMAND");
}
```

You should now be able to create a new student and view that student in the application. Here is a sample run of the program:

```
Main Menu
1. List Student IDs
```

```
2. Create New Student
3. View a Student
4. Remove a Student
5. Exit
Please select from the above choices.
2
=== Create Student ===
Please enter Student ID
0002
Please enter First Name
Jane
Please enter Last Name
Awesome
Please enter Cohort
Java Jan 2021
Student successfully created.  Please hit enter to continue

Main Menu
1. List Student IDs
2. Create New Student
3. View a Student
4. Remove a Student
5. Exit
Please select from the above choices.
3
=== Display Student ===
Please enter the Student ID.
0002
0002
Jane Awesome
Java Jan 2021

Please hit enter to continue

Main Menu
1. List Student IDs
2. Create New Student
3. View a Student
4. Remove a Student
5. Exit
Please select from the above choices.
```

REMOVING A STUDENT USE CASE

We'll move on to Remove Student next. Our final use case will again follow the same pattern as before.

ClassRosterDaoFileImpl

Here we will implement the removeStudent() method. This method is simple as well. We just ask the students Map to remove the Student object mapped with the given ID. Modify your removeStudent() method to look like the following:

```
@Override
public Student removeStudent(String studentId) {
    Student removedStudent = students.remove(studentId);
    return removedStudent;
}
```

ClassRosterView

For this use case, we need to add two methods to our view: one to display the Remove Student banner and one to display the results of our remove. We will reuse the getStudentIdChoice() method that was created in a previous step. Add the methods in Listing 27.15 to your view.

LISTING 27.15

The Remove Student Methods

```
public void displayRemoveStudentBanner () {
    io.print("=== Remove Student ===");
}

public void displayRemoveResult(Student studentRecord) {
    if(studentRecord != null){
      io.print("Student successfully removed.");
    }else{
      io.print("No such student.");
    }
    io.readString("Please hit enter to continue.");
}
```

ClassRosterController

Here we need to create the `removeStudent()` method. This method will ask the view to display the Remove Student banner and ask the user for the ID of the student to be removed. It will then ask the DAO to remove the student and capture the returned student. Finally, we will pass the record to the view to display the results. Add the method in Listing 27.16 to your controller.

LISTING 27.16

The `removeStudent()` Method

```java
private void removeStudent() {
    view.displayRemoveStudentBanner();
    String studentId = view.getStudentIdChoice();
    Student removedStudent = dao.removeStudent(studentId);
    view.displayRemoveResult(removedStudent);
}
```

Finally, we have to make a call to `removeStudent()` in the run method when the user selects menu option 4. Update the `switch` statement in your run method to look like this:

```java
switch (menuSelection) {
    case 1:
        listStudents();
        break;
    case 2:
        createStudent();
        break;
    case 3:
        viewStudent();
        break;
    case 4:
        removeStudent();
        break;
    case 5:
        keepGoing = false;
        break;
    default:
        io.print("UNKNOWN COMMAND");
}
```

You should now be able to remove a student from the system. Here is a sample run of the program showing the steps after a student has been added:

```
Main Menu
1. List Student IDs
2. Create New Student
3. View a Student
4. Remove a Student
5. Exit
Please select from the above choices.
1
=== Display All Students ===
0003: Jamal Fantastic
Please hit enter to continue.

Main Menu
1. List Student IDs
2. Create New Student
3. View a Student
4. Remove a Student
5. Exit
Please select from the above choices.
4
=== Remove Student ===
Please enter the Student ID.
0003
Student successfully removed.
Please hit enter to continue.

Main Menu
1. List Student IDs
2. Create New Student
3. View a Student
4. Remove a Student
5. Exit
Please select from the above choices.
1
=== Display All Students ===
Please hit enter to continue.

Main Menu
1. List Student IDs
2. Create New Student
3. View a Student
4. Remove a Student
5. Exit
Please select from the above choices.
```

You have now completed all the use cases for the application. You should now be able to add, display, and remove students in the system. In our next step, we'll clean up the unknown command and exit processing.

HANDLING UNKNOWN COMMAND AND EXITING

We still have some things to clean up in the controller and the view. We need to add code to handle unknown commands and exiting. After we do this, we can remove the `ConsoleIO` member field from the controller because all user interaction will be handled through the view, as it should be.

ClassRosterView

Add the two methods in Listing 27.17 to your view. These will print messages when we exit or run into an unknown situation.

LISTING 27.17

Added ClassRosterView Methods

```
public void displayExitBanner() {
    io.print("Good Bye!!!");
}

public void displayUnknownCommandBanner() {
    io.print("Unknown Command!!!");
}
```

ClassRosterController

Here we will add two methods: unknownCommand() and exitMessage(). These methods ask the view to display the appropriate message to the user. Add the methods in Listing 27.18 to your controller.

LISTING 27.18

Added `ClassRosterController` Methods

```
private void unknownCommand() {
    view.displayUnknownCommandBanner();
}

private void exitMessage() {
    view.displayExitBanner();
}
```

Finally, we need to call these methods from the run() method. Modify your run() method to look like Listing 27.19.

LISTING 27.19

The Updated `run()` Method

```
public void run() {
    boolean keepGoing = true;
    int menuSelection = 0;
    while (keepGoing) {

        menuSelection = getMenuSelection();

        switch (menuSelection) {
            case 1:
                listStudents();
                break;
            case 2:
                createStudent();
                break;
            case 3:
                viewStudent();
                break;
            case 4:
                removeStudent();
                break;
```

```
                case 5:
                    keepGoing = false;
                    break;
                default:
                    unknownCommand();
            }

        }
        exitMessage();
    }
```

Now all references to UserIO are gone from the controller, so we can remove the UserIO member field.

WORKING WITH DEPENDENCY INJECTION

At this point, our application is shaping up nicely. Everything is well organized into a Model-View-Controller pattern, and our classes are well designed. One of the critical pieces in good application design is the concept of loose coupling. As has been mentioned, one technique that helps with loose coupling is programming to interfaces. We have two places in our application where we use interfaces to help with loose coupling.

- ClassRosterDao

- UserIO

We use these interfaces and their associated implementations because we can anticipate needing different implementations of each. For example, in this project, we could create a DAO that persists student data to a file. We could imagine an implementation that only stored student data in memory or an implementation that stores student data in a database. As far as the controller is concerned, each implementation looks the same because the controller programs to the DAO interface and not to a particular implementation.

Although we are programming to the ClassRosterDao interface in the controller and to the UserIO interface in the view, we still hard-code our choice for implementation.

In our ClassRosterController:

```
private ClassRosterDao dao = new ClassRosterDaoFileImpl();
```

In the ClassRosterView:

```
private UserIO io = new UserIOConsoleImpl();
```

Even after all that work to create an interface and a well-designed private implementation, the controller and view are still tightly coupled to a specific implementation of the interface, so all our hard work has not paid off yet.

What we really need is a way to tell the controller and the view which implementation of the ClassRosterDao and UserIO interfaces, respectively, to use. This concept is known as *dependency injection*. We'll implement a version of it in this lesson.

Implementation

It is time to see what all this looks like in practice. Here we will refactor our application to use dependency injection by doing the following:

1. Remove the hard-coded reference to ClassRosterDaoFileImpl and ClassRoster-View in the controller.

2. Remove the hard-coded reference to UserIOConsoleIMpl in the view.

3. Implement a constructor in the controller that has a ClassRosterDao parameter and a ClassRosterView parameter and uses the incoming values to initialize the ClassRosterDao and ClassRosterView member fields.

4. Implement a constructor in the view that has a UserIO parameter and uses the incoming value to initialize the UserIO member field.

5. Add code to the main method in the App class that wires everything up and kicks off the program.

ClassRosterController

Our first step is to remove the code that initializes the view and dao member fields in the controller so that we are left with just their declarations. Modify ClassRosterController so the declarations look like this:

```
private ClassRosterView view;
private ClassRosterDao dao;
```

Now we must implement a constructor that initializes these members. Add the following constructor to your ClassRosterController:

```
public ClassRosterController(ClassRosterDao dao, ClassRosterView view) {
    this.dao = dao;
    this.view = view;
}
```

NOTE At this point, the app won't be working since we need to make a few more changes. Do not panic if you try to run your app and it is not working.

Note we are passing the view and the DAO into the controller. Even though we have only one implementation of these interfaces now, it could be that in the future there will be other implementations. The App class has the responsibility to tell the controller what implementations to use. This decouples the controller from knowing about which implementations of the DAO and view exist. The controller can know how to use those interfaces without worrying about how they are implemented.

ClassRosterView

We'll modify ClassRosterView in the same way we modified the controller. First, remove the code that initializes the io member field. Modify ClassRosterView so the declaration looks like this:

```
final UserIO io;
```

Now we must implement a constructor that initializes the io member field. Add the following constructor to your ClassRosterView:

```
public ClassRosterView(UserIO io) {
    this.io = io;
}
```

App

We have all the components modified for dependency injection, so now we must modify the main method in our App class so that it configures, instantiates, and assembles the classes in our application. Our code will do the following:

1. Declare a UserIO variable and initialize it with a UserIOConsoleImpl reference.
2. Declare and instantiate a ClassRosterView object, passing the UserIO created in the previous step into the constructor.
3. Declare a ClassRosterDao variable and initialize it with a ClassRosterDaoFileImpl reference.
4. Instantiate a ClassRosterController, passing the ClassRosterDao and ClassRosterView objects into the constructor.
5. Call the run method on the controller to kick things off.

Modify the main method in your App class to look like this:

```
public static void main(String[] args) {
    UserIO myIo = new UserIOConsoleImpl();
    ClassRosterView myView = new ClassRosterView(myIo);
    ClassRosterDao myDao = new ClassRosterDaoFileImpl();
    ClassRosterController controller =
            new ClassRosterController(myDao, myView);
    controller.run();
}
```

> **NOTE** You need to add imports for your classes as well.

That does it. You now have an application that uses a form of dependency injection to keep the components loosely coupled. It is possible also to create an interface that includes all the methods we want to see in our view and then make the ClassRosterView class implement the underlying interface. That way, if we decide to implement an actual user interface for our application through the web, we can implement the view class for a web application.

HANDLING APPLICATION EXCEPTIONS

In the next few steps, we'll see how to use application-specific exceptions, and we'll implement the file persistence feature of the application.

ClassRosterDaoException

Now we'll create the application-specific exception for our project. As we discussed earlier, the purpose of this exception is to allow us to hide the underlying implementation exceptions so that we don't leak implementation details from our DAO.

As demonstrated in the UML diagram for our application in Figure 27.8, ClassRosterDaoException extends Exception.

This is common practice when creating specific exceptions for your application. By extending Exception, we inherit all the capabilities of Exception and then can add any special features that we want to add. In our case, we won't add any new features, because we want our exception to act just like Exception. Extending Exception allows us to translate and/or wrap any implementation-specific exception that can get thrown, which is exactly the feature we are interested in. You can also get this by extending RuntimeException as well. Remember that when we extend Exception, our new exception will be a checked exception.

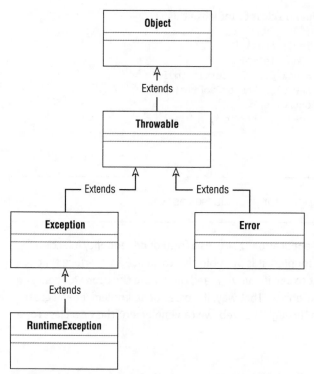

Figure 27.8 `ClassrosterDaoException` extends `Exception`

Create the `ClassRosterDaoException` class in the `com.sg.classroster.dao` package and make it look like Listing 27.20.

LISTING 27.20

The `ClassRosterDaoException` Class

```
public class ClassRosterDaoException extends Exception{

    public ClassRosterDaoException(String message) {
        super(message);
    }

    public ClassRosterDaoException(String message, Throwable cause) {
        super(message, cause);
    }

}
```

Let's analyze this code a bit. First, notice that we use the `extends` keyword to indicate that we are extending `Exception`. This is standard, but it is a good example of where you will use inheritance fairly often.

Next, notice that we have two constructors. One takes just a string `message`, and the other takes a string `message` and a `Throwable` cause. Also notice that each of these constructors turns around and calls the matching constructor on the `Exception` class by calling `super()`. All constructors call `super` implicitly, but in our case we are explicating calling `super`. We do this because we want to call particular constructors in the `super` class, not the default `super()` constructor.

We will use the first constructor in cases where something is wrong in our application, but it isn't caused by another exception. For example, maybe our application has some validation rules for student data input and one of the fields doesn't pass validation. In that case, we could throw a new `ClassRosterDaoException` with a message describing the problem.

We will use the second constructor in cases where something is wrong in our application that is caused by another exception in the underlying implementation. In these cases, we catch the implementation-specific exception (for example `FileNotFoundException`). In the `catch` block, we would create a new `ClassRosterDaoException` and pass in a new message and the exception that caused the original problem, and then we throw the newly created `ClassRosterDaoException`. We have effectively wrapped the original exception with our application-specific exception.

One more question remains: Why is the type of the second parameter of the second constructor `Throwable` and not `Exception`?

As it turns out, `Exception` extends `Throwable`. If we reduced the scope of what the constructor could take, then it wouldn't be overriding. We want to be compliant with the existing constructor of `Exception` as opposed to creating an unintentional overload. Here is an excerpt from the Javadoc for `Exception`:

```
public class Exception extends Throwable
```

The class `Exception` and its subclasses are a form of `Throwable` that indicates conditions that a reasonable application might want to catch.

> **NOTE** Now you have a better idea of how exceptions are used and handled in Java. Right now, all this information probably seems a bit overwhelming, but with time and practice, you'll become more comfortable with these concepts and techniques.

ADDING FILE PERSISTENCE

In the final step of the code-along, we will add code to persist the student information to a file. The DAO code for this will follow the algorithm described in Lesson 24. We need to make the following changes:

1. Add methods to the DAO to read student data from a file.

    - Add a method to unmarshal a line of text into a `Student` object.

    - Add a method to iterate over a file line by line, and load students into our Map.

2. Add a method to the DAO to write student data to a file.

    - Add a method to marshal a student into a line of text.

    - Add a method to iterate over all students in our Map and write each to a file.

3. Modify the public methods of the DAO to read from and write to the file when appropriate.

4. Modify the DAO interface to account for the exceptions that can be thrown by the implementation.

5. Modify the controller to account for and handle exceptions thrown by the DAO.

6. Add a method to our view for displaying error messages to the user.

ClassRosterDaoFileImpl

There are several changes we will need to make in `ClassRosterDaoFileImpl`. We'll cover each of these changes in the following sections.

Constants

We will use the file format described in Lesson 24. Each line in our file will consist of the student ID, first name, last name, and cohort, separated by two colons like this:

```
<studentid>::<first name>::<last name>::<cohort>
```

Here's an example:

```
0001::Joe::Cool::Java - Jan 2021
0002::Jane::Awesome::Java - April 2019
0003::Jamal:Fantastic::.NET - Jan 2021
```

To start, we'll create two constants in our DAO: one for the name of the file that holds all the student data and one for the delimiter (two colons). Add the following constants near the top of your ClassRosterDaoFileImpl class:

```
public static final String ROSTER_FILE = "roster.txt";
public static final String DELIMITER = "::";
```

unmarshalStudent

Our next step is to create a method that can translate a line of text into a Student object. This method will follow the pattern described earlier, and the process is also described in Lesson 24.

1. Take in a String line to break apart for student information.

2. Split the String into chunks at the :: delimiter.

3. Create a new Student object.

4. Use the first value from the split String to set the student ID (this is passed into the constructor of the new Student object).

5. Use the second value from the split String to set the student's first name.

6. Use the third value from the split String to set the student's last name.

7. Use the fourth value from the split String to set the cohort value.

Add the method in Listing 27.21 to your ClassRosterDaoFileImpl.

LISTING 27.21

unmarshalStudent() Method

```
private Student unmarshalStudent(String studentAsText){
    // studentAsText is expecting a line read in from our file.
    // For example, it might look like this:
    // 1234::Ada::Lovelace::Java-September1842
    //
    // We then split that line on our DELIMITER - which we are using as ::
    // Leaving us with an array of Strings, stored in studentTokens.
    // Which should look like this:
    // ------------------------------------
    // |    |   |        |                 |
    // |1234|Ada|Lovelace|Java-September1842|
    // |    |   |        |                 |
    // ------------------------------------
```

```
//  [0]   [1]     [2]         [3]
String[] studentTokens = studentAsText.split(DELIMITER);

// Given the pattern above, the student Id is in index 0 of the array.
String studentId = studentTokens[0];

// Which we can then use to create a new Student object to satisfy
// the requirements of the Student constructor.
Student studentFromFile = new Student(studentId);

// However, there are 3 remaining tokens that need to be set into the
// new student object. Do this manually by using the appropriate setters.

// Index 1 - FirstName
studentFromFile.setFirstName(studentTokens[1]);

// Index 2 - LastName
studentFromFile.setLastName(studentTokens[2]);

// Index 3 - Cohort
studentFromFile.setCohort(studentTokens[3]);

// We have now created a student! Return it!
return studentFromFile;
}
```

You should note that we use the `String.split` method to split each line in the file into an array of `String`s. When the `split` method splits a `String` on the given delimiter, it throws the delimiter away. Carefully read the comments in the previous code for details.

loadRoster

Our next step is to create a method that reads the roster file into memory. This method will follow the algorithm described in Lesson 24.

1. Open the file for reading.
2. For each line in the file, do the following:
   a. Read the line into a `String` variable.
   b. Pass the line to our `unmarshalStudent()` method to parse it into `Student`.
   c. Put the newly created and initialized `Student` object into the `students` `Map`.
3. Close the file.

Add the method in Listing 27.22 to your `ClassRosterDaoFileImpl`.

LISTING 27.22

The loadRoster() Method

```
private void loadRoster() throws ClassRosterDaoException {
    // create an initial scanner
    Scanner scanner = null;

    try {
        // Change scanner to read from file
        scanner = new Scanner(
                new BufferedReader(
                        new FileReader(ROSTER_FILE)));
        // currentLine holds the most recent line read from the file
        String currentLine;
        // currentStudent holds the most recent student unmarshaled
        Student currentStudent;
        // Go through ROSTER_FILE line by line, decoding each line into a
        // Student object by calling the unmarshalStudent method.
        // Process while we have more lines in the file
        while (scanner.hasNextLine()) {
            // get the next line in the file
            currentLine = scanner.nextLine();
            // unmarshal the line into a Student
            currentStudent = unmarshalStudent(currentLine);

            // We are going to use the student id as the map key for our
            // student object.
            // Put currentStudent into the map using student id as the key
            students.put(currentStudent.getStudentId(), currentStudent);
        }
    } catch (FileNotFoundException e) {
        throw new ClassRosterDaoException(
                "-_- Could not load roster data into memory.", e);
    }

    // close scanner
    finally{
        if (scanner!=null) {
            scanner.close();
        }
    }
}
```

Pay close attention to the following:

- At the top of this method, in the `try-catch` block, we catch the `FileNotFoundException` and translate it into a `ClassRosterDaoException`.
- We use a `Scanner` to read each line from the file one by one (this was demonstrated in Lesson 24).

marshalStudent

Now we'll create the method that organizes the student information from an in-memory object into a line of text so that it can then be written properly into a file. This method will also follow the pattern described earlier and the process outlined in Lesson 24.

However, most importantly, we must preserve the order of information when we translate our student into text because we are eventually expecting to unmarshal it back into a student again. The write method must be the equal and opposite balance to the read method:

1. Take in a student.
2. Create a `String` consisting of student ID, first name, last name, and cohort (in that order), separated by the :: delimiter.

Add the method in Listing 27.23 to your `ClassRosterDaoFileImpl`.

LISTING 27.23

The `marshalStudent()` Method

```java
private String marshalStudent(Student aStudent){
    // We need to turn a Student object into a line of text for our file.
    // For example, we need an in-memory object to end up like this:
    // 4321::Charles::Babbage::Java-September1842

    // It's not a complicated process. Just get out each property,
    // and concatenate with our DELIMITER as a kind of spacer.

    // Start with the student id, since that's supposed to be first.
    String studentAsText = aStudent.getStudentId() + DELIMITER;

    // add the rest of the properties in the correct order:

    // FirstName
    studentAsText += aStudent.getFirstName() + DELIMITER;
```

```
    // LastName
    studentAsText += aStudent.getLastName() + DELIMITER;

    // Cohort - don't forget to skip the DELIMITER here.
    studentAsText += aStudent.getCohort();

    // We have now turned a student to text! Return it!
    return studentAsText;
}
```

writeRoster

Now we'll create the method that writes the student information from memory to a file. Again, we will follow the algorithm outlined in Lesson 24.

1. Open the file for writing.
2. Go through the Student objects in the students Map one by one.
3. For each Student, do the following:
   a. Turn a Student to text, using our marshalStudent() method, spaced by our delimiter.
   b. Write the String to the output file.
4. Close the file.

Add the method in Listing 27.24 to your ClassRosterDaoFileImpl.

LISTING 27.24

The writeRoster() Method

```
private void writeRoster() throws ClassRosterDaoException {
    // NOTE FOR APPRENTICES: We are not handling the IOException, but
    // we are translating it to an application-specific exception and
    // then simply throwing it (i.e., "reporting" it) to the code that
    // called it.  It is the responsibility of the calling code to
    // handle any errors that occur.
    PrintWriter out = null;

    try {
        out = new PrintWriter(new FileWriter(ROSTER_FILE));
        // Write out the Student objects to the roster file.
        // NOTE TO APPRENTICES: We could just grab the student map,
```

```
        // get the Collection of Students, and iterate over them but we've
        // already created a method that gets a List of Students, so
        // we'll reuse it.
        String studentAsText;
        List<Student> studentList = new ArrayList(students.values());
        for (Student currentStudent : studentList) {
            // turn a Student into a String
            studentAsText = marshalStudent(currentStudent);
            // write the Student object to the file
            out.println(studentAsText);
            // force PrintWriter to write line to the file
            out.flush();
        }
    } catch (IOException e) {
        throw new ClassRosterDaoException(
                "Could not save student data.", e);
    }
    finally{
        // Clean up
        if (out!=null){
            out.close();
        }
    }
}
```

Pay close attention to the following:

1. At the top of this method, in the try-catch block, we catch the IOException and translate it into a ClassRosterDaoException.

2. We're using a PrintWriter to write to the file (this was demonstrated in Lesson 24).

3. We flush the PrintWriter buffer each time through the for loop to force it to write the student to the file.

4. We close the PrintWriter at the end.

addStudent

Now that we have the loadRoster and writeRoster methods in place, we need to modify addStudent, getAllStudents, getStudent, and removeStudent so that they read from and write to the file as appropriate.

Add a call to loadRoster and to writeRoster and add the throws ClassRosterDaoException declaration to addStudent so it looks like Listing 27.25.

LISTING 27.25

The addStudent() Method

```
@Override
public Student addStudent(String studentId, Student student)
 throws ClassRosterDaoException {
    loadRoster();
    Student newStudent = students.put(studentId, student);
    writeRoster();
    return newStudent;
}
```

This method reads all the Student objects from the file and loads them into our map. It then adds the new Student object to our map and then writes all the student information to the file to make sure the change is persisted.

Notice that this now causes an error because the addStudent method declaration in the ClassRosterDao interface does not allow the declaration of new or broader checked exceptions. We'll fix that later in this lesson.

getAllStudents

Add a call to loadRoster and add the throws ClassRosterDaoException declaration to getAllStudents so it looks like Listing 27.26.

LISTING 27.26

The getAllStudents() Method

```
@Override
public List<Student> getAllStudents()
 throws ClassRosterDaoException {
    loadRoster();
    return new ArrayList(students.values());
}
```

This method reads all the Student objects from the file, gets them out of the map, and then returns an ArrayList of the Student objects to the caller. Notice that this now causes an error because the getAllStudents method declaration in the ClassRosterDao interface does not specify that it throws a ClassRosterDaoException. We'll fix that later in this lesson.

getStudent

Add a call to `loadRoster` and add the `throws ClassRosterDaoException` declaration to `getStudent` so it looks like Listing 27.27.

LISTING 27.27

The getStudent() Method

```
@Override
public Student getStudent(String studentId)
  throws ClassRosterDaoException {
    loadRoster();
    return students.get(studentId);
}
```

This method reads all the `Student` objects from the file, gets the requested student out of the map, and then returns the `Student` object to the caller. Notice that this now causes an error because the `getStudent` method declaration in the `ClassRosterDao` interface does not specify that it throws a `ClassRosterDaoException`. Again, we will fix that later in this lesson.

removeStudent

Add a call to `loadRoster` and to `writeRoster` and add the `throws ClassRosterDaoException` declaration to `removeStudent` so it looks like Listing 27.28.

LISTING 27.28

The removeStudent Method

```
@Override
public Student removeStudent(String studentId)
  throws ClassRosterDaoException {
    loadRoster();
    Student removedStudent = students.remove(studentId);
    writeRoster();
    return removedStudent;
}
```

This method ensures that all Student objects are read in from the file and loaded into our map. Then the method removes the specified Student object from our map, writes the updated students map to the file, and returns the removed Student object to the caller.

Notice that this now causes an error because the removeStudent method declaration in the ClassRosterDao interface does not specify that it throws a ClassRosterDaoException. Again, we will fix that later in this document.

ClassRosterDao

Now we need to go fix the ClassRosterDao interface. We'll add the throws ClassRosterDaoException declaration to each of the methods. Modify ClassRosterDao to look like Listing 27.29. With this change, the controller will fail to compile until we update it as well.

LISTING 27.29

The Updated ClassRosterDao Interface

```
public interface ClassRosterDao {
    /**
     * Adds the given Student to the roster and associates it with the
     * given student id. If there is already a student associated with the
     * given student id it will return that student object; otherwise it
     * will return null.
     *
     * @param studentId id with which student is to be associated
     * @param student student to be added to the roster
     * @return the Student object previously associated with the given
     * student id if it exists, null otherwise
     * @throws ClassRosterDaoException
     */
    Student addStudent(String studentId, Student student)
      throws ClassRosterDaoException;

    /**
     * Returns a List of all Students on the roster.
     *
     * @return Student List containing all students on the roster.
     * @throws ClassRosterDaoException
     */
```

```
        List<Student> getAllStudents()
          throws ClassRosterDaoException;

        /**
         * Returns the student object associated with the given student id.
         * Returns null if no such student exists
         *
         * @param studentId ID of the student to retrieve
         * @return the Student object associated with the given student id,
         * null if no such student exists
         * @throws ClassRosterDaoException
         */
        Student getStudent(String studentId)
          throws ClassRosterDaoException;

        /**
         * Removes from the roster the student associated with the given id.
         * Returns the student object that is being removed or null if
         * there is no student associated with the given id
         *
         * @param studentId id of student to be removed
         * @return Student object that was removed or null if no student
         * was associated with the given student id
         * @throws ClassRosterDaoException
         */
        Student removeStudent(String studentId)
          throws ClassRosterDaoException;
    }
```

ClassRosterView

We need to add one more method to our view to display the given error message to the user. We'll use this method in the controller to display any error messages we encounter. Add the following method to your ClassRosterView:

```java
public void displayErrorMessage(String errorMsg) {
    io.print("=== ERROR ===");
    io.print(errorMsg);
}
```

ClassRosterController

The DAO is all taken care of, but the changes we made broke our controller. All the methods in our controller that call DAO methods now have compile errors because they do not have any code to handle the new `ClassRosterDaoExceptions` that the DAO is now throwing. We'll fix this in two steps.

1. We'll add `throws ClassRosterDaoException` to the `createStudent`, `viewStudent`, `removeStudent`, and `listStudents` methods.

2. We'll add a `try–catch` block in the `run` method.

Modify the private methods in `ClassRosterController` to look like Listing 27.30.

LISTING 27.30

The Updated ClassRosterController

```java
private int getMenuSelection() {
    return view.printMenuAndGetSelection();
}

private void createStudent() throws ClassRosterDaoException {
    view.displayCreateStudentBanner();
    Student newStudent = view.getNewStudentInfo();
    dao.addStudent(newStudent.getStudentId(), newStudent);
    view.displayCreateSuccessBanner();
}

private void listStudents() throws ClassRosterDaoException {
    view.displayDisplayAllBanner();
    List<Student> studentList = dao.getAllStudents();
    view.displayStudentList(studentList);
}

private void viewStudent() throws ClassRosterDaoException {
    view.displayDisplayStudentBanner();
    String studentId = view.getStudentIdChoice();
    Student student = dao.getStudent(studentId);
    view.displayStudent(student);
}

private void removeStudent() throws ClassRosterDaoException {
    view.displayRemoveStudentBanner();
    String studentId = view.getStudentIdChoice();
    Student removedStudent = dao.removeStudent(studentId);
    view.displayRemoveResult(removedStudent);
}
```

```
private void unknownCommand() {
    view.displayUnknownCommandBanner();
}

private void exitMessage() {
    view.displayExitBanner();
}
```

Now we'll add a try-catch block to the controller's run method so we can react to the ClassRosterDaoExceptions that potentially get thrown by our code. When we encounter an exception, we'll just tell the view to print out the error message for us. Modify your run method to look like Listing 27.31.

LISTING 27.31

The Updated run Method

```
public void run() {
    boolean keepGoing = true;
    int menuSelection = 0;
    try {
        while (keepGoing) {

            menuSelection = getMenuSelection();

            switch (menuSelection) {
                case 1:
                    listStudents();
                    break;
                case 2:
                    createStudent();
                    break;
                case 3:
                    viewStudent();
                    break;
                case 4:
                    removeStudent();
                    break;
                case 5:
                    keepGoing = false;
                    break;
                default:
                    unknownCommand();
            }
```

```
        }
        exitMessage();
    } catch (ClassRosterDaoException e) {
        view.displayErrorMessage(e.getMessage());
    }
}
```

Create roster.txt

The final step in the code-along is to create the `roster.txt` file where our student data will be stored. To do this, switch to the Files tab (found next to the Projects tab), right-click the *ClassRoster* folder, and select *New* and then *Other*, as shown in Figure 27.9.

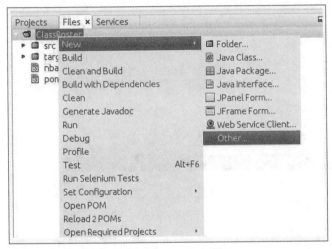

Figure 27.9 Adding the `roster.txt` file

That will display the New File dialog. In the Categories pane, select *Other*. In the Choose File Type pane, select *Empty File*, and click *Next*, as shown in Figure 27.10.

This will display the New Empty File dialog. Enter **roster.txt** in the File Name text entry field and click *Finish*, as shown in Figure 27.11.

Now `roster.txt` should show up on the Files tab, as shown in Figure 27.12.

Finally, open `roster.txt` and remove all empty lines from the file. For some reason, NetBeans creates an empty line in its empty file. If you don't remove this line from `roster.txt`, you will get an `ArrayIndexOutOfBoundsException` when your program tries to read `roster.txt`.

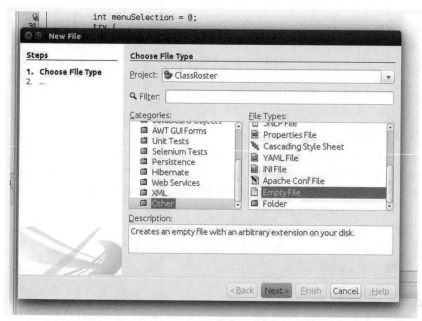

Figure 27.10 Selecting the file type

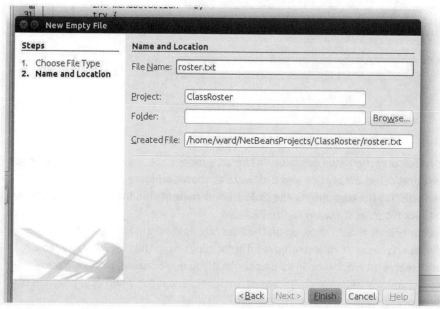

Figure 27.11 Entering the filename and location

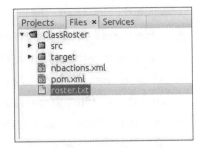

Figure 27.12 The roster.txt file has been added

SUMMARY

You have created your first MVC CRUD application. Remember to follow the steps we took to build this application as you build the exercises included with this lesson. Make sure you use the code you wrote here as a template, or guide, for your future projects.

EXERCISES

These exercises help you practice in your own application what you have reviewed in this lesson. These are to do on your own.

> **Exercise 1:** Your Own DVD Library
> **Exercise 2:** Electronic Address Book

> **NOTE** This exercise will be referenced again in a future lesson where you will extend what you build here.

Exercise 1: DVD Library Update

The purpose of this exercise is to demonstrate your proficiency in what you've learned up to this point, including basic Java syntax involving console input and output, basic file input and output, basic string/text manipulation, flow of control statements, expressions, and basic data structures such as arrays, lists, and maps. Additionally, you will demonstrate your proficiency in implementing the MVC design pattern and dependency injection.

In this exercise, you will create a program that stores information about a DVD collection. The program must do the following:

- Allow the user to add a DVD to the collection
- Allow the user to remove a DVD from the collection

- Allow the user to edit the information for an existing DVD in the collection
- Allow the user to list the DVDs in the collection
- Allow the user to display the information for a particular DVD
- Allow the user to search for a DVD by title
- Load the DVD library from a file
- Save the DVD library back to the file when the program completes
- Allow the user to add, edit, or delete many DVDs in one session

Additionally, you should follow the MVC design pattern and follow the agile approach checklist outlined in Appendix D.

Your DVD data transfer object should have the following fields:

- Title
- Release date
- MPAA rating
- Director's name
- Studio
- User rating or note (allows the user to enter additional information, e.g., "Good family movie")

Exercise 2: Electronic Address Book

The objective of this exercise is to continue to practice designing programs that consist of more than one class, implement the MVC pattern presented in this course, and use Java Collections and Maps. In this exercise, design a program that acts as an electronic address book. This program should do the following:

- Allow the user to add addresses to the address book
- Allow the user to remove addresses from the address book
- Allow the user to see how many addresses are in the book
- Allow the user to list all the addresses in the book
- Allow the user to find an address by last name

Design an Address class to hold address information. Design an AddressBookDao class that holds Address objects. It should also have methods to do the following:

- Add an address
- Remove an address

- Find an address by last name
- Return a count of addresses in AddressBookDao
- Return all the addresses in AddressBookDao

Design an AddressBookController class. This class should do the following:

- Orchestrate all activities of the program.
- Use the view and UserIOClass from a previous exercise to handle all console input and output. You might need to modify the view.
- Use the AddressBookDao class to store Address objects.

You should also add code to allow the user to edit an address and to initialize your address book from a file. Finally, add code to allow the user to save an address back to the file.

The following provides ideas as a sample for the UI for the application:

```
==========
Initial Menu:
        Please select the operation you wish to perform:
                1. Add Address
                2. Delete Address
                3. Find Address
                4. List Address Count
                5. List All Addresses

Add Address Menu:
        Please Enter First Name:
        Please Enter Last Name:
        Please Enter Street Address:
        .
        .
        .
        Address added.  Press 1 to go to Main Menu.

Delete Address Menu:
        Please enter last name of address to delete:

        John Doe
        123 Main Street
        Hometown, OH, 12345

        Really Delete?
        Address Deleted.  Press 1 to go to Main Menu.
```

Find Address Menu:
        Please enter last name of address to find:

        Sally Jones
        45 Elm Street
        Applegrove, OH 44321

        Press 1 to go to Main Menu.

List Address Count Menu:
        There are 45 addresses in the book. Press 1 to go to Main Menu.

List Addresses Menu:
        John Doe
        123 Main Street
        Hometown, OH, 12345

        Sally Jones
        45 Elm Street
        Applegrove, OH 44321

        .

        .

        .

        Press 1 to go to Main Menu.

PART IV

Intermediate Java

Lesson 28
Exploring the Service Layer

This lesson introduces the service layer to our tiered/MVC application design. The service layer sits between the controller and the data access object (DAO) and contains the business logic for the application. We'll discuss why service layers are needed, their role in an application, and how they relate to the other application components.

LEARNING OBJECTIVES

By the time you finish this lesson, you will be able to:
- Explain the role of the service layer
- Create semantic exceptions
- Design a service layer application programming interface (API)

THE ROLE OF THE SERVICE LAYER

So far we have the model, view, and controller components in our tiered application design. Let's review some of the MVC rules we've seen in earlier lessons.

- The model is responsible for persisting, retrieving, and ferrying data around the application.

- The controller is the orchestrator of our application: it knows what needs to be done and when it needs to be done, but it doesn't do any of the work. All work is done by other components.
- The view knows how to display what it receives, but it can't do any calculations.

This works well for CRUD applications. If all you need to do is create, read, update, and delete data and there is no business logic in your application, you are all set. But what if you need business logic? What if you need to make calculations such as tax and shipping on an order? What if you need to validate inputs such as a credit card number or shipping address? What if we need to coordinate the activities of more than one DAO? Where do we put all this code?

The MVC pattern as we know it now has no place for any of this type of code. This is where the service layer comes in: it is all about doing work. The *service layer* is responsible for checking business rules, doing calculations, coordinating interactions with the DAOs, and performing other similar activities.

The term *service layer* is a bit of a misnomer. Generally speaking, the service layer is just a Java class that implements a service layer functionality. In that sense, it is just like the other components of our application; it just has a different role to play in the system.

The introduction of the service layer changes the MVC rules some because we insert the service layer in between the controller and the DAOs. This means that the controller is no longer allowed to talk directly to the DAOs. The controller now must use the service layer to communicate with the DAOs, which means that the service layer becomes both the business logic and the persistence API for the rest of the application. The service layer is the only component in the system that is allowed to talk to the DAOs. Our MVC tiered design now looks like Figure 28.1.

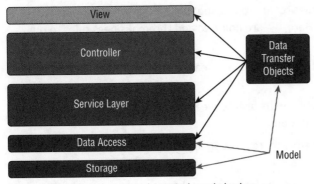

Figure 28.1 Our updated MVC tiered design

SERVICE LAYER EXCEPTIONS

In this lesson, we introduce the concept of semantic or application logic exceptions. These exceptions represent violations of validation or business logic. For example, we will create an exception for the Class Roster application that is thrown if the user tries to create a `Student` object with an existing ID. These exceptions are implemented just like application-specific exceptions in that they extend `Exception` and they have two constructors. The only difference is that they signal a different type of error. We will see in the following sections how these become an integral part of the service layer interface/API.

SERVICE LAYER API DESIGN

The first step in creating a service layer is to define what you want the service layer to do and create an interface for that functionality. We probably won't have more than one implementation for our service layer (like we will have for our DAOs), but creating an interface for the service layer gives us that option later if we need it. That said, the main reason we create the service layer interface is that it forces us to design the API/contract for our service layer up front: we have to think about what the interface is, how it will be used, and how we signal success and failure.

To demonstrate this process, we will design the Class Roster service layer interface. In the next lesson, we will implement the service layer in the Class Roster project. The service layer for Class Roster will be similar to the interface for the underlying DAO, but there will be several changes because of the business rules we are going to introduce to the application and enforce in the service layer.

NEW BUSINESS RULES

If we didn't have new business rules to add to the application, we would have no reason to create a service layer. Here, we are going to add three business rules to our application.

- The application should not allow the user to create a student with an ID that already exists in the system.

- The application should not allow the user to create a student that has empty values for First Name, Last Name, or Cohort.

- The application will record an entry to an audit log every time a `Student` object is created or removed from the system.

As mentioned earlier, we will design the interface for the new service layer here, and we will implement the new service layer as part of the next lesson in this course.

CREATE A STUDENT

This is where the biggest change will be. In the current implementation, the DAO method for creating a student simply takes the student and saves it no matter what. This is perfectly fine—the DAO is supposed to be fast and stupid, and it is supposed to do what you tell it to do, no questions asked.

We want the service layer method that creates a student to be a bit more sophisticated; it must enforce our three business rules. In this step, we are declaring the method in the service layer interface, but our method declaration must somehow indicate that these rules will be enforced. Let's see how this works.

Define the Method Signature

First, we must define the signature of our method. We are going to call this method createStudent(). It will not have any parameters. Note that this is different from the addStudent() method in the underlying DAO interface, which takes a student ID and a Student object. This is perfectly acceptable. The service layer doesn't have to mirror the DAO interface methods. Here is our method signature:

```
createStudent()
```

Define the Return Type

Next, we must define the return type of our method. The createStudent() method will return nothing. This is different from the addStudent() method in the underlying DAO interface, which returns a Student object if the given student ID already exists. There is no need to return a student object from the createStudent() service layer method because our business rules do not allow us to create a student with a duplicate student ID.

> **NOTE** You could return a Boolean from createStudent() to indicate that the method was successful. Additionally, in most real-world applications, you would programmatically generate a student ID rather than having the user provide it.

Define the Errors That Might Occur in This Method

Finally, we must define any errors that might occur when this method is executed. There are three things that might go wrong.

- The ID of the given Student object might already exist

- First Name, Last Name, or Cohort values might be missing

- Something might go wrong when the DAO tries to read from or write to the underlying data store

If any of these things occur, the method must throw an exception that lets the caller know the nature of the error. To do this, we must create two new exception types.

- ClassRosterDuplicateIdException for the duplicate student ID error

- ClassRosterDataValidationException for the data validation error

We have an existing exception for the third error—ClassRosterDaoException— but, in hindsight, this exception seems a bit specific. We will rename/refactor this from ClassRosterDaoException to ClassRosterPersistenceException so that it applies to any persistence error, not just problems that occur in a DAO.

This gives us the following code to define createStudent():

```
void createStudent(Student student) throws
    ClassRosterDuplicateIdException,
    ClassRosterDataValidationException,
    ClassRosterPersistenceException;
```

One thing you may have noticed is that there is nothing in the declaration of this method to indicate that our third business rule—writing to the audit log every time a Student object is created or removed in the system—is enforced. This is because that particular business rule is part of the private implementation of the service layer. This rule does not affect how the service layer methods are used by other parts of the application, so it does not show up as part of the public interface of the service layer.

SERVICE LAYER METHODS FOR GETTING STUDENTS

For our class roster application, we will need methods for getting students. These will include getting all students, getting a single student, and removing a student.

Get All Students

The service layer method for getting all students will be identical to the method getAllStudents() in the underlying DAO interface, because we don't have any business logic or validation to perform here. These types of methods are known as pass-through methods, and you will generally have a few of these in your service layer interfaces.

```
List<Student> getAllStudents() throws ClassRosterPersistenceException;
```

Get a Single Student

The method to get a single student, getStudent(), will also be a pass-through method, as shown in the following:

```
Student getStudent(String studentId) throws
ClassRosterPersistenceException;
```

Remove a Student

The method to remove a student, removeStudent(), is not a pass-through because we must write to the audit log when a Student object is removed from the system; however, the declaration of this method is the same as the underlying DAO interface method.

```
Student removeStudent(String studentId) throws
    ClassRosterPersistenceException;
```

SUMMARY

In this lesson, we introduced the service layer and discussed how it fits into a tiered MVC application structure. The key takeaways from this document are as follows:

- The service layer is responsible for the business logic of an application.
- The service layer sits between the controller and the DAOs. When introduced into an application, the controller should use the service layer for all DAO access.
- Application-specific exceptions are used to signal violations of business rules. These exceptions are part of the public interface, or API, of the service layer.
- Service layers generally have some methods that simply turn around and call a matching DAO method—these are known as pass-through methods.

In the following lesson, we will go deeper by starting with what we learned in this lesson on the service layer and applying it to our Class Roster application.

Lesson 29

Pulling It All Together: Coding the Class Roster Service Layer

It's time again to pull together what we've learned by implementing the Class Roster service layer that we designed in the previous lesson into an application. We will continue with the Class Roster application we updated in Lesson 27.

PROGRAM OBJECTIVES

Essentially, we will be coding the business rules into our application by following these steps:

- Create the service layer interface.
- Create new application-specific exceptions.
- Refactor/rename the existing `ClassRosterDaoException`.
- Implement the service layer interface.
- Modify the controller to use the new service layer.

- Modify the dependency injection code in App to account for the new service layer component.
- Add the audit log feature.
  - Create the Audit DAO interface.
  - Create the Audit DAO file implementation.
  - Modify the service layer to use the Audit DAO.
  - Modify the dependency injection code in App to account for the new Audit DAO component.

CREATE A SERVICE LAYER INTERFACE

The first step in updating our Class Roster application is to create the service layer interface that we designed in the previous lesson. We are going to have several classes and interfaces related to our service layer, so we will create a new com.sg.classroster. service package in the same way we've added packages before. To do this, open the ClassRoster project, right-click the com.sg.classroster package, and select New ➤ Java Package, as shown in Figure 29.1.

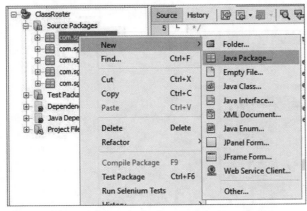

Figure 29.1 Adding a new Java package

Type the name of the new package (**com.sg.classroster.service**) next to *Package Name* in the New Java Package window, as shown in Figure 29.2. Click the *Finish* button when you are done.

Now that the package has been created, it is time to create the interface. In the package explorer, right-click the com.sg.classroster.service package and select New ➤ Java Package, as shown in Figure 29.3.

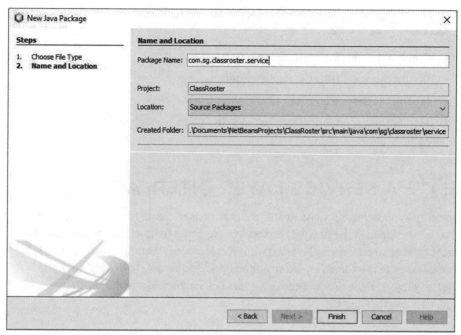

Figure 29.2 Naming the Java package

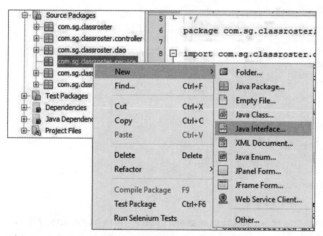

Figure 29.3 Creating a new Java interface

When the New Java Interface dialog box appears, type **ClassRosterServiceLayer** into the Class Name text box, as shown in Figure 29.4. Click the *Finish* button when you are done.

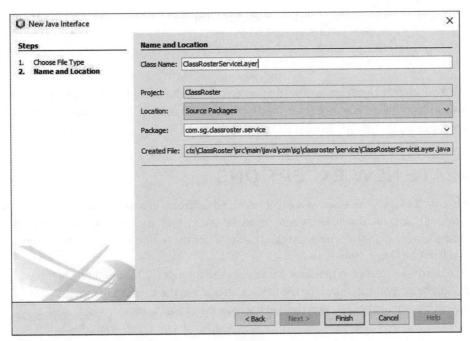

Figure 29.4 Naming the new Java interface

Finally, we need to define the methods we designed in Lesson 28. Add code to your ClassRosterServiceLayer interface so that it looks like Listing 29.1.

LISTING 29.1

The ClassRosterServiceLayer Interface

```java
public interface ClassRosterServiceLayer {

    void createStudent(Student student) throws
            ClassRosterDuplicateIdException,
            ClassRosterDataValidationException,
            ClassRosterPersistenceException;

    List<Student> getAllStudents() throws
            ClassRosterPersistenceException;

    Student getStudent(String studentId) throws
            ClassRosterPersistenceException;
```

```
    Student removeStudent(String studentId) throws
            ClassRosterPersistenceException;

}
```

You'll notice that NetBeans is now showing errors. This is because we haven't created the new exceptions or refactored/renamed the existing exception. We'll do that in the next step.

CREATE NEW EXCEPTIONS

Now we need to create our two new exceptions and refactor/rename the existing exception. At this point, you should know how to create new classes, packages, and interfaces in NetBeans (as shown in the previous step). The details of these NetBeans creation operations will not be shown from here on out.

Exceptions are created in the same package as the component that potentially throws them. So, the exceptions thrown by the service layer are in the service package and the exception thrown by the DAO is in the dao package in our application.

ClassRosterDuplicateIdException

Create a new class in the com.sg.classroster.service package called **ClassRoster-DuplicateIdException**. This class will extend Exception and will have two constructors (just like the ClassRosterDaoException you implemented in the previous section). When complete, your new class should look like Listing 29.2.

LISTING 29.2

The ClassRosterDuplicateIdException Class

```java
public class ClassRosterDuplicateIdException extends Exception {

    public ClassRosterDuplicateIdException(String message) {
        super(message);
    }

    public ClassRosterDuplicateIdException(String message,
            Throwable cause) {
        super(message, cause);
    }

}
```

ClassRosterDataValidationException

Create a new class in the com.sg.classroster.service package called **ClassRosterData-ValidationException**. This class will be similar to ClassRosterDuplicateIdException. When complete, your new class should look like Listing 29.3.

LISTING 29.3

The `ClassRosterDataValidationException` Class

```java
public class ClassRosterDataValidationException extends Exception {

    public ClassRosterDataValidationException(String message) {
        super(message);
    }

    public ClassRosterDataValidationException(String message,
            Throwable cause) {
        super(message, cause);
    }
}
```

Refactor/Rename ClassRosterDaoException

Now we need to refactor/rename ClassRosterDaoException to ClassRosterPersis-tenceException. This change does not add or remove any functionality from our program, but it does better signal the intent of this exception and better encapsulates the private implementation of the service layer.

In NetBeans, right-click *ClassRosterDaoException* in the com.sg.classroster.dao package in the Project Explorer and select Refactor ➤ Rename, as shown in Figure 29.5.

Type **ClassRosterPersistenceException** into the New Name text box of the Rename Class dialog box, as shown in Figure 29.6. Click the *Refactor* button when done.

Finally, we have to return to the ClassRosterServiceLayer interface and import ClassRosterPersistenceException. Open ClassRosterServiceLayer.java, right-click any white space in the file, and select Fix Imports, as shown in Figure 29.7. This will import ClassRosterPersistenceException and fix the final error in NetBeans.

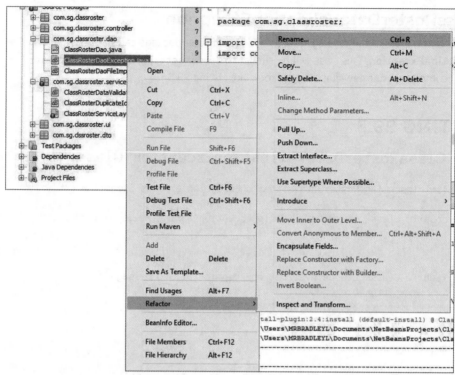

Figure 29.5 Refactoring a name

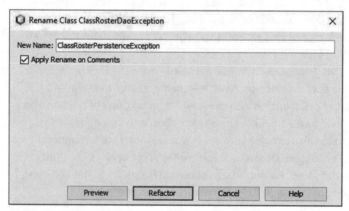

Figure 29.6 Renaming the class

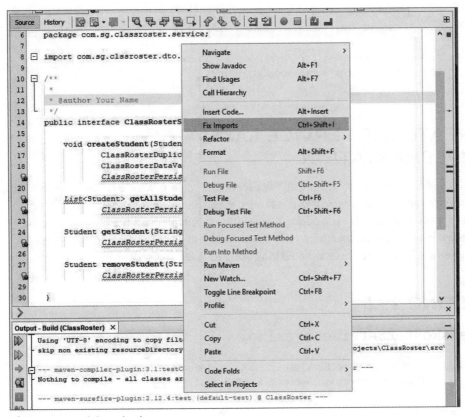

Figure 29.7 Fixing the imports

Now `ClassRosterServiceLayer` should look like Listing 29.4 with no errors.

LISTING 29.4

The Fixed ClassRosterServiceLayer

```
public interface ClassRosterServiceLayer {

    void createStudent(Student student) throws
            ClassRosterDuplicateIdException,
            ClassRosterDataValidationException,
            ClassRosterPersistenceException;

    List<Student> getAllStudents() throws
            ClassRosterPersistenceException;
```

```
    Student getStudent(String studentId) throws
            ClassRosterPersistenceException;

    Student removeStudent(String studentId) throws
            ClassRosterPersistenceException;
}
```

CREATE THE SERVICE LAYER IMPLEMENTATION

With the service layer interface and all the exceptions in place, we are ready to implement the service layer. Create a new Java class called ClassRosterServiceLayerImpl in the com.sg.classroster.service package. Have this class implement the ClassRosterServiceLayer interface and then have NetBeans implement all of the abstract methods of the interface for you. Your class should look like Listing 29.5 when you are done.

LISTING 29.5

ClassRosterServiceLayerImpl

```java
public class ClassRosterServiceLayerImpl implements
        ClassRosterServiceLayer {

    @Override
    public void createStudent(Student student) throws
            ClassRosterDuplicateIdException,
            ClassRosterDataValidationException,
            ClassRosterPersistenceException {
        throw new UnsupportedOperationException("Not supported yet.");
    }

    @Override
    public List<Student> getAllStudents() throws
            ClassRosterPersistenceException {
        throw new UnsupportedOperationException("Not supported yet.");
    }

    @Override
    public Student getStudent(String studentId) throws
            ClassRosterPersistenceException {
        throw new UnsupportedOperationException("Not supported yet.");
    }
```

```
@Override
public Student removeStudent(String studentId) throws
        ClassRosterPersistenceException {
    throw new UnsupportedOperationException("Not supported yet.");
}
}
```

Constructor and DAO Member

Now that we have the shell of our service layer implementation, we can start adding some functionality. The service layer needs to use the DAO for Student object CRUD operations, so we will add a member field of type ClassRosterDao to our service layer implementation. The member field will be initialized through the service layer implementation constructor. Add the following code to the top of your ClassRosterServiceLayerImpl class:

```
private final ClassRosterDao dao;

public ClassRosterServiceLayerImpl(ClassRosterDao dao) {
    this.dao = dao;
}
```

Validating Student Data

One of the business rules that we must enforce in the service layer is that every student in the system must have values for First Name, Last Name, and Cohort. If any of these fields is empty, the Student object should not be persisted. To help with this, we will create a method that does this validation for us. If the given Student object fails validation, this method will throw a ClassRosterDataValidationException. We will use this method during the Create Student process. Add the private method in Listing 29.6 to the bottom of your ClassRosterServiceLayerImpl class.

LISTING 29.6

The Private validateStudentData() Method

```
private void validateStudentData(Student student) throws
        ClassRosterDataValidationException {

    if (student.getFirstName() == null
            || student.getFirstName().trim().length() == 0
            || student.getLastName() == null
```

```
            || student.getLastName().trim().length() == 0
            || student.getCohort() == null
            || student.getCohort().trim().length() == 0) {

        throw new ClassRosterDataValidationException(
                "ERROR: All fields [First Name, Last Name, Cohort] are required.");
    }
}
```

Here, we are checking each field in the given object to see, first, that it is not null and, second, that it is neither empty or just whitespace. This is necessary because a null string and an empty string are not the same things in Java. If any of the fields is either null or empty/whitespace only, this method throws a ClassRosterDataValidationException.

> **NOTE** For added safety, we should also check to make sure that the student name does not contain the delimiter we are using when storing and retrieving data, in our case : :.

Create Student

We are now ready to implement the Create Student logic. In this method, we must do the following:

1. Ensure that the incoming student ID does not already exist.

2. Validate that all the fields in the incoming Student object have values.

3. Pass the incoming Student object to the DAO so that it can persist it.

Modify the createStudent method in your ClassRosterServiceLayerImpl class so that it looks like Listing 29.7.

LISTING 29.7

The Modified createStudent() Method

```
@Override
public void createStudent(Student student) throws
        ClassRosterDuplicateIdException,
        ClassRosterDataValidationException,
        ClassRosterPersistenceException {

    // First check to see if there is already a student
```

```
    // associated with the given student's id
    // If so, we're all done here.
    // Throw a ClassRosterDuplicateIdException
    if (dao.getStudent(student.getStudentId()) != null) {
        throw new ClassRosterDuplicateIdException(
                "ERROR: Could not create student.  Student Id "
                + student.getStudentId()
                + " already exists");
    }

    // Now validate all the fields on the given Student object.
    // This method will throw an
    // exception if any of the validation rules are violated.
    validateStudentData(student);

    // We passed all our business rules checks so go ahead
    // and persist the Student object
    dao.addStudent(student.getStudentId(), student);
}
```

Get All Students

This method is straightforward because it is a pass-through method. We simply turn around and call the getAllStudents method on the DAO and return the results. Modify the getAllStudents method in your ClassRosterServiceLayerImpl class so that it looks like Listing 29.8.

LISTING 29.8

The Modified getAllStudents() Method

```
@Override
public List<Student> getAllStudents() throws ClassRosterPersistenceException {
    return dao.getAllStudents();
}
```

Get One Student

This is another pass-through method. We simply turn around and call the getStudent method on the DAO and return the results. Modify the getStudent method in your ClassRosterServiceLayerImpl class so that it looks like Listing 29.9.

LISTING 29.9

The Modified getStudent() Method

```
@Override
public Student getStudent(String studentId) throws
ClassRosterPersistenceException {
    return dao.getStudent(studentId);
}
```

Remove Student

Finally, we'll implement the removeStudent method. This is a pass-through method as well (for now; we will add code to write to the audit log in a later step). We simply turn around and call the removeStudent method on the DAO and return the results. Modify the removeStudent method in your ClassRosterServiceLayerImpl so that it looks like Listing 29.10.

LISTING 29.10

The Modified removeStudent() Method

```
@Override
public Student removeStudent(String studentId) throws
ClassRosterPersistenceException {
    return dao.removeStudent(studentId);
}
```

MODIFY THE CONTROLLER

We are now ready to modify the controller so that it uses our new service layer instead of directly using the DAO. We do this in the following steps:

1. Replace the member field of type ClassRosterDao with a member field of type ClassRosterServiceLayer.

2. Modify the constructor, replacing the ClassRosterDao parameter with a ClassRosterServiceLayer parameter.

3. Replace all the calls to DAO methods with calls to service layer methods.

Replace Member Field

Replace the field declaration for the `ClassRosterDao`:

```
private ClassRosterDao dao;
```

with a declaration for the `ClassRosterServiceLayer`:

```
private ClassRosterServiceLayer service;
```

Modify Constructor

Now we must modify the constructor so that it initializes the new `ClassRosterServiceLayer` instead of the now removed `ClassRosterDao`. Modify the constructor in your `ClassRosterServiceLayerImpl` class so that it looks like Listing 29.11.

LISTING 29.11

The Modified `ClassRosterController()` Method

```
public ClassRosterController(ClassRosterServiceLayer service,
ClassRosterView view) {
    this.service = service;
    this.view = view;
}
```

Replace Calls to DAO Methods with Calls to the Service Layer Method

The changes we made in the previous two steps are now causing compilation errors in four of our controller methods. Update these listings with the changes in Listings 29.12 through 29.15 to fix these errors.

LISTING 29.12

The Modified `listStudents()` Method

```
private void listStudents() throws ClassRosterPersistenceException {
    List<Student> studentList = service.getAllStudents();

    view.displayStudentList(studentList);
}
```

LISTING 29.13

The Modified viewStudent() Method

```java
private void viewStudent() throws ClassRosterPersistenceException {
    String studentId = view.getStudentIdChoice();
    Student student = service.getStudent(studentId) ;
    view.displayStudent(student);
}
```

LISTING 29.14

The Modified removeStudent() Method

```java
private void removeStudent() throws ClassRosterPersistenceException {
    view.displayRemoveStudentBanner();
    String studentId = view.getStudentIdChoice();
    service.removeStudent(studentId);
    view.displayRemoveSuccessBanner();
}
```

LISTING 29.15

The Modified createStudent() Method

```java
private void createStudent() throws ClassRosterPersistenceException {
    view.displayCreateStudentBanner();
    boolean hasErrors = false;
    do {
        Student currentStudent = view.getNewStudentInfo();
        try {
            service.createStudent(currentStudent);
            view.displayCreateSuccessBanner();
            hasErrors = false;
        } catch (ClassRosterDuplicateIdException |
                ClassRosterDataValidationException e) {
            hasErrors = true;
            view.displayErrorMessage(e.getMessage());
        }
    } while (hasErrors);
}
```

The changes to `createStudent` are more extensive than the previous three methods. Notice that we are now calling `service.createStudent`. You'll remember from the design of our service layer interface that this method throws two additional exceptions: `ClassRosterDuplicateIdException` and `ClassRosterDataValidationException`. Our program can handle these two errors by displaying an error message to the user and then reprompting for the student data.

To do this, we use a combination of a Boolean flag (`hasErrors`), a do-while loop, and a try-catch construct. If the call to `createStudent` causes an exception, we display the error message to the user and set the `hasErrors` flag to `true`, which will cause the do-while loop to execute again. This prompts the user for the requested input again. If the call to `createStudent` does not cause an exception, the program displays the success banner and sets the `hasErrors` flag to `false`, which will cause the do-while loop to stop repeating.

The `catch` block in this `createStudent` demonstrates the syntax for handling more than one type of exception in a single `catch` block. This syntax is straightforward: instead of listing one exception type followed by an identifier, list all the exception types to be handled in the `catch` block separated by the bitwise OR (|) operator followed by a single identifier, as shown in the example.

> **NOTE** While you can handle more than one exception in a single `catch` block, there is one rule. None of the exceptions in the single `catch` block can be in the same hierarchy. For example, (`FileNotFoundException` | `IOException`) would not be legal.

MODIFY THE APP

The changes we made to the controller have caused compilation errors in the App class because we changed the signature of the controller's constructor. Recall that the App class is responsible for wiring or assembling the components of our application. We'll make two changes to the App class.

- Add code to instantiate the service layer (and pass the DAO into its constructor).
- Modify the code that instantiates the controller to pass the service layer instance to the constructor.

Modify the main method of your App class so that it looks like Listing 29.16.

LISTING 29.16

The Updated main() Method

```
public static void main(String[] args) {
    UserIO myIo = new UserIOConsoleImpl();
    ClassRosterView myView = new ClassRosterView(myIo);
    ClassRosterDao myDao = new ClassRosterDaoFileImpl();
    ClassRosterServiceLayer myService = new ClassRosterServiceLayerImpl(myDao);
    ClassRosterController controller = new ClassRosterController(myService, myView);
    controller.run();
}
```

That completes the addition of the first two business rules. Now we will add the audit log feature.

ADD THE AUDIT LOG FEATURE

The audit log feature will be implemented in four steps:

1. Creation and implementation of the Audit DAO interface and implementation class
2. Changes to the service layer to write to the Audit Log when creating and removing students in the system
3. Modifying the App class to create and wire the Audit DAO into the service layer
4. Creating the empty audit.txt file

Audit DAO Interface and Implementation

The Audit DAO is simple. It has just one method that writes an entry to the log file. Because this method can run into problems writing to the audit file, it throws ClassRosterPersistenceException. Create a new Java interface called ClassRosterAuditDao in the com.sg.classroster.dao package and add code so it looks like this:

```
public interface ClassRosterAuditDao {

    public void writeAuditEntry(String entry) throws
ClassRosterPersistenceException;

}
```

Now create a new Java class called `ClassRosterAuditDaoFileImpl` in the com.sg. `classroster.dao` package and modify the file so it looks like Listing 29.17.

LISTING 29.17

ClassRosterAuditDaoFileImpl

```java
public class ClassRosterAuditDaoFileImpl implements ClassRosterAuditDao {

    public static final String AUDIT_FILE = "audit.txt";
    @override
    public void writeAuditEntry(String entry) throws
ClassRosterPersistenceException {
        PrintWriter out;

        try {
            out = new PrintWriter(new FileWriter(AUDIT_FILE, true));
        } catch (IOException e) {
            throw new ClassRosterPersistenceException("Could not persist audit
information.", e);
        }

        LocalDateTime timestamp = LocalDateTime.now();
        out.println(timestamp.toString() + " : " + entry);
    }
}
```

There are some things to note about this implementation.

You should note that we are opening the audit file in *append mode* so that each entry will be appended to the file rather than overwriting everything that was there before. We accomplish this by setting the second parameter of the `FileWriter` constructor to `true`.

```java
new FileWriter(AUDIT_FILE, true)
```

Also, note that we are using a `LocalDateTime` object to create a timestamp for our audit log entries. Don't worry too much about `LocalDateTime` now—just use it as shown here. We will learn about the Java Date-Time API in a later lesson.

Modify the Service Layer

Now that the Audit DAO is implemented, we need to modify the service layer to use the Audit DAO to write to the audit log. We'll do this in four steps.

1. Add a member field of type ClassRosterAuditDao.

2. Modify the ClassRosterServiceLayerImpl constructor so that it initializes the ClassRosterAuditDao member field.

3. Modify the createStudent method to write an audit log message when a student is successfully created.

4. Modify the removeStudent method to write an audit log message when a student is removed.

Add Member Field

First, we'll add a member field of type ClassRosterAuditDao to our service layer implementation. Add the following line to the top of your ClassRosterServiceLayer-Impl class:

```
private final ClassRosterAuditDao auditDao;
```

Modify the Constructor

Now we must add code to the constructor to initialize the auditDao member field. Modify your ClassRosterServiceLayerImpl constructor so that it looks like Listing 29.18.

LISTING 29.18

ClassRosterServiceLayerImpl

```
public ClassRosterServiceLayerImpl(ClassRosterDao dao, ClassRosterAuditDao auditDao) {
    this.dao = dao;
    this.auditDao = auditDao;
}
```

Now that the Audit DAO has been declared and initialized, it is ready for use.

Modify createStudent

The changes to createStudent are straightforward. We simply need to ask the Audit DAO to write an entry to the log after the student has been successfully added to the DAO.

Modify your `createStudent` method so that it looks like Listing 29.19 (note that we've added only one line to the end of the method).

LISTING 29.19

The Modified createStudent() Method

```
public void createStudent(Student student) throws
        ClassRosterDuplicateIdException,
        ClassRosterDataValidationException,
        ClassRosterPersistenceException {

    // First check to see if there is already a student
    // associated with the given student's id
    // If so, we're all done here.
    // Throw a ClassRosterDuplicateIdException
    if (dao.getStudent(student.getStudentId()) != null) {
        throw new ClassRosterDuplicateIdException(
                "ERROR: Could not create student.  Student Id "
                + student.getStudentId()
                + " already exists");
    }

    // Now validate all the fields on the given Student object.
    // This method will throw an
    // exception if any of the validation rules are violated.
    validateStudentData(student);

    // We passed all our business rules checks so go ahead
    // and persist the Student object
    dao.addStudent(student.getStudentId(), student);

    // The student was successfully created, now write to the audit log
    auditDao.writeAuditEntry(
            "Student " + student.getStudentId() + " CREATED.");
}
```

Modify removeStudent

Now we will make similar changes to the method. Modify your `removeStudent` method so that it looks like Listing 29.20.

LISTING 29.20

The Modified `removeStudent()` Method

```
public Student removeStudent(String studentId) throws
ClassRosterPersistenceException {
    Student removedStudent = dao.removeStudent(studentId);
    // Write to audit log
    auditDao.writeAuditEntry("Student " + studentId + " REMOVED.");
    return removedStudent;
}
```

Again, we are simply writing an entry to the audit log after a student has been successfully removed from the system.

Modify App

Finally, we must modify the App class so that it instantiates the new Audit DAO and wires it into the service layer. Modify the main method in your App class so that it looks like Listing 29.21.

LISTING 29.21

The Modified `App main()` Method

```
public static void main(String[] args) {
    // Instantiate the UserIO implementation
    UserIO myIo = new UserIOConsoleImpl();
    // Instantiate the View and wire the UserIO implementation into it
    ClassRosterView myView = new ClassRosterView(myIo);
    // Instantiate the DAO
    ClassRosterDao myDao = new ClassRosterDaoFileImpl();
    // Instantiate the Audit DAO
    ClassRosterAuditDao myAuditDao = new ClassRosterAuditDaoFileImpl();
    // Instantiate the service layer and wire the DAO and Audit DAO into it
    ClassRosterServiceLayer myService = new ClassRosterServiceLayerImpl(myDao, myAuditDao);
    // Instantiate the Controller and wire the service layer into it
    ClassRosterController controller = new ClassRosterController(myService, myView);
    // Kick off the Controller
    controller.run();
}
```

SUMMARY

In this lesson, you have seen how a service layer is implemented. The important things to remember from this exercise are the following:

- The service layer sits between the controller and the DAO and contains the business logic of the program.
- The service layer can (and often does) interact with more than one DAO. In our example, the service layer interacted with both the `ClassRosterDao` (for CRUD operations on `Student` objects) and the `AuditDao` (for writing to the audit log).
- Adding a service layer to an application affects several components. In our example, we had to modify the controller and the `App` classes to account for the new component. It is strongly recommended that you take the "back to front" approach that we followed in this example.

  - Create the service layer interface and implementation.
  - Modify the controller to use the new service layer.
  - Modify the `App` class to instantiate the new service layer and wire it into the application.

Lesson 30
Doing Unit Testing

We now have a complete application, which is pretty cool! But how do we know we're done? How do we know that we've met all the requirements of the project? And how do we know that there are no errors? Unit testing is a technique that can help us answer these questions.

In this lesson, we will introduce the concept of unit testing, look at the JUnit automated unit testing framework, see how we can test both stateless and stateful code, and do a code-along where we add unit tests to the Class Roster application.

LEARNING OBJECTIVES

By the end of this lesson, you will be able to:

- Explain what unit testing is
- Differentiate between black-box and glass-box (or white-box) testing
- Differentiate between stateful and stateless components
- Describe test-driven development

- Trace the process of Red/Green/Refactor
- Explain the usage of test stubs
- Use JUnit to create, run, and document unit tests
- Explain how the Given/When/Then approach to unit testing works
- Describe what makes a good unit test
- Trace the unit testing design and implementation process

UNIT TESTING

Software is tested at several different points during the development of a project. *Unit testing* involves testing the lowest-level components of an application and is done by the software development team. The developer responsible for developing a particular component is also generally responsible for creating the unit tests for that component.

Modern unit testing involves the use of automated testing frameworks. The de facto standard for Java development is the JUnit testing framework, which we will be using in this lesson. These automated tests are run as part of the build process, and if the tests don't pass, the build fails. We do this to make sure, to the extent possible, that new code doesn't break existing code.

Unit testing is just the beginning of the testing story for a software project. As the project goes on, the entire application is tested as part of integration and system testing. The QA team will test the entire system in a combination of manual and automated tests using a variety of specialized QA testing frameworks. In addition to these functional tests, the application may undergo performance testing (especially if it is a web application) to ensure that the application runs normally under load. The final step in the testing process is user acceptance testing. This is where the client puts the final version of the application through its paces and signs off that it meets all requirements.

> **NOTE** Since this is a development course, we will concentrate on unit and integration testing using the JUnit testing framework.

TYPES OF UNIT TESTING

There are some different approaches to unit testing, some different types of code to be unit tested, and some terminology that we need to discuss before we look at JUnit and dive into creating tests.

Black-Box vs. Glass-Box Testing

Black-box testing tests only the *functionality* of a particular component without knowing anything about how the component is implemented. In our examples, black-box testing tests the interface, or contract, of the component. The purpose of this type of testing is to ensure that a given component does what it promises to do.

Glass-box (commonly referred to as *white-box*) testing does take the implementation of a component into account. The tests are designed so that each code path through the component is exercised. The tiered/MVC application design approach followed in this course puts a premium on programming to interfaces so that the functionality can be separated from the implementation, so we will use the black-box testing approach.

Stateful vs. Stateless Components

Generally, there are two types of code that we can test: code that has no state (i.e., causes no side effects, called *stateless*) and code that does. Code that has no state or side effects acts like a mathematical function. If you put the same inputs into this code, it will always produce the same result. Examples of this type of code include all the static methods on the Java Math class. If you put 100 into the Math.sqrt method, it will always return 10 whether you call it once or call it 350 times.

Code that does have state (i.e., causes side effects, called *stateful*) is different. The results of a particular method call, even with identical inputs, might be different depending on what happened previously. For example, the first time you add a student to the Class Roster program with a student ID of 0001, the system persists the Student object without error. If you try to do that a second time, the system will throw an exception; thus, you have the same input, but you get a different result.

From a practical standpoint, this means we must be mindful to put things in a known state before testing stateful code, whereas we can test stateless code in any order we want.

Test-Driven Development and Red/Green/Refactor

Test-Driven Development (TDD) is a software development approach where the unit tests for a component are written before the component is implemented. In this approach, the interface and shell implementation (where each method throws UnsupportedOperation-Exception) are the only components created before the unit tests are written. After these (all failing) unit tests are written, the developer goes back to the component and starts to replace the UnsupportedOperationExceptions with actual code. Once all unit tests pass, the developer is done.

This approach is called Red/Green/Refactor. The name refers to the fact that the test results will initially be Red (for failing) but will turn Green as the actual code is implemented. Once all tests are Green (passing) the developer is free to refactor the code to make it more concise or efficient. Since the test suite already exists, the developer can be sure that any refactoring done to the code doesn't break anything. You will have the opportunity to try TDD in some of the exercises ahead.

Test Stubs

Test stubs allow us to simulate some components of the system to make the testing of other components easier. For example, when testing the business logic in our service layer, we will stub out both the `ClassRosterDao` and the `ClassRosterAuditDao` components. It is not necessary for the DAOs to actually read from and write to files when testing the service layer, so we'll replace the file implementations with stub implementations containing canned data.

JUnit

JUnit is the de facto standard automated unit test framework in the Java universe. There are other options out there, but JUnit has, by far, the largest mindshare.

JUnit has good integration with NetBeans, Eclipse, IntelliJ, and Maven. The unit tests are part of the Maven build by default, and if any of the tests fail, the build fails. JUnit makes it easy to create unit test suites for your Java components.

Here we will discuss some of the features of the JUnit framework and discuss how unit tests should be approached. This includes test setup and teardown (also called *cleanup*) as well as annotations and asserts.

Test Setup and Teardown

To help get the code being tested into a known good state, the JUnit framework provides `Setup` and `tearDown` hooks that will run before and after your tests. These come in two flavors. First, there are the `Setup`/`tearDown` methods that run only once. The `Setup` method runs right before your JUnit test class is created, and the `tearDown` method runs right after your JUnit test class is destroyed. These can be useful for specialized situations.

The more common (and more useful) `Setup` and `tearDown` methods run before and after each individual test in your test suite. These methods allow you to ensure that your code is in a known good state before every test case is run and that everything is cleaned up when the test has completed. You will have the opportunity to use these methods in the code-along and in your labs.

Annotations

The current version of JUnit is *annotation* driven. That means that the classes containing the unit test code are just plain old Java objects (POJOs). In older versions, your test class had to extend a JUnit base class, but this is no longer the case. Simply mark your class with JUnit annotations and JUnit will know what to do. NetBeans will generate the shell of your JUnit test class for you, so you do not have to remember all the annotations. One that you will use all the time, however, is the `@Test` annotation. You must mark each of your test methods with this annotation if you want JUnit to execute it. We'll see this in action later in this lesson.

Asserts

JUnit provides a set of static helper methods that allow you to test different conditions in your tests. These are known as *assertions*. These methods allow you to assert things like the following:

- A Boolean condition is false.
- A Boolean condition is true.
- An object reference is null.
- An object reference is not null.
- Two values are equal.
- Two objects are equal.

If the assertion is wrong, the method throws an `AssertionError`, and the test case fails. We will use these assertions in the code-along, and you will use them in your unit test suites throughout the rest of the course.

GIVEN/WHEN/THEN

The general approach that we will take for unit testing our code is called Given/When/Then.

First, we put the code in a known good state and create all necessary test data (Given). Then we write a test that acts—this test uses the arranged data to execute the code we are testing (When). Finally, we assert that the results are what we expect (Then).

STATELESS UNIT TESTING

Now that we've provided an overview of the concepts associated with unit testing, we will discuss what makes a good unit test and the process you should use when unit testing. Here, we concentrate on the techniques used for testing stateless code, which, if you recall, is a type of code that produces the same output for the same input, regardless of how often it is run. We are going to focus on the following:

- Describing what makes a good unit test
- Tracing the unit testing design and implementation process

What Makes a Good Unit Test?

A good unit test must cover all the different categories of input and output combinations that are possible in a given piece of code. This does not mean you need to test every possible input/output combination. In some cases, that is impossible.

Rather, this means you must design tests that cover each class and each branch of code, making a best effort to not miss any. We'll see an example of this later. Having said that, your tests should be efficient, but not redundant, addressing each class and branch of code (or combination) uniquely. Multiple tests of the same kind of inputs are a waste of effort.

Designing a Test Plan

A test plan is a way of documenting the scope and approach of a particular group (often called a *suite*) of tests. As a whole, a test plan should encompass all types of valid inputs, as well as edge and boundary conditions, and occasionally invalid potential inputs. Some of these may seem abstract, so let's consider a concrete example by designing tests for the method presented in Listing 30.1.

LISTING 30.1

The areTheLlamasHappy Method

```
/**
 * A method to determine if the provided trampolines will result in
 * happy llamas.
 *
 * When llamas get together they like to bounce on trampolines.
 * However, llamas are very particular about the proper number of
 * trampolines,
 * and are usually only happy if there are between 24 to 42 (inclusive!).
 * This only changes if the trampolines are made of ultra-bouncey NASA
 * fabric.
 * In those cases, while they still require at LEAST 24, the llamas figure
 * the more trampolines the better!
 *
 * return true if the llamas will be happy with their trampolines,
 * or false otherwise.
 *
 * @param ultraBouncy True if trampolines are made of UltraBouncy NASA
 * fabric.
 * @param trampolines The number of trampolines
 * @return boolean indicating if the llamas are happy
 */

public static boolean areTheLlamasHappy(boolean ultraBouncy, int trampolines){
    // implementation removed!
    return true;
}
```

NOTE We are designing tests for a method without knowing anything about the method's internal code. As long as we know the *expected* behavior of a method, we can design (and even implement) tests!

Designing a test plan for a method means we have to decide on values for its input parameters and expected return value as a result of using those input parameters. In the case of the method areTheLlamasHappy, there are two input parameters, a Boolean and an integer, as well as a Boolean return type.

These three things thus become the focus of our test design, and in general we should work to cover all the types of inputs that put us in bounds (making the llamas happy) and out of bounds (making the llamas unhappy), and we need to test boundary conditions as well. The boundaries in this case are 24 and 42 trampolines and normal or ultra-bouncy trampoline fabric.

This means a practical test plan would combine input values for our parameters in effective ways, pairing a number of normal trampolines below, at, and above our boundary numbers, and then doing the same but with the ultra-bouncy trampolines.

Happy Llama Test Plan

Here's an example of what that could look like for Happy Llamas:

Normal Trampoline Tests

- `areTheLlamasHappy(false, 10)` → `false`
- `areTheLlamasHappy(false, 24)` → `true`
- `areTheLlamasHappy(false, 30)` → `true`
- `areTheLlamasHappy(false, 42)` → `true`
- `areTheLlamasHappy(false, 50)` → `false`

Ultra-Bouncy Trampoline Tests

- `areTheLlamasHappy(true, 10)` → `false`
- `areTheLlamasHappy(true, 24)` → `true`
- `areTheLlamasHappy(true, 30)` → `true`
- `areTheLlamasHappy(true, 42)` → `true`
- `areTheLlamasHappy(true, 50)` → `true`

Examining the inputs, we have chosen a number of trampolines that fall below, at, and above the lower boundary for our llama logic of 24 and followed suit with the upper boundary of 42. These five resulting values were then paired first with the Boolean representing normal fabric and then again with the ultra-bouncy.

This simple combination already expands into the result of 10 separate tests, a good first step, but a bare minimum to prove functionality. If we were to design a more exhaustive test plan, it would be good to test other values including numbers of llamas including the negative, extremely large, or those values immediately above and below the boundaries. However, this sort of exhaustive testing quickly becomes just that—exhausting. So, we need to carefully balance good coverage of tests and effective return on effort.

> **NOTE** It is *always* a good idea to take the time to develop a test plan first before you begin writing your code. You are less likely to forget input and output combinations if you take the time to plan them first.

IMPLEMENTING UNIT TESTS

Implementing a test plan is often as simple as creating a new Java class to act as our JUnit test suite. While you can create test classes manually, it is often easier to use the auto-generation technology that is part of most IDEs. This way, your IDE will often take care of connecting external dependencies like JUnit into your project automatically.

Creating the Test Class

To create a test plan in NetBeans, you can use the following steps:

1. In NetBean's Project view, right-click the class you want to test (for example, `HappyLlamas.java`).
2. Select *Tools* and then *Create/Update Tests*.
3. Walk through the wizard to create a new JUnit class.
   - The name should look similar to `com.tsg.HappyLlamasTest`. Note that `com.tsg` will match the Java package you used for your `HappyLlamas` class.
   - Ensure that *Test Packages* is selected in the Location drop-down.
   - Generated Code Checkbox List should have nothing selected.
   - Method Access Levels Checkbox List should have nothing selected.
   - Generated Comments Checkbox List should have nothing selected.
4. Click OK.

Once you complete the wizard, you should be left with a new Java class similar to Listing 30.2. You'll find this class listed under the Test Packages folder on the Projects tab.

LISTING 30.2

The New Java Test Class

```
public class HappyLlamasTest {

    public HappyLlamasTest() {
```

```
    }

    @Test
    public void testSomeMethod() {

    }
}
```

Once you have generated the code in Listing 30.2, implementing our test suite is simply a matter of writing new test methods, similar in definition to `testSomeMethod`. These will be public void methods that are annotated with the `@Test`. Within these methods we will have to set up our inputs, call the method we are testing, capture the return, and assert that it conforms to the expected return value.

NOTE The `areTheLlamasHappy` method under test is a stateless, static method. If your IDE wizard generated `setUp` or `tearDown` methods in the previous step, there is no need to use them. You can remove them from your test class if you are doing stateless unit testing.

Writing Happy Llama Tests

As we walk through an example of how to implement tests from our test plan, the following are important things to remember:

- JUnit test methods are just Java methods, but they have specific requirements for structure.
  - All tests *must* have an `@Test` annotation or JUnit won't know to run it as part of the test suite.
  - Test methods should always be public, return no value, and have an empty parameter list. It's just the names of our test methods that will change. However, starting from JUnit 5, these constraints were relaxed, and JUnit 5 requires test classes to have any visibility except for private.
  - Name your test cases so that you can tell what they are testing. This is less a requirement than a good idea.

- Each test method should test only one input/output combination. This makes it much easier to debug your tests when they fail.

- Use the assertXxxx methods to determine whether the test results are what you expected. (For example, calling areTheLlamasHappy with false and 10 should return false, so we could use the method assertFalse to test the return value.)

Let's look at an example test for our first test case from earlier:

- areTheLlamasHappy(false, 10) → false

Listing 30.3 provides the code for the implementation of this test.

LISTING 30.3

Testing for False, 10

```
@Test
public void testNormalTrampoline10() {
    // GIVEN - for simple methods, this means setting up the parameters
    boolean isNasaFabric = false;
    int numTrampolines = 10;

    // WHEN - for simple methods, this generally means calling the method
    // under test
    // and then capturing its return to assert on
    boolean result = areTheLlamasHappy(isNasaFabric, numTrampolines);

    // THEN - basically just a conditional that proves the result is what
    // you expect it to be, plus an extra message to display if it doesn't
    // match.
    //
    // There are a wide variety of assert types. Here we
    // just want to assert that it returned false, but we could have also
    // used
    // assertEquals and passed in a false value.

    assertFalse( result , "10 Llamas w/ Normal Trampolines Should Be
Unhappy!" );
    }
```

This test method follows the Given/When/Then model discussed earlier. First, it allocates variables for each of the method's parameters and assigns them the values picked out in the test plan. Next, it calls the method using those variables as parameters and captures the result. Finally, it uses an *assert* method to check the return value from the method, in this case asserting that the value should be false.

A similar pattern can be used to implement the rest of the tests in our test suite, and once saved to a JUnit test class, it (and any others) can be run as part of a project-built process to verify the behavior of the method under test.

> **NOTE** When adding the test to your test file, you might need to also include an import for the method's code. You've added imports to your project in previous lessons, so this process should be familiar.

Running JUnit Tests

You can run the unit tests by first doing a Clean & Build ( ), and then, as shown in Figure 30.1, right-click your project in the project view and select *Test* from the drop-down. This will run all unit tests associated with your project.

This should populate the Test Results window, as shown in Figure 30.2, and allow you to drill down into specific tests and see the results.

> **NOTE** If you close the Test Results window by accident, the easy way to reopen it in NetBeans is to navigate to Window ➤ IDE Tools ➤ Test Results.

The test files themselves are in the Test Packages project folder, and you can trigger an individual test file by right-clicking the appropriate test file and selecting *Test File*. This will only run the tests described in that file. In Figure 30.3, we can see that the selection would only run the `HappyLlamaTests.java` file.

The Test Results window will list all the tests you chose to run (in the individual test file or for the project as a whole). You can choose to expand or collapse individual test results by clicking the + symbol (Windows) or arrow (Mac) next to a test in the list. You can see the Test Results window in Figure 30.4, which shows that three of the tests for HappyLlamasTest passed but seven others failed.

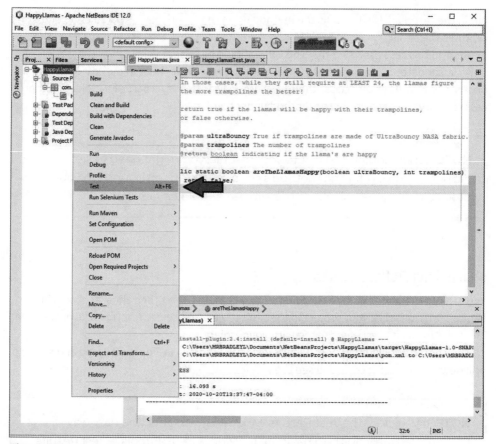

Figure 30.1 Running the tests

> **NOTE** If you don't see the passed tests, you can click the check mark in the green circle to the left to show them. The icons on the left toggle what is shown in the test results.

If you double-click a test in the Test Results window, you will jump to the code for the test case in question, and you can see more information about the test that failed, or even set a breakpoint to debug the test.

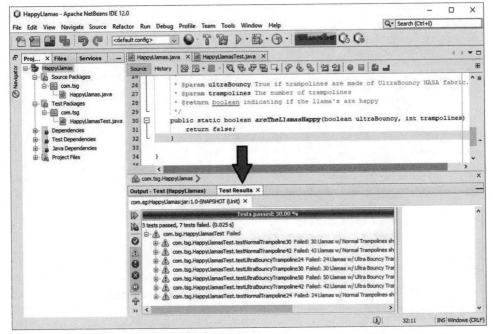

Figure 30.2 The Test Results window

IMPORTANT NOTE

With NetBeans version 10 and newer, there were some issues with the test methods triggering correctly during the testing step of the build process. This can be fixed by adding the following to the project's pom.xml file. This is usually added after the properties node.

```
<build>
    <plugins>
        <plugin>
            <artifactId>maven-surefire-plugin</artifactId>
            <version>2.19.1</version>
            <dependencies>
                <dependency>
                    <groupId>org.junit.platform</groupId>
                    <artifactId>junit-platform-surefire-provider</artifactId>
                    <version>1.1.0</version>
                </dependency>
            </dependencies>
        </plugin>
    </plugins>
</build>
```

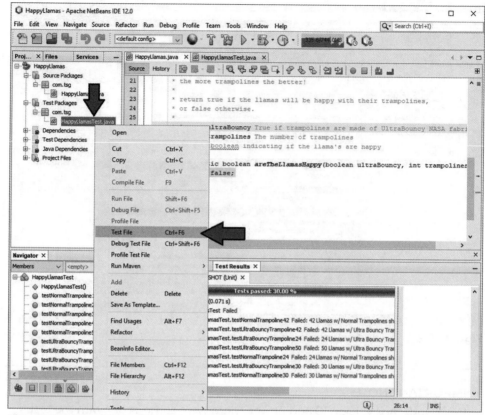

Figure 30.3 Running a single test file

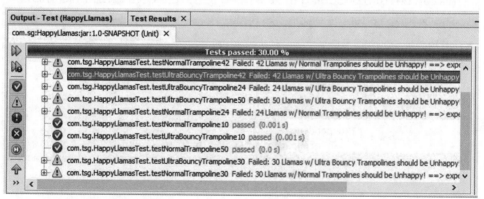

Figure 30.4 The test results

SUMMARY

This was a quick introduction to some of the concepts associated with unit testing in the software development process as well as a discussion of the design and implementation of unit tests for stateless code using the JUnit framework. The following are the main take-aways for this lesson:

- Unit testing involves testing the lowest-level components of a software application. It is the responsibility of the developer to create unit tests for every class, and this is usually done with an automated unit testing framework like JUnit.

- Black-box testing tests only the promised functionality of a given software component and does not take the implementation details into account. Glass-box testing (sometimes called white-box testing) does take the implementation details into account. Glass-box tests are designed to exercise all possible paths in the component under testing.

- Special consideration must be given when testing stateful software so that the component is in a known good state before each test is run; no such consideration is necessary when testing stateless components.

- We use the Given/When/Then approach to unit testing.

  Given: Put the system in a known good state and create any test data needed.

  When: Run the code under test using the test data set up in the Given step.

  Then: Check to see whether the actual result matches the expected result for the test.

- Test-Driven Development (TDD) is a development approach that builds the unit tests for a component before the implementation of that component is created. This approach is also known as Red/Green/Refactor.

- Test stubs can be used to make unit testing certain components easier.

- You should write a test plan and figure out all the input/output combinations necessary for testing a method before you write any code.

- Each test method in your unit test class should test as few things as possible while still being a valid test. Make your test methods as granular as possible.

- Any method marked with the `@Test` annotation will be run by JUnit as a part of the test suite.

- Your test methods must be marked with the @Test annotation, public, return nothing, and have no parameters.
- JUnit has a number of assertXxxx methods that should be used in your tests to assert that the actual result matches the expected result.

Now that you are familiar with stateless Java code, in the next lesson, we will create test suites for stateful Java code.

Lesson 31
Testing Stateful Code

In this lesson, we will look at techniques for unit testing stateful code. We will use many of the same techniques we learned for testing stateless code, but there will be additional work in setting up our tests, and we must be mindful of the order in which we test things.

We will also unit test the service layer for the Class Roster application with a new testing technique called *stubbing*. We will use stubbed versions of the DAOs in the unit tests for the service layer. This lesson will also explain the motivation and techniques for testing a service layer using stubbed DAOs.

LEARNING OBJECTIVES

By the end of this lesson, you will be able to:

- Differentiate between testing stateless and stateful code
- Use the setup and teardown methods in JUnit
- Use arrange, act, assert for stateful code
- Test the `ClassRoster` DAO
- Test that the creation of a student with an existing student ID does not work
- Test that all fields of a student object cannot be empty

UNIT TESTING STATEFUL CODE

Testing stateful code is a bit more complicated than testing stateless code because, depending on the state of the code, the same set of inputs can produce a different output. For example, say you are testing the account portion of a banking application. Some of the account components include functionality to deposit money, withdraw money, and check the account balance. Now suppose you are testing this component and you want to test the deposit method. You set up your test to add $100 to the account. After depositing the $100, you want to check the balance to make sure the $100 was deposited correctly. So, you call the method to get the account balance. What should the balance be? Should it be $100?

Herein lies the complexity of testing stateful code. You have no way of knowing what the balance of the account should be if you don't know what the balance was before you started your test. What if you deposit $100 more into the account? What should the balance be now? Clearly, it should be $100 more than it was before, but if we don't know the state of the system before the test, we have no way of knowing what that value should actually be. Because we don't know the state or what the values should be, this code is stateless, which means we need a different way of testing.

The following points illustrate the main differences between testing stateless code and stateful code:

- You must put the system in a known good state before testing stateful code. If you do not do this, you will have no way to check to see whether the actual result of the test matches your expected result. This is not necessary for stateless code.

- You must be mindful of the order in which you test things in stateful code. Calling the same method with the same parameters three times in a row may produce three different results if the code is stateful. Stateless code produces the same result no matter how many times in a row it is called.

- The expected results from a particular method call might depend on if and/or how many times *a different method was called* in stateful code. For example, the expected result from the method that gets the bank account balance depends on how many times the deposit and withdraw methods were called and the parameters used in those calls. In other words, calling one method can change the result of calling another method. This does not happen with stateless code.

You must take all of this into account when designing and implementing tests for stateful code, which makes it more difficult than testing stateless code. In the rest of this lesson, we will see how JUnit can help us with some of these difficulties, and we will implement the unit test suite for the Class Roster DAO and service layer.

SEPARATING PRODUCTION AND TEST DATA

In our Class Roster application, the DAO's only job is to store and retrieve student information without altering that data in any way. Our tests will simply make sure that the DAO stores and retrieves students as advertised.

However, our DAO implementation is tightly intertwined with the file system, and using the DAO will actively modify the data currently stored in the working application. As such, it is important that we create a way to separate the production or working data from the test data. This will require an update to your DAOImpl class to first change the ROSTER_FILE variable to a declaration, and the addition of new constructor methods to allow this separation.

First, let's change the ROSTER_FILE variable so that it exists as a declaration, not a declaration and assignment. Instead, we will use our DAOImpl constructors to assign the filename to our constant variable. This also means we need to remove ROSTER_FILE's static keyword since different instances of ClassRosterDaoFileImpl might be using different files, and thus the ROSTER_FILE becomes better suited as a nonstatic variable associated with that instance.

Update the ROSTER_FILE variable declaration in ClassRosterDaoFileImpl to the following statement:

```
private final String roster_file;
```

Note that because ROSTER_FILE is no longer a constant, we've changed its name to lowercase. Next add the constructors in Listing 31.1 to ClassRosterDaoFileImpl.

LISTING 31.1

The New ClassRosterDaoFileImpl Constructors

```
public ClassRosterDaoFileImpl(){
    roster_file = "roster.txt";
}

public ClassRosterDaoFileImpl(String rosterTextFile){
    roster_file = rosterTextFile;
}
```

This has created a pair of constructors. The first, no-args constructor is providing the earlier default behavior that ClassRosterDaoFileImpl was originally built upon, which is instantiation and the assignment of roster.txt to the roster_file variable. However, the second, overloaded constructor has allowed us to create ClassRosterDaoFileImpl instances that use another file, thus allowing the file reference to be injected upon construction. This is something that will be perfect for test setup and ensuring that we don't overwrite our production application data.

Adding hashCode and equals to Student

To make testing easier, we implement the equals and hashCode methods for the Student object. This will allow us to easily compare two Student objects to see if the values of their fields match.

Both equals and hashCode are methods inherited from the Object class. The default implementation of equals simply compares the heap location of two Student references to see if they are pointing to the same place on the heap, equating whether or not they are literally the same object. While useful, during testing it would be more useful to have the method work similarly to the String's overloaded version, where when comparing two Students' contents, if the same, those two Student objects would be considered equal.

We will only use the equals method for our tests. This requires that if two objects are equal, then the hashCode values for each object must also match. As such, we must also implement the hashCode method. We won't get into all the details here, but essentially, the hashCode of an object is a unit integer value that represents the state of that object. In short, two objects that are equal to one another must have the same hashCode value.

Luckily, NetBeans (and every other IDE) will generate these methods for us and will help ensure that they are implemented correctly. In fact, NetBeans won't let you generate one without the other.

> **IMPORTANT NOTE**
>
> If you override either `equals` or `hashCode`, you are expected to override the other, and you should use the same properties in both. Failure to do so can cause irregular or breaking issues in Java code.

Simply follow these steps to add `equals` and `hashCode`:

1. Open the Student class and right-click the class name to get a pop-up menu. Select the *Insert Code* option in the menu.

2. Select *equals()* and *hashCode()* from the list of options.

3. Select all four checkboxes in both sections. All the `Student` properties are important for this.

4. Click the *Generate* button.

You should end up with two methods that look similar to the ones in Listing 31.2. Make sure all the properties are accounted for in yours, but don't worry if the numbers are a little different. The numbers are autogenerated, and it is not as important that they match exactly with the ones in our example.

LISTING 31.2

Student's New equals and hashCode Methods

```java
@Override
public int hashCode() {
    int hash = 7;
    hash = 89 * hash + Objects.hashCode(this.firstName);
    hash = 89 * hash + Objects.hashCode(this.lastName);
    hash = 89 * hash + Objects.hashCode(this.studentId);
    hash = 89 * hash + Objects.hashCode(this.cohort);
    return hash;
}

@Override
public boolean equals(Object obj) {
    if (this == obj) {
        return true;
    }
    if (obj == null) {
        return false;
```

```
        }
        if (getClass() != obj.getClass()) {
            return false;
        }
        final Student other = (Student) obj;
        if (!Objects.equals(this.firstName, other.firstName)) {
            return false;
        }
        if (!Objects.equals(this.lastName, other.lastName)) {
            return false;
        }
        if (!Objects.equals(this.studentId, other.studentId)) {
            return false;
        }
        if (!Objects.equals(this.cohort, other.cohort)) {
            return false;
        }
        return true;
    }
```

Now that you have these methods, you can assert on whole Student objects to check their equality with another Student object.

Adding toString to Student

It is also recommended to add an overridden toString method to your Student class to help with test failure messages. This toString method is added mostly for convenience. Often in error messages, JUnit will print out information about the object that failed a test. It helps if that information is readable to us, but the default toString method only really serializes the object's class name and hashcode. Both are interesting pieces of information, but not often particularly usable. Overriding this method can allow us to print out all the object's property values instead, which can allow for much better insight into issues when reading test logs.

To add your new toString method, follow the same process we used earlier for adding the equals and hashcode methods. Right-click the Student class name and select Insert Code. From the menu, select toString to display the code generation dialog. From the dialog, select all the fields and then click the *Generate* button to add the code that will be similar to Listing 31.3.

LISTING 31.3

Example of Student's New toString Method

```
@Override
public String toString() {
    return "Student{" + "firstName=" + firstName + ", lastName=" + lastName +
", studentId=" + studentId + ", cohort=" + cohort + '}';
}
```

Creating the Test Class

Our next step is creating the JUnit test class that will hold our test suite for our DAO. To do this, we follow similar steps to the ones done in the stateless testing exercises.

1. In NetBeans's Project view, right-click the `ClassRosterDaoFileImpl` class.

2. Select *Tools*, and then select *Create/Update Tests*.

3. Walk through the wizard to create a new JUnit class.

   - The name should look similar to `classroster.dao.ClassRosterDao-FileImplTest`.
   - Ensure that *Test Packages* is selected in the Location drop-down.
   - Generated Code Checkbox List should have everything selected.
   - Method Access Levels Checkbox List should have nothing selected.
   - Generated Comments Checkbox List should have nothing selected.

4. Click *OK*.

Once you complete the wizard, you should be left with a new Java class similar to Listing 31.4. This class is the shell of our new test suite, and we will be creating new tests to replace the `testSomeMethod` method with real tests.

LISTING 31.4

ClassRosterDaoFileImplTest

```
public class ClassRosterDaoFileImplTest {

    public ClassRosterDaoFileImplTest() {
    }
```

```java
@BeforeAll
public static void setUpClass() {
}

@AfterAll
public static void tearDownClass() {
}

@BeforeEach
public void setUp() {
}

@AfterEach
public void tearDown() {
}

@Test
public void testSomeMethod() {
    fail("The test case is a prototype.");
}

}
```

The Set Up and Tear Down Methods

The JUnit Framework gives us four methods, or rather four annotations, to help get the code we are testing into a known good state.

- setUpClass annotated with @BeforeAll
  - This static method is run once at the time the test class is initialized and can be used to set up external resources.
- tearDownClass annotated with @AfterAll
  - This static method is run once after all the tests have been run and can be used to clean up external resources.
- setUp annotated with @BeforeEach
  - This nonstatic method is run once before each test method in the JUnit test class. It can be used to set things to a known good state before each test.
- tearDown annotated with @AfterEach
  - This nonstatic method is run once after each test method in the JUnit test completes. It can be used to clean up after each test.

We will use the setUp method to put our system into a known good state before each test. Setting the system to a known good state in setUp gives us everything we need right now.

To do this, we're going to add in a new ClassRosterDao property declaration to our test class and then use the setUp in the JUnit class to reference the new overloaded constructor we built in the ClassRosterDaoFileImpl with a newly created file to ensure that we aren't messing up production data and that our testDAO is effectively empty.

Update your to ClassRosterDaoFileImplTest method, as shown in Listing 31.5, to declare our new testDao object, remove the unneeded setup/teardown methods and template method, and fill setUp with our initialization code.

LISTING 31.5

Updated ClassRosterDaoFileImplTest Method

```
public class ClassRosterDaoFileImplTest {

    ClassRosterDao testDao;

    public ClassRosterDaoFileImplTest() {
    }

    @BeforeEach
    public void setUp() throws Exception{
        String testFile = "testroster.txt";
        // Create a new FileWriter for the test roster file
        new FileWriter(testFile);
        testDao = new ClassRosterDaoFileImpl(testFile);
    }
}
```

This way, before every test run, we will have created a new blank testroster.txt file using the FileWriter and then used that as our fileName when instantiating our testDao. Both ensure that we are starting with a fresh, empty DAO object and minimize our interference with the normal application's data stored in the roster.txt file.

Arrange/Act/Assert for Stateful Code

We must add two general steps to the Arrange part of the unit testing process for stateful code.

1. Put the system in a known good state using the JUnit setUp method.

2. Create test data and add it to the system before each test is run. This can be done either in the setUp method (if the test data should be the same for all tests) or in each individual test method.

The Act and Assert parts of the testing process are identical to those for testing stateless code:

- **Act:** Call the method under test with the correct test inputs
- **Assert:** Verify that the expected result matched the actual result

---

> **NOTE** As you learned in the previous lesson, Arrange/Act/Assert is also referred to as Given/When/Then.

CLASS ROSTER DAO TEST DESIGN

Our ClassRosterDao has four methods that we must test.

- Add Student
- Get Student
- Get All Students
- Remove Student

When designing tests for these methods in our DAO, we need to make sure we design and implement tests for each method. In most cases, we will use more than one per test to "arrange" our DAO's state correctly before we assert on it.

First, we must consider what the effects of each method will be on the DAO and then how we can use the other tools (DAO methods) available to us to determine whether the state was correctly changed. Let's start this process with the addStudent method.

Add Student

Let's look at the DAO interface method and comment, which is shown in Listing 31.6, before we get started on designing a test for this method.

LISTING 31.6

The DAO Interface Method and Comment

```
/**
 * Adds the given Student to the roster and associates it with the given
 * student id. If there is already a student associated with the given
 * student id it will return that student object, otherwise it will
 * return null.
 *
 * @param studentId id with which student is to be associated
 * @param student student to be added to the roster
 * @return the Student object previously associated with the given
 * student id if it exists, null otherwise
 */
Student addStudent(String studentId, Student student)
    throws ClassRosterPersistenceException;
```

Reading through both the method and its JavaDoc comment, let's list some of the information we can gather about this method and its potential testing requirements. Here is what we know about addStudent:

- To call this method, we will need a studentId String and a Student object.

- After calling this method with those parameters, the student should now be stored within ClassRosterDaoFileImplTest and be associated with the given studentId.

- If there was no student in the DAO already with that studentId, the return should be null.

- However, if there *was* a student stored under that ID, then the previous Student associated will be returned.

- There is also a chance that this method could throw a ClassRosterPersistenceException, which implies it is touching a data store (we know it should be reading and writing to the file).

All this data is something we should already know, but it is always a good idea to double- and even triple-check your assumptions when beginning the testing process.

Looking at our gathered information, the first two bullet points are particularly important for our testing purposes. In this case, they focus on the fact that addStudent changes the state by adding a new or replacing an existing student within the DAO.

However, just the state change isn't the only thing we need to focus on. We need to also understand how to assert and *prove* that the state change happened correctly. In this case, we use other methods to measure the effect that this method call had on the state—the change of students stored within the DAO.

Remember, the `ClassRosterDaoFileImplTest` has three other methods: `getStudent`, `getAllStudents`, and `removeStudent`. Technically, each one of these could be used to verify the effect that calling the `addStudent` method has on the DAO, but `getStudent` is particularly well suited in that it allows us to simply retrieve the student from the DAO and examine it.

Get Student

Before we use it in a test, let's refresh ourselves with what `getStudent` does. Listing 31.7 presents the current code for `getStudent`.

LISTING 31.7

The getStudent Interface Method and Comments

```
/**
 * Returns the student object associated with the given student id.
 * Returns null if no such student exists
 *
 * @param studentId ID of the student to retrieve
 * @return the Student object associated with the given student id,
 * null if no such student exists
 */
Student getStudent(String studentId)
    throws ClassRosterPersistenceException ;
```

We know the following things about `getStudent`:

- To call this method, we will need a `studentId` `String`.

- The return should be a `Student` object. In theory, this is a student previously stored under that ID.

- If there was no student in the DAO with that studentId, the return should be null.
- There is also a chance that this method could throw a ClassRosterPersistenceException, which again implies touching a persistent data store.

ClassRosterDaoTest: Adding and Getting a Student

Our Add/Get Student test is straightforward. We know that the DAO is in an empty state since we created a new empty instance within our setUp method.

1. The first step of this test is to create a new Student object (Arrange).

2. Then we add that student to the DAO (Act).

3. Next, we get the student back out of the DAO and put it in another variable (Act).

4. Finally, we check to see that the data within the stored student is equal to the retrieved student from the DAO (Assert).

Listing 31.8 presents our test code.

LISTING 31.8

The testAddGetStudent Test Code

```
@Test
public void testAddGetStudent() throws Exception {
    // Create our method test inputs
    String studentId = "0001";
    Student student = new Student(studentId);
    student.setFirstName("Ada");
    student.setLastName("Lovelace");
    student.setCohort("Java-May-1845");

    //  Add the student to the DAO
    testDao.addStudent(studentId, student);
    // Get the student from the DAO
    Student retrievedStudent = testDao.getStudent(studentId);

    // Check that the data is equal
    assertEquals(student.getStudentId(),
            retrievedStudent.getStudentId(),
            "Checking student id.");
    assertEquals(student.getFirstName(),
            retrievedStudent.getFirstName(),
            "Checking student first name.");
    assertEquals(student.getLastName(),
```

```
                    retrievedStudent.getLastName(),
                    "Checking student last name.");
        assertEquals(student.getCohort(),
                    retrievedStudent.getCohort(),
                    "Checking student cohort.");
    }
```

Our first test is now complete, but we've only touched two of our DAO methods, and we only used the test with one Student object. Let's do another.

Get All Students

Let's look at the DAO interface method and comment before we get started on designing a test for the getAllStudents method. This is shown in Listing 31.9.

LISTING 31.9

The getAllStudents Interface Method and Comments

```
/**
 * Returns a List of all Students on the roster.
 *
 * @return Student List containing all students on the roster.
 */
List<Student> getAllStudents()
        throws ClassRosterPersistenceException;
```

This is an easier method to consider. It takes in no parameters and simply returns a list of students within the DAO. To properly test this method, we're going to have to use it along-side addStudent and maybe removeStudent to change what is contained within the list.

ClassRosterDaoTest: Adding and Getting All Students

This test is slightly more complicated than the previous Add/Get test, but not by much. Here we are focusing on testing the two methods addStudent and getAllStudents and verifying that each method works. To do this properly, we should really use multiple Student objects. In this test, we do the following:

1. Create and add two Student objects to the DAO (Arrange).

2. Get all the Student objects from the DAO (Act).

3. Check to see that the DAO returned the two objects (Assert).

Listing 31.10 shows the resulting test code.

LISTING 31.10

The `testAllGetAllStudents` Test Code

```java
@Test
public void testAddGetAllStudents() throws Exception {
    // Create our first student
    Student firstStudent = new Student("0001");
    firstStudent.setFirstName("Ada");
    firstStudent.setLastName("Lovelace");
    firstStudent.setCohort("Java-May-1845");

    // Create our second student
    Student secondStudent = new Student("0002");
    secondStudent.setFirstName("Charles");
    secondStudent.setLastName("Babbage");
    secondStudent.setCohort(".NET-May-1845");

    // Add both our students to the DAO
    testDao.addStudent(firstStudent.getStudentId(), firstStudent);
    testDao.addStudent(secondStudent.getStudentId(), secondStudent);

    // Retrieve the list of all students within the DAO
    List<Student> allStudents = testDao.getAllStudents();

    // First check the general contents of the list
    assertNotNull(allStudents, "The list of students must not be null.");
    assertEquals(2, allStudents.size(),"The list of students should have 2
students.");

    // Then the specifics
    assertTrue(testDao.getAllStudents().contains(firstStudent),
            "The list of students should include Ada.");
    assertTrue(testDao.getAllStudents().contains(secondStudent),
            "The list of students should include Charles.");

}
```

IMPORTANT NOTE

The test in Listing 31.10 will fail unless you properly completed the `equals`/hashCode additions to your Student class discussed earlier in this lesson.

Remove Student

Let's look at the DAO interface method and comment for removing a student before we get started on designing a test for this method. Listing 31.11 shows the removeStudent interface method.

LISTING 31.11

The `removeStudent` Interface Method and Comments

```
/**
 * Removes from the roster the student associated with the given id.
 * Returns the student object that is being removed or null if
 * there is no student associated with the given id
 *
 * @param studentId id of student to be removed
 * @return Student object that was removed or null if no student
 * was associated with the given student id
 */
Student removeStudent(String studentId);
```

We know the following things about removeStudent:

- To call this method, we will need a studentId String.
- The return should be a Student object. In theory, this is a student that was previously stored under that ID.
- If there was no student in the DAO with that studentId, the return should be null.
- The state effect of this on the DAO is that the returned student should no longer be within the DAO.
- There is another mention of a ClassRosterPersistenceException, which implies more persistent data storage.

ClassRosterDaoTest: Adding and Removing Students

In this test, we do the following:

1. Create and add two Student objects to the DAO (Arrange).
2. Remove one of the students from the DAO (Act).
3. Check to see that there is only one student left in the DAO (Assert).
4. Check to see that the DAO returns null if we try to retrieve the removed student (Assert).

5. Remove the other student from the DAO (Act).

6. Check to see that there are no students in the DAO (Assert).

7. Check to see that the DAO returns null if we try to retrieve the removed student (Assert).

Even though this is only one test, as shown in Listing 31.12, we are acting and asserting several times. This is perfectly fine. You can act and assert as many times as needed to fully execute the test case.

LISTING 31.12

The `testRemoveStudent` Test Code

```java
@Test
public void testRemoveStudent() throws Exception {
    // Create two new students
    Student firstStudent = new Student("0001");
    firstStudent.setFirstName("Ada");
    firstStudent.setLastName("Lovelace");
    firstStudent.setCohort("Java-May-1945");

    Student secondStudent = new Student("0002");
    secondStudent.setFirstName("Charles");
    secondStudent.setLastName("Babbage");
    secondStudent.setCohort(".NET-May-1945");

    // Add both to the DAO
    testDao.addStudent(firstStudent.getStudentId(), firstStudent);
    testDao.addStudent(secondStudent.getStudentId(), secondStudent);

    // remove the first student - Ada
    Student removedStudent = testDao.removeStudent(firstStudent.
getStudentId());

    // Check that the correct object was removed.
    assertEquals(removedStudent, firstStudent, "The removed student should
be Ada.");

    // Getall the students
    List<Student> allStudents = testDao.getAllStudents();

    // First check the general contents of the list
    assertNotNull( allStudents, "All students list should be not null.");
```

```
        assertEquals( 1, allStudents.size(), "All students should only have 1
    student.");

        // Then the specifics
        assertFalse( allStudents.contains(firstStudent),
                    "All students should NOT include Ada.");
        assertTrue( allStudents.contains(secondStudent),
                    "All students should NOT include Charles.");

        // Remove the second student
        removedStudent = testDao.removeStudent(secondStudent.getStudentId());
        // Check that the correct object was removed.
        assertEquals( removedStudent, secondStudent,
                        "The removed student should be Charles.");

        // retrieve all of the students again and check the list.
        allStudents = testDao.getAllStudents();

        // Check the contents of the list - it should be empty
        assertTrue( allStudents.isEmpty(),
                    "The retrieved list of students should be empty.");

        // Try to get both students by their old id. They should be null.
        Student retrievedStudent = testDao.getStudent(firstStudent.
    getStudentId());
        assertNull(retrievedStudent, "Ada was removed, should be null.");

        retrievedStudent = testDao.getStudent(secondStudent.getStudentId());
        assertNull(retrievedStudent, "Charles was removed, should be null.");

    }
```

UNIT TESTING THE SERVICE LAYER

In this part of the lesson, we will unit test the service layer for the Class Roster application. As mentioned at the beginning of this lesson, we will use a new testing technique called *stubbing*.

Planning the Test Design

The main purpose of the unit test suite for the service layer is to test that the business rules are being applied properly. For completeness, we will also test the pass-through methods of the service layer. We will test these business rules:

- Creation of a Student object with an existing student ID is prohibited.
- All fields on the Student object must have nonempty values.

These business rules are enforced in the createStudent method of the DAO. We will need three test cases:

- Create valid student. All fields have values, and the student does not have an existing student ID.
- Create a student with an existing student ID.
- Create a student with one or more empty field values.

We will also implement tests for getAllStudents, getStudent, and removeStudent. These tests will be similar to the tests we created for the matching DAO methods in a previous step.

Creating the Test Class

You should remember this step from our DAOImpl testing step. We will create a JUnit test class that will hold our test suite for our service layer. Do the following:

1. In the NetBeans Project view, right-click the ServiceLayerImpl class.
2. Select *Tools*, and then select *Create/Update Tests*.
3. Walk through the wizard to create a new JUnit class.
    - The name should look similar to classroster.service.ClassRosterService-LayerImplTest.
    - Ensure that *Test Packages* is selected in the *Location* drop-down.
    - Generated Code Checkbox List should have everything selected.
    - Method Access Levels Checkbox List should have nothing selected.
    - Generated Comments Checkbox List should have nothing selected.

4. Once these steps are finished, click the OK button.

Completing the wizard should leave you with a new Java test class, as shown in Listing 31.13, where we will write our service layer test suite.

LISTING 31.13

`ClassRosterServiceLayerImplTest`

```java
public class ClassRosterServiceLayerImplTest {

    public ClassRosterServiceLayerImplTest() {
    }

    @BeforeAll
    public static void setUpClass() {
    }

    @AfterAll
    public static void tearDownClass() {
    }

    @BeforeEach
    public void setUp() {
    }

    @AfterEach
    public void tearDown() {
    }

    @Test
    public void testSomeMethod() {
        fail("The test case is a prototype.");
    }
}
```

Creating the DAO Stubs

The service layer is not responsible for storing or retrieving Student objects. That is the job of the DAO. This means we don't have to (or want to) test the actual persistence of Student objects in this test suite. We only want to test the business rules and the integration between the service layer and the DAO.

Given this fact, we can use stubbed versions of our DAOs to test the functionality of the service layer. Since we are programming to interfaces and using constructor-based dependency injection, it will be easy to use the stubbed versions of the DAOs instead of the file-based implementations.

A *stubbed version* of a component simply returns canned data for any method call. We can set up a stubbed version of a component to act just about any way we want or need it to. Let's take a look at the stubbed implementation of our DAOs.

ClassRosterAuditDaoStubImpl

The `ClassRosterAuditDaoStubImpl` implementation shown in Listing 31.14 is simple. The `writeAuditEntry` method does nothing. This allows the service layer to make the call to the Audit DAO, but nothing will get written to the audit log file.

This is a testing class and belongs inside our test packages, not our development sources. Therefore, to create this testing stub, proceed with the following steps:

1. In the NetBeans Project view, right-click the `ClassRosterServiceLayerImplTest`'s test package.

2. Select *New* and then *Java Class.*

3. Name it **ClassRosterAuditDaoStubImpl**.

4. Click the *Finish* button.

5. Update the internal code to the shell implementation in Listing 31.14.

LISTING 31.14

The `ClassRosterAuditDaoStubImpl` Shell Implementation

```
public class ClassRosterAuditDaoStubImpl implements ClassRosterAuditDao {

    @Override
    public void writeAuditEntry(String entry) throws
ClassRosterPersistenceException {
        //do nothing . . .
    }
}
```

ClassRosterDaoStubImpl

This `ClassRosterDaoStubImpl` implementation is a bit more complicated than the Audit DAO stub implementation, but it is still quite straightforward. The stub implementation has the following features:

- A member field of type `Student`
  This represents the one and only student in the DAOStub.

- Constructor
  We have two. One is a no-arg constructor that instantiates a hard-coded student for our stub. The other allows a test student to be injected via the constructor by a test class.

- addStudent
  This returns our onlyStudent field if the ID matches our onlyStudent's ID. Otherwise, it returns null. Note that there is no persistence. The incoming Student parameter is never added to the DAOStub or persisted in any way.

- getAllStudents
  This method simply returns a List containing the one and only student.

- getStudent
  This returns our onlyStudent field if the ID matches our onlyStudent's ID; otherwise, it returns null.

- removeStudent
  This returns our onlyStudent field if the ID matches our onlyStudent's ID; otherwise, it returns null. Note that this does not change or remove our only Student existence within our DAOStub.

To create this stub, follow similar steps as the AuditDaoStub previously, and then fill out your ClassRosterDaoStubImpl with the code in Listing 31.15.

LISTING 31.15

ClassRosterDaoStubImpl

```
public class ClassRosterDaoStubImpl implements ClassRosterDao {

    public Student onlyStudent;

    public ClassRosterDaoStubImpl() {
    onlyStudent = new Student("0001");
        onlyStudent.setFirstName("Ada");
        onlyStudent.setLastName("Lovelace");
        onlyStudent.setCohort("Java-May-1845");
    }

    public ClassRosterDaoStubImpl(Student testStudent){
        this.onlyStudent = testStudent;
     }
```

```java
@Override
public Student addStudent(String studentId, Student student)
            throws ClassRosterPersistenceException {
    if (studentId.equals(onlyStudent.getStudentId())) {
        return onlyStudent;
    } else {
        return null;
    }
}

@Override
public List<Student> getAllStudents()
            throws ClassRosterPersistenceException {
    List<Student> studentList = new ArrayList<>();
    studentList.add(onlyStudent);
    return studentList;
}

@Override
public Student getStudent(String studentId)
            throws ClassRosterPersistenceException {
    if (studentId.equals(onlyStudent.getStudentId())) {
        return onlyStudent;
    } else {
        return null;
    }
}

@Override
public Student removeStudent(String studentId)
            throws ClassRosterPersistenceException {
    if (studentId.equals(onlyStudent.getStudentId())) {
        return onlyStudent;
    } else {
        return null;
    }
}
```

Test Setup

By using stubbed DAOs for these tests, we have essentially defined the state of our test system. Since the DAOs are the properties that belong to our service layer, their state represents the state of our service layer. That means if we can start these DAOs in a good state, so will our service layer. Since our stubs start in a predefined state, we will begin testing our service layer with the assumption that it contains a Class Roster DAO with exactly one student.

Although we don't have to do any work to put our code in a known good state, we do have to create the service layer object and wire in our stub DAOs. This code is similar to the code we have in the App class of the Class Roster application. Update the top of your ClassRosterServiceLayerImplTest with the setup in Listing 31.16.

LISTING 31.16

Create the Service Layer Object and Wire a Stub DAO

```
private ClassRosterServiceLayer service;

public ClassRosterServiceLayerImplTest() {
    ClassRosterDao dao = new ClassRosterDaoStubImpl();
    ClassRosterAuditDao auditDao = new ClassRosterAuditDaoStubImpl();

    service = new ClassRosterServiceLayerImpl(dao, auditDao);
}
```

Test Implementation

Finally, we will look at our test implementations. These include testCreateValidStudent, testCreateStudentDuplicateId, testGetAllStudents, testGetStudent, and testRemoveStudent.

testCreateValidStudent

The testCreateValidStudent test shown in Listing 31.17 is quite straightforward. We are simply asserting that the creation of a valid student (no duplicate student ID and values for all fields that the only hard-coded student in our DaoStub) does not cause an exception to be thrown.

LISTING 31.17

The testCreateValidStudent test

```
@Test
public void testCreateValidStudent() {
```

```
    // ARRANGE
    Student student = new Student("0002");
    student.setFirstName("Charles");
    student.setLastName("Babbage");
    student.setCohort(".NET-May-1845");
    // ACT
    try {
        service.createStudent(student);
    } catch (ClassRosterDuplicateIdException
        | ClassRosterDataValidationException
            | ClassRosterPersistenceException e) {
    // ASSERT
        fail("Student was valid. No exception should have been thrown.");
    }
}
```

testCreateStudentDuplicateId

The testCreateStudentDuplicateID test shown in Listing 31.18 asserts that a ClassRosterDuplicateIdException is thrown when trying to create a student with an existing student ID. In this case, we know that the stubbed implementation of the Class Roster DAO has an existing student with an ID of 0001 so we attempt to create a new student with that student ID. Since we expect an exception to be thrown by this call, we surround it with a try/catch.

- If the call executes and no exception is thrown, we fail the test with a message saying we expected an exception to be thrown.

- If the expected exception is thrown, we simply return. Since there are no errors or exceptions, this lets the JUnit test framework know that this test passed.

- If a different exception is thrown, the test will fail.

LISTING 31.18

The testCreateStudentDuplicateId Test

```
@Test
public void testCreateDuplicateIdStudent() {
    // ARRANGE
    Student student = new Student("0001");
    student.setFirstName("Charles");
    student.setLastName("Babbage");
    student.setCohort(".NET-May-1845");
```

```
    // ACT
    try {
        service.createStudent(student);
        fail("Expected DupeId Exception was not thrown.");
    } catch (ClassRosterDataValidationException
            | ClassRosterPersistenceException e) {
    // ASSERT
        fail("Incorrect exception was thrown.");
    } catch (ClassRosterDuplicateIdException e){
        return;
    }
}
```

testCreateStudentInvalidData

The `testCreateStudentInvalidData` test shown in Listing 31.19 is similar to the test for duplicate student ID. Here we ensure that we don't have a duplicate student ID and then also leave one of the fields blank. We use the same `try/catch` techniques as shown in the previous example except we are looking for a different exception.

LISTING 31.19

The `testCreateStudentInvalidData` Test

```
@Test
public void testCreateStudentInvalidData() throws Exception {
    // ARRANGE
    Student student = new Student("0002");
    student.setFirstName("");
    student.setLastName("Babbage");
    student.setCohort(".NET-May-1845");

    // ACT
    try {
        service.createStudent(student);
        fail("Expected ValidationException was not thrown.");
    } catch (ClassRosterDuplicateIdException
            | ClassRosterPersistenceException e) {
    // ASSERT
        fail("Incorrect exception was thrown.");
    } catch (ClassRosterDataValidationException e){
        return;
    }
}
```

testGetAllStudents

In the `testGetAllStudents` test shown in Listing 31.20, since we know that the stubbed Class Roster DAO contains only one student, we assert that only one student is returned from the `getAllStudents` service layer method.

LISTING 31.20

The `testGetAllStudents` Test

```
@Test
public void testGetAllStudents() throws Exception {
    // ARRANGE
    Student testClone = new Student("0001");
        testClone.setFirstName("Ada");
        testClone.setLastName("Lovelace");
        testClone.setCohort("Java-May-1845");

    // ACT & ASSERT
    assertEquals( 1, service.getAllStudents().size(),
                                "Should only have one student.");
    assertTrue( service.getAllStudents().contains(testClone),
                        "The one student should be Ada.");
}
```

testGetStudent

For the `testGetStudent` test shown in Listing 31.21, since we know that the stubbed Class Roster DAO only contains one Student with Student ID = 0001, we assert that a Student is returned when we ask for Student ID 0001 and that no student is returned when we ask for Student ID 0042.

LISTING 31.21

The `testGetStudent` Test

```
@Test
public void testGetStudent() throws Exception {
    // ARRANGE
    Student testClone = new Student("0001");
        testClone.setFirstName("Ada");
        testClone.setLastName("Lovelace");
        testClone.setCohort("Java-May-1845");
```

```
    // ACT & ASSERT
    Student shouldBeAda = service.getStudent("0001");
    assertNotNull(shouldBeAda, "Getting 0001 should be not null.");
    assertEquals( testClone, shouldBeAda,
                            "Student stored under 0001 should be Ada.");

    Student shouldBeNull = service.getStudent("0042");
    assertNull( shouldBeNull, "Getting 0042 should be null.");

}
```

testRemoveStudent

The behavior of the removeStudent method is that it will remove the student and return the associated Student object if a student exists for the given student ID. Otherwise, it will do nothing and return null. In the testRemoveStudent test shown in Listing 31.22, we assert that a Student object is returned when we remove student ID 0001 and that null is returned when we remove student ID 0042.

LISTING 31.22

The testRemoveStudent Test

```
@Test
public void testRemoveStudent() throws Exception {
    // ARRANGE
    Student testClone = new Student("0001");
        testClone.setFirstName("Ada");
        testClone.setLastName("Lovelace");
        testClone.setCohort("Java-May-1845");

    // ACT & ASSERT
    Student shouldBeAda = service.removeStudent("0001");
    assertNotNull( shouldBeAda, "Removing 0001 should be not null.");
    assertEquals( testClone, shouldBeAda, "Student removed from 0001 should
be Ada.");

    Student shouldBeNull = service.removeStudent("0042");
    assertNull( shouldBeNull, "Removing 0042 should be null.");

}
```

SUMMARY

In this lesson, we discussed and demonstrated the techniques for unit testing stateful code. We then completed the unit tests for the Class Roster service layer and saw how stubbed implementations can be used to test other components. The following are the main points to remember from this lesson:

- You must put stateful code into a known good state before unit testing it.
- You must be mindful of the order in which you test and call methods for stateful code. Calls to one method can affect the results from other methods.
- JUnit provides set up and tear down methods to help put stateful code into a known good state.
- Implementing the `equals` and `hashCode` methods on your DTOs can make unit testing a lot easier. Remember that you must use the same fields to calculate equality and the hash code for your objects.
- Stubbed implementations of components such as DAOs can be used to test components that use them.
- Hard-coded stubbed component implementations have a fixed state.
- When testing components (such as the service layer) that depend on other components (such as DAOs), you must wire the dependencies together as part of your overall test setup.
- The combination of a `try/catch` block and the JUnit static method called `fail` can be used to test conditions where an exception is expected.

EXERCISES

Many people learn best by doing, so this section includes exercises using what you learned in this lesson and previously in this course.

Exercise 1: Testing the Address Book app

Exercise 2: Testing the DVD Library program

Exercise 1: Testing the Address Book App

Design and implement a complete set of unit tests for the DAO of the Address Book application that you created in Lesson 27. Use the lesson notes as a guide and pattern your test suite after the test suite created in the Class Roster unit test code-along earlier in this lesson.

Exercise 2: Testing the DVD Library

Design and implement a complete set of unit tests for the DAO of the DVD Library application that you created in Lesson 27. Use the information from this lesson as a guide and pattern your test suite after the test suite created in the Class Roster application.

Lesson 32
Including Magic Numbers and Enums

We use enums to define a set of predefined, related constants. Some common examples include the months of the year and days of the week. In this shorter lesson, we'll look at how to create and use enums. *Enums* are a construct that allows us to define a group of related constants.

LEARNING OBJECTIVES

By the end of this lesson, you will be able to:

- Explain what a magic number is and why enums are better
- Create enums
- Use enums

MAGIC NUMBERS

A *magic number* is a value that is hard-coded into your code but does not have a clear meaning. For example, suppose we had an order-entry system. As each order is processed, it could have a status of Quoted, Purchased, Shipped, or Delivered.

In languages that do not provide enums, a developer will often simply assign a numeric code to each status, so you could end up looking at code such as what is shown in Listing 32.1.

LISTING 32.1

Coding without an Enum

```
public void shipOrder(Order order) {
    if(order.getStatus() == 2) { // purchased
        // ship it

        // move to shipped status
        o.setStatus(3);
    }
}
```

With the comments, the code is clearer, but without the comments, a developer unfamiliar with the order status codes would not know what 2 and 3 mean. This listing might work now, but what happens if a change is needed? Software tends to change over time, so what would we do when we need to add steps in the middle?

For example, what would happen if we needed to add a Gift Wrap stage in between Purchased and Shipped? In that case, the order of steps could end up being 1, 2, 5, 3, 4. The larger the workflow becomes and the more insertions and deletions are made, then the more unwieldy hard-coding numbers actually becomes.

This is where enums become useful.

ENUMS

As mentioned, enums are a construct that allows us to define a group of related constants. In other words, we can define a controlled vocabulary for the constants we are interested in. For example, we can use an enum to define the order status options in the previous example, define the days of the week, or even identify the different shifts at a factory.

You have already seen that constants are far better than hard-coded magic numbers in your code. Enums take constants a step further in that they are all grouped together and are type safe. It is also easier to see which enum values are valid and which are not.

There are many sophisticated things that can be done with enums; many of them are not available in other languages, but these features are beyond the scope of this lesson and beyond your needs at this stage of your development career. We will concentrate on using enums as better constants.

Creating Enums for Fixed Constants

Defining a Java enum is similar to defining a class or interface. For example, we could define an enum to be used as a set of fixed constants for the basic math operators: addition, subtraction, multiplication, and division. This enum could then be used in a simple math program.

Creating an enum for use as a set of constants is straightforward. Simply list each item in the enum vocabulary in a comma-separated list in the body of the enum like this:

```
public enum MathOperator {
    ADD, SUBTRACT, MULTIPLY, DIVIDE
}
```

NOTE Because the enum items are constants, they should be named in all caps.

Using Enums

One of the advantages of using enums over regular constants is that an enum is a proper type. This means we can use a particular enum type in the formal parameter list of a method and in `switch` statements.

To illustrate this, we will create a class that performs simple math operations on two integers. This class has one method—`calculate()`—that has three parameters:

- The operation to perform
- Operand 1
- Operand 2

We then assign each of the enum values to a specific operation using a `switch` statement, as shown in Listing 32.2.

LISTING 32.2

Using a Switch and Enum Together

```java
public class IntMath {

    public int calculate(MathOperator operator, int operand1, int operand2) {

        switch(operator) {
            case ADD:
                return operand1 + operand2;
            case SUBTRACT:
                return operand1 - operand2;
            case MULTIPLY:
                return operand1 * operand2;
            case DIVIDE:
                return operand1 / operand2;
            default:
                throw new UnsupportedOperationException();
        }
    }
}
```

Here are some things to note about this code:

- The first formal parameter of this method is of type MathOperator, which is the enum type that we just created. This guarantees that the only values allowed as operators are ADD, SUBTRACT, MULTIPLY, and DIVIDE.

- When using an enum in a switch statement, the values in the case statements must be unqualified—in other words, ADD versus MathOperator.ADD.

- The return statements in each case negate the need for break statements.

- We have chosen to throw an UnsupportedOperationException if we don't recognize the operator.

Listing 32.3 presents an application class that uses the MathOperator enum along with the IntMath class.

LISTING 32.3

Using the IntMath Class

```java
public class App {

    public static void main(String[] args) {
```

```
    IntMath num1 = new IntMath();
    int result;

    result = num1.calculate(MathOperator.ADD, 10, 5);
    System.out.println("Add: " + result);

    result = num1.calculate(MathOperator.SUBTRACT, 10, 5);
    System.out.println("Subtract: " + result);

    result = num1.calculate(MathOperator.MULTIPLY, 10, 5);
    System.out.println("Multiply: " + result);

    System.out.println("Divide: " + num1.calculate(MathOperator.DIVIDE, 10, 5));
  }
}
```

In this listing, you can see that an `IntMath()` object is created called num1. It is then used to do calculations. The type of calculation will be based on the `MathOperator` enum that was created. You can see that using `MathOperator.ADD` results in the ADD case in Listing 32.2 being called. Using `MathOperator.SUBTRACT` results in the corresponding SUB-TRACT case being used. The end result is that the use of the enum makes it clear what the listing is trying to accomplish. When the program is executed, the results should look like the following:

```
Add: 15
Subtract: 5
Multiply: 50
Divide: 2
```

Getting Values from an Enum

Many times, we might use an enum that has been defined in a different file. As such, we might not be aware of the values it contains. In Java, when an enum is created by the compiler, a method called `values()` is added to the enum. This method allows you to access the values that the enum contains.

In Listing 32.4, we illustrate a simple use of the `values()` method using an enhanced `for` loop to show all the entries in an enum of months.

LISTING 32.4

The Month Enum

```
public class Test {
    enum Month { JANUARY, FEBRUARY, MARCH,
```

```
              APRIL, MAY, JUNE,
              JULY, AUGUST, SEPTEMBER,
              OCTOBER, NOVEMBER, DECEMBER }

    public static void main(String[] args) {
        for (Month m : Month.values())
            System.out.println(m);
    }
}
```

In the listing, an enhanced loop cycles through the values in the Month enum and prints each entry.

```
JANUARY
FEBRUARY
MARCH
APRIL
MAY
JUNE
JULY
AUGUST
SEPTEMBER
OCTOBER
NOVEMBER
DECEMBER
```

> **NOTE** In Listing 32.4, you can clearly see the values in the enum in the code. This is done as a simple example to show you how values() can be used.

ENUM MEMBERS

The Month enum in Listing 32.4 presents a common but basic usage of enums using constant values. Enums, however, can do a lot more by including additional members, specifically fields and methods. Members of an enum are implicitly declared as public static members that cannot be changed. In Listing 32.5, the Month enum is expanded to provide more functionality.

LISTING 32.5

The Expanded Month Enum

```java
package com.tsg.moreenumfun;

public enum Month {
    JANUARY(1, 31),
    FEBRUARY(2, 28),
    MARCH(3, 31),
    APRIL(4, 30),
    MAY(5, 31),
    JUNE(6, 30),
    JULY(7, 31),
    AUGUST(8, 31),
    SEPTEMBER(9, 30),
    OCTOBER(10, 31),
    NOVEMBER(11, 30),
    DECEMBER(12, 31);

    private int order;
    private int days;

    Month(int order, int days) {
        this.order = order;
        this.days = days;
    }

    int numberOfDays() {
        return days;
    }

    int monthToNumber() {
        return order;
    }

    String monthToSeason() {

        String season;

        switch (this) {
            case JANUARY:
            case FEBRUARY:
            case MARCH:
                season = "Winter";
                break;
```

```
        case APRIL:
        case MAY:
        case JUNE:
            season = "Spring";
            break;
        case JULY:
        case AUGUST:
        case SEPTEMBER:
            season = "Summer";
            break;
        case OCTOBER:
        case NOVEMBER:
        case DECEMBER:
            season = "Fall";
            break;
        default:
            season = "Unknown";
            break;
    }
    return season;
    }
}
```

When we review Listing 32.5, we can see that the enum looks a lot like other classes with a few key differences. First, it is declared with the enum keyword. This sets the type as an enum instead of a standard class. Second, the members of the enum, both fields and methods, are all declared by default as public final. This means that once defined, they cannot be changed.

In the listing, we didn't just define the value for the enum items, such as JANUARY; we also included defining values for each. In this case, we included two additional numbers. The first is the order in which the month appears in the year, and the second is the number of days the month contains. We included these in parentheses after each month's entry. To maintain the value for the enum, we declared two private variables to hold the values as well as declared a constructor to assign the values.

```
private int order;
private int days;

Month(int order, int days) {
    this.order = order;
    this.days = days;
}
```

As you can see, we store the values as order and days. With the constructor, we assign the initializing value into the private variables of our existing enum. To access these values, we have created member functions that can be used. We can do more than just access these values from within our enum, which is illustrated by the monthToSeason( ) method that determines the season and returns it.

Listing 32.6 is a short listing that uses the updated Month enum and its methods.

LISTING 32.6

Using the Month Enum

```
package com.tsg.moreenumfun;

public class MoreEnumFun {

    public static void main(String[] args) {

        Month month;
        month = Month.JANUARY;

        System.out.println("Month: " + month.numberOfDays());
        System.out.println("====");

        for (Month i : Month.values()) {
            System.out.println("Month: " + i + " - " + i.monthToNumber()
                    + " - " + i.numberOfDays() + " - " + i.monthToSeason());
        }
    }
}
```

In this listing, a variable called month is defined as a Month enum. This value is then assigned a value from the enum, in this case Month.January. Following the assignment, a simple call to System.out.println displays the number of days within the month we assigned—in this case, 31 days.

In addition to showing how a month can be declared, assigned, and displayed, the listing also uses an enhanced for loop to show how you can cycle through the enum and see not only the entries but also the values associated to each entry. When Listing 32.6 is executed, the following is displayed:

```
Month: 31
====
Month: JANUARY - 1 - 31 - Winter
```

```
Month: FEBRUARY - 2 - 28 - Winter
Month: MARCH - 3 - 31 - Winter
Month: APRIL - 4 - 30 - Spring
Month: MAY - 5 - 31 - Spring
Month: JUNE - 6 - 30 - Spring
Month: JULY - 7 - 31 - Summer
Month: AUGUST - 8 - 31 - Summer
Month: SEPTEMBER - 9 - 30 - Summer
Month: OCTOBER - 10 - 31 - Fall
Month: NOVEMBER - 11 - 30 - Fall
Month: DECEMBER - 12 - 31 - Fall
```

Of course, the point of an enum is to be able to access these values as constants within your listings, more so than simply printing the values out.

> **NOTE** In Listing 32.6, the value of Month.JANUARY is assigned to the month variable. If you try assigning a value that is not listed in the enum, you will get an error. For example, assigning month = Month.HALLOWEEN would be invalid because HALLOWEEN is not a valid entry in Month.

SUMMARY

That's all there is to it. We introduce this topic here because, as we begin to use other libraries, we see enums more and more, and we want you to understand how they work.

The important takeaways from this lesson are the following:

- Enums are used as a way to group related constants.
- Enums are first-class types and can be used as formal parameters to methods and in switch statements.
- Items in an enum should be in all caps since they are constants.
- Enums are used widely, and you will start to see them in other APIs and frameworks as we program larger applications.

EXERCISES

The following exercises will help you practice what you are learning about enums in this lesson. These are to do on your own.

Exercise 1: How Many Days until Friday?
Exercise 2: Playing Cards

Exercise 1: How Many Days until Friday?

In this exercise, create an enum for every day of the week. Then, create an App class that asks the user to enter a day of the week and then use a `switch` statement and your enum to print out how many days there are until Friday.

Exercise 2: Playing Cards

Create two enums: one that contains the four suits in a card deck (CLUBS, DIAMONDS, HEARTS, and SPADES) and a second one that contains the names of the ranks of cards such as ACE, TWO, THREE, etc.

Use your newly created enums in a listing that should randomly select a card by selecting a random suit and a rank and then display the card to the console. Here's an example:

```
ACE CLUBS
```

Once you've completed printing a card, modify your listing to select and print five cards randomly. Your output could look something like the following:

```
Drawing a hand of cards:
THREE DIAMONDS
KING CLUBS
SIX CLUBS
FOUR HEARTS
NINE HEARTS
```

Lesson 33
Manipulating Dates and Times

The Java Date-Time API is a big API with a large number of features. In this lesson we will introduce the Date-Time API and show what is needed to get started.

The version of the Date-Time API that we cover in this lesson was introduced in Java 8 and addresses many shortcomings of what was available prior to that version for the date-time classes. The problems with the previous API led to the rise of several third-party Date-Time API implementations. The newer Java API incorporates features of these third-party APIs.

NOTE The Date-Time API is just like any other API in that it consists of several different packages and classes, all of which have Javadocs explaining how they are to be used. We encourage you to explore the API and grab additional features as you need them.

LEARNING OBJECTIVES

By the end of this lesson, you will be able to:
- Use the correct ISO calendar standard
- Differentiate between human time and machine time
- Differentiate between local and zone classes
- Differentiate between periods and duration
- Create LocalDates
- Calculate dates in the future and the past
- Calculate the time between two dates
- Format dates
- Convert the `Date` and `GregorianCalendar` objects

ISO CALENDAR

The Java Date-Time API uses standard 8601 from the International Organization for Standardization (ISO 8601) for representing dates and times. ISO 8601 is meant to normalize the differences in date/time formats across the globe and is based on the Gregorian calendar that was introduced in 1582. The basic format is as follows:

```
YYYY-MM-DDThh:mm:ss
```

Time is represented using the 24-hour clock. Although ISO 8601 is the default format, the Date-Time API gives us several ways to format dates and times as needed for our applications. We will see examples of this later in the lesson.

HUMAN TIME AND MACHINE TIME

The Java Date-Time API has two ways to represent time: human time and machine time.

Human time is familiar to us. It consists of units such as years, months, days, hours, minutes, and seconds. As the name implies, human time is regular calendar and clock time.

Machine time is a bit different. Machine time is a timeline (measured down to nanosecond intervals) that starts on January 1, 1970, which is known as the *epoch*. Positive numbers represent time after the epoch, and negative numbers represent time before the epoch. There are utility methods that convert from machine time to human time, and vice versa.

LOCAL AND ZONED CLASSES

The Java Date-Time API provides classes that work with time zone information and others that just deal with dates and times without taking time zones into account. They are easy to tell apart: ZonedDateTime takes the time zone into account, whereas LocalDate-Time does not.

We will be using LocalDateTime and LocalDate throughout this course, but you should be aware of the zoned date/time classes, especially if you work at a global company where time zones can be critical.

PERIODS AND DURATION

The Java Date-Time API has two ways to measure time periods: duration and period. Durations are measured in machine time (seconds and nanoseconds), whereas periods are measured in human time (years, months, and days). We will see examples of using a period to calculate the difference between two dates later in this lesson. The basic principles of using duration are basically the same. This method keeps track of how much time there is between two points in time.

WORKING WITH LocalDate OBJECTS

Now that we have discussed some of the basics of the Java Date-Time API, we are ready to look at some code. We'll start by creating a LocalDate object. It is a good class to start with if you just need to use a simple date.

Creating LocalDates

LocalDate objects are created using one of the supplied *factory methods* rather than using the LocalDate constructor. A factory method is simply a method that creates a new object for us when called. The two most commonly used LocalDate factory methods are now and parse.

The first example in Listing 33.1 creates a new LocalDate object containing today's date.

LISTING 33.1

Creating a LocalDate with the Current Date

```
import java.time.LocalDate;

public class App {
    public static void main(String[] args) {
```

```
            LocalDate ld = LocalDate.now();
            System.out.println(ld);
    }
}
```

Note that to use the `LocalDate` object, we needed to import `java.time.LocalDate`. When this program is executed, we see that the current date is displayed similar to the following:

```
2020-10-06
```

As can be seen, this program was executed on October 6, 2020. What happens, however, if we want a date other than the current date? In Listing 33.2 two more examples of setting values into our LocalDate object are presented.

LISTING 33.2

Initializing LocalDate Values

```
import java.time.LocalDate;
import java.time.format.DateTimeFormatter;

public class App {
    public static void main(String[] args) {

        LocalDate ld = LocalDate.now();
        System.out.println(ld);

        ld = LocalDate.parse("2021-03-01");
        System.out.println(ld);

        ld = LocalDate.parse("02/07/2021", DateTimeFormatter.ofPattern(
        "MM/dd/yyyy"));
        System.out.println(ld);
    }
}
```

This listing leaves the call to `LocalDate.now()`, but then adds two new examples. In the first new example, we create a new `LocalDate` object containing the date represented by a well-formed ISO 8601 string, which is passed in the `parse()` method of the `Local-Date` object.

```
ld = LocalDate.parse("2021-03-01");
```

In the output from running the listing, we can see that the date was assigned and displayed as expected and that 2021-03-01 is the second date printed when you run the program.

```
2020-10-06
2021-03-01
2021-02-07
```

What happens if we want to capture a date in a different format than the standard yyyy-mm-dd ISO 8601 format? The third example presented in the listing creates a new LocalDate object containing the date represented by a well-formed date string of the pattern MM/dd/yyyy.

```
ld = LocalDate.parse("02/07/2021", DateTimeFormatter.ofPattern("MM/dd/yyyy"));
```

Notice that this version of the parse() method requires both the date string and a parameter specifying the pattern of the incoming date. To do this, we use the static ofPattern() method on the DateTimeFormatter. Because the DateTimeFormatter code is in a different package from LocalDate, we need to import java.time.format.Date-TimeFormatter to use it.

When we run the listing, you can see from the output that was displayed earlier that our entered date of 02/07/2021 was displayed; however, it was displayed in the standard ISO format of 2021-02-07.

NOTE When creating the format string for month, you might have noticed that the format string uses capital Ms instead of lowercase. DateTimeFormatter uses a capital M for identifying months and a lowercase m for identifying minutes.

Converting Dates to and from Strings

Often, we will get dates from a file or other sources that are not stored in a LocalDate format but rather are presented as a simple string of text. In such cases, we are likely to want to convert these from a String format into a date within our programs so that we can do date calculations on them.

To convert a date from a string, we can use the same parse() method we used in the previous listing and simply pass it our date, as shown in Listing 33.3.

LISTING 33.3

Converting a Date to and from a String

```java
import java.time.LocalDate;

public class App {
    public static void main(String[] args) {

        String isoDate = "2021-12-25";

        LocalDate ld = LocalDate.parse(isoDate);
        System.out.println("ld = " + ld);
        System.out.println("isoDate = " + isoDate);
    }
}
```

In this listing, a `String` is created called `isoDate` and assigned a value of `2021-12-25`. We could have also read this same value from a file, asked the user to enter the date value, or obtained the value in a variety of other ways and placed it into our string. We then pass the `String` value in `isoDate` to the `parse()` method of `LocalDate`, which converts it to an `isoDate`. The listing then prints the value of both the `LocalDate` (`ld`) object and the `String` (`isoDate`).

```
ld = 2021-12-25
isoDate = 2021-12-25
```

To convert a date to a `String` is a simple matter of calling the `toString()` method on the `LocalDate` object. Using our values from the previous listing, it would be as simple as this:

```java
isoDate = ld.toString();
```

Formatting Dates

Although ISO 8601 is the default date format for the Java Date-Time API, dates can be displayed in a variety of formats. To do this, we use a combination of the `LocalDate.format()` method and the `DateTimeFormatter` class.

In Listing 33.2, you saw the `DateTimeFormatter` class used to display a date in the MM/dd/yyyy format using the `parse()` method of the `LocalDate` object. The following also formats a `LocalDate` into a String with the date pattern MM/dd/yyyy:

```java
DateTimeFormatter formatter = DateTimeFormatter.ofPattern("MM/dd/yyyy");
```

```
LocalDate ld = LocalDate.parse("02/07/2021", formatter);
String formatted = ld.format(formatter);
```

What is happening in this code is that a DateTimeFormatter is being created called formatter. This is a layout or pattern that can be used to format our date.

The DateTimeFormatter will then be passed to the parse() method of LocalDate along with a date value to create a LocalDate in the second line. In the final line, we are assigning the value returned from calling the format() method on our LocalDate object (ld) to our formatted String, formatted. However, we are also passing the formatted() method to the formatter we had created. This will result in the returned date being formatted with that formatter. As a result, if we were to print the value of formatted, it would look like this:

02/07/2021

Listing 33.4 takes the formatting we just did to the next level. In this listing, we format a date using special characters in a couple of different patterns.

LISTING 33.4

Going Crazy Formatting Dates

```
import java.time.LocalDate;
import java.time.format.DateTimeFormatter;

public class App {

    public static void main(String[] args) {

        LocalDate ld = LocalDate.parse("2020-12-25");
        String formatted;

        System.out.println("Starting date: " + ld);

        formatted = ld.format(DateTimeFormatter.ofPattern("MM=dd=yyyy+=+=+="));
        System.out.println(formatted);

        formatted = ld.format(DateTimeFormatter.ofPattern("==> MM/yyyy <=="));
        System.out.println(formatted);
```

```
        formatted = ld.format(DateTimeFormatter.ofPattern("yyyy-dd-MM-dd-yyyy"));
        System.out.println(formatted);
    }
}
```

When you run this listing, you see our date printed in a variety of manners.

```
Starting date: 2020-12-25
12=25=2020+=+=+=
==> 12/2020 <==
2020-25-12-25-2020
```

You can see in this formatted output that the values for month, day, and year are placed into the corresponding letters and that the symbols that were used are simply displayed.

Using Localization

There is one more example worth reviewing at this time, which involves the ofLocalized-Date() method of the DateTimeFormatter we've been using. This method uses localization information from the system to determine how the date should be formatted. The format for using the method is as follows:

```
ld.format(DateTimeFormatter.ofLocalizedDate(FormatStyle.FULL));
```

In this case, a predefined style is passed to the ofLocalizedData() method. The predefined style is a FormatStyle enum. In this case, FormatStyle.FULL is the style being passed. When called, the previous line will result in a date value that looks like this (depending on the localization information on your computer, this may look different for you):

```
Friday, December 25, 2020
```

To use FormatStyle enum, we will need to import java.time.format.FormatStyle. This will give you access to the different predefined formats shown in Listing 33.5.

LISTING 33.5

Using Localized Date Formats

```
import java.time.LocalDate;
import java.time.format.DateTimeFormatter;
import java.time.format.FormatStyle;
```

```java
public class App {

    public static void main(String[] args) {

        LocalDate ld = LocalDate.parse("2020-12-25");

        System.out.println("Starting date: " + ld);

        String formatted = ld.format(
                DateTimeFormatter.ofLocalizedDate(FormatStyle.FULL));
        System.out.println(formatted);

        System.out.println(
            ld.format(DateTimeFormatter.ofLocalizedDate(FormatStyle.LONG)));
        System.out.println(
            ld.format(DateTimeFormatter.ofLocalizedDate(FormatStyle.
MEDIUM)));
        System.out.println(
            ld.format(DateTimeFormatter.ofLocalizedDate(FormatStyle.SHORT)));
    }
}
```

When you execute this listing, you should see something similar to the following:

```
Starting date: 2020-12-25
Friday, December 25, 2020
December 25, 2020
Dec 25, 2020
12/25/20
```

> **NOTE** Again, the localization function localizes the date format to your system. As such, your output might vary from what is displayed.

GETTING THE TIME WITH LocalDateTime

We have focused on LocalDate up to this point; however, at times you might also want to capture the time. You can get both the date and the time by using a LocalDateTime object. For the most part, this object works like the LocalDate object, except that you will also get time information.

Listing 33.6 is concise and illustrates the use of LocalDateTime.

LISTING 33.6

Getting the Local Time

```java
import java.time.LocalDateTime;
import java.time.format.DateTimeFormatter;

public class App {

    public static void main(String[] args) {

        LocalDateTime ldt = LocalDateTime.now();

        System.out.println(ldt);

        String formatted =
                ldt.format(DateTimeFormatter.ofPattern("yyyy-MM-dd hh:mm:ss"));
        System.out.println(formatted);
    }
}
```

With the exception of using `LocalDateTime` instead of `LocalDate`, this listing operates like the previous listings. We declare a `LocalDateTime` called `ldt` to which we assign the current date and time by calling the `now()` method. We then print out the value.

Because the value isn't as nicely presented as we'd like, the listing then calls the `format()` method in the same manner we did earlier. We pass a pattern through the `DateTimeFormatter` to state in what format we want our output. In this case, we present the year, month, and day followed by a space and then the hour, minutes, and seconds. The resulting output for both the formatted date and time and unformatted are as follows:

```
2020-10-06T20:26:23.583
2020-10-06 08:26:23
```

If we were to run the program now, the date and time would be the current date and time.

As you can see, the features mentioned with `LocalDate` work equally well with `LocalDateTime`. If you wanted only the time, without the date, then you could use the `DateTimeFormatter` with a pattern such as `hh:mm:ss`.

> **NOTE** Remember, when formatting dates and times with the `ofPattern()` method, you use capital `M` for month and lowercase `m` for minutes.

WORKING WITH DATE CALCULATIONS

When working with dates, we often need to do more than just convert them from strings and format them for display. There are times we need to manipulate dates. This might be adjusting dates by adding to them, such as adding two weeks to a due date for a library book. Alternatively, it might be that we need to do calculations on dates, such as subtracting a due date from the current date to see how long something is past due (or how long until it is due).

Fortunately, the `LocalDate` provides methods that makes doing such calculations easy. We'll cover adjusting dates and then doing calculations for determining the time between dates.

Calculating Dates in the Future and Past

`LocalDate` provides a number of methods that lets you move a date forward into the future or backward into the past. This can be done by adding or subtracting years, months, weeks, or days to a date. The variety of methods provided by `LocalDate` include the following:

- `plusYears()`
- `plusMonths()`
- `plusWeeks()`
- `plusDays()`
- `minusYears()`
- `minusMonths()`
- `minusWeeks()`
- `minusDays()`

To use these methods, simply pass in the number of years, months, or days that you want to add or subtract from the existing date, and the method will return a new `Local-Date` object. It is as easy as it sounds. For example, the following code subtracts (moves back in time) eight days from the `ld` date and assigns the new date to the `past` object.

```
LocalDate past = ld.minusDays(8);
```

Listing 33.7 presents a simple use of the `plusYear()` method to let you know what day of the week New Year's Day will be for each of the next 10 years.

LISTING 33.7

The Day of the Week for New Year's Day

```java
import java.time.LocalDate;
import java.time.format.DateTimeFormatter;
import java.time.format.FormatStyle;

public class App {

    public static void main(String[] args) {

        LocalDate ld = LocalDate.parse("2021-01-01");
        System.out.println("Starting date: " + ld);
        System.out.println("==========================");

        for (int i = 0; i < 10; i++) {
            System.out.println(
                ld.format(DateTimeFormatter.ofLocalizedDate(FormatStyle.FULL)));

            ld = ld.plusYears(1);
        }
    }
}
```

The output from running this listing is as follows:

```
Starting date: 2021-01-01
==========================
Friday, January 1, 2021
Saturday, January 1, 2022
Sunday, January 1, 2023
Monday, January 1, 2024
Wednesday, January 1, 2025
Thursday, January 1, 2026
Friday, January 1, 2027
Saturday, January 1, 2028
Monday, January 1, 2029
Tuesday, January 1, 2030
```

You can use the other methods in the same manner. Clearly, the methods starting with minus move a date back in time. Those that start with plus move dates forward.

Calculating the Time between Two Dates

LocalDate also provides an easy way to determine the amount of time between two dates via the until() method. The until() method compares two dates and returns a Period object representing the difference in time between the two dates. Listing 33.8 presents an example of using a LocalDate variable and comparing it to another date using the Period class to store the difference. To use the Period class, you'll need to import java.time.Period.

LISTING 33.8

The Difference between Dates

```
import java.time.LocalDate;
import java.time.Period;

public class App {
    public static void main(String[] args) {

        LocalDate ld = LocalDate.now();
        LocalDate otherDate = LocalDate.parse("2022-01-01");

        Period diff = ld.until(otherDate);

        System.out.println("Starting date: " + ld);
        System.out.println("Other date:    " + otherDate);
        System.out.println("===========================");

        System.out.println("Difference: " + diff );
    }
}
```

What you see in looking at Listing 33.8 is that we place the current date into our Local-Date variable called ld. We then place a second date into our otherDate variable. In this case, we are placing 2022-01-01, which is New Year's Day 2022, into the variable. Using the following line of code, we then determine the difference between the two dates:

```
Period diff = ld.until(past);
```

When the listing was executed, it produces the following information:

```
Starting date: 2020-10-06
Other date:    2022-01-01
==========================
Difference: P1Y2M26D
```

> **NOTE** Because we are comparing to the current date (`LocalDate.now()`), your output will be different.

When I ran the listing, you can see that the difference is 1 year, 2 months, and 26 days; however, this information is presented in a manner that is a bit cryptic. Fortunately, the `Period` class has getter methods for the years, months, and days values that make up the time difference between the two dates.

- `getYears()`
- `getMonths()`
- `getDays()`

Listing 33.9 presents an update to Listing 33.8 that has an output that is much easier to understand.

LISTING 33.9

Getting Differences Piece by Piece

```java
import java.time.LocalDate;
import java.time.Period;

public class App {

    public static void main(String[] args) {
        LocalDate ld = LocalDate.now();
        LocalDate otherDate = LocalDate.parse("2022-01-01");

        Period diff = ld.until(otherDate);

        System.out.println("Starting date: " + ld);
        System.out.println("Other date:    " + otherDate);
        System.out.println("==========================");
```

```
        System.out.println("Difference: " + diff );
        System.out.println("Years: " + diff.getYears());
        System.out.println("Months: " + diff.getMonths());
        System.out.println("Days: " + diff.getDays());
    }
}
```

The output is much clearer, as shown here:

```
Starting date: 2020-10-06
Other date:    2022-01-01
=========================
Difference: P1Y2M26D
Years: 1
Months: 2
Days: 26
```

WORKING WITH LEGACY DATES

In the final section of this lesson, we will look at conversion from the legacy Date and GregorianCalendar objects to LocalDate objects. These two types of date objects were used in older versions of Java, so we might come across them.

Converting Date Objects

The conversion of a legacy Date object into a LocalDate object involves two steps. First, you must convert the Date into a ZonedDateTime object and from there into a LocalDate.

The first step (converting the Date to the ZonedDateTime) consists of several pieces.

1. We convert the Date into an Instant. Essentially, we are converting the Date from human time into machine time.

2. We then convert the Instant derived from the legacy Date into a ZonedDateTime object using the static ofInstant() method. Here, we are essentially converting the machine time Instant back into a human time ZonedDateTime object. Notice that we must also pass a time zone ID into the ofInstant() method, so we use the system default of the machine the code is running on.

The second step is more straightforward. We simply call the toLocalDate() method of our ZonedDateTime object. Listing 33.10 shows the conversion of a Date object into a LocalDate object.

LISTING 33.10

Converting from Date to LocalDate

```
import java.time.LocalDate;
import java.time.ZoneId;
import java.time.ZonedDateTime;
import java.util.Date;

public class App {
    public static void main(String[] args) {

        LocalDate ld;
        Date legacyDate = new Date();

        // Step 1
        ZonedDateTime zdt = ZonedDateTime.ofInstant(
                legacyDate.toInstant(), ZoneId.systemDefault());
        // Step 2
        ld = zdt.toLocalDate();

        System.out.println(legacyDate);
        System.out.println(ld);
    }
}
```

The comments within the listing show the two steps described earlier. Also note that we needed to include a few additional imports for the new objects that are being used. When you run this listing, you see basic output, which is the original value of the Date object followed by the value of the newly created LocalDate object. The values match, which is what we want.

```
Wed Oct 07 11:14:43 EDT 2020
2020-10-07
```

Converting a GregorianCalendar Object

Converting from a GregorianCalendar object to a LocalDate is much easier. In this case, GregorianCalendar includes a method to convert to a ZonedDateTime object called, appropriately, toZoneDateTime(). Once converted, you can then follow the second step from earlier to convert the ZonedDateTime to a LocalDate, as shown in Listing 33.11.

LISTING 33.11

Converting from GregorianCalendar to LocalDate

```java
import java.time.LocalDate;
import java.time.ZonedDateTime;
import java.util.GregorianCalendar;

public class App {
    public static void main(String[] args) {

        LocalDate ld;
        GregorianCalendar legacyCalendar = new GregorianCalendar();

        // Step 1
        ZonedDateTime zdt = legacyCalendar.toZonedDateTime();
        // Step 2
        ld = zdt.toLocalDate();

        System.out.println(legacyCalendar);
        System.out.println(ld);
    }
}
```

When you look at the output from this listing, you'll notice that the Gregorian calendar default format for printing contains a lot of information, which makes its printout somewhat unusable. Even so, once converted, we get the LocalDate we've come to expect. The following is the output from this listing:

```
java.util.GregorianCalendar[time=1602084052565,areFieldsSet=true,areAllFie
ldsSet=true,lenient=true,zone=sun.util.calendar.ZoneInfo[id="America/New_
York",offset=-18000000,dstSavings=3600000,useDaylight=true,transitions=235,
lastRule=java.util.SimpleTimeZone[id=America/New_York,offset=-18000000,dstS
avings=3600000,useDaylight=true,startYear=0,startMode=3,startMonth=2,start
Day=8,startDayOfWeek=1,startTime=7200000,startTimeMode=0,endMode=3,endMont
h=10,endDay=1,endDayOfWeek=1,endTime=7200000,endTimeMode=0]],firstDayOfWee
k=1,minimalDaysInFirstWeek=1,ERA=1,YEAR=2020,MONTH=9,WEEK_OF_YEAR=41,WEEK_
OF_MONTH=2,DAY_OF_MONTH=7,DAY_OF_YEAR=281,DAY_OF_WEEK=4,DAY_OF_WEEK_IN_
MONTH=1,AM_PM=0,HOUR=11,HOUR_OF_DAY=11,MINUTE=20,SECOND=52,MILLISECOND=565,Z
ONE_OFFSET=-18000000,DST_OFFSET=3600000]
2020-10-07
```

> **NOTE** Your output will be different, depending on the day you run the program.

SUMMARY

The Java Date-Time API introduced way back in Java 8 was a great improvement over previous versions. It is a large and powerful API, and we have really just scratched the surface. We have shown the basics of the API in this lesson, and these basics will get you through the course, but there are many useful features that we leave to you to discover. The best way to learn an API is to read the documentation and then write some code that uses the API to see how it behaves—in other words, just play with the API.

The important takeaways from this lesson are the following:

- The Java Date-Time API uses the ISO-8601 date format.
- The Java Date-Time API can represent time in human time and machine time.
- Machine time is represented as a timeline (down to nanosecond intervals) since the epoch (which is January 1, 1970).
- Periods of time are measured using two classes: `Duration`, which uses machine time, and `Period`, which uses human time.
- `LocalDate` and `LocalDateTime` objects are instantiated using factory methods instead of constructors. The two most commonly used factory methods are `now()` and `parse()`.
- Java Date-Time objects can be formatted in a variety of ways.
- `LocalDate` provides methods to calculate dates in the future or the past based on an existing `LocalDate` object.
- The Java Date-Time API provides methods to help convert to and from legacy date and time APIs.

EXERCISES

The following are exercises to help you practice what you are learning about working with dates and times in this lesson. These are to do on your own.

Exercise 1: Birthday Calculator
Exercise 2: It's the End of the World as We Know It
Exercise 3: Tracking Your Time

Exercise 1: Birthday Calculator

For this exercise, create an application to help people report on birthdays. Your birthday calculator application should do the following:

- Ask someone for their birthday, for example 01/01/2002.

- Tell them the day of the week their birthday falls on.

- Then tell them the day of the week it falls on this year.

- Next tell them what day it is today and the number of days until their next birthday.

- And then tell them what their age will be.

The following is example output your application could produce:

```
Welcome to the Magical BirthDAY Calculator!

What's your birthday?
01-01-2002
That means you were born on a TUESDAY!
This year it falls on a MONDAY...
And since today is 12-30-2021, there are only 2 more days until the next one!
Bet you're excited to be turning 20!
```

Exercise 2: It's The End of the World as We Know It

There are several predictions as to when the world will end. The following are some of the predicted dates:

- December 31, 2129

- January 1, 3239 (approximately)

- January 1, 2026 (approximately)

- January 1, 2028 (approximately)

Write a program that determines how much time remains between now and each of these predictions.

NOTE You can search online for *list of dates for apocalyptic events* to determine additional dates to try.

Exercise 3: Tracking Your Time

Write a program that tracks the amount of time it takes you to read the next lesson in this course. One approach to doing this is to do the following:

1. Run the program when you are ready to start the lesson.

2. Have the program capture the date and time when it starts.

3. Within a loop, create a prompt that asks, "Are you done with the lesson (y/n)?"

4. If the user responds with "n," then provide the current time, indicate how many hours and minutes they've been working on the lesson, and prompt them again to ask if they are done.

5. If the user responds with "y," then provide the ending date and time and tell them how many total minutes they spent on the lesson.

6. If they answer something other than "n" or "y," then you'll want to tell them that they need to respond with "n" or "y."

Lesson 34
Using the BigDecimal Class

In this lesson, we will look at the `BigDecimal` class. This class is used to represent arbitrary precision decimal numbers. It provides ways to set the number of significant digits and configure how numbers should be rounded. This class should be used for all calculations involving currency.

Like some of the other classes and libraries we have covered, we will introduce you to `BigDecimal` and show what you need to get started. We won't cover every capability of the class, but we will give you enough information so that you can explore the remaining capabilities on your own.

LESSON OBJECTIVES

By the end of this lesson, you will be able to:
- Explain `BigDecimal`
- Describe scale as it applies to `BigDecimal`
- Explain considerations for rounding modes

EXPLORING BIGDECIMAL

The Javadoc documentation for BigDecimal is pretty technical and can be a bit intimidating. In this section, we explore some of the ideas behind BigDecimal, and in the next section, we look at some code samples.

BigDecimal is an immutable type (just like String). That means that a BigDecimal object's value cannot be changed once it is set. From a practical standpoint, that means you must set the result of any BigDecimal operation to another BigDecimal variable. We will see examples of this in the code examples later in this lesson.

Constructing BigDecimals

There are several different constructors that you can use to create instances of BigDecimal. Most of them are straightforward, but we want to discuss two of them here: the String constructor and the double constructor.

It seems intuitive to use a double value to create a BigDecimal instance. After all, they are both decimal numbers, right? Well, the problem with using a double to create a BigDecimal stems from the imprecise nature of doubles, which is why BigDecimal was created in the first place.

For example, you would expect that passing in 0.1 to the constructor of BigDecimal would create a BigDecimal with the value of exactly 0.1, but you would be wrong. Not all values can be represented exactly as a double. For example, you would expect 0.1 to be stored when constructing an instance with BigDecimal(0.1); however, what could actually end up being stored is the following:

0.1000000000000000055511151231257827021181583404541015625

This odd value is stored because the 0.1 value being used with the constructor is not exactly 0.1 in the system, even though it appears that way when being passed in.

So, it is *not* a good idea to use the BigDecimal double constructor. Take a look at Listing 34.1, which illustrates how to create a BigDecimal called myNumber with an assigned double value of 0.1.

LISTING 34.1

Using a Double with BigDecimal

```
import java.math.BigDecimal;

public class MyBigDecimal {
    public static void main(String[] args) {
```

```
        double x = 0.1;
        BigDecimal myNumber = new BigDecimal(x);
        System.out.println(myNumber);
    }
}
```

If you enter and execute this listing, you'll confirm that the output is not 0.1, just as the Oracle documentation claimed.

0.1000000000000000055511151231257827021181583404541015625

What should we do if we need to create a BigDecimal with the exact value of 0.1? This is where the String constructor helps us. It may seem nonintuitive to create a BigDecimal from a String; however, if we pass the String "0.1" into the BigDecimal constructor, it will create a BigDecimal equal to exactly 0.1. Again, according to the Oracle documentation:

The String constructor, on the other hand, is perfectly predictable: writing new BigDecimal ("0.1") creates a BigDecimal which is *exactly* equal to 0.1, as one would expect. Therefore, it is generally recommended that the String constructor be used in preference to this [the double constructor] one.

Listing 34.2 is short, but it confirms the Oracle documentation.

LISTING 34.2

Using a String with BigDecimal

```
import java.math.BigDecimal;

public class MyBigDecimal {
    public static void main(String[] args) {

        BigDecimal myNumber = new BigDecimal("0.1");
        System.out.println(myNumber);
    }
}
```

This time, BigDecimal is assigned a string value that is displayed when you run the program. The result is what we want, which is simply:

0.1

> **NOTE** None of the other `BigDecimal` constructors (`int`, `long`, `BigDecimal`) have the problem of imprecision.

Understanding Scale

When working with `BigDecimals`, it is important to understand scale. The *scale* value is the number of digits to the right of the decimal point. For example, when dealing with currency calculations, we will use a value of 2 for the scale.

Understanding Rounding Modes

Another concept to be aware of when working with numbers and doing mathematical operations is rounding. The `BigDecimal` class has several rounding modes. The rounding mode you should use will be dependent upon the business rules for your application. Different industries and applications have different rules. This is generally *not* a decision that should be made by anyone on the development team. Table 34.1 lists the modes that are available.

The rounding modes and the scale value that are right for your application are completely dependent on your business rules. Often, these settings will be related to the generally accepted accounting principles for your particular industry; sometimes tax law

Table 34.1 BigDecimal Rounding Modes

Rounding Mode	Description
CEILING	Rounds toward positive infinity
DOWN	Rounds toward zero
FLOOR	Rounds toward negative infinity
HALF_DOWN	Rounds toward the nearest neighbor unless both neighbors are equidistant, in which case it rounds down
HALF_EVEN	Rounds toward the nearest neighbor unless both neighbors are equidistant, in which case it rounds toward the even neighbor
HALF_UP	Rounds toward the nearest neighbor unless both neighbors are equidistant, in which case it rounds up
UNNECESSARY	Asserts that the requested operation has an exact result so there is no need to round
UP	Rounds away from zero

determines them. In any case, the development team should never make these decisions without knowing the business rules.

> **NOTE** You can import java.math.RoundingMode to get the RoundingMode enum values.

WORKING WITH BIGDECIMAL

Now that we have some background information, we will take a closer look at BigDecimal in action. In Listings 34.1 and 34.2, you saw BigDecimal values created using a double and a string, respectively. These values were created and set with default scaling values. For example, when the value of "0.1" was assigned to myNumber in Listing 34.2, the scale value was set to the number of positions to the right of the decimal, which was 1.

Setting Scale

What happens if we want to set the scale to a different value? Listing 34.3 helps illustrate the use of BigDecimal's setScale() method to set the scale.

LISTING 34.3

Changing the Scale of a BigDecimal Object

```java
import java.math.BigDecimal;

public class App {
    public static void main(String[] args) {

        BigDecimal aNum = new BigDecimal("23.45");
        BigDecimal bNum = aNum.setScale(4);

        System.out.println("aNum = " + aNum);
        System.out.println("bNum = " + bNum);

        System.out.println("aNum scale = " + aNum.scale() );
        System.out.println("bNum scale = " + bNum.scale() );
    }
}
```

This code should be easy to follow with what we already know. A BigDecimal object called aNum is created, and the value of "23.45" is assigned to it. We then assign this value to a second BigDecimal object called bNum; however, we called the setScale() method to use a scale of 4.

The listing then prints out the value stored within both aNum and bNum. This is followed by a call to another BigDecimal method called scale(), which returns the scale value for a variable.

Take a look at the output:

```
a = 23.45
b = 23.4500
a scale = 2
b scale = 4
```

We can see that the value of aNum was set to 23.45 as expected, and its scale matched the number of places to the right of the decimal, which is 2. You can also see that since the value assigned to bNum was stated to have a scale of 4, when bNum was displayed, it included four positions to the right of the decimal, and as expected, the scale value shown is indeed 4.

Setting Scale without Rounding Mode

Look at Listing 34.3 again. What would you expect to happen if you changed the assignment to bNum to the following?

```
BigDecimal bNum = aNum.setScale(1);
```

In this line of code, we attempt to create a new BigDecimal object called bNum and assign it a value from aNum, but with a scale of 1.

This produces an error.

While you might expect the value of 23.4 to be assigned to bNum, this is not what happens. Rather, your code generates an exception because we didn't tell the method what rounding mode to use when getting rid of the second digit to the right of the decimal point.

Rounding BigDecimals

Table 34.1 listed the rounding modes that can be used to let BigDecimal know how to round a number. Listing 34.4 updates Listing 34.3 to show bNum being scaled to one position instead of two.

LISTING 34.4

Setting Scale with Rounding Mode HALF_UP

```java
import java.math.BigDecimal;
import java.math.RoundingMode;

public class App {
    public static void main(String[] args) {

        BigDecimal aNum = new BigDecimal("23.45");
        BigDecimal bNum = aNum.setScale(1, RoundingMode.HALF_UP);

        System.out.println("aNum = " + aNum);
        System.out.println("bNum = " + bNum);

        System.out.println("aNum scale = " + aNum.scale() );
        System.out.println("bNum scale = " + bNum.scale() );
    }
}
```

In this example, we add the rounding mode value of HALF_UP when setting the scale to 1. Now BigDecimal knows how to properly round when getting rid of the second digit to the right of the decimal point. Not only do we avoid an exception, but we get the output with a scale of one position, as expected. We also see that bNum's decimal value was rounded up.

```
aNum = 23.45
bNum = 23.5
aNum scale = 2
bNum scale = 1
```

If we wanted to have rounding go down, we could swap out the RoundingMode for HALF_DOWN:

```java
BigDecimal bNum = aNum.setScale(1, RoundingMode.HALF_DOWN);
```

If we change this line of code in Listing 34.4 and run it again, the output would be as follows:

```
aNum = 23.45
bNum = 23.4
aNum scale = 2
bNum scale = 1
```

As we can see, the value of bNum results in 23.4 instead of 23.5. The value was rounded down.

DOING CALCULATIONS WITH BigDecimals

When doing math calculations with BigDecimals, we need to use the methods included with the class rather than the math operators. The basic methods are as follows:

- add
- subtract
- multiply
- divide

For example, to add bNum to aNum, we would do the following:

```
BigDecimal result = aNum.add(bNum);
```

This would put the sum of the two numbers into the BigDecimal object called result. Subtracting and multiplying would work the same way as shown in Listing 34.5.

LISTING 34.5

Basic Math with BigDecimals

```
import java.math.BigDecimal;

public class App {
    public static void main(String[] args) {

        BigDecimal aNum = new BigDecimal("10");
        BigDecimal bNum = new BigDecimal("6");
        BigDecimal result

        result = aNum.add(bNum);
        System.out.println("Adding: " + result);
```

```
        result = aNum.subtract(bNum);
        System.out.println("Subtracting: " + result);

        result = aNum.multiply(bNum);
        System.out.println("Multiplying: " + result);
    }
}
```

As you can see, the code is straightforward. The values of 10 and 6 are placed into Big-Decimal objects, and adding, subtracting, and multiplying are each done. The results are what we would expect.

```
Adding: 16
Subtracting: 4
Multiplying: 60
```

Dividing BigDecimals

You might have noticed that the last example didn't include division. When we add, subtract, or multiply numbers, things are relatively clean. For example, you don't need to worry about the possibly of increasing decimal places.

When we divide numbers, it is possible for the number of decimal places to increase. In simple terms, 10 divided by 2 is 5, which is nice and clean. In fact, we could divide 10 by 4, which results in 2.5, which adds a decimal place but is still a result we can work with.

What happens, however, when we divide 10 by 6?

In this case, the result is 1.6666. The result is a nonterminating decimal. Because the decimal value doesn't end, the BigDecimal value won't know how to store the value unless you tell it. Consider the following:

```
aNum = new BigDecimal("10");
bNum = new BigDecimal("6");
result = aNum.divide(bNum); // Exception!
```

The calculation of result will throw an exception. In fact, it will throw an Arithmetic-Exception exception because result would contain an infinitely repeating value to the right of the decimal point. To avoid this issue, we need to set a value for a rounding mode, as shown in Listing 34.6.

LISTING 34.6

Division with Various Rounding Modes

```java
import java.math.BigDecimal;
import java.math.RoundingMode;

public class App {
    public static void main(String[] args) {

        BigDecimal aNum = new BigDecimal("10");
        BigDecimal bNum = new BigDecimal("6");
        BigDecimal result;

        result = aNum.divide(bNum, RoundingMode.HALF_UP);
        System.out.println("Adding: " + result);

        result = aNum.divide(bNum, 2, RoundingMode.HALF_UP);
        System.out.println("Subtracting: " + result);

        result = aNum.divide(bNum, 2, RoundingMode.DOWN);
        System.out.println("Multiplying: " + result);
    }
}
```

When you execute this listing, you get the following output:

```
2
1.67
1.66
```

In this listing, you can see that division is done three times. The first time, two values are passed to the `divide()` method of aNum. First is the number that will be used to divide, bNum, and the second is the rounding mode, which in this case is HALF_UP. You can see in this case that the result is that 10 divided by 6 is equal to 2. The result was rounded to the same scale as our original number, in this case, aNum.

In the second and third calls to the `divide()` method on aNum, three values are passed. The first is the number that will be used to divide, bNum again. These two times, however, bNum is followed by a scale value before including the rounding mode. You can see that the first rounding mode is set to round HALF_UP. The second is set to round DOWN, which is what our output reflects.

SUMMARY

The BigDecimal class provides Java developers with a convenient way to deal with decimal numbers in a predictable fashion. The important takeaways from this lesson are the following:

- Scale refers to the number of digits to the right of the decimal point.

- BigDecimal provides several different rounding modes.

- It is important to set the rounding mode when performing division operations because the operation may result in an infinitely repeating value to the right of the decimal point.

- BigDecimal objects are immutable.

EXERCISES

The following exercises will help you practice what you have learned about using the BigDecimal class. These are to do on your own.

Exercise 1: Interest Calculator

Exercise 2: Car Lot Service Layer

Exercise 1: Interest Calculator

In this exercise, write an interest calculator program that works as described in this example.

John has $500 to invest. Sue knows of a mutual fund plan that pays 10% interest annually, compounded quarterly. That is, every three months, the principal is multiplied by 2.5% (the 10% annual rate divided by 4 because it is compounded 4 times per year), and the result is added to the principal.

More generally, the new amount each quarter is equal to the following:

```
CurrentBalance * (1 + (QuarterlyInterestRate / 100))
```

Write a program that will tell John how much money will be in the fund after a specified number of years. Make the program general; that is, it should prompt for the following inputs and use those inputs in the calculations.

- Annual interest rate

- Initial amount of principal

- The number of years the money is to stay in the fund

The output should include the following for each year:

- The year number
- The principal at the beginning of the year
- The total amount of interest earned for the year
- The principal at the end of the year

The following is an example of output that you could have your program produce:

```
How much do you want to invest? 500
How many years are you investing? 10
What is the annual interest rate % growth? 10

Calculating...
Year 1:
Began with $500.00
Earned $51.91
Ended with $551.91

Year 2:
Began with $551.91
Earned $57.30
Ended with $609.20

Year 3:
Began with $609.20
Earned $63.24
Ended with $672.44

    ...
```

If you are adventurous, you can update your program with the following additional changes:

- Change the program so that interest is compounded monthly.
- Change the program so that the user can choose from quarterly, monthly, or daily interest compound periods.

Exercise 2: Car Lot Service Layer

Create a service layer that could be used in a simulated car lot program. Remember, the service layer handles the business logic for a larger application. This car lot's business lot expects the layer to do some purchase validation, discounting, and filtering.

Your service layer should implement the interface in Exercise Listing 34.2A.

EXERCISE LISTING 34.2A

CarLotService

```
public interface CarLotService {

    public Car getACar(String VIN);
    public List<Car> getAllCars();
    public List<Car> getCarsByColor(String color);
    public List<Car> getCarsInBudget(BigDecimal maxPrice);
    public List<Car> getCarByMakeAndModel(String make, String model);

    public BigDecimal discountCar(String VIN, BigDecimal percentDiscount)
        throws NoSuchCarException;

    public CarKey sellCar(String VIN, BigDecimal cashPaid)
        throws NoSuchCarException,
        OverpaidPriceException,
        UnderpaidPriceException;
}
```

As you can see, there are several business-based methods that must be defined:

- Given a VIN, it should be able to get a single Car.
- It should be able to get all the Car objects and return them in a List.
- Given a color, it should be able to return all the available Car objects of that color in a List.
- Given a max price, it should be able to return a List of all available Car objects at or under that price.
- Given a make and model, it should be able to return a List of all the available Car objects.
- Given a VIN and a discount amount (i.e., 15%), this method should discount the car's price (updating the official price records of that car) and then return the new final price.
    - If there is no car that matches, it should throw a NoSuchCarException.
- Given a VIN and a cash Amount, it should "buy": checking if the price matches, removing the car from the lot, and returning the associated CarKey.
    - If there is no car that matches, it should throw a NoSuchCarException.

- If they gave too much money, it should throw an `OverpaidPriceException`.
- If they gave too little money, it should throw an `UnderpaidPriceException`.

Assume that you also have access to the DAO and DTOs in Exercise Listings 34.2B through 34.2D.

NOTE These are references. You should not need to change or add nondescribed properties or methods.

EXERCISE LISTING 34.2B

CarLotDAO

```
public interface CarLotDAO {
    public Car addCar(String VIN, Car car);

    public Car getCar(String VIN);
    public List<Car> getCars();

    public void editCar(String VIN, Car car);

    public Car removeCar(String VIN);
}
```

EXERCISE LISTING 34.2C

Car DTO

```
public class Car {
    private String VIN;
    private String make;
    private String model;
    private String color;

    private BigDecimal price;
    private long odometerMiles;
```

```
    private CarKey key;

    // plus getters, setters & appropriate constructors
}
```

EXERCISE LISTING 34.2D

CarKey DTO

```
public class CarKey {
    private String VIN;
    private boolean laserCut;

    // plus getters, setters & appropriate constructors
}
```

Working with Lambdas and Streams

Streams, in conjunction with lambdas, allow developers to process data from Collections in a powerful way. In this lesson, we will cover a lot of terminology and look at these features to see how we can use them to simplify our code and make it more efficient.

LEARNING OBJECTIVES

By the end of this lesson, you will be able to:

- Identify tasks you can use aggregate operations for
- Describe pipelines
- Explain streams as they relate to pipelines
- Compare streams to iteration
- Explain lambdas
- Use filter with streams
- Use map with streams
- Use collect with streams
- Use forEach with streams

USING AGGREGATE OPERATIONS

When we use Collections to store objects in our programs, we generally need to do more than simply put the objects in the Collection: we also need to store, retrieve, remove, and update these objects.

Aggregate operations use lambdas to perform actions on the objects in a Collection. For example, you can use aggregate operations to:

- Print the names of all the people in a Collection of Address objects
- Return all of the Address objects for people from Akron, Ohio
- Return all of the Address objects for people from Akron, Ohio, grouped by ZIP code
- Calculate and return the average age of servers in your inventory (provided the Server object has a purchase date field)

These tasks can be accomplished by using aggregate operations along with pipelines and streams.

UNDERSTANDING PIPELINES AND STREAMS

A *pipeline* is simply a sequence of aggregate operations. A *stream* is a sequence of items (*not* a data structure) that carries items from the source through the pipeline. Pipelines include a data source, zero or more intermediate operations, and a terminal operation.

A *data source* is most commonly a Collection, but it could be an array, the return from a method call, or some sort of I/O channel. *Intermediate operations*, such as a filter operation, accept a stream and produce a new stream. A filter operation takes in a stream and then produces another stream that contains only the items matching the criteria of the filter. There are some intermediate operations that accept one type of stream and convert it to another type of stream.

Finally, a *terminal operation* is an operation that returns a nonstream result. This result could be a primitive type (for example, an integer), a Collection, or no result at all. For example, the operation might just print the name of each item in the stream.

> **NOTE** A data source and terminal operation are required for a pipeline to execute.

STREAMS VS. ITERATION

We will see that some aggregate operations (e.g., forEach) look like iterators, but there are fundamental differences.

- Aggregate operations process items from a stream, not directly from a Collection.
- Aggregate operations support lambda expressions as parameters.

That said, anything we do with streams can also be accomplished by using normal loops and iteration. It might just take a lot more code.

EXPLORING LAMBDAS

Lambdas in programming are anonymous functions or methods. The term *anonymous* here simply means that we don't define them with a specific name. They do still take in parameters, have a body, and can return data.

In Java, lambda expressions are not anonymous. Lambda expressions are implementations of functional interfaces. A functional interface is simply an interface with a single abstract method. An example of a functional interface is the Runnable or the Comparable interface.

Lambda expressions can be passed into methods as a parameter, which essentially allows us to pass methods into methods. We have only seen examples of passing data into methods, so you may be asking yourself when this might be useful. Lambdas are particularly useful with the stream and aggregate operation features of Java. Aggregate operations such as filter and forEach require the caller to pass in a lambda that defines how the objects in the stream should be filtered or processed.

> **NOTE** In Java, lambda expressions allow us to treat code as data.

WORKING WITH STREAM AND LAMBDA SYNTAX

We've covered a lot of terminology, but now we will look at the syntax and usage of lambdas in streams. To illustrate how we typically use them, we will create several lambdas with commonly used stream methods. To that end, we will first define an object to use in these streams.

To help with our illustration, we will use the Person class shown in Listing 35.1 in our code. We will then use this class with the stream methods.

LISTING 35.1

The Person Class

```
package com.tsg.lambdafun;

public class Person {

    private String name;
    private int age;

    Person (String n, int a){
        name = n;
        age = a;
    }
    Person (){
        name = "empty";
        age = 0;
    }

    public String getName() {
        return name;
    }

    public void setName(String name) {
        this.name = name;
    }

    public int getAge() {
        return age;
    }

    public void setAge(int age) {
        this.age = age;
    }
}
```

The forEach() Stream Method

The first terminal operation we'll review is the forEach() method. This method doesn't actually return anything. Instead, it allows us to run code against each and every object in the stream. The lambda passed in this example implements the functional interface Consumer, which includes the abstract method accept (docs.oracle.com/javase/8/docs/api/java/util/function/Consumer.html).

One use for the forEach() method is to print out everything in the List.

```
people.stream()
    .forEach((p) -> System.out.println(p.getName + " : " + p.getAge()));
```

In this example, we start the stream as usual with the stream() method and then call forEach() on the stream. Inside the forEach(), our lambda takes in each object and puts it into a println.

Let's say we want to print the name on one line and the age on the next; we can make a multiline lambda using curly braces, as illustrated in Listing 35.2.

LISTING 35.2

Using forEach() to Loop through a Stream

```
package com.tsg.lambdafun;

import java.util.ArrayList;
import java.util.List;

public class App {

    public static void main(String[] args) {

        List<Person> people = new ArrayList<>();

        people.add( new Person("Alfred", 17));
        people.add( new Person("Henrey", 18));
        people.add( new Person("George", 19));
        people.add( new Person("Joe", 27));
        people.add( new Person("Zelda", 7));

        for (Person currentPerson : people) {
            System.out.print(currentPerson.getName());
            System.out.print(" - ");
            System.out.println(currentPerson.getAge());
        }

        System.out.println("======");
```

```
people.stream()
  .forEach((currentPerson) -> {
      System.out.print(currentPerson.getName());
      System.out.print(" - ");
      System.out.println(currentPerson.getAge());
  });
}
}
```

This listing creates a List containing several Person objects using the Person class from Listing 35.1. The list is then printed to the screen using a for loop to show its contents. Our interest now, however, is to use the stream() method to print out each person. You can see that this is being done as well. The forEach() method selects each person and then uses three lines to print out the values for the name and age with a dash in the middle.

As you can see from the following output, printing the list with the stream() results in the same output as printing it with a for loop:

```
Alfred - 17
Henrey - 18
George - 19
Joe - 27
Zelda - 7
======
Alfred - 17
Henrey - 18
George - 19
Joe - 27
Zelda - 7
```

You should note that when we use a multiline lambda, we need to include a semicolon at the end of lines and a return statement if the functional interface has a return value. If we use a multiline lambda in a filter or map, we also need to make sure to return a value from the lambda. The return is assumed on the single-statement lambdas, but is required in multistatement lambdas.

Combining the forEach() with the filter() method we covered in the previous section, you can see in Listing 35.3 how to use the stream to filter the people List first by age and then by the first letter.

LISTING 35.3

Using filter() with a Stream

```java
package com.tsg.lambdafun;

import java.util.ArrayList;
import java.util.List;

public class App {

    public static void main(String[] args) {

        List<Person> people = new ArrayList<>();

        people.add( new Person("Alfred", 17));
        people.add( new Person("Henrey", 18));
        people.add( new Person("George", 19));
        people.add( new Person("Joe", 27));
        people.add( new Person("Zelda", 7));

        System.out.println("==> Age 18 or greater ==");
        people.stream()
            .filter((currentPerson) ->
                    currentPerson.getAge() >= 18)
            .forEach((currentPerson) -> {
               System.out.print(currentPerson.getName());
               System.out.print(" - ");
               System.out.println(currentPerson.getAge());
        });

        System.out.println("==> Names start with G ==");
        people.stream()
            .filter((currentPerson) ->
                    currentPerson.getName().startsWith("G"))
            .forEach((currentPerson) -> {
               System.out.print(currentPerson.getName());
               System.out.print(" - ");
               System.out.println(currentPerson.getAge());
        });
    }
}
```

The first part of this listing again sets up a List of Person objects called people. The stream() method is then used as is the forEach() to cycle through each person. The difference this time is that the filter() method is also used. The first time stream() is called, we filter based on the age being greater than or equal to 18. The following time we filter based on the name starting with G. The output from the listing reflects these filters in action.

```
==> Age 18 or greater ==
Henrey - 18
George - 19
Joe - 27
==> Names start with G ==
George - 19
```

The filter Stream Method

The first stream method we will look at is filter(). This method does just what it says: it filters a stream down to contain only the objects we want it to. The lambda that we define for it is a Boolean check. Anything that returns true from the check stays in the stream; everything else is discarded from the stream.

> **NOTE** A lambda that returns true or false in Java can also be called a *predicate*. The lambdas passed into filter operations are predicate implementations. Predicates take one parameter and return a Boolean primitive. Other types of predicates include BiPredicate, which takes two parameters: IntPredicate, which takes an int parameter; and LongPredicate, which takes a long parameter.

To start, we will look at filtering a stream of Person objects to include only the people who are old enough to vote, 18 years old or older. We will assume we are starting from a List of Person objects called people.

```
people.stream()
    .filter((p) -> p.getAge() >= 18)
```

We first use the stream method on the List to turn it into a stream, and then we call the filter method on that. Inside the filter method we see our lambda.

```
(p) -> p.getAge() >= 18.
```

Let's break this line of code down. The p is the parameter of the lambda. It will hold each Person object as we evaluate it in the stream. Since it is just a parameter name, it can be anything. We just decided to call it p here since it represents a person. The arrow operator (->) is used only for lambdas to separate the parameters from the body of the lambda. Finally is the body.

```
p.getAge() >= 18
```

This is the statement that will be evaluated. Anything that returns true from this statement stays in the stream.

Now let's say we want to filter the original List down to people whose names start with J.

```
people.stream()
    .filter((p) -> p.getName().startsWith("J"))
```

This would have the same setup as the previous example: stream method calls and then filter method call with our lambda inside. Because startsWith() returns true or false on its own, we don't need to make it any more complicated than just calling that method.

What if we wanted to combine our previous two examples and look for people who are greater than or equal to 18 and have a name that starts with J? Because the filter method returns a stream, we just chain these calls together as follows:

```
people.stream()
    .filter((p) -> p.getAge() >= 18)
    .filter((p) -> p.getName().startsWith("J"))
```

We first filter down to people over the age of 18 and then filter that down to people whose names start with J. At the end of this statement we have a stream of people who are older than 18 and whose names start with J.

You typically want to handle situations like this using two (or more) separate filters, rather than combining the two into a single filter method call, because it keeps your code more readable.

The map Stream Method

Sometimes when we process data with streams, we care about only one piece of the data and we don't need the rest. There are also times when we simply need to convert a piece of our data to something different. The map() method allows us to switch the stream to contain only the data that can sometimes be easier to process. We use the map() stream method when we want to convert the type that is being held in the stream.

> **NOTE** The map method doesn't have anything to do with the Map class. The map method takes a function as a parameter. The input function is a functional interface that takes as input a generic parameter and returns a generic value.

For an initial example, let's say we want to get all the names out of our List of Person objects.

```
people.stream()
    .map((p) -> p.getName())
```

We turn our List into a stream with the stream() method and then call our map() method.

Inside the map() method, we use a lambda to return a piece of data with its type being the type of the stream. In this case, by returning the name of the Person object, the stream is now a stream of String objects, instead of a stream of Person objects. If we wanted to continue working on the stream, the lambdas would now take in Strings.

There are also special map methods if we want to map into ints, doubles, or longs. We can use mapToInt(), mapToDouble(), or mapToLong() (respectively) to specifically change the stream into those types. In fact, those create special stream types (IntStream, DoubleStream, and LongStream) that let us use methods such as average(), sum(), min(), or max() on the stream.

As an example of that, let's say we want to get the average age of all the Person objects in our List.

```
int averageAge = people.stream()
                    .mapToInt((p) -> p.getAge())
                    .average();
```

The map() method can also be combined with the filter() method, or any other stream method. Let's get a stream of all the names of Persons over 18:

```
people.stream()
    .filter((p) -> p.getAge() >= 18)
    .map((p) -> p.getName())
```

We first filter the list down to just Person objects with an age of 18 or more and then map the stream so it is now a stream of String objects that are the names of our people.

The collect Stream Method

The filter( ) and map( ) methods both return a stream. We need to change the stream back into a List to pass it around and use it in our code properly. The collect( ) method lets us do that.

When we use the collect( ) method, we pass into it a Collector type, which we can generate using static methods in the Collectors class.

First let's look at collecting our stream into a List.

```
List<Person> overEighteen = people.stream()
                    .filter((p) -> p.getAge() >= 18)
                    .collect(Collectors.toList());
```

We first create the stream with the stream( ) method and then use filter to keep only Person objects over the age of 18 in the stream. We then finally use collect( ) to put them into a List. The Collectors.toList( ) call specifically puts the remaining things in the stream into a List. Listing 35.4 pulls this together into a working program using our Person class.

LISTING 35.4

Using the collect() Method

```
package com.tsg.lambdafun;

import java.util.ArrayList;
import java.util.List;
import java.util.stream.Collectors;

public class App {

    public static void main(String[] args) {

        List<Person> people = new ArrayList<>();

        people.add(new Person("Alfred", 17));
        people.add(new Person("Henrey", 18));
        people.add(new Person("George", 19));
        people.add(new Person("Joe", 27));
        people.add(new Person("Zelda", 7));
        people.add(new Person("Zoe", 27));
```

```
        List<Person> oldPeople = people.stream()
                .filter((p) -> p.getName()
                .startsWith("Z")).collect(Collectors.toList());

        oldPeople.stream()
                .forEach((currentPerson) -> {
                    System.out.print(currentPerson.getName());
                    System.out.print(" - ");
                    System.out.println(currentPerson.getAge());
                });
    }
}
```

When you execute this listing, you get the following results:

```
Zelda - 7
Zoe - 27
```

An important thing to note is that when we assign the filtered stream back into a List, the original List people will not change. The act of streaming a List will not change the original List.

Another way we might want to collect our stream is into a Map. Let's say we want to organize our Person List into sublists based on age.

```
Map<Integer, List<Person>> peopleAges = people.stream()
        .collect(Collectors.groupingBy((p) -> p.getAge()));
```

In the call Collectors.groupingBy((p) -> p.getAge()), we specify what we want the key for the Map to be and how we are organizing our List: in this case, by age. So, for each distinct age, we will have a List of Person objects.

Further Syntax

There are many more things you can do with streams, but the methods we discussed here are what you will typically use with them. If you are interested in researching what else can be done with streams, take a look at the Stream Javadoc, which you can find at docs.oracle.com/en/java/javase/11/docs/api/java.base/java/util/stream/Stream.html. You can also find a summary of the package at docs.oracle.com/en/java/javase/11/docs/api/java.base/java/util/stream/package-summary.html.

SUMMARY

Streams, aggregate operations, and lambdas are powerful features in Java. They allow us to easily accomplish tasks that used to be difficult. In this lesson, you learned that streams, aggregate operations, and lambdas can provide you with powerful tools for processing data. The following main takeaways from this lesson:

- Streams are associated with Collections of objects. A stream is a sequence of items; it is not a data structure.

- Stream objects are processed through a pipeline, which consists of zero or more intermediate operations and exactly one terminal operation.

- Processing items from a stream is similar to iteration except that stream iteration is all internal; there is no way for the calling code to control the iteration process.

- There are many methods in the Stream class that allow us to process data using lambdas, but we primarily use filter(), map(), collect(), and forEach().

EXERCISES

The following exercises help you practice what you are learning regarding lambdas and streams. These are to do on your own.

Exercise 1: Only the Young
Exercise 2: DVD Library Update

Exercise 1: Only the Young

Make the following modifications to the code presented in the listings in this lesson to get each of the following results:

- Modify Listing 34.3 to print only the people who are younger than 18.

- Modify the listing to print only the people younger than 18 who have a name that begins with A.

- Create a new List using collect() that contains only the people younger than 17. Print your results to confirm.

Exercise 2: DVD Library Update

Your task in this exercise is to change the implementation of the first version of DVD Library you did in Lesson 27 to take advantage of the lambda, stream, and aggregate features of Java.

You should add the following features to your program:

- Find all movies released in the last *N* years.

- Find all the movies with a given MPAA rating.

- Find all the movies by a given director.

- When searching by director, the movies should be sorted into separate data structures by MPAA rating.

- Find all the movies released by a particular studio.

- Find the average age of the movies in the collection.

- Find the newest movie in your collection.

- Find the oldest movie in your collection.

- Find the average number of notes associated with movies in your collection.

In your implementation you should include an interface for your DAO that contains all the methods specified here plus all the methods in version 1 of your DAO. Also include an implementation class that implements the DVDLibrary interface using lambdas, streams, and aggregates and makes all necessary changes to the Controller, View, and App classes.

PART V

Advanced Java

Lesson 36

Working with the Spring Framework

Spring is a collection of libraries that provide support for JVM-based enterprise applications. We will use the Spring framework portion of the larger Spring ecosystem in this lesson. The Spring framework provides support for dependency injection, MVC web applications, RESTful web services, authentication/ authorization, and database connectivity.

In this lesson, we will look at dependency injection with Spring and how to accomplish it using XML configuration files or annotation-based configuration.

LEARNING OBJECTIVES

By the end of this lesson, you will be able to:

- Explain how dependency injection (DI) and programming to interfaces work together
- Explain why the Spring framework is used
- Outline the four main strategies of Spring
- Define plain old Java objects (POJOs)
- Implement DI using XML configuration
- Implement DI using annotation-based configuration

DEPENDENCY INJECTION AND PROGRAMMING TO INTERFACES

As we have covered in previous lessons, *dependency injection* is a design pattern that implements a form of *inversion of control*. In fact, these two terms are used interchangeably.

The "inversion" of control in this case is that client objects are no longer responsible for instantiating the objects (also known as *services*) on which they depend. Instead, the dependencies are handed to (i.e., injected into) the client objects by some other entity. Dependencies are handed to the client through either constructors or setter methods.

Of course, we have been using this pattern for a while now. We have built our components so that their dependencies are handed to them via their constructors. We assemble (or wire) the application in our App class. This arrangement works pretty well, but our configuration is still hard-coded in our App class. If we want to change anything, we have to modify the App class and recompile. The Spring framework allows us to externalize this configuration into XML files or use annotations to define our DI.

Using dependency injection has the following advantages:

- Allows for loose coupling between the client and the concrete implementation of the service.
- Allows the externalization (to configuration files) of the system's configuration information. This allows for configuration changes without forcing a recompilation of the application.
- Allows for more flexible parallel development. Developers can program against the interface and use stubbed or mock implementations while the real implementation of the component is being built.

WHY SPRING?

Spring was originally created as a reaction against the growing complexity of the Java frameworks that existed at the time. The first version of the Spring framework was written by Rod Johnson and was released in conjunction with a development book he wrote in 2002. The official 1.0 version was released in March 2004, and the project has been going strong ever since. Its sole purpose was (and is) to simplify the programming and creation of Java applications. We'll start with the base feature of dependency injection because the other features (e.g., MVC, web services, security, and database support) build on this foundation.

When Spring started, the main framework for building enterprise Java applications was the Enterprise Java Bean (EJB) specification. This specification required complicated deployment descriptors and lots of extra plumbing code. Over time Java developers began looking for a simpler, cleaner way to build complex applications, and this is where Spring came into its own. Over time, the EJB specification has become much simpler and now Spring and JEE (of which the EJB specification is a part) share much in common.

While the Spring Framework has done much to simplify enterprise Java programming from the beginning, it has not been completely free from criticism. Like any software, it has evolved over time, getting better with each release. The first couple of releases relied heavily on XML-based configuration to the extent that sometimes it felt as if you were writing programs in XML. In later releases, annotation and Java-based configuration options were added to the framework. This gave developers many configuration options and allowed them the freedom to choose the right configuration tool for the job. In this course, we will use both XML and annotation-driven configuration.

One of the more recent releases of Spring introduced Spring Boot, which enables automatic configuration based on what libraries are packaged with or available to your application. Spring Boot relies heavily on the "convention over configuration" approach where little or no configuration is required for standard situations. Of course, even with this approach, developers are free to override any configuration setting in the application using XML, Java, or annotations.

UNDERSTANDING THE SPRING APPROACH

In addition to providing loose coupling via DI, Spring provides us with a lightweight development approach using plain old Java objects and templates that can replace boilerplate code.

Plain Old Java Objects

Many frameworks (both historical and current) require you to extend their classes to take advantage of their features. This often leads to code that is bound to the framework, essentially locking you into a particular vendor's solution.

Spring strives to be minimally invasive to your code base in that it allows you to use plain old Java objects instead. POJOs can be largely free of framework-specific code, which makes the code more testable (since it can be tested outside the framework) and easier to move to another framework if desired.

The Spring framework includes a container known as the Inversion of Control (IoC) container. The IoC container is responsible for creating objects needed by an application as well as configuring and managing the objects through their lifecycle.

The Spring container uses the POJO classes and the configuration data to configure and run an application. The Spring framework provides two containers that support DI.

- **BeanFactory container:** The simplest container with basic support for DI.

- **ApplicationContext container:** Built on top of the BeanFactory to provide more enterprise-specific functionalities. The ApplicationContext container includes all the functionality of the BeanFactory, so it is recommended to use it over the BeanFactory container.

All the objects managed by the Spring container are called *beans*. The Spring container is responsible for instantiating, assembling, and managing objects (also called *beans*).

The container uses configuration metadata to know which objects to instantiate, assemble, and configure. We can use XML to represent the configuration metadata (more on this later in the lesson). It is also possible to do that through annotations or through Java code.

Templates

Spring uses templates to reduce the need for boilerplate code in your applications. Listing 36.1 contains code that talks to a database without using Spring's JDBC template. Don't worry about understanding all of the code in this listing.

LISTING 36.1

No Spring

```
public Employee getEmployeeById(long id) {
    Connection conn = null;
    PreparedStatement stmt = null;
```

```java
        ResultSet rs = null;
        try {
            conn = dataSource.getConnection();
            stmt = conn.prepareStatement(
                    "select id, firstname, lastname, salary from "
                    + "employee where id=?"); //select employee
            stmt.setLong(1, id);
            rs = stmt.executeQuery();
            Employee employee = null;
            if (rs.next()) { //this will create an object from the data
                employee = new Employee();
                employee.setId(rs.getLong("id"));
                employee.setFirstName(rs.getString("firstname"));
                employee.setLastName(rs.getString("lastname"));
                employee.setSalary(rs.getBigDecimal("salary"));
            }
            return employee;
        } catch (SQLException e) { // what should be done here?

        } finally {
            if (rs != null) { //clean up mess
                try {
                    rs.close();
                    catch(SQLExeception e) {}
                }

                if (stmt != null) {
                    try {
                        stmt.close();
                    } catch (SQLException e) {
                    }
                }

                if (conn != null) {
                    try {
                        conn.close();
                    } catch (SQLException e) {
                    }
                }
            }

            return null;
        }
    }
```

Listing 36.2 shows code that does the same thing using a Spring JDBC template. Even if you don't fully understand the code (which you certainly won't at this point), it is clear that the example in Listing 36.2 is much cleaner than the first example.

LISTING 36.2

With Spring

```
public Employee getEmployeeById(long id) {
    return jdbcTemplate.queryForObject (
    "select id, firstname, lastname, salary " + // SQL Query
    "from employee where id=?",
    new RowMapper<Employee>() {
            Public Employee mapRow(ResultSet rs, //Map results to object
                int rowNum) throws SQLException {
                Employee employee = new Employee();
                employee.setId(rs.getLong("id"));
                employee.setFirstName(rs.getString("firstname"));
                employee.setLastName(rs.getString("lastname"));
                employee.setSalary(rs.getBigDecimal("salary"));
                return employee;
            }
        },
    id); //specify query parameter
}
```

Spring templates allow the developer to concentrate on the business logic instead of repetitious resource management and error handling code.

PULLING IT ALL TOGETHER: SPRING DI IN ACTION

To take a look at how we can implement Spring DI, we will use a prewritten MVC project with the same setup we've been using already. You can download the file, Book Tracker using the following URL: www.wiley.com/go/jobreadyjava under the "Downloads" link.

Save this file to your computer and extract its contents. Open the extracted project in your IDE for use in this code-along. If you run this program, you will see that it allows you to enter and view book details. It uses a simple menu structure.

```
Main Menu
1. View Books
```

```
2. View Book Details
3. Add Book
4. Update Book
5. Delete Book
6. Exit
Please select an option:
```

You can add books and then view, update, or delete them. The code for each of these options is included and works as expected.

NOTE Code for exception handling is not included in the program, so if you enter bad information, such as a character when a number is expected, the program will throw an exception.

Spring DI with XML

First, let's look at the XML-based setup. To start with, we need to add a dependency into our pom.xml file so that Maven will include the appropriate Spring libraries in our project. Listing 36.3 shows the markup to add to your project's pom.xml file.

LISTING 36.3

The Dependency Markup to Add to pom.xml

```
<dependencies>
    <dependency>
        <groupId>org.springframework</groupId>
        <artifactId>spring-context</artifactId>
        <version>5.2.2.RELEASE</version>
    </dependency>
</dependencies>
```

Once this is in the project, you need to build the project to ensure that the libraries are downloaded.

XML Configuration File

Next, we need to create a new folder in our project for the XML configuration file. Inside your project, go to the `src/main` folder and create a `resources` folder. Inside this folder, create a new file called `applicationContext.xml`.

We will configure the DI in the XML file, but we need to start by adding the markup in Listing 36.4 to `applicationContext.xml`.

LISTING 36.4

Markup to Add to applicationContext.xml

```xml
<?xml version="1.0" encoding="UTF-8"?>
<beans xmlns="http://www.springframework.org/schema/beans"
        xmlns:xsi="http://www.w3.org/2001/XMLSchema-instance"
        xsi:schemaLocation="
                http://www.springframework.org/schema/beans
                http://www.springframework.org/schema/beans/spring-
beans.xsd">


</beans>
```

These tags help set up the file so Spring can read it in and understand everything else that comes inside.

We now need to add in `<bean>` tags that will identify each of our different classes and how they tie together. These tags should be nested inside the `<beans>` element we just created.

First, we have some simple classes that have no dependencies themselves.

```xml
<bean id="io" class="com.sg.booktracker.ui.UserIOConsoleImpl"/>
```

```xml
<bean id="dao" class="com.sg.booktracker.dao.BookDaoMemoryImpl"/>
```

We will use the `id` field to reference each class in other parts of the XML, and the `class` field is the fully qualified name of the class we want to inject. Notice that we make beans out of the `Impl` versions, rather than creating beans for interfaces.

Now we can add in the beans for the rest of the classes, adding in the dependencies as they are necessary. Listing 36.5 shows the markup.

LISTING 36.5

The Beans for the Other Classes

```xml
<bean id="view" class="com.sg.booktracker.ui.BookView">
    <constructor-arg ref="io"/>
</bean>

<bean id="service" class="com.sg.booktracker.service.BookService">
    <constructor-arg ref="dao"/>
</bean>

<bean id="controller" class="com.sg.booktracker.controller.BookController">
    <constructor-arg ref="service"/>
    <constructor-arg ref="view"/>
</bean>
```

The bean tags here are not self-closed because we need to add in our dependencies.

- Because each of these classes has a constructor that takes in the dependency, we add in constructor-arg tags.

- Inside that tag, the ref field references the id of the class that needs to be injected.

- We also set up all our dependencies: our view takes in the UserIO class, our service takes in the DAO, and our controller takes in our service and view.

Update the App Class

The last part of the XML setup is to update the main method in our App class with the markup in Listing 36.6.

LISTING 36.6

The XML for Updating main Method in App Class

```java
public static void main(String[] args) {

    ApplicationContext appContext
            = new ClassPathXmlApplicationContext("classpath:application-
Context.xml");
```

```
        BookController controller = appContext.getBean("controller",
BookController.class);
        controller.run();
    }
```

NOTE At this point, if you run the code and get any errors, make sure you rebuild the project so the appropriate dependencies are pulled.

The first line here loads our XML file. The resources directory is an easy one for Java to read data in from, so just indicating our XML is in the classpath is enough. The `Application-Context` and `ClassPathXMLApplicationContext` classes come in from the Spring library, so they will need to be imported.

After we have that loaded up, we just need to ask it to get the controller bean, which references the ID in the XML. Behind the scenes it will build everything it needs in memory to give us the controller, including any dependencies and their dependencies.

If you make these same changes in the provided code, you should be able to see it run. If there are any mistakes in the XML, you will probably get some ugly stack traces in the console. Review them closely: the mistakes are there, but it's not always easy to read.

Spring DI with Annotations

Now we will look at doing Spring DI with annotations. This is the way you will typically see it in done. The XML method still works, but annotation-based configuration is how most development is set up these days.

Starting with a new copy of the project, we add the same dependency to the `pom.xml` file, which is shown in Listing 36.7.

LISTING 36.7

Dependencies for Annotation-Based Configuration

```xml
<dependencies>
    <dependency>
        <groupId>org.springframework</groupId>
        <artifactId>spring-context</artifactId>
        <version>5.2.2.RELEASE</version>
    </dependency>
</dependencies>
```

Make sure to do a build so the libraries are downloaded and added to the project, and then we are ready to start adding in annotations.

Class Annotations

Each class that was a bean in the XML setup needs to be annotated in this step; the annotations are how Spring figures out which classes to instantiate.

We will start with the `UserIOConsoleImpl`. At the top of the class, just before the class declaration, we need to add in the `@Component` annotation.

```
@Component
public class UserIOConsoleImpl implements UserIO {
```

This is the primary annotation we use to tell Spring to instantiate this class in memory so it can be injected elsewhere. The annotation comes from the Spring library we added, so it will need to be imported. Since this class doesn't have any dependencies of its own, this is all we need to do.

We will similarly annotate the `BookDaoMemoryImpl` class.

```
@Component
public class BookDaoMemoryImpl implements BookDao {
```

We are once again only dealing with the `Impl` versions of classes, so we do not need to annotate any interfaces.

Next, we will start annotating classes that have actual dependencies, which means we will add in another annotation. Let's start with the `BookView` class annotations presented in Listing 36.8.

LISTING 36.8

BookView Class Annotations

```
@Component
public class BookView {

    private UserIO io;

    @Autowired
    public BookView(UserIO io) {
        this.io = io;
    }
}
```

We once again add in the @Component annotation before the class declaration, but we have now also added in the @Autowired annotation before the constructor. This tells Spring that when a BookView is created, it should look for something that is-a UserIO in memory to inject. Since we annotated the UserIOConsoleImpl class, that class will be in memory and available to inject.

If we did not have this constructor, we could also put the @Autowired annotation directly on the io field.

```
@Component
public class BookView {

    @Autowired
    private UserIO io;
```

Both ways are valid, and both work. The @Autowired annotation comes from our Spring library, so it will need to be imported.

We will do the same thing for our other classes, BookService and BookController, as shown in Listing 36.9.

> **NOTE** Using constructor autowiring will avoid null resources at runtime. If Spring can't find a bean to inject, the context load will fail if using the constructor. On the field, you could get a null value.

LISTING 36.9

Annotations for BookService and BookController

```
@Component
public class BookService {

    private BookDao dao;

    @Autowired
    public BookService(BookDao dao) {
        this.dao = dao;
    }
```

```
@Component
public class BookController {

    private BookService service;
    private BookView view;

    @Autowired
    public BookController(BookService service, BookView view) {
        this.service = service;
        this.view = view;
    }
}
```

Even though the BookController constructor takes in two parameters, the @Autowired annotation will still work. Spring can figure out what needs to be injected.

With the annotations all set up, we can now modify the main method in our App class to start everything up, as shown in Listing 36.10.

LISTING 36.10

Modified main Method

```
    public static void main(String[] args) {
    AnnotationConfigApplicationContext appContext = new AnnotationConfig-
ApplicationContext();
        appContext.scan("com.sg.booktracker");
        appContext.refresh();

        BookController controller = appContext.getBean("bookController",
BookController.class);
        controller.run();
    }
```

This looks similar to the XML main method in the previous step, but it starts up in a different way. The appContext in this version is an AnnotationConfigApplicationContext class, which will need to be imported from the Spring library.

Once we have that instantiated, we need to tell it where to start scanning our project for annotations. Your package structure needs to be set up correctly for this to work. You typically want to start scanning from the package your App is in, in this case com .sg.booktracker. When we call the refresh method on the next line, Spring checks all classes it can find in that package and any child packages for annotations. Anything that is an @Component is created in memory with dependencies injected where it sees @Autowired.

We can then ask for our `BookController` so we can start the program. Since we didn't set any IDs for our classes when we annotated them, their default IDs are their names converted to camel case, in this situation `bookController` for `BookController`. Once we have that class, we can run it, and everything should work.

SUMMARY

In this lesson, we looked at what the Spring framework is and how we can use it for dependency injection. Here are important points to remember:

- We have to add our external libraries as dependencies to our Maven POM file.
- The Spring application context can be set up using XML or annotations.
- To use the Spring application context, we need to read in the XML file or scan for annotations.
- Annotations are the more common option in Java development these days.

Lesson 37
Introducing Maven

We have been using Maven to build our projects in NetBeans, but we have not discussed the advantages of using Maven over the build management tools that are built into the IDE. The IDE tools work reasonably well for small, individual projects that don't depend on too many external libraries, but they have the following drawbacks for larger, multideveloper projects:

- Everyone on the team must use NetBeans.
- All external JAR files must be referenced directly in the project and must be manually copied to each developer's machine.
- There is no good way to manage the versions of the required external libraries.
- There is no way to build the project outside of NetBeans. This severely limits the options the team has for automated build machines and for building and deploying the project to QA, performance test, and production environments.

Maven helps address these issues. Maven is a project management framework that provides IDE-independent build and dependency management tools.

LEARNING OBJECTIVES

By the end of this lesson, you will be able to:
- Describe Maven
- Explain the project object model (POM)
- Explain how Maven uses dependency management
- Outline the Maven lifecycle

WHAT IS MAVEN?

Maven bills itself as a *project management framework*. It strives to manage a project's build, reporting, and documentation from one place.

Maven's build management is declarative rather than task oriented. It has a built-in lifecycle, so you simply declare what you want to do, not how to do it. Maven also has declarative dependency management, so you tell Maven what libraries (including version numbers) you need, and it will make sure those libraries are available to your code.

Maven does a lot of things, so covering what it can do is a big subject on its own. In this lesson, we will concentrate on using the built-in Maven lifecycle and the dependency management features to make our projects easier to build and to share with our team.

PROJECT OBJECT MODEL

Maven is based on the project object model (POM). The POM is defined in an XML file called pom.xml. This file contains the declarations for all libraries on which the project depends and can contain declarations of the Java version to use and other project-level settings. Listing 37.1 shows a typical POM file.

LISTING 37.1

A Typical Mavin POM.xml File

```
<project xmlns="http://maven.apache.org/POM/4.0.0"
         xmlns:xsi="http://www.w3.org/2001/XMLSchema-instance"
```

```xml
    xsi:schemaLocation=
       "http://maven.apache.org/POM/4.0.0 http://maven.apache.org/xsd/maven-
4.0.0.xsd">
  <modelVersion>4.0.0</modelVersion>

  <groupId>com.sg</groupId>
  <artifactId>MeanMedianMode</artifactId>
  <version>1.0-SNAPSHOT</version>
  <packaging>jar</packaging>

  <name>MeanMedianMode</name>
  <url>http://maven.apache.org</url>.

  <properties>
    <project.build.sourceEncoding>UTF-8</project.build.sourceEncoding>
  </properties>

  <dependencies>
    <dependency>
      <groupId>junit</groupId>
      <artifactId>junit</artifactId>
      <version>5.6.0</version>
      <scope>test</scope>
    </dependency>
  </dependencies>

    <build>
       <finalName>mean-median-mode</finalName>
       <plugins>
          <plugin>
             <groupId>org.apache.maven.plugins</groupId>
             <artifactId>maven-compiler-plugin</artifactId>
             <version>3.8.1</version>
             <configuration>
                 <source>1.8</source>
                 <target>1.8</target>
             </configuration>
          </plugin>
       </plugins>
    </build>
</project>
```

Let's analyze the POM file. First, it is important to remember that this file is generated by NetBeans when you create your project. We'll just look at the parts of the file that you might want to modify.

Project Identification

The following code contains the tags that identify your project to Maven:

```
<groupId>com.sg</groupId>
<artifactId>MeanMedianMode</artifactId>
<version>1.0-SNAPSHOT</version>
<packaging>jar</packaging>

<name>MeanMedianMode</name>
```

We learned about most of this in the first part of this course, but it is worth covering each of these tags again.

- **groupID:** Traditionally, the `groupId` is the base package of your project, but this is not a requirement. The `groupId` is meant to identify the organization with which the project is associated.

- **artifactId:** The `artifactId` is the name that will be given to the file into which this project is packaged.

- **SNAPSHOT:** The version indicates the version of the project. It defaults to `1.0-SNAPSHOT` in NetBeans, but you can set this to any value.

- **packaging:** The `packaging` tag indicates how you would like the project to be packaged. For now, this will always be `jar`, which stands for Java Archive. If you were doing web applications, then this would be `war`, which stands for Web Archive.

- **name:** The `name` tag is, essentially, the name of this project. It does not have to match the `artifactId` discussed earlier.

Dependencies

The following tags indicate the external Java libraries on which your application depends:

```
<dependencies>
  <dependency>
    <groupId>junit</groupId>
    <artifactId>junit</artifactId>
    <version>5.6.0</version>
    <scope>test</scope>
  </dependency>
</dependencies>
```

Each library on which we depend has a separate dependency tag nested in the dependencies tag. In this case, we rely on version 5.6.0 of the JUnit library. Note that each dependency entry is described using the same tags used to describe our project to

Maven: `groupId`, `artifactId`, and `version`. The `scope` tag can be used to limit where and how a particular library will be used. In this case, the value `test` indicates that the JUnit library should be used only when running unit tests but should not be included when packaging or installing the project.

Build Settings

The build tag contains settings affecting how the project will be built.

```
<build>
  <finalName>mean-median-mode</finalName>
    <plugins>
        <plugin>
            <groupId>org.apache.maven.plugins</groupId>
            <artifactId>maven-compiler-plugin</artifactId>
            <version>3.8.1</version>
            <configuration>
                <source>1.8</source>
                <target>1.8</target>
            </configuration>
        </plugin>
    </plugins>
</build>
```

With the build tags, we are interested in the `target` and `source` tags of the compiler plugin. The `source` tag indicates the Java version that should be used for the source code of the `project`, and the `target` tag indicates the version of the JVM on which the project should be run.

DEPENDENCY MANAGEMENT

One of the great features of Maven is *dependency management*. This means that Maven will manage all the external libraries (packaged as JAR files) that you need to use in your program. You may have noticed that we're using the term *dependency* here in a different way than we did when we talked about the Spring Framework. The Spring Framework helps us manage how the components of our application relate to and depend on each other at the class and object levels through dependency injection. Maven, on the other hand, helps us manage the external Java libraries that we rely on at a project level.

Without Maven, the developer is responsible for manually identifying, downloading, and including the JAR files of all the libraries on which the project depends. The developer is also responsible for storing and managing these JAR files.

When using Maven, the developer is still responsible for identifying the libraries on which the project depends, but Maven automatically fetches all dependencies into a central repository on your machine (located in the ~/.m2 directory). All Maven projects on your machine share this repository, which means that each library is downloaded only once.

As an added bonus, Maven also handles *transitive dependencies* automatically. For example, if you declare (in your POM) that your project depends on Library A and it turns out that Library A depends on Libraries B and C, Maven will automatically download all three libraries into your local repository. You do not have to specify (or even be aware) that Library A requires Libraries B and C.

MAVEN LIFECYCLE

Maven's project lifecycle is defined but is flexible. You can change it if you need to but, for most projects, the predefined lifecycle is sufficient. The lifecycle consists of several stages, which are known as *goals*. These goals are simply the kinds of actions (like compiling and running unit tests) that we need to take as we build a software project. NetBeans hides much of this from us, but these goals are run behind the scenes when we ask NetBeans to build and run our applications.

Developers tend to use the following goals extensively:

- **compile**: Compiles the project source code
- **test-compile**: Compiles the project test source code
- **test**: Runs the project unit tests
- **package**: Builds and packages the project
- **install**: Installs the project package into the local .m2 repository (the project package can then be used in other projects)

SUMMARY

In this lesson, we took a closer look at Maven and discussed its benefits for larger projects. The main takeaways for this lesson are the following:

- Maven is an IDE independent build management tool.
- Maven is a declarative framework. It allows you to say what you want to have done without specifying how it will be done.
- The Maven build is represented in the project object model, which is defined in the pom.xml file.

- Maven manages the external libraries on which your project depends. This includes management of transitive dependencies.

- Maven has a predefined lifecycle made up of several stages called *goals*.

- Using Maven, instead of the built-in IDE build management tools, gives software teams more flexibility in choosing which IDE (or IDEs) will be used and allows easy integration with automated build and deployment servers.

NOTE You can find more on Apache Maven at `https://maven.apache.org/`.

Lesson 38

Pulling It All Together: Building the Class Roster with Spring

In this lesson, we pull together the code to convert our Class Roster application into a Spring application. In the new version, we will have Spring do the dependency injection and application wiring that we currently do by hand in the App class and the service layer unit test. Using the Spring DI container is a foundational Spring skill. Almost all other Spring features (security, AOP, MVC, REST) take advantage of the core Spring DI container, which means that this is something you'll do in just about every Spring project you encounter.

PROGRAM OBJECTIVES

We'll convert our Class Roster application by doing these tasks:

- Add the Spring libraries to the POM file
- Add the shell Spring configuration files to the project
- Convert the DI and application wiring code currently in the App class into Spring
- Convert the unit tests to use Spring

INCLUDE THE SPRING LIBRARIES

To take advantage of the Spring framework, we must ensure that the Spring framework library is included in the Maven POM. As we discussed in the Maven lesson, you must include a dependency entry for each library we want to include in our project.

Open your pom.xml file and verify that it includes the code dependencies, as shown in Listing 38.1.

LISTING 38.1

The pom.xml File

```xml
<?xml version="1.0" encoding="UTF-8"?>
<project xmlns="http://maven.apache.org/POM/4.0.0" xmlns:xsi="http://www.
w3.org/2001/XMLSchema-instance" xsi:schemaLocation="http://maven.apache.org/
POM/4.0.0 http://maven.apache.org/xsd/maven-4.0.0.xsd">
    <modelVersion>4.0.0</modelVersion>
    <groupId>com.sg</groupId>
    <artifactId>ClassRoster</artifactId>
    <version>1.0-SNAPSHOT</version>
    <packaging>jar</packaging>
    <dependencies>
        <dependency>
            <groupId>org.springframework</groupId>
            <artifactId>spring-context</artifactId>
            <version>5.3.0.RELEASE</version>
        </dependency>
        <dependency>
            <groupId>org.junit.jupiter</groupId>
            <artifactId>junit-jupiter-api</artifactId>
            <version>5.6.0</version>
            <scope>test</scope>
        </dependency>
        <dependency>
```

```
            <groupId>org.junit.jupiter</groupId>
            <artifactId>junit-jupiter-params</artifactId>
            <version>5.6.0</version>
            <scope>test</scope>
        </dependency>
        <dependency>
            <groupId>org.junit.jupiter</groupId>
            <artifactId>junit-jupiter-engine</artifactId>
            <version>5.6.0</version>
            <scope>test</scope>
        </dependency>
    </dependencies>
    <properties>
        <project.build.sourceEncoding>UTF-8</project.build.sourceEncoding>
        <maven.compiler.source>1.8</maven.compiler.source>
        <maven.compiler.target>1.8</maven.compiler.target>
    </properties>
</project>
```

In particular, you want to check for the following dependency:

```
<dependency>
    <groupId>org.springframework</groupId>
    <artifactId>spring-context</artifactId>
    <version>5.3.0.RELEASE</version>
</dependency>
```

As long as the Spring framework dependency is inside the `<dependencies>` node, everything should be good, even if the individual dependencies are in a different order in your file.

How Do I Know What My Dependency Entry Should Be?

The libraries that will be used in this lesson are available in online Maven repositories. This is true of the vast majority of open source libraries. The question is, how do I know what the Maven dependency entry is supposed to be? There are two good approaches for finding this out.

Go to the project website: Many project websites have the Maven dependency entry right there. Simply copy and paste the entry into your POM file. For example, the Maven entry for the Spring core framework is found on Spring Boot's Maven Plugin page at docs.spring.io/spring-boot/docs/current/maven-plugin/usage.html.

Search for the dependency on Google or another search engine: For example, a search for *JUnit maven dependency* yields this page as its top result: junit ➤ junit ➤ Maven Repository (`mvnrepository.com/artifact/junit/junit/`), which contains the Maven dependency entry for JUnit 5.

> **NOTE** We use JUnit just as an example. NetBeans automatically adds the JUnit dependency to your POM when you create a new unit test.

ADD SPRING CONFIGURATION FILES

Now that we have access to the Spring libraries, we will start to put things in place that will allow us to use the libraries. Our first step will be the addition of the *application context* configuration files. Recall that one way to define (configure) the Spring DI container and application context is through an XML configuration file. Our convention is to list all the beans in the file `applicationContext.xml`, but this is not a requirement. You can call the file anything you want. To start, we'll just add the skeleton of the file to our project.

Create a file called `applicationContext.xml` in the `src/main/resources` folder of your project (you may have to create the folder) and copy the code content from Listing 38.2 into it.

LISTING 38.2

applicationContext.xml

```
<?xml version="1.0" encoding="UTF-8"?>
<beans xmlns="http://www.springframework.org/schema/beans"
       xmlns:xsi="http://www.w3.org/2001/XMLSchema-instance"
       xmlns:context="http://www.springframework.org/schema/context"
       xmlns:tx="http://www.springframework.org/schema/tx"
       xmlns:aop="http://www.springframework.org/schema/aop"
       xsi:schemaLocation="http://www.springframework.org/schema/beans
          http://www.springframework.org/schema/beans/spring-beans.xsd

    <!-- Bean definitions go here -->

</beans>
```

Note that this is an empty template for the applicationContext file, which is pre-populated with Spring XML namespace entries for the Spring container as well as some additional Spring features. Use this as a starting point for all of your Spring configuration files. Also note that all bean wiring definitions will appear after the "Bean definitions go here" comment and before the closing </beans> tag.

Do exactly the same thing in the src/test/resources folder of your project. You may have to create this folder manually. This applicationContext.xml file will allow us to have a separate configuration for our unit tests.

CONVERT THE APP CLASS TO USE SPRING

Now we are ready to convert the manual dependency injection code in our App class to use Spring for dependency injection. Essentially, we're going to move the code in the main method (shown in Listing 38.3) of App into the applicationContext.xml file.

LISTING 38.3

The Updated App Class main Method

```
public static void main(String[] args) {
        UserIO myIo = new UserIOConsoleImpl();
        ClassRosterView myView = new ClassRosterView(myIo);
        ClassRosterDao myDao = new ClassRosterDaoFileImpl();
        ClassRosterAuditDao myAuditDao =
            new ClassRosterAuditDaoFileImpl();
        ClassRosterServiceLayer myService =
            new ClassRosterServiceLayerImpl(myDao, myAuditDao);
        ClassRosterController controller =
            new ClassRosterController(myService, myView);
        controller.run();

    }
```

After we do that, we'll replace the code currently in App with code that instantiates the Spring DI container, gets the controller from the Spring DI container, and then calls run on the controller.

Defining Beans

The code that we currently have in the `main` method of the `App` class is responsible for instantiating each of the objects in our application. This requires knowing the dependencies between the components and passing the correct objects into appropriate constructors when instantiating the classes. Spring allows us to remove this knowledge from our Java code and externalize it to the `applicationContext.xml` file. We will define the relationships between all our components in the `applicationContext.xml` file, and we will let the Spring DI container handle the instantiation of our objects. We will simply instantiate the Spring container and ask it to hand us our controller.

Before we start modifying our `applicationContext.xml` file, we need to discuss some of the tags and attributes that we'll be using to define our beans.

- **The bean tag:** This is the XML tag we use to define the objects we want the Spring container to instantiate for us.

- **The id attribute:** This is the XML attribute that we use to tell the Spring container what alias to give a particular bean that it instantiates. It is similar to the key in a Map. We can ask for a reference to the object by passing the `id` attribute to the Spring application context, and it will hand us back the requested reference.

- **The class attribute:** This is the fully qualified name of the class that we want the Spring container to instantiate for us. Remember, this must be the fully qualified name of the class. You must explicitly include the full package name.

- **The constructor-arg tag:** This tag is nested in the `bean` tag and is used to indicate that we want Spring to pass a parameter into the constructor when instantiating the bean.

- **The ref attribute:** We use this attribute to refer to a previously defined bean. The value of the `ref` attribute must be the `id` of another bean in the `applicationContext.xml` file.

Modify the `applicationContext.xml` file in `src/main/resources` so that it looks like Listing 38.4.

LISTING 38.4

Modified applicationContext.xml File

```xml
<?xml version="1.0" encoding="UTF-8"?>
<beans xmlns="http://www.springframework.org/schema/beans"
       xmlns:xsi="http://www.w3.org/2001/XMLSchema-instance"
       xmlns:context="http://www.springframework.org/schema/context"
```

```
    xmlns:tx="http://www.springframework.org/schema/tx"
    xmlns:aop="http://www.springframework.org/schema/aop"
    xsi:schemaLocation="http://www.springframework.org/schema/beans
        http://www.springframework.org/schema/beans/spring-beans.xsd

<!-- Bean definitions go here -->
<bean id="userIO" class="com.sg.classroster.ui.UserIOConsoleImpl"/>

<bean id="view" class="com.sg.classroster.ui.ClassRosterView">
    <constructor-arg ref="userIO"/>
</bean>

<bean id="classRosterDao"
        class="com.sg.classroster.dao.ClassRosterDaoFileImpl"/>

<bean id="auditDao"
        class="com.sg.classroster.dao.ClassRosterAuditDaoFileImpl"/>

<bean id="serviceLayer"
        class="com.sg.classroster.service.ClassRosterServiceLayerImpl">
    <constructor-arg ref="classRosterDao"/>
    <constructor-arg ref="auditDao"/>
</bean>

<bean id="controller"
        class="com.sg.classroster.controller.ClassRosterController">
    <constructor-arg ref="serviceLayer"/>
    <constructor-arg ref="view"/>
</bean>

</beans>
```

This userIO entry tells the Spring container to instantiate an instance of our UserIO-
ConsoleImpl class and to make it available in the application context under the alias
userIO. Notice that we only have the id and class attributes for this bean because this
class does not depend on any other components. In other words, we don't need to tell
Spring to pass any parameters into the constructor of the UserIOConsoleImpl class.

The view entry tells the Spring container to instantiate an instance of our
ClassRosterView class and to make it available in the application context under the alias
view. Notice that, in addition to the id and class attributes, we have a nested constructor-arg tag inside this bean tag. The constructor-arg tag allows us to tell the Spring
container to pass a parameter into the constructor. We use the ref attribute of the constructor-arg tag to tell Spring we want to pass the userIO bean as a parameter to the
ClassRosterView constructor.

The classRosterDao entry tells the Spring container to instantiate an instance of our ClassRosterDaoFileImpl class and to make it available in the application context under the alias classRosterDao.

The auditDao entry tells the Spring container to instantiate an instance of our ClassRosterAuditDaoFileImpl class and to make it available in the application context under the alias auditDao.

The serviceLayer entry tells the Spring container to instantiate an instance of our ClassRosterServiceLayerImpl class and to make it available in the application context under the alias serviceLayer. Notice that, in addition to the id and class attributes, we have two nested constructor-arg tags inside this bean tag. We use the ref attribute of the first constructor-arg tag to tell Spring we want to pass the classRosterDao bean as a parameter of the ClassRosterServiceLayerImpl constructor. We use the ref attribute of the second constructor-arg tag to tell Spring we want to pass the auditDao bean as a parameter of the ClassRosterServiceLayerImpl constructor.

The controller entry tells the Spring container to instantiate an instance of our ClassRosterController class and to make it available in the application context under the alias controller. Notice that, in addition to the id and class attributes, we have two nested constructor-arg tags inside this bean tag. We use the ref attribute of the first constructor-arg tag to tell Spring we want to pass the serviceLayer bean as a parameter of ClassRosterController constructor. We use the ref attribute of the second constructor-arg tag to tell Spring we want to pass the view beans as a parameter of the ClassRosterController constructor.

Modifying the App Class

Now that we have the Spring application context defined, we can replace the code currently in the main method of the App class with code that instantiates the application context, retrieves the controller from the context, and then invokes the run method on the controller.

Modify the main method of your App class so it looks like Listing 38.5 (make sure to just comment out the existing code so you can compare it to the new code).

LISTING 38.5

Modified main Method in App Class

```
public static void main(String[] args) {
    // UserIO myIo = new UserIOConsoleImpl();
    // ClassRosterView myView = new ClassRosterView(myIo);
```

```
// ClassRosterDao myDao = new ClassRosterDaoFileImpl();
// ClassRosterAuditDao myAuditDao =
//       new ClassRosterAuditDaoFileImpl();
// ClassRosterServiceLayer myService =
//       new ClassRosterServiceLayerImpl(myDao, myAuditDao);
// ClassRosterController controller =
//       new ClassRosterController(myService, myView);
// controller.run();

ApplicationContext ctx =
    new ClassPathXmlApplicationContext("applicationContext.xml");
ClassRosterController controller =
    ctx.getBean("controller", ClassRosterController.class);
controller.run();
}
```

The Java object that holds the application context that we defined in the `applica-tionContext.xml` file is of type `ApplicationContext`. The particular implementation of `ApplicationContext` that we use is called `ClassPathXmlApplicationContext`, and we pass the name of our Spring application context configuration file to the constructor of `ClassPathXmlApplicationContext`. In our case, that is `applicationContext.xml`.

We can retrieve the beans instantiated by the Spring application context by using the `getBean` method. This method takes two parameters. The first parameter is the `id` of the bean you want to retrieve. In our case, it is `controller`. The second parameter is the type of the bean you want to retrieve. Because the Spring application context can instantiate and hold on to objects of any type, it uses `Object` references for all of them. When we retrieve a reference from the application context, we must tell the Spring container the underlying type of the reference we want to retrieve so that the container can cast it to the correct type for us.

> **NOTE** There is another version of getBean that just takes one parameter (the `id` of the object). This version returns an `Object` reference, so you have to explicitly cast the object to the correct type manually.

CONVERT THE UNIT TESTS TO USE SPRING

We must go through a similar process to convert our unit tests to use the Spring applica-tion context. We will only convert the service layer unit tests to use the Spring context because the service layer is the only component that uses dependency injection.

As we did with the code in the `main` method of our `App` class, here we are going to move the code from the constructor of our `ClassRosterServiceLayerTest` class (shown in Listing 38.6) to the `applicationContext.xml` file.

LISTING 38.6

ClassRosterServiceLayerTest

```java
public ClassRosterServiceLayerTest() {
        // wire the Service Layer with stub implementations of the Dao and
        // Audit Dao
        ClassRosterDao dao = new ClassRosterDaoStubImpl();
        ClassRosterAuditDao auditDao = new ClassRosterAuditDaoStubImpl();

        service = new ClassRosterServiceLayerImpl(dao, auditDao);
}
```

Defining Beans

Modify the `ApplicationContext.xml` file in the `src/resources` folder so that it looks like Listing 38.7.

LISTING 38.7

Modified ApplicationContext.xml File

```xml
<?xml version="1.0" encoding="UTF-8"?>
<beans xmlns="http://www.springframework.org/schema/beans"
       xmlns:xsi="http://www.w3.org/2001/XMLSchema-instance"
       xmlns:context="http://www.springframework.org/schema/context"
       xmlns:tx="http://www.springframework.org/schema/tx"
       xmlns:aop="http://www.springframework.org/schema/aop"
       xsi:schemaLocation=
         "http://www.springframework.org/schema/beans
          http://www.springframework.org/schema/beans/spring-beans.xsd

      <!-- Bean definitions go here -->
      <bean id="classRosterDao"
        class="com.sg.classroster.dao.ClassRosterDaoFileImpl"/>

      <bean id="classRosterDaoStub"
        class="com.sg.classroster.dao.ClassRosterDaoStubImpl"/>
```

```
<bean id="auditDaoStub"
   class="com.sg.classroster.dao.ClassRosterAuditDaoStubImpl"/>

<bean id="serviceLayer"
   class="com.sg.classroster.service.ClassRosterServiceLayerImpl">
    <constructor-arg ref="classRosterDaoStub"/>
    <constructor-arg ref="auditDaoStub"/>
</bean>

</beans>
```

This is similar to the `applicationContext.xml` file used for the application itself, but there are some important differences.

- We only define beans for the DAOs and the service layer because these are the only components used for this set of tests.
- We define beans for the stubbed-out versions of the Class Roster DAO and the Audit DAO.
- We pass the stubbed-out versions of the DAOs to the service layer constructor.

Modifying the Test Class Constructor

Now that we have the application context defined, we can modify the constructor of our unit test to use the application context instead of the code we currently have. Modify the constructor of your `ClassRosterServiceLayerTest` class so that it looks like Listing 38.8.

LISTING 38.8

Modified `ClassRosterServiceLayerTest` Constructor

```
public ClassRosterServiceLayerTest() {
    // wire the Service Layer with stub implementations of the Dao and
    // Audit Dao
    // ClassRosterDao dao = new ClassRosterDaoStubImpl();
    // ClassRosterAuditDao auditDao =
    //          new ClassRosterAuditDaoStubImpl();
    //
    // service = new ClassRosterServiceLayerImpl(dao, auditDao);

    ApplicationContext ctx =
        new ClassPathXmlApplicationContext("applicationContext.xml");
```

```
        service =
            ctx.getBean("serviceLayer", ClassRosterServiceLayer.class);
}
```

This looks similar to the modifications we made to the `main` method of the `App` class except that we are retrieving the service layer object from the context instead of the controller. Also note that we're not calling a method on the service layer here, but rather we are simply assigning the returned reference to the `service` class member.

EXCEPTION CONDITIONS

The Spring container is a powerful tool that helps us build flexible, loosely coupled applications. This is a great thing, but it does add more moving parts to our environment. One consequence of externalizing dependencies to an XML configuration file is that any errors contained in the configuration file are not detectable until runtime, because the compiler has no way of catching these errors.

Here are some common errors that you might encounter:

- **Misspelled bean class attribute:** All bean classes must be specified by their correctly spelled, fully qualified class name. If you misspell this, the Spring container will throw an error indicating that the bean cannot be instantiated.

- **Misspelled bean id in ref attribute:** When you refer to another bean (in a ref attribute), it must appear exactly as it did in the original bean definition.

- **Malformed XML:** The `applicationContext.xml` file must be composed of well-formed XML. These are the easiest errors to catch and diagnose. The error message usually tells you the line and column where the error occurred.

- Using the `value` attribute when you meant to use the `ref` attribute in constructor or setter injection. Remember that the value attribute passes the literal value of the attribute to the constructor or setter, whereas the ref passes a reference to the object referred to by the attribute value.

These types of error message will show up in the NetBeans console output.

Another way to provide configuration metadata for the Spring container is through the use of annotations or Java code. These two alternatives provide a better way to deal with the previous errors since the metadata is written in Java code.

SUMMARY

Once you have made the changes described in this lesson, you will be able to run your unit tests and your application just as you did before. We made no changes to functionality; we simply refactored the project by replacing the code we wrote that manually did dependency injection and replaced it with the Spring dependency injection container. Use this project as a template for future Maven/Spring projects.

Here are the important points to remember:

- We have to add dependency entries for all external libraries to the Maven POM file. Specifically, for this project, we added entries for Spring Core.

- The Spring container (known as the *application context*) is configured via an XML file that contains definitions for all the objects we want Spring to control.

- Maven makes a distinction between the application and test environments. We must have a Spring configuration file for each environment.

- We place the Spring configuration files on the classpath. In our Maven projects, we place these files in either *Other Sources* or *Other Test Sources*.

- To use the Spring container, we must instantiate an implementation of `Application-tionContext` (in our case, we use `ClassPathXmlApplicationContext`). The `ApplicationContext` will read the Spring configuration file and instantiate all configured objects. We then ask the `ApplicationContext` for references to these objects by name rather than instantiating them ourselves.

EXERCISES

This exercise helps you practice what you are learning about using the Spring framework. This is to do on your own.

Exercise 1: DVD Library

Exercise 1: DVD Library

Convert your DVD Library application to use the Spring DI container. Use what you learned in this lesson as a guide and pattern for your approach.

PART VI

Appendices

Appendix A: Code Checklist

This document can be used as a guide to help you prepare your code. Many organizations have similar lists with more detail to guide you through preparing your code before sharing with a team. Go through the items on this checklist before you consider your code to be complete.

FUNCTIONALITY

- Make sure your code compiles.
- Double-check that the application performs per specification.
- Have unit tests to verify that the application performs per specifications.
    - Use positive unit tests to exercise code as intended.
    - Use negative unit tests to intentionally misuse the code and verify robust error handling and bounds of input values.
    - Step through all possible code paths in the debugger.
- Confirm that code analysis tools in your IDE do not report warnings.

STYLE

- Use a consistent style.
    - Ensure that classes, methods, and variables are named with appropriate letter casing and code blocks are indented properly.
- Follow the Single Responsibility Principle.
    - Strive to separate large functions into collections of smaller functions that perform single tasks.
    - Strive to make classes cohesive so that each class has one area of responsibility that it handles completely.

- Use comments appropriately.
  - Use comments sparingly; intent should be clear from your naming conventions.
  - Use comments to clarify your intent if it might not be clear, for example, when there is a legitimately complicated section of code to satisfy a business rule or requirement.
  - Do not use comments to make up for poorly written code; they should enhance already readable code.
  - Do not comment the obvious.

Appendix B: Java Concepts Study List

The following is a list of basic Java concepts that you learned within this book. You should know and be comfortable discussing these topics in preparation for technical interviews and your first days on the job.

VARIABLES

- What is a variable?
- What is a variable declaration?
- What is a variable assignment?
- What does the `final` keyword mean?
- What does it mean to cast a variable?

METHODS

- What makes up a method's signature?
- What is a method parameter?
- What is a method body?
- What does the `static` keyword mean?
- What does the `final` keyword mean?
- What does the term `override` mean?
- What does the term `overload` mean?

ARRAYS

- What is an array?
- What does an array hold?
- What are the limitations of an array?
- Is an array an object?
- The first value in an array can be found at what index?
- What is an `ArrayIndexOutOfBoundException`?

MAKING DECISIONS

- What is a Boolean expression?
- What is a `switch` statement?
- What is an `if` statement?
- What is an `else` statement?
- What is an `else if` statement?

LOOPS

- What is a loop?
- What is a `for` loop?
- What is a `for-each` loop?
- What can a `for` loop do that a `for-each` loop cannot?
- What is a `while` loop?
- What is a `do-while` loop?
- What is the difference between a `while` loop and a `do/while` loop?

JAVA/JVM

- How is the `import` keyword used?
- What is a package?
- What is Javadoc?
- What is the stack?

- What kinds of variables are created there?
- What is garbage collection?
- How does the garbage collector know when to return memory to the heap?
- Is the Java language pass by value or pass by reference?
- What does pass by value mean?
- What does pass by reference mean?
- What is a `NullPointerException`?

OBJECTS

- What is a class?
- What is an object?
- What is the heap?
- What is scope?
- What is an accessor?
- What is a mutator?
- What is a constructor?
- What does the `public` keyword mean?
- What does the `static` keyword mean?
- What does the `private` keyword mean?
- What does the `abstract` keyword mean?
- How is `abstract` used in conjunction with classes?
- What is polymorphism?
- What does encapsulation mean?
- What does it mean if a class is cohesive?
- What is the single responsibility principle?
- What is data hiding?
- What does the term `generic` mean?
- What are the two categories of nested classes?
- What is a local class?
- What is a static nested class?

- What level of access to the properties and methods of the enclosing class does a static nested class have?
- Under what conditions can a local class access variables in the enclosing scope?
- What is the default constructor?

INTERFACES

- What is an interface?
- How do interfaces help achieve polymorphism?

INHERITANCE

- What is inheritance?
- What does it mean if one class is derived from another class?
- What does it mean if one class extends another class?
- How does inheritance help achieve polymorphism?
- What is a base class?
- What is an abstract base class?
- What is a superclass?
- What is a subclass?
- What is specialization?

N-TIER DESIGN

- What does MVC stand for? What is it?
- What is a model?
- What is a controller?
- What is a view?
- What is a DAO?
- What does it mean to be loosely coupled?
- Why is it a good idea to split your applications into layers?

COLLECTIONS

- What is an `ArrayList`?
- What is a `List`? How is it different from an `ArrayList`?
- What is a `HashMap`?
- What is a `Map`? How is it different from a `HashMap`?
- What is a `Collection`?
- What is an iterator?

EXCEPTIONS

- What is an exception?
- What is an unchecked exception?
- What is a checked exception?
- What is a runtime exception?
- What does a `finally` block do?
- What is a `try/catch`?
- What does the `throws` keyword mean?

LAMBDAS/STREAMS

- What is a lambda?
- What is a stream (in the context of the new Java 8 Collection API)?
- What are aggregate operations?
- What is a pipeline?
- What is a functional interface?

SPRING CORE

- What are the four design principles of Spring?
- What is dependency injection?
- What is constructor injection?
- What is setter injection?

Appendix C: Agile Approach Checklist for Console CRUD Applications

This appendix outlines an approach that can be used to break down a project and implement it in a stepwise and agile way. This will allow you to deliver demonstrable, testable code in small increments.

> **NOTE** A hypothetical address book application is used as an example when describing this approach.

ASSUMPTIONS

Our applications are mainly concerned with creating, reading, updating, and deleting (CRUD) data to and from persistent storage (files or databases).

- Our programs (even the simple ones) must be split into tiers or layers as practice for more complicated problems. This leads us to create projects with the following features:
  - Data transfer objects (DTOs), also known as domain objects (e.g., `Address`)
  - A data access object that handles storing data in memory and reading and writing data from persistent storage (e.g., `AddressBookDao`)
  - Some kind of user interface (e.g., the console)
  - Logic that orchestrates the objects in the program (this will be found in the controller)

REQUIREMENT STEPS

Step 1

Create user stories from the problem statement and/or requirements. For Address Book, they would be as follows:

- Add an address
- View an address
- Delete an address
- Edit an address
- List all addresses
- Show the number of addresses in the address book
- Save to file
- Read from file

DESIGN STEPS

Step 2

Analyze the problem statement and identify the required classes. For Address Book, we have the following:

- Address (DTO)
- AddressBookDao (data access object)
- UserIO (helper used by the View class to interact with the console)
- View class (used by Controller to handle user interaction)
- AddressBookController (this class orchestrates the program)
- App (this class has a main method that instantiates AddressBookController and calls the execute method)

Step 3

Flesh out the classes by defining properties and methods for each.

Step 4

Create a flowchart for the user interaction process (e.g., displaying menus and reacting to user menu choices).

Step 5

Create a file format to match the identified domain object(s) (e.g., `Address`). For example, for storing addresses, we might have something like this:

```
<firstName>::<lastName>::<streetAddress>::<city>::<state>::<zip>
```

CONSTRUCTION STEPS

Step 6

Create a menu system (in the execute method of `AddressBookController`) with stubbed-out code for each menu choice.

For example, when the user presses the choice to add an address, the system simply prints a message saying, "Add Address: To Be Implemented." This can be delivered to the user for testing and feedback.

Step 7

Pick a user story to implement, for example "Add address." For this story, we'll need to do the following:

1. Create the `Address` class (domain object).
2. Create the `AddressBookDao` class.
   a. Include a `HashMap` or `ArrayList` to hold the `Address` objects as a class-level variable.
   b. Implement the `addAddress(...)` method.
3. Add code into the `AddressBookController` to do the following:
   a. Instantiate `AddressBookDao` object for storing `Address` information.
   b. Read in address information from the user.
   c. Create a new `Address` object.

    d. Put address information from the user into the `Address` object.

    e. Add the new `Address` object to the `AddressBookDao`.

Each user story will be different, and the first one is always the most work. Repeat step 7 for each user story.

Index

removing, 67

setting, 64–66, 224–226

compilation errors, 61–62

logic errors, 63

methods, 265

running debugger, 226–234

runtime errors, 63

stepping through code, 226, 259–264

syntax errors, 61–62

variables, 229–232

WindowMasterDebug. java, 223–224

decisions

if statements, 139–142

if-else statements, 142–146

study list, 707

declaring interfaces, 349–350

declaring variables, 106

WindowMaster, 129–130

default keyword, 79

default methods, 350

delegation, 304

dependency injection, 669

dependency management, Maven, 686–687

derived classes, 375–376

design patterns, 449

diamond operator ( ), 398

do keyword, 79

doc comments, 76

doIt( ) method, 261–265

dot operator (.), 308

double keyword, 79

doubles, random, 210–212

do-while loops, 174–175

DTOs (data transfer objects), 448

dynamic data types, 81

E

EJB (Enterprise Java Bean), 670

elaboration phase (agile development), 452–453

else keyword, 79

else-if statements, switch logic, 154

encapsulation, 303

delegation, 304

exceptions, 465

enum keyword, 79

enums, 608–609

fixed contants, 609

IntMath class, 610–611

members, 612–616

Month, 611–612

switches and, 610

using, 609–611

values, 611–612

equality operators, 140

equals( ) method, 155–158, 580–582

error handling, 535–536

arrays, 293

errors

compilation, 61–62

compiletime, 456

logic, 63

runtime, 63, 456

syntax, 61–62

exception handling, 456

catching, 459

catch block, 461–462

finally block, 462–464

try block, 459–460

specifying, 459

exceptions

checked, 459

Class Roster application, Spring framework, 700

object-oriented languages, 301
objects, 74
    behavior, 302
    classes, compared, 307
    dot operator (.), 308
    DTOs (data transfer objects), 448
    identity, 302
    instantiation, 311–312
    POJOs (plain old Java objects),
        671
    scanner objects, 106–107
    state, 302
    study list, 707–708
    types, 302
`ofLocalizedDate( )` method, 625
one-dimensional arrays, 274
OpenJDK
    AdoptOpenJDK, 7–10
    installing, 5–6
        macOS, 13–17
        Windows, 6–13
operands, 85
operators, 84
    arithmetic operators
        - (subtraction), 86
        / (division), 86
        + (additive), 86
        * (multiplication), 86
        % (remainder), 86
    binary operators, 86–87
        = (simple assignment), 86
    bitwise and bit shift operators
        & (bitwise AND), 87
        ^ (bitwise exclusive OR), 87
        | (bitwise inclusive OR), 87
        & (bitwise AND), 87
        ^ (bitwise exclusive OR), 87
        | (bitwise inclusive OR), 87
        << (signed left shift), 87

>> (signed right shift), 87
        >>> (unsigned right shift), 87
    bitwise operators, 149
    comparison operators
        == (equal to), 86
        != (not equal to), 86
        < (less than), 86
        == (equal to), 86
        != (not equal to), 86
        < (less than), 86
        <= (less than or equal to),
            86
        > (greater than), 86
    conditional, 147–149, 150–151
    conditional operators
        && (conditional AND), 87
        || (conditional OR), 87
        && (conditional AND), 87
        || (conditional OR), 87
    equality, 140
    exclusive-or, 149
    mathematical, 89–92
    precedence, 88–89
        conditional operators, 148
    relational, 140
    ternary, 87–88, 150–151
    unary, 85–86
`Opinionator` class, 217
`Opinionator.java`, 218–219
Oracle JDK, 4
`OutFile.txt` file, 437–438
overloading methods, 371–372
overriding methods, 373–375

P

`package` keyword, 79
package-private access, 367
packages, 449–450

T